TALCOTT PARSONS

Theorist of Modernity

edited by
Roland Robertson and
Bryan S. Turner

SAGE Publications

London • Newbury Park • New Delhi

First published 1991

Chapter 2 is reprinted from *Theory, Culture & Society*, 6 (1989)
© Theory, Culture & Society Ltd 1989

Chapter 3 also appeared in that issue and is reprinted here by permission of the
Harvard University Archives

Chapter 9 appears in *American Journal of Sociology*, 96 (5) (March 1991)
© 1991 by The University of Chicago

SAGE Publications Ltd
6 Bonhill Street
London EC2A 4PU

SAGE Publications Inc
2455 Teller Road
Newbury Park, California 91320

SAGE Publications India Pvt Ltd
32, M-Block Market
Greater Kailash – I
New Delhi 110 048

Published in association with *Theory, Culture & Society*, Department of
Administrative and Social Studies,Teesside Polytechnic

British Library Cataloguing in Publication data

Talcott Parsons: Theorist of modernity.—
    (Theory, culture and society)
    I. Robertson, Roland   II. Turner, Bryan S.
    III. Series
    301.01092

    ISBN 0-8039-8513-4
    ISBN 0-8039-8514-2 pbk

Library of Congress catalogue card number 90-53709

Typeset by Best-set Typesetter Ltd.
Printed in Great Britain by Dotesios Ltd, Trowbridge, Wiltshire

CONTENTS

THE CONTRIBUTORS

Harold J. Bershady is Professor of Sociology at the University of Pennsylvania. His work concentrates on the theory of action, the sociology of knowledge, and cultural and moral sociology. In addition to several essays, he has written or edited *Ideology and Social Knowledge* (1973), *Social Class and Democratic Leadership* (1989) and *Max Scheler on Knowing, Feeling and Valuing in Social Life* (1991).

Arthur W. Frank is Associate Professor of Sociology, University of Calgary, Alberta, Canada. His papers and reviews have appeared in *Theory, Culture & Society*, *Symbolic Interaction*, and other journals. He is the author of *At the Will of the Body* (1991), and his current research concerns the experience of illness as an aspect of the sociology of the body.

Mark Gould is Professor of Sociology and Chair of the Department of Sociology and Anthropology at Haverford College, Haverford, Pennsylvania. He is the author of *Revolution in the Development of Capitalism: The Coming of the English Revolution* (1987). His current work involves an attempt to reconstruct microeconomic theory sociologically.

Frank J. Lechner teaches sociology at Emory University, Atlanta, Georgia. His research focuses on sociological theory, world system analysis, and problems in the sociology of religion. Recent articles of his deal with secularization and fundamentalism. He is currently at work on studies of antimodernism and solidarity.

Donald N. Levine is Peter B. Ritzma Professor of Sociology at the University of Chicago and editor of The Heritage of Sociology series published by the University of Chicago Press. His most recent book is *The Flight from Ambiguity: Essays in Social and Cultural Theory*.

Victor Lidz studied and collaborated with Talcott Parsons for nineteen years and has published a number of articles dealing with the general theory of action. He is now affiliated with the Center for Addiction Research, University of Medicine and Dentistry of New Jersey, Camden, New Jersey.

Jens Kaalhauge Nielsen is completing a major study of Parsons's intellectual biography in the course of his doctoral research at Yale University.

Roland Robertson is Professor of Sociology at the University of Pittsburgh. His books include *International Systems and the Modernization of Societies* (with J.P. Nettl), *The Sociological Interpretation of Religion*, *Meaning and Change* and (forthcoming) *Globalization*. He has published many influential essays on various aspects of globalization, modernization and identity. He has also co-edited (with William Garrett) *Religion and Global Order* (1991).

Bryan S. Turner is Professor of Sociology at the University of Essex. He has published a number of volumes on sociological theory, sociology of religion and medical sociology, including (with Robert J. Holton) *Talcott Parsons on Economy and Society* (1986), *Medical Power and Social Knowledge* (1987) and (with Robert J. Holton) *Max Weber on Economy and Society* (1989). He edited *Theories of Modernity and Postmodernity* (1990).

ACKNOWLEDGEMENTS

Chapters 2 and 3 appeared originally in *Theory, Culture & Society*, 6 (4), 1989. We are grateful to Dr Clark Elliott of Harvard University and Professor Charles Parsons of Harvard University for permission to publish Talcott Parsons's 'A Tentative Outline of American Values' from the vast collection of his unpublished writings in the Harvard University Archives, Nathan M. Pusey Library, Cambridge, Massachusetts. The location in the Harvard University Archives is the series 'Manuscripts of Books and Major Theoretical Works', call number HUG (FP), 42. 45.2, box 7, folder: 'American Society: Tentative Outline'. Our introduction to this volume is an extensively revised version of 'Talcott Parsons and Modern Social Theory: An Appreciation', which also appeared in the *Theory, Culture & Society* special issue on Parsons in 1989. Donald Levine's chapter on Simmel and Parsons has been accepted previously for publication in *American Journal of Sociology*; we are grateful for permission to reprint this article. Arthur Frank's chapter on Parsons's sick role was originally given as a public lecture at the Second International Conference on the Future of Adult Life at Leeuwenhorst in the Netherlands in 1990. We would like to thank Robin McElheny of the Harvard University Archives and Steve Dunwell for permission to use the photograph of Talcott Parsons on the next page. We are grateful to Stephen Barr for his support in producing this collection. Finally, our thanks are offered to our wives Kate and Karen who exercised patience throughout.

Roland Robertson
Bryan S. Turner

1

AN INTRODUCTION TO TALCOTT PARSONS: THEORY, POLITICS AND HUMANITY

Roland Robertson and
Bryan S. Turner

Talcott Parsons, who died in 1979 in Munich, is widely regarded as the most significant and influential twentieth-century American sociologist. Nevertheless, the status of his legacy and the scientific value of his work are topics of considerable debate and controversy. Parsons is still too frequently the target of naive and unidimensional criticism, which typically ignores the range and scope of his theoretical, empirical and moral interests. In many respects, the problem of interpreting Parsons is thus only in its infancy. Although there is a complex intellectual 'industry' which is concerned with 'reading Max Weber' (Tribe, 1989), the discourse for reading Parsons has yet to be fully established. In this collection, however, Frank Lechner and Roland Robertson start the task of outlining a number of critical steps towards such a reading by relating Parsons's work to the general problem of global modernity. In this introduction, we want to outline the principal aspects of Parsons's sociology and the significance of his contributions.

Following Parsons's death, there has been a considerable revival of interest in Parsonian sociology; clearly there is a major re-evaluation of his work and a reappraisal of conventional criticisms of it under way (Alexander, 1984; 1987; Buxton, 1985; Camic, 1989; Hamilton, 1983; Holmwood, 1983a; 1983b; Holton and Turner, 1986; Münch, 1981; 1987; 1988; Sciulli and Gerstein, 1985). A number of writers, especially Jeffrey C. Alexander, have detected a 'new theoretical movement' in sociology, which is in part a consequence of this reappraisal. Bryan S. Turner in this book considers aspects of this theoretical movement within the context of cultural rivalry between Germany and America. Part of the paradox of the Parsonian legacy is that, while his work has been extremely influential, it is also conventional for sociologists to reject the work of Parsons on theoretical, methodological and ideological grounds. Although Parsons's work cannot be ignored, 'the conventional attitude toward his theory is one of critical aloofness' (Münch, 1981: 710).

In this introduction to the sociology of Talcott Parsons, we attempt to contribute to this global re-evaluation of Parsonian sociology. We shall briefly review Parsons's sociology, examine critical responses to his work and attempt to evaluate the character of the contemporary reappraisal of his intellectual status. We also show how the various chapters in this study relate to this appreciation of Parsons. In this book as a whole, therefore, we have attempted to bring together a number of essays by established sociologists who were colleagues or contemporaries of Parsons, and essays by younger social theorists, in order to get a balanced view of Parsonian sociology across a number of academic generations. We also include what we regard as a major paper by Parsons on the American value system. Part of our evaluation of Parsons thus relates to his essential commitment to America as a special type of civilization. In our conclusion, we attempt to show how Parsons continues to be relevant to a range of critical issues in contemporary sociological theory.

Although Parsons's own work was voluminous, a substantial amount of it has yet to be published from the Harvard University Archives. We are pleased to re-publish Parsons's essay on the American value system which first appeared in *Theory, Culture & Society* (Parsons, 1989). We are equally pleased to include Victor Lidz's introduction to Parsons's essay on the American value system, which shows how this issue of the nature of American civilization was central to Parsons's entire intellectual endeavour. Roland Robertson's discussion of Parsons's views on American religion and its global-historical significance further reinforces this inter-pretation. Parsons's optimistic sense of American uniqueness and global relevance contrasts sharply with much contemporary postmodern writing on American commercialism and cultural shallowness in, for example, the work of Jean Baudrillard (1988).

We can anticipate further publications from the Harvard archive as the current appreciation of the scope of Parsons's sociology gains momentum. These new publications are important, because they can provide a more detailed view of Parsons's development and dispel misunderstandings of alleged divisions in his intellectual evolution (Parsons, 1990). For example, Jeffrey C. Alexander's commentary (1990) on Parsons's study of social institutions is an important corrective to many current misunderstandings of notions of functionalism in the 'early' Parsons.

The broad details of Parsons's academic career are relatively well known. He was born in 1902 in Colorado Springs, Colorado, the son of a Congregational minister. Parsons's early life was influenced by Protestant social reform values which to some extent coloured his early interest in what we might call the moral dimension of sociological analysis. He entered Amherst College in 1920 to study biology and philosophy. Although his intention was to follow a medical career, he became influenced by the institutional economics which was taught at Amherst by Walter Hamilton (Parsons, 1970). These two interests (the bio-medical sciences and institutional economics) in fact guided much of his sociological work throughout his career. In 1924 he left Amherst to spend a year at the London School of Economics where he studied sociology in an academic environment shaped by the ideas of L.T. Hobhouse, Morris Ginsburg, R.H. Tawney, Harold Laski and Bronislaw Malinowski. It was Malinowski, the Polish social anthropologist, 'who proved to be the most important influence' (Parsons, 1970: 826) in intellectual terms, and again these early influences continued to have a significant impact on Parsons's later work, for he retained a life-long interest in cultural anthropology, notably in the work of Clyde Kluckhohn. Parsons obtained a scholarship to work at the University of Heidelberg (1925–6), where he decided to write a dissertation on 'the concept of capitalism in recent German literature', concentrating on the work of Lujo Brentano, Werner Sombart and Max Weber. 'It started with Karl Marx, but ended with Max Weber,' Parsons (1981: 184) remarked. Although Max Weber had been dead for five years, his influence was still substantial in the Heidelberg intellectual community and Parsons soon entered 'this particular intellectual circle' (Parsons, 1981: 183). He became particularly interested in Weber's analysis of the relationship between religious values and economic change, within the context of Kantian philosophy and the German *Methodenstreit*.

It was Parsons who eventually translated Weber's famous essays on *The Protestant Ethic and the Spirit of Capitalism* in 1930, with R.H. Tawney providing the foreword (Weber, 1930). In retrospect, it has become rather too easy to dismiss Parsons's interpretation of Weber as a 'founding father' of structural-functionalism (Lassman and Velody, 1989). In fact Parsons's view of Weber as an action theorist clearly recognized the Kantian origins of Weber's notions of rationality, affectivity and personality. Parsons appreciated the centrality of religious values in Weber's analysis of the development of modern personalities in rational capitalism; it is not the case that Parsons attempted to appropriate Weber to simplistic functionalism, because Parsons understood only too well the tensions in Weber's sociology around the analysis of modernity (Turner, 1990). However, it is clearly the case that Parsons's interpretations of Weber's sociology were contentious (Sica, 1988).

Later, in 1947 with A.M. Henderson, Parsons translated selections of Weber's *Wirtschaft und Gesellschaft* with the English title *The Theory of Social and Economical Organization*. Parsons's translations of Weber and his commentary on and theoretical analysis of European social theorists played a crucial role in changing the character of American sociology which since its inception in the 1880s had been dominated by a mixture of pragmatism, positivistic philosophy, social reformist values (Vidich and Lyman, 1985) and a commitment to problem-solving empirical research. Apart from the specific and still disputed influence of Herbert Spencer (Peel, 1971; Coser, 1971: 126; Wilson, 1968), American sociology retained a largely national and home-grown character, its leading representatives including Lester Ward, William Sumner, Robert Park, Charles Cooley, Albion Small, William Thomas and Franklin Giddings. Even though some of the latter group took seriously certain strands of German philosophy and sociology, such as Park's appreciation of Simmel, there was relatively little systematic discussion or comparison of continental European sociological theory until Pitirim Sorokin's *Contemporary Sociological Theories* (1928), Sorokin himself being a fairly recent immigrant from Russia. In any case, much of American sociology was guided by the optimistic view that the research findings of applied sociology could directly inform the political process to bring about a reform of the urban environment (Faris, 1945). Parsons's interest in the analytical problems which are involved in the relationship between sociology and economics provided a sharp contrast to the amalgam of scientism (Bannister, 1987) and social journalism which informed American sociology, and it is not surprising therefore that Parsons came to be regarded as a 'convert' (Timasheff 1957: 183) to Weberian sociology.

Even Alvin Gouldner, who was one of Parsons's major critics in *The Coming Crisis of Western Sociology* (1970), had to admit after Parsons's death that more than any other American sociologist, Parsons helped to destroy American intellectual parochialism and isolationism, attacking the American penchant for positivism and hostility to theory (Gouldner, 1979). Harold J. Bershady in his chapter takes up some additional aspects of Parsons's location within the American tradition, specifically in terms of the contrast between German and American orientations to social theory and intellectual life generally.

In 1931, following a brief return to Amherst, Parsons became an economics tutor at Harvard, where he consolidated his interest in institutional economics and in the interaction between sociological and economic theory. These intellectual concerns led him into studies of Vilfredo Pareto, the Italian economist and sociologist, and Alfred Marshall, the English economist. While his interest in institutional economics was by then well established and his focus on Pareto had developed out of discussions with L.J. Henderson at Harvard, his subsequent turn to the work of Emile Durkheim – notably *The Division of Labour in Society* – was largely self-generated, in defiance of both the anti-Durkheim arguments of Malinowski and Ginsberg to which he had been exposed at the London School of Economics (Parsons, 1981: 184) and American rejection of Durkheim's collectivism. These interests were the background to Parsons's development of what came to be known as 'the voluntaristic theory of action', which resulted in his first major publication in 1937, *The Structure of Social Action* (Parsons, 1937).

Two principal ideas formed the intellectual structure of *The Structure of Social Action*. First, Parsons argued that rational theories of economic action cannot explain social order, because it is perfectly rational for economic agents to use force and fraud to achieve their egoistic ends. Parsons argued that conventional economic theories of rational behaviour cannot solve the Hobbesian problem of order without *ad hoc* and unstable theoretical assumptions about for example 'the hidden hand' of economic forces resolving the conflicts of the social order. In this collection of essays, Victor Lidz draws attention to the complexity of Parsons's analysis of social solidarity and social integration. To solve analytically the problem of social order – to explain how social order is possible – one needs to assume the presence of normative, non-rational constraints which themselves are to be considered as partly constitutive of action itself. It is precisely in this respect that James S. Coleman's study of sociological theory attempts to turn back the theoretical clock (Coleman, 1990), which does not mean that Parsons should be regarded as having said the last significant word on this question of social order, values and rational action.

The second main argument of *The Structure of Social Action* was that European social theory, particularly in the work of Weber, Pareto, Marshall and Durkheim, had converged on a voluntaristic theory of action, precisely because these theories could not resolve the tension between a rationalistic theory of action and a sociological explanation of social order. The analytical goal of *The Structure of Social Action* was therefore very ambitious: to establish the general basis for an integrated voluntaristic theory of action for the whole of the social sciences. In this respect Parsons anticipated many contemporary developments towards an integrated, interdisciplinary programme of social science. Indeed, the implications of Parsons's voluntaristic theory of action and his subsequent analysis of the subsystems of system theory for interdisciplinarity and multidisciplinarity in curriculum reform have yet to be widely recognized. While Parsons had become well known primarily as a sociologist, he argued with increasing explicitness for a coordinated programme of social-scientific work. In fact, at the end of his life, he showed much interest in a programme which included all disciplinary approaches to both the natural and human worlds (Parsons, 1978: 352–433; Klausner and Lidz, 1986). Writing with respect to Parsons's empirical work of the 1940s on fascism, aggression and racism, Baum and Lechner argue persuasively that even by that early date Parsons had accumulated sufficient 'professional experience to show that serious theoretical work could no longer be done with information-saving assumptions about the nature of man, regardless what nature, homo religious, homo economics, homo psychoanalytical, or whatever' (Baum and Lechner, 1981: 291).

Over the years Parsons's arguments in *The Structure of Social Action* have been heavily challenged (Camic, 1989). For example, much attention has been given to Parsons's failure to deal with American pragmatism and early symbolic interactionism. In arguing, for instance, that the pragmatist critique of rationalistic individualism was particularly cogent, Hans Joas (1987: 83) comments that Parsons literally did not devote a single word to the accomplishments of John Dewey's and George Herbert Mead's pragmatist social philosophy, or to the pioneering methodological achievements of the Chicago School of sociology and the theoretical implications of their large-scale investigations.

Parsons is thus found to be partly responsible for the lag in the European appreciation of American pragmatism and symbolic interactionism. Whether sustained attention to sociological pragmatists such as Cooley, Thomas and Mead would have made a significant difference to the general arguments of Parsons's account of voluntaristic action in *The Structure of Social Action* is indeed an interesting theme. But Parsons himself did attempt on a number of occasions to incorporate aspects of the more theoretical work of the philosophical Chicagoans into his intellectual endeavours – notably in his essay on Cooley (Parsons, 1968).

Despite these periodic engagements with pragmatism and symbolic interactionism, we do not believe that Parsons finally or successfully came to terms with these particular dimensions of the American intellectual tradition. In this respect, we would follow Jürgen Habermas (1987) in criticizing Parsons for his failure to develop an adequate understanding of the pragmatics of communicative interaction. Perhaps the critical issue in Parsons's failure to engage with pragmatic philosophy was his neglect of the important work of Charles Peirce, who has in any case only very recently been taken seriously by social scientists. However, it is equally interesting that, while Habermas has addressed a range of philosophical problems which Parsons failed to tackle, Habermas has yet to develop an adequate analysis of the interaction between civilizations and social systems which is sociologically convincing. In other words, while Habermas's idea of communicative action is adequate at the level of individual or group interaction, it is not adequate as a framework for understanding macro-sociologically the relations between whole civilizations, societies and transnational collectivities. Thus, Parsons's work on the evolution of societies and the modern global system points in a much more definitely sociological and realistic direction towards such an understanding than do Habermas's philosophical and idealist endeavours.

One other problem with Parsons's analysis of the convergence of sociological theory towards a voluntaristic framework of action was its selectivity. On the one hand, Parsons almost entirely neglected the work of Karl Marx, which he persistently regarded as simply another version of utilitarian positivism. On the other hand, Parsons did not include a chapter, which in fact he had drafted, on Georg Simmel, whom some would regard as the major figure in twentieth-century German social theory. In this volume, Mark Gould addresses the question of Marx in Parsons's sociology, while Donald Levine considers Parsons's relationship to Simmel.

While in retrospect it is obvious that *The Structure of Social Action* was a major contribution to the development of sociological theory, Parsons's career at Harvard was relatively slow to develop, partly as a consequence of the opposition to Parsons from the chairman of sociology, Sorokin, who was later, in *Sociological Theories of Today* (1966), to describe Parsons's work as 'full of sham scientific slang devoid of clear meaning, precision and elementary elegance' (Sorokin, 1966: 56). However, by the late 1930s and early 1940s a group of graduate students had collected around Parsons, who in the long term came to be very influential in American sociology – people such as Robert Merton, Kingsley Davis, Robin Williams, Edward Devereux, Wilbert Moore, Florence Kluckhohn and Bernard Barber. This relatively slow development of Parsons's institutional career – not to speak of the later institutionalized hostility to it in many quarters – has to be set against criticism that Parsons enjoyed a permanently privileged position in sociology (Goudsblom, 1988).

During the Second World War and its aftermath, much of Parsons's work was concentrated on the problems of the learned professions in modern society, the social conditions which support democratic politics, and conversely therefore on the origins of the fascist dictatorships in Europe. The latter interest was obviously a direct response to the momentous world events of the 1930s and 1940s. In contrast, the interest in the professions which began in the mid-1930s followed rather directly from Parsons's concern with the debate about capitalism and socialism, his argument being that the professional conformed to 'neither the common conception of a self-interested, profit-maximizing capitalist relation nor the conception of a socialistic relation . . . ' (Parsons, 1981: 185). However, Parsons's most significant publication after *The Structure of Social Action* was *The Social System* (1951), a controversial book which was heavily influenced by the work of the Henderson-Mayo group on social processes and social stability and which was responsible for much of the negative view of Parsons which peaked in the late 1960s. Parsons was also increasingly influenced by American anthropological work on values, while his intense exposure to the work of Sigmund Freud was crucial to his mounting interest in the processes of socialization and internalization as explanations of individual adjustment to social requirements and social cohesion generally. In short, Parsons was concerned to understand within a Freudian paradigm the complex 'civilizing' processes which connect the individual and the society, without any reification in his theoretical development of the concepts of self and society.

In the same year as the publication of *The Social System*, Parsons, in collaboration with Edward Shils, published *Toward a General Theory of Action*, which combined many of his psychological and sociological interests. These two works came to be important in the development of so-called functionalist sociology, which was central to American sociology in the 1950s and 1960s. Whereas *The Structure of Social Action* had been somewhat neglected, Parsons's work in the 1950s was widely discussed (often critically) and Parsons himself became a much more influential figure, being for example elected as president of the American Sociological Association in 1949. His observations on 'some problems confronting sociology as a profession' (1959) probably represent the high-water mark of action-system theory as a dominant paradigm in American sociology.

Thus *The Social System* was an attempt to integrate and to extend the work which Parsons had done in collaboration with a number of other social scientists and psychologists in the Harvard University Department of

Social Relations in the 1940s. Parsons saw the book as an attempt to systematize the voluntaristic theory of action by combining insights from Freudian psychoanalysis, political science and institutional economics with many features of social anthropology (as developed in the work of Durkheim and Malinowski). *The Social System, Toward a General Theory of Action* and (in 1953 with Robert Bales and Edward Shils) the very technical and formalistic *Working Papers in the Theory of Action* established the main contours of Parsons's sociological interests in his so-called 'middle period' (Alexander, 1984). These three studies elaborated the notion that there are fundamental choices involved in all types of action (the pattern variables), the idea that all social systems have to confront four basic systemic problems (the four subsystems of the AGIL framework, namely the adaptive, goal attainment, integrative and latency functions), the theory of the sick role in medical sociology, the analysis of the relationship between affective and instrumental leadership, the analytical characterization of the professions and finally the theory of social equilibrium as the outcome of the successful internalization and institutionalization of general cultural values. Parsons's sociology came to assume a fundamental coherence which, while drawing on the traditions of Tönnies, Durkheim and Weber, was an undoubtedly original approach to the analysis of culture and society (Chazel, 1974). These basic ideas came to constitute what was called with considerable reservation on Parsons's part 'structural-functional sociology'. It was this functionalist paradigm which became the target of most of the criticism of Parsonian sociology (Cohen, 1968; Rex, 1961).

Parsons's structural-functionalism was criticized on four main grounds. First, it was held to be incompatible with his earlier voluntaristic theory of action, as spelled out in *The Structure of Social Action*, because the notion – which was essentially Kantian (Bershady, 1973) – that human agents select goals through normative choices was incompatible with the idea that human social relations are structured in a systematic fashion as a consequence of the functional imperatives of the social system. One persistent charge against Parsons therefore has been that his work is diachronically inconsistent (Dawe, 1978; Scott, 1963). More substantively, but in similar vein, Parsons's work on the social system and the relationship between society and personality (Parsons, 1964a) led to mounting claims that he presented what Dennis Wrong (1961) in a much-cited essay called 'an over-socialized conception of man'. In his almost completely neglected reply to Wrong, Parsons (1962) argued that the individual had to be understood in sociological terms as 'institutionalized individualism'. Although we do not have the opportunity to develop this point here, we believe that Parsons's understanding of institutionalized individualism as an historical form in some respects anticipated Michel Foucault's subsequent development of the idea of 'technologies of the self' and the 'cultivation of the self' which was a departure from subjectivist views of personality (Foucault, 1988: 43). Parsons did not work with ahistorical and fixed notions of 'self' and 'society'. In Parsons's response to these issues, we can note a crucial feature of Parsons's sociology as a whole, namely its dependence on a Durkheimian tradition – that is, Parsons's conception of the institutionalized individual as the product of changes in the social structure reproduced the tradition of Durkheim and not the tradition of Weber. Parsons thus remained a Durkheimian rather than a Weberian scholar.

The second main criticism of Parsons's work claimed that it was too abstract and general to be of any real value in either sociological explanation or description. The earliest influential critique of this kind was presented by Parsons's former student Robert Merton (1967) in the late 1940s. Subsequently C. Wright Mills (1959) attempted to show that so-called 'Grand Theory' was incapable of addressing the real problems of history and social structure, and merely disguised a list of essentially simple and mundane observations about social life. In more recent criticism, it is ironic that Parsons has been charged with a failure to develop a social theory which is sufficiently abstract to avoid psychological reductionism. For example, Niklas Luhmann has attempted to develop a general theory of social relations which explicitly rejects any reference to the psychological characteristics of individual human subjects (Luhmann, 1982).

Given the status of C. Wright Mills's critical sociology on the Left, Parsons was almost by definition labelled as necessarily conservative, which constitutes the third main criticism of his work. Parsons's implicit and not infrequently explicit celebration of American values in the postwar and Cold War periods was regarded as morally objectionable. More specifically, Parsons was charged with providing a sociology which was a highly suspect ideological justification of American power, wealth and inequality. For example, Andrew Hacker (1961) argued that Parsons's liberal defence of American democracy failed to comprehend the massive reproduction of inequality by the American class system, the existence of powerful vested interests and the continuity of a power elite which negated the democratic foundation of the American political system. Parsons, who had critically reviewed Mills's *The Power Elite* (Parsons, 1957), simply could not understand, according to Hacker, what Mills was saying about American power-relations. In a similar fashion, one of the most influential, not to say abrasive, attacks on Parsonian sociology was undertaken by Gouldner (1970) in *The Coming Crisis of Western Sociology*, in which he challenged Parsons's naive optimism about the possibility of a gradual perfection of capitalist society. Gouldner noted that Parsons's implicit criticism of the classical sociological tradition in fact centred on the question of pessimism. Whereas Marx and Weber represented in different ways deterministic and pessimistic accounts of capitalism through theories of human alienation and rationalization (Löwith, 1982), Parsons's voluntarism and his more concrete diagnoses of contemporary societies represented an optimistic and voluntaristic view of social reality. Thus

Gouldner (1970: 183) attacked Parsons because much of his 'later theoretical work is shaped by these two powerful impulses clearly manifest in his earliest work: (1) by his effort to generalize the anti-Marxist critique, and, (2) at the same time, by his effort to overcome the determinism, the pessimism, and, indeed, the anti-capitalism of these critics of Marxism.'

Of course, attempting to assess Parsons's political and ideological position over the 'merits' of capitalism in relation to Soviet-style socialism has become increasingly complex in the aftermath of the collapse of organized socialism in Eastern Europe and Russia after the 'revolutions' of 1989–90. In retrospect, Parsons's critique of Soviet socialism appears increasingly justified against those critics who regarded Parsons as simply a Cold War warrior. Such issues, in particular Parsons's activities in post-war European reconstruction, are analysed in this book in detail by Jens Kaalhauge Nielsen.

The prominence which Mills in the 1960s, and Gouldner in the 1970s, enjoyed in radical sociology meant that Parsonian sociology was virtually excluded (apart from being an object of critical and ritualistic attack) from the social science curriculum of European universities, while by the mid-1970s there was widespread exclusion of his work from many universities in the USA. It is important to keep in perspective Parsons's impact on American sociology, since Parsonian functionalism has often been regarded by its critics as the hegemonic paradigm of sociology in capitalistic America, which in fact it has never been, despite the diffuse functionalism of the late 1950s and early 1960s.

Such criticisms of Parsons had their analytical root in the basic argument, the fourth of the major forms of attack, that Parsons's sociology could not address the general problem of power in a way which was analytically satisfying and sensitive to empirical circumstances, a claim often expressed in the argument that Parsons had no theory of conflict, particularly in view of his concern with the equilibrium (or homeostasis) of the social system (Black, 1961; Dahrendorf, 1958). While Parsons had developed the idea of 'social strain' (Parsons, 1963) in relation to fascist and other authoritarian political movements, it was claimed that Parsons had no genuine understanding of the centrality of conflict in the formation and dissolution of social groups, and furthermore that he had no conception of power but only a notion of influence – an issue which is partly addressed by Victor Lidz in this volume. This critique of Parsons was associated with the notion that as European sociology was imported into the American sociological profession, the centrality of power, conflict, ideology and interest in the work of writers like Weber had been systematically excluded in favour of an emphasis on values, cultural integration, liberal politics and social stability (Cohen et al., 1975; Horowitz, 1983: 173–90). Conflict theory (Coser, 1956; Dahrendorf, 1959; Rex, 1961) emerged as a major alternative to the theoretical strategy of Parsonian structural-functionalism which, according to its critics, was based upon the importance of consensus over values as the foundation of social order and stability. In recent years there has been some recognition of the value of Parsons's theory of power, which clearly emphasized the productive, expandable and enabling features of power as a medium of exchange. Foucault's view of power as decentralized and productive has a peculiar and ironic relationship to the legacy of Parsons (Clegg, 1989).

This critique of Parsons's analysis of power as a medium of exchange and control was in fact very closely related to the final major criticism of structural-functionalism, namely that it could not offer a powerful theory of social change or that the theory of change which emerged from functionalism was in fact a modern version of evolutionary, teleological explanations which presupposed a biological analogy with the differentiation of organic life (Haines, 1987; Peel, 1969). In spite of such charges Parsons was a very influential figure in the crystallization of societal modernization theory and its applications to the Third World countries of Africa, Asia and Latin America in the 1960s (Almond and Coleman, 1960; Vallier, 1970; Evans, 1988: 111). With the rise of dependency and world-systems approaches in the late 1960s and early 1970s, however, Parsons came under further attack – most vociferously among Latin Americans and Latin Americanists – for spreading the idea that individual Third World societies could modernize autonomously via cultural change and processes of differentiation (Cockcroft et al., 1972), as opposed to the dependency and world-system view that it is the economic structure of the world as a whole which determines the fortunes of individual societies. Regrettably, in this barrage of criticism of 'modernization' theory, Parsons's (1971) own attempt to analyse and describe the global 'system of societies' went virtually unnoticed; although it has to be conceded that he largely omitted the Third World from his work on that theme.

These critical responses to Parsonian sociology did much to challenge the influence of Parsons's structural-functionalist analysis as a sociological paradigm and Parsons was of course forced to respond to these objections in a series of publications in which he addressed the problems of 'over-socialization' (Parsons, 1962), power (Parsons, 1969), social stratification (Parsons, 1970) and social change (Parsons, 1966). In our view (and we will return to this issue shortly), the kinds of criticism of Parsons's structural-functionalism which we have indicated obscured the essential character of his sociology and furthermore failed to address, or take notice of, important developments in Parsons's own sociology, which, for example, began to address important issues in the educational systems of modern societies – specifically, the significance of the university in democratic systems (Parsons and Platt, 1973), the 'expressive revolution' of the 1960s and, as we have noted, the increasing salience of the world-system of societies (Parsons, 1971). Criticisms of Parsons have also usually failed to trace his final concerns with the 'human condition', where he addressed his sociological perspective to the problems of death, health and disease, and 'the gift of life' (Parsons, 1978). While Parsons's critics remained focused on problems of conflict and change, he continued to be one of the most prolific and innovative contributors to social theory in the twentieth century. For example, he began to elaborate a theory of the symbolic parallels between money in the production of wealth and sex in the production of people, both being media of exchange (Parsons, 1979). Heiner Ganssmann (1988), in an otherwise informed study of 'money – a symbolically generalized medium', curiously ignores this as part of Parsons's theory. Indeed, Parsons's stature as a *general* theorist of social relations and cultural patterns has yet to be properly evaluated, let alone questioned.

Our argument is that the debate around structural-functionalism obscured the essential character of Parsonian sociology as a contribution to action-systems theory. What then were the essential issues in Parsons's sociological contribution?

First, the critical focus on the problem of values has obscured Parsons's contribution to economic sociology and in particular his contribution to action theory as a basis for both economic and sociological analysis (Holton and Turner, 1986; Turner, 1989). Parsons's economic sociology, which continued to be of major importance throughout his career (Parsons and Smelser, 1956; Parsons, 1976), represents one of the most systematic and theoretically coherent attacks on rationalist models in economic action theory and in the social sciences generally. Parsons's status in economic theory (as contrasted with his obvious prominence in sociology) is perhaps usefully illustrated by the fact that he was Marshall lecturer in economics at Cambridge University in 1953 (Parsons, 1986). Secondly, Parsons's sociology continued to be guided by his interest in medical sciences and, despite a long history of criticism, his sick-role theory represents one of the most enduring features of contemporary medical sociology, offering a critical, interdisciplinary approach to health and illness by combining a sociology of action with Freudian transference theory (Turner, 1987). The importance of Parsons's medical sociology is critically evaluated in relation to contemporary social theory in this volume by Arthur Frank. Thirdly, the scope and power of Parsonian sociology as a comparative historical perspective is borne out by a consideration of his contribution to the sociology of religion where, unlike conventional sociological approaches, Parsons retained a strong interest in comparative religious studies – a tradition which to a large extent he inherited from Weber (Parsons, 1963). Parsons was one of the very few sociologists in the classical tradition to develop an interest in religion in industrial society and to recognize that 'secularization' was a complex process in which religious institutions continued to play a major role in so-called secular society, despite their overt institutional erosion. Parsons played an influential role in contemporary sociology in keeping the analysis of the sacred as a central aspect of analytical sociological enquiry (Lidz, 1982; Robertson, 1982). Finally, his consistent and increasingly multifaceted concern with the problem of social order was not in fact a merely static, analytic or conservative interest, but was rather part of a broader concern with the historical and comparative conditions for political change in circumstances of increasing complexity which would permit the development of individual freedoms and collective stability.

While this focus may well be described as liberal, Parsons was clearly very far removed from political conservatism, as Nielsen's contribution to this volume amply demonstrates. It is now increasingly clear that Parsons made an important contribution to postwar reconstruction in Germany and, to a lesser extent, Japan. He remained a profound critic of fascism and right-wing social movements. It is therefore appropriate that some recent interpretations of Parsons have given such prominent notice to his political sociology (Buxton, 1985). The restoration of these often neglected features of Parsons's sociology to prominence amounts to the assertion that Parsons was a major contributor to an empirical sociology of modernization rather than simply an abstract theorist of social systems. This empirical focus in Parsons's sociology (on the family, on economic processes, on the state, on the university system and generally on social citizenship) is a crucial feature of his work and provides an alternative perspective to the idea of Parsons as the Grand Theorist. Of course, Parsons in the dedication to his wife Helen in *The Social System* had referred to himself as 'an incurable theorist', but his theoretical interests were clearly focused on specific empirical issues and it is a major injustice to dismiss his work as Mills does in terms of a collection of abstract generalizations which have no empirical or moral content. If Durkheim developed Kantian philosophy into the sociology of knowledge, Parsons's sociology can be seen as an empirical translation of the categorial imperative of brotherly love into the arena of political life. Moreover, it is our view that Parsons's 'will to generalize' developed largely and increasingly out of his fascination with historical and comparative diversity and difference. More specifically, Parsons's interest in the analytical aspects of order pivoted upon his acute sensitivity to empirical 'disorder'. Having said that, it has also to be remarked that Parsons never resolved the perennial methodological problem as to just how much and in what form one should refer directly in one's writing to empirical phenomena in order to make a theoretical point.

Our characterization of Parsonian sociology as empirical leads us finally into a commentary on the so-called neofunctionalist movement (Alexander, 1985), or the 'new theoretical movement' (Alexander, 1988), or more generally to the Parsons revival. Given the critical attack on Parsons's work in the 1950s and 1960s, and the more recent critical evaluation of Alexander (Sica, 1983), the sympathetic revival of attention to Parsons in the 1980s is particularly striking. In this volume, Bryan S. Turner provides an overview and evaluation of some of these theoretical developments and debates. In Germany Jürgen Habermas (1981) and Niklas Luhmann (1982) have both been drawn into an extensive discussion of Parsonian sociology. In particular, the three principal divisions in Luhmann's, basically phenomenological, theory (the theory of systems, the analysis of evolution and the study of communication) all derive from, or have their roots in, Parsons's systems theory (Beyer, 1984). Indeed, it is an exquisite irony that Habermas, as the leading representative of critical theory, should have been recently criticized for being too closely associated with Parsonian functionalism in combining hermeneutics and structural functionalism (Joas, 1988). Other important contributions have been made by Richard Münch (1988), who has analysed the impact of Kant's critique of practical reason on Parsons's action theory. Further commentators (Sciulli, 1988) have noticed an important convergence between Parsons's views on democratic pluralism and Habermas's theory of communicative action, leading to a new interest in the question of 'societal constitutionalism'.

In this introduction we have given some prominence to the claim that Parsons's sociology was driven by specific empirical and political concerns, especially those associated with the socio-political and cultural problems of modern American civilization. In short, we have emphasized the idea of Parsons as a modernist with a specific concern for the cultural core of the American socio-cultural system. This emphasis on empirical issues has been adopted to counteract the mistaken allegation that Parsonian sociology was merely abstract Grand Theory. However, we do not want thereby to play down the obvious fact that Parsons's analytical concerns with the nature of social action were central to his intellectual career, nor that some of his technical work in that regard is tedious. We have noted that one index of his stature in sociological theory is that Parsons is probably the only American theorist whom Habermas and Luhmann feel the need to debate and criticize. Why then is Parsons significant as a sociological theorist? We offer four broad answers to the question: why read Parsons?

First, there is something admirable in sustained and systematic sociological theory which is directed towards consciously established objectives. There is a general coherence to Parsons's sociology which he sustained over a lifetime. In this introduction, we have referred only to a limited number of his theoretical and empirical interests and to how these were organized. In a fuller evaluation, it would be necessary to examine how Parsons integrated the theory of social differentiation, media of exchange, and pattern variables into his general theory. As a systematic theorist, Parsons's career might therefore be regarded as an exemplar, not of how to do sociology, but of how to be a sociologist.

Secondly, Parsons's theoretical work is important because it remains one of the very few attempts to locate what would be the minimal requirements for a genuinely general theory of the social sciences as such. Parsons wanted to establish the fundamental and elementary theoretical components of action theory which would become a general analytical paradigm for all the sciences of human action (in contrast to theories of behaviour). The unit act, the notions of interaction and social relations, the theory of social systems and so forth were contributions to a general theory of action which would embrace economics, sociology, political science, anthropology and psychology. In other words, Parsons sought a theoretical strategy whereby, *inter alia*, the insights of Freudian psychoanalysis, Marshallian and Keynesian economics, Durkheimian sociology, Meadian and Piagetian social psychology, the anthropology of Malinowski and Kroeber, and the philosophy of Kant could be brought within a single, but complex and evolving, theoretical system.

Thirdly, Parsons wanted to utilize this theory to make possible informed and systematic work on 'actually existing' capitalism as well as on 'actually existing' pre-1989 socialism, the collapse of which, mainly in a democratic direction, Parsons predicted on a number of occasions (Parsons, 1964b). In this volume, Parsons's paper on American values shows how he was working towards a comprehensive sociological analysis of an entire society, America, which must be regarded, from both the Right and the Left, as the most complex society yet to have emerged in the history of the human world. While it is often held up as the focus of criticism for those who oppose capitalism in its entirety, America is also one of the most progressive and revolutionary of societies in Western civilization. As we have already noted, the apparent shift in much of the old Soviet bloc towards markets, liberal values and political pluralism gives, in our view, a new impetus to the study of Parsonian sociology. Like Weber, Parsons had an appreciation of the historical irony of unintended consequences in social change. Thus, although the American polity offers great opportunities for liberal change, it coexists with massive inequality, racism and brutality.

Finally, Parsons's critique of utilitarian rationalist economism remains one of the most cogent attacks on the core logic of the positivistic variant of social science, which is as valid today as it was when Parsons published *The Structure of Social Action* in 1937. In contemporary social theory, there are still many variants of the utilitarian position, including rational choice theory, various forms of exchange theory and a number of other versions of economism, which embrace many of the assumptions which Parsons radically criticized in the 1930s. Parsons's critique provides a method of combining value-analysis with mainstream sociological theory, thereby also offering a possible solution to the fact-value distinction. Parsons's work cannot be criticized in terms of some simplistic adherence to a value-relevant and value-neutral dichotomy. This aspect of his sociology is very clearly illustrated by his philosophical relationship to the Kantian formulation of the categorical imperatives.

In North America the re-evaluation of Parsons has taken the form of on the one hand accepting much of the critical rejection of Parsons, and on the other attempting to develop aspects of Parsonian sociology in order to cope with the analysis of conflict, change and development. Much of this revival involves an enthusiasm for the theory of differentiation as a theoretical basis for the analysis of modern societies (for example Alexander, 1987; Colomy, 1985; Smelser, 1985). This attempt on the part of neofunctionalism simultaneously to accept the criticism of Parsons's sociology while also advancing Parsonian sociology involves a number of obvious tensions. For example, Alexander, having considered the conflict-theory critique of Parsons, concludes that 'Parsons's perspective does not focus on integration alone nor does it assume consensus. To the contrary, it effectively articulates some of the most basic social antagonisms. Moreover, this change theory is firmly rooted in Parsons's more general empirically-oriented work and in the multidimensional presuppositions that inform it' (Alexander, 1984: 71). Furthermore, Alexander, having considered Parsons's political sociology as a whole, suggests that 'taken together, his writings present a sustained inquiry into the particular national patterns of Western development and the threat to this development posed by the radical right' (Alexander, 1984: 71–2). If this sympathetic appraisal of Parsons is correct (and we believe that it is), then the argument that we need to go beyond Parsons seems at least premature. Thus if this defence of Parsons could be sustained, there is little ground for believing that we are already in a 'post-Parsonian' world of sociology (Alexander, 1987: 375). In any case, Alexander has already argued that 'functionalism' was never a particularly good description of Parsons's sociological theory (Alexander, 1985: 8). If 'functionalism' was an inappropriate description, is there any real merit in 'neofunctionalism' as a label? In our view there are some important continuities between Parsons's world and the contemporary situation. As a conclusion to this introductory essay, we wish to outline briefly the central core of Parsons's legacy, relating it to contemporary discussions of postmodernism.

Parsons's sociology was structured by two separate but related questions. The first question is: how can individual autonomy by sustained without authoritarian regulation? It was to this issue that the voluntaristic theory of action was ultimately directed. François Bourricaud's *The Sociology of Talcott Parsons* (1981) is essential for understanding this aspect of Parsons's theory, primarily because he represents Parsons as arguing that the greater the complexity of a social system the more it depends for its viability on the voluntaristic inputs of individuals. The second question is: how can social order be maintained in a world which is increasingly differentiated, pluralistic and necessarily conflictual? It was the theory of the social system which attempted to address this issue. However, it is clear that these two questions and their solutions are highly interrelated (as Alexander has argued) since the autonomy of the individual becomes both more possible but also more complex in a world of increasing value differentiation. As we know, Parsons proposed a number of solutions to these issues, but an important ingredient within his approach was that values have to become more general in order to embrace greater complexity, and social structures have to become more differentiated to respond to more complex demands. Although, broadly speaking, Parsons thought that the Western legacy of liberalism, which he traced back through Christianity to ancient Greek cultures, had an important contribution to make globally to these problems, his sociology was not nationalistic in any narrow sense. By contrast, contemporary sociology is unfortunately typically nationalistic and parochial in its interests (Moore, 1966). It is known that there are certain problems in Parsons's sociology related, for example, to his views on Russia as a modern system (Holton and Turner 1986: 224–5).

We can now specify Parsons's problematic more precisely. We can see his overall interest as an inquiry into the conditions which make progressive political life possible globally and the conditions which make individual life meaningful and autonomous within social systems which are increasingly complex. It is for this reason that we believe Parsons's sociology is directly relevant to the issues of a postmodern society, insofar as we think of postmodernism in terms of fragmentation, complexity, diversity and difference. In this respect postmodernism is largely the effect of a high level of structural and cultural differentiation and pluralism, which were clearly problems to which Parsons addressed himself through a long career. Finally, while classical sociology often responded to modernism in terms of nostalgic romanticism, Parsons faced the complexities, promises and dangers of the modern world with a completely modernistic mentality. In this respect Parsons is one of the few genuinely modern and global minds of the twentieth century.

References

Alexander, J.C. (1984) *Theoretical Logic in Sociology*, vol. 4, *The Modern Reconstruction of Classical Thought: Talcott Parsons*. London: Routledge & Kegan Paul.

Alexander, J.C. (ed.) (1985) *Neofunctionalism*. Beverly Hills: Sage.

Alexander, J.C. (1987) *Twenty Lectures: Sociological Theory since World War II*. New York: Columbia University Press.

Alexander, J.C. (1988) 'The New Theoretical Movement', pp. 77–101 in N.J. Smelser (ed.), *Handbook of Sociology*. Newbury Park: Sage.

Alexander, J.C. (1990) 'Commentary: Structure, Value, Action', *American Sociological Review*, 55 (3): 339–45.

Almond, G.A. and Coleman, J.S. (1960) *The Politics of the Developing Areas*. Princeton, NJ: Princeton University Press.

Bannister, R.C. (1987) *Sociology and Scientism: the American Quest for Objectivity 1880–1940*. Chapel Hill: University of North Carolina Press.

Baudrillard, J. (1988) *America*. London: Verso.

Baum, R.C. and Lechner, F.J. (1981) 'National Socialism: Towards an Action-Theoretical Interpretation', *Sociological Inquiry*, 51 (3/4): 281–305.

Bershady, H.J. (1973) *Ideology and Social Knowledge*. Oxford: Blackwell.

Beyer, P. (1984) 'Introduction' to Niklas Luhmann, *Religious Dogmatics and the Evolution of Societies*. New York: Edwin Mellen Press, pp. v–xlvii.

Black, M. (1961) 'Some Questions about Talcott Parsons' Theories', pp. 268–88 in M. Black (ed.), *The Social Theories of Talcott Parsons*. Englewood Cliffs, NJ: Prentice-Hall.

Bourricaud, F. (1981) *The Sociology of Talcott Parsons*. Chicago and London: University of Chicago Press.

Buxton, W. (1985) *Talcott Parsons and the Capitalist Nation-State: Political Sociology as a Strategic Vocation*. Toronto: University of Toronto Press.

Camic, C. (1989) 'Structure after 50 Years: the Anatomy of a Charter', American Journal of Sociology, 95 (1): 38–107.

Chazel, F. (1974) La Théorie analytique de la société dans l'œuvre de Talcott Parsons. Paris: Mouton.

Clegg, S. (1989) Frameworks of Power. London: Sage.

Cockcroft, D., Frank, A.G. and Johnson, D. (1972) Dependence and Underdevelopment. Garden City, NY: Anchor Books.

Cohen, J., Hazelrigg, L.E. and Pope, W. (1975) 'De-Parsonizing Weber: a Critique of Parsons's Interpretation of Weber's Sociology', American Sociological Review, 40 (2): 229–41.

Cohen, P.S. (1968) Modern Social Theory. London: Heinemann Educational Books.

Coleman, J.S. (1990) Modern Social Theory. Cambridge, Mass.: Harvard University Press.

Colomy, P. (1985) 'Uneven Structural Differentiation: Toward a Comparative Approach', pp. 131–56 in Alexander (1985).

Coser, L. (1956) The Functions of Social Conflicts. New York: Free Press.

Coser, L. (1971) Masters of Sociological Thought. New York: Harcourt Brace Jovanovich.

Dahrendorf, R. (1958) 'Out of Utopia', American Journal of Sociology 64 (2): 115–27.

Dahrendorf, R. (1959) Class and Class Conflict in an Industrial Society. London: Routledge & Kegan Paul.

Dawe, A. (1978) 'Theories of Social Action', pp. 362–417 in T. Bottomore and R. Nisbet (eds), A History of Sociological Analysis. London: Heinemann.

Evans, P.M. (1988) John Fairbank and the American Understanding of Modern China. New York: Blackwell.

Faris, R.E.L. (1945) 'American Sociology', pp. 538–61 in G. Gurvitch and W.E. Moore (eds), Twentieth Century Sociology. New York: The Philosophical Library.

Foucault, M. (1986) The History of Sexuality. The Care of the Self. Harmondsworth: Penguin Books.

Foucault, M. (1988) 'Technologies of the Self', pp. 16–49 in L.H. Martin, H. Gutman and P.H. Hutton (eds), Technologies and the Self. London: Tavistock.

Ganssmann, H. (1988) 'Money – a Symbolically Generalized Medium of Communication? On the Concept of Money in Recent Sociology', Economy and Society, 17 (3): 285–316.

Goudsblom, J. (1988) 'The Sociology of Norbert Elias: its Resonance and Significance', Theory, Culture & Society, 4 (2–3): 323–37.

Gouldner, A.W. (1970) The Coming Crisis of Western Sociology. New York: Basic Books.

Gouldner, A.W. (1979) 'Talcott Parsons', Theory and Society, 8 (Dec.): 299–302.

Habermas, J. (1981) 'Talcott Parsons: Problems of Theory Construction', Sociological Inquiry, 51 (3–4): 173–96.

Habermas, J. (1987) The Theory of Communicative Action, vol. 2, The Critique of Functionalist Reason. Cambridge: Polity Press.

Hacker, A. (1961) 'Sociology and Ideology', pp. 289–310 in M. Black (ed.), The Social Theories of Talcott Parsons, a Critical Examination, Englewood Cliffs, NJ: Prentice-Hall.

Haines, V.A. (1987) 'Biological and Social Theory: Parsons's Evolutionary Theme', Sociology, 21 (1): 19–39.

Hamilton, P. (1983) Talcott Parsons. London: Tavistock.

Holmwood, J.M. (1982) Review of Alexander, Theoretical Logic in Sociology, vol. 1, Sociology, 16 (4): 599–601.

Holmwood, J.M. (1983a) Review of Alexander, Theoretical Logic in Sociology, vol. 2, Sociology, 17 (3): 392–4.

Holmwood, J.M. (1983b) 'Talcott Parsons and the Development of his System', British Journal of Sociology, 34 (4): 573–90.

Holton, R.J. and Turner, B.S. (1986) Talcott Parsons on Economy and Society. London and New York: Routledge & Kegan Paul.

Horowitz, I.L. (1983) C. Wright Mills. New York: Free Press.

Joas, H. (1987) 'Symbolic Interactionism', in A. Giddens and J. Turner (eds), Social Theory Today. Stanford: Stanford University Press.

Joas, H. (1988) 'The Unhappy Marriage of Hermeneutics and Functionalism', *Praxis International*, 8 (1): 34–51.

Klausner, S.Z. and Lidz, V.M. (1986) *The Nationalization of the Social Sciences.* Philadelphia: University of Pennsylvania Press.

Lassman, P. and Velody, I. with Martins, H. (eds) (1989) *Max Weber's 'Science as a Vocation'.* London: Unwin Hyman.

Lidz, V. (1982) 'Religion and Cybernetic Concepts in the Theory of Action', *Sociological Analysis*, 43 (4): 287–305.

Loubser, J.J., Baum, R.C., Effrat, A. and Lidz, V. (1976) *Explorations in General Theory in Social Science*, 2 vols. New York: Free Press.

Löwith, K. (1982) *Max Weber and Karl Marx.* London: Allen & Unwin.

Luhmann, N. (1982) *The Differentiation of Society.* New York: Columbia University Press.

Lyotard, J.F. (1986) *The Postmodern Condition: a Report on Knowledge.* Manchester: Manchester University Press.

Merton, R.K. (1967) *On Theoretical Sociology.* New York: Free Press.

Mills, C.W. (1959) *The Sociological Imagination.* Harmondsworth: Penguin.

Moore, W.E. (1966) 'Global Sociology: the World as a Singular System', *American Journal of Sociology*, 71 (5): 475–82.

Münch, R. (1981) 'Talcott Parsons and the Theory of Action, I: the Structure of the Kantian Core', *American Journal of Sociology*, 86 (3): 709–40.

Münch, R. (1987) 'Parsonian Theory Today: in Search of a New Synthesis', pp. 116–55 in A. Giddens and J. Turner (eds), *Social Theory Today.* Stanford: Stanford University Press.

Münch, R. (1988) *Theory of Action: Towards a New Synthesis Going beyond Parsons.* London: Routledge & Kegan Paul.

Parsons, T. (1937) *The Structure of Social Action.* New York: McGraw-Hill.

Parsons, T. (1951) *The Social System.* London: Routledge & Kegan Paul.

Parsons, T. (1957) 'The Distribution of Power in American Society', *World Politics*, 10: 123–43.

Parsons, T. (1959) 'Some Problems Confronting Sociology as a Profession', *American Sociological Review*, 29 (4): 547–59.

Parsons, T. (1961) 'Some Considerations on the Theory of Social Change', *Rural Sociology*, 26 (3): 219–39.

Parsons, T. (1962) 'Comment on "The Oversocialized Conception of Man" by Dennis Wrong', *Psychoanalysis and Psychoanalytic Review*, 10: 322–34.

Parsons, T. (1963) 'Social Strains in America: a Postscript', pp. 231–8 in D. Bell (ed.), *The Radical Right.* New York: Doubleday.

Parsons, T. (1964a) *Social Structure and Personality.* New York: Free Press.

Parsons, T. (1964b) 'Communism and the West: the Sociology of Conflict', pp. 390–9 in A. Etzioni and E. Etzioni (eds), *Social Change: Sources, Patterns and Consequences.* New York: Basic Books.

Parsons, T. (1965) 'Unity and Diversity in the Modern Intellectual Disciplines: the Role of the Social Sciences', *Daedalus* (Winter). Repr. in *Sociological Theory and Modern Society*, pp. 166–91. New York: Free Press, 1967.

Parsons, T. (1966) *Societies: Evolutionary and Comparative Perspectives.* Englewood Cliffs, NJ: Prentice-Hall.

Parsons, T. (1968) 'Cooley and the Problem of Internalization', pp. 48–67 in A.J. Reiss, Jr (ed.), *Cooley and Sociological Analysis.* Ann Arbor: University of Michigan Press.

Parsons, T. (1969) *Politics and Social Structure.* New York: Free Press.

Parsons, T. (1970) 'On Building Social System Theory, a Personal History', *Daedalus*, 99: 826–81.

Parsons, T. (1971) *The System of Modern Societies.* Englewood Cliffs, NJ: Prentice-Hall.

Parsons, T. (1976) 'Clarence Ayer's Economics and Sociology', pp. 175–9 in W. Breit and W. Patton Culbertson Jr (eds), *Science and Ceremony.* Austin, Texas: University of Texas Press.

Parsons, T. (1978) *Action Theory and the Human Condition.* New York: Free Press.

Parsons, T. (1979) 'Religions and Economic Symbolism in the Western World', *Sociological Inquiry*, 49 (2–3): 1–48.

Parsons, T. (1981) 'Revisiting the Classics throughout a Long Career', pp. 183–94 in B. Rhea (ed.), *The Future of the Sociological Classics*. London: Allen & Unwin.

Parsons, T. (1986) 'The Integration of Economic and Sociological Theory. The Marshall Lectures'. *Research Reports from the Department of Sociology*, Uppsala University, 4: 1–69.

Parsons, T. (1989) 'A Tentative Outline of American Values', *Theory, Culture & Society*, 6 (4): 577–612.

Parsons, T. (1990) 'Prolegomena to a Theory of Social Institutions', *American Sociological Review*, 55 (3): 319–33.

Parsons, T., Bales, R.F. and Shils, E.A. (1953) *Working Papers in the Theory of Action*. New York: Free Press.

Parsons, T. and Platt, G.M. (1973) *The American University*. Cambridge, MA: Harvard University Press.

Parsons, T. and Shils, E. (eds) (1951) *Toward a General Theory of Action*. Cambridge MA: Harvard University Press.

Parsons, T. and Smelser, N.J. (1956) *Economy and Society: a Study in the Integration of Economic and Social Theory*. London: Routledge & Kegan Paul.

Peel, J.D.Y. (1969) 'Spencer and the Neo-evolutionists', *Sociology*, 3 (2): 173–92.

Peel, J.D.Y. (1971) *Herbert Spencer, the Evolution of a Sociologist*. London: Heinemann Educational Books.

Rex, J. (1961) *Key Problems of Sociological Theory*. London: Routledge & Kegan Paul.

Robertson, R. (1970) *The Sociological Interpretation of Religion*. Oxford: Blackwell.

Robertson, R. (1977) 'Talcott Parsons', pp. 284–300 in T. Raison (ed.), *The Founding Fathers of Social Science*. London: Scolar.

Robertson, R. (1982) 'Parsons on the Evolutionary Significance of American Religion', *Sociological Analysis*, 43 (4): 307–25.

Robertson, R. (1991) 'Globality, Global Culture and Images of World Order', in H. Haferkamp and N.J. Smelser (eds), *Social Change and Modernity*. Berkeley, CA: University of California Press.

Sciulli, D. (1988) 'Foundations of Societal Constitutionalism', *British Journal of Sociology*, 34 (3): 377–408.

Sciulli, D. and Gerstein, D. (1985) 'Social Theory and Talcott Parsons in the 1980s', *Annual Review of Sociology*, 11: 369–87.

Scott, J.F. (1963) 'The Changing Foundations of the Parsonian Action Scheme', *American Sociological Review*, 28 (5): 716–35.

Sica, A. (1983) 'Parsons, Jr', *American Journal of Sociology*, 89 (1): 200–19.

Sica, A. (1988) *Weber, Irrationality and Social Order*. Berkeley, CA: University of California Press.

Smelser, N.J. (1985) 'Evaluating the Model of Structural Differentiation in Relation to Educational Change in the Nineteenth Century', pp. 113–30 in Alexander (1985).

Sorokin, P.A. (1928) *Contemporary Sociological Theories*. New York: Harper & Row.

Sorokin, P.A. (1966) *Sociological Theories of Today*. New York: Harper & Row.

Timasheff, N.S. (1957) *Sociological Theory, its Nature and Growth*. New York: Random House.

Tribe, K. (ed.) (1989) *Reading Weber*. London: Routledge.

Turner, B.S. (1987) *Medical Power and Social Knowledge*. London: Sage.

Turner, B.S. (1989) 'Some Reflections on Cumulative Theorizing in Sociology', pp. 131–47 in J.H. Turner (ed.), *Theory Building in Sociology*. Newbury Park: Sage.

Turner, B.S. (1990) 'Periodization and Politics in the Postmodern', pp. 1–13 in B.S. Turner (ed.), *Theories of Modernity and Postmodernity*. London: Sage.

Vallier, I. (1970) *Catholicism, Social Control and Modernization in Latin America*. Englewood Cliffs, NJ: Prentice-Hall.

Vidich, A.J. and Lyman, S.M. (1985) *American Sociology: Worldly Rejections of Religion and their Directions*. New Haven: Yale University Press.

Weber, M. (1930) *The Protestant Ethic and The Spirit of Capitalism*, tr. T. Parsons. London: Allen & Unwin.

Weber, M. (1947) *The Theory of Social and Economic Organization*, tr. T. Parsons and A.H. Henderson. New York: Oxford University Press.

Wiener, J. (1989) 'Talcott Parsons' Role: Bringing Nazi Sympathizers to the US', *The Nation*, 6 March: 1–2.

Wilson, R. (1968) *In Quest of Community: Social Philosophy in the United States 1860–1920*. New York: Knopf.

Wrong, D. (1961) 'The Oversocialized Conception of Man in Modern Sociology', *American Sociological Review*, 26 (2): 183–92.

Zuckerman, H. (1988) 'The Sociology of Science', pp. 511–74 in N.J. Smelser (ed.), *Handbook of Sociology*. Newbury Park: Sage.

2

THE AMERICAN VALUE SYSTEM: A COMMENTARY ON TALCOTT PARSONS'S PERSPECTIVE AND UNDERSTANDING

Victor Lidz

The American society project

The working paper entitled 'A Tentative Outline of American Values' is part of a relatively little known yet important aspect of Talcott Parsons's work. For more than thirty years, from the late 1940s until just days before his death, when he completed the draft of a large volume, Parsons hoped to write a major interpretive study of American society. Displeased with what he regarded as ideological distortions in the common understandings of American society, not least among many of the nation's most famous intellectuals, Parsons endeavoured to use his own analytical framework to establish a rigorous orientation for objective interpretation.

Parsons's project on American society took shape in the years following the Second World War, when he took a particular interest not only in the nation's religious traditions and democratic institutions, but also in its complicated and ambivalent adjustment to a role of leadership in the international arena (Parsons, 1955). He was especially concerned to explore the ways in which social science might prove helpful to the nation in making difficult institutional changes during a period of social strain (Parsons, 1986).

In the late 1940s Parsons began to use research funds to hire graduate assistants to investigate a wide range of problems concerning American values, social structure, social problems, and patterns of institutional change (Parsons Papers). For a period of twenty years or more, research on general institutional arrangements in American society remained a major focus of the work he assigned to a succession of assistants, including Jesse Pitts, Robert Bellah, Kaspar Naegele, Jan Loubser, Winston White, Leon Mayhew and others, including, in a later phase, myself. Parsons also began to teach a general course about American society for advanced undergraduate and graduate students, and then continued to teach it on a fairly regular basis for roughly thirty years. A general course on American society, given in collaboration with Harold Bershady, was the most heavily enrolled of the classes he taught at the University of Pennsylvania in the mid-1970s after his retirement from Harvard.

Parsons's research on American society provided a basis for several occasional essays on various aspects of American culture and institutions during the mid-1950s. Some of these essays, notably ' "McCarthyism" and American Social Tension: a Sociologist's View', better known by the title under which it was later published, 'Social Strains in America' (Parsons, 1955), and 'The Distribution of Power in American Society' (Parsons, 1957), were well received at the times of their publication. Many readers found the theoretically grounded analysis of American social conditions that they projected to be highly persuasive, even though they contrasted sharply with views commonly held by academics and intellectuals of the period. For Parsons, these essays represented a promising start to his project of developing a comprehensive interpretation of American society with a distinctive foundation in technical sociological theory.

The publication of these essays brought Parsons self-consciously into tension with fashionable intellectual opinion in the world of journalists and humanistic scholars. Although journalists and literary intellectuals made fun of sociological jargon, their analyses of American social conditions were crude and misleading, Parsons believed, when compared with the kind of sociology he and many other professionals practised.[1] A large proportion of the nation's most prominent intellectuals had believed that McCarthyism represented an American form of fascism. But, using notions of relative deprivation and social strain to analyse the thrust of a social movement, Parsons had argued that McCarthyism more closely resembled the indigenous tradition of populism and should be linked to resentments over long-term processes of change that had diminished the social position of small business proprietors and small-town ways of life (Parsons, 1955). Parsons foresaw that the depth of these resentments was limited and that McCarthyism, though a serious challenge to civil liberties, would prove to be a passing tumult rather than, in the manner of European fascism, a force generating a reactionary overturn in the nation's political structure and status order. In developing this analysis, Parsons believed that he had vindicated sociology as a discipline and shown up an element of hysteria in the circles of literary intellectuals. He had also become newly sensitive to the limitations of intellectual fashion. As the American society project evolved over the next several years, it became for Parsons an effort to demonstrate the analytical power of technical, theoretically sophisticated sociology. That power was to be highlighted to a large degree through contrasts with the less disciplined interpretations of journalists and literary/humanistic scholars.

Despite the successes of his essays on American society, Parsons did not sustain the underlying research project. He found that his duties as chairman of the interdisciplinary Department of Social Relations at Harvard and a series of other writing commitments competed with his ambitions to write a major work on American society. In the late 1940s and early 1950s these commitments had involved work on *Toward a General Theory of Action* (Parsons and Shils, 1951) and *The Social System* (Parsons, 1951). In the mid-1950s he was working on *Working Papers in the Theory of Action* (Parsons et al., 1953), *Family, Socialization and Interaction Process* (Parsons and Bales, 1955), and *Economy and Society* (Parsons and Smelser, 1956). Although he maintained his interest in the American society project, he repeatedly permitted it to be pushed into the background by writing projects that focused on general sociological theory.

Parsons believed that his theoretical projects were producing rapid advances of strategic importance to the social sciences as a whole. He also felt that general theory addressing basic categories of sociological analysis comprised the kind of work to which he personally had a special calling. Moreover, his ambitions for a new analysis of American society seemed to depend on just the sort of macrosocial theory that was then progressing rapidly in his other writing. The four-function paradigm, its application to the identification of four primary subsystems of society, and its use as a framework for analysing the general equilibrium processes of society were all ideas that underwent crucial development during the mid-1950s and early 1960s. Because of fairly obvious implications of these theoretical developments, it appeared that maintaining immediate concentration on them should in the long run benefit the American society project as well.

Parsons accordingly confined his writing on American society to a few essays dealing with social conditions that held particular interest for him, such as the system of social stratification (Parsons, 1953), institutions of family and kinship (Parsons and Bales, 1955, esp. Ch. 1), medical institutions (Parsons and Fox, 1953) and the rise of McCarthyism. The project of writing a general interpretive volume was postponed, although it still figured prominently in his plans for the future. The course on American society and the research of his assistants on various aspects of American social structure became continuing pledges of a future book.

In the meantime, the use of social science to gain a comprehensive understanding and critical perspective on American social life had attained a special importance in the nation's culture. It had, in a sense, become a major intellectual genre. A number of interpretations of American society, including *The Lonely Crowd* (Riesman, 1950), *The Power Elite* (Mills, 1956), *The Sane Society* (Fromm, 1956), the volumes of the 'Yankee City' series (Warner, 1963), *America as a Civilization* (Lerner, 1957), *The Authoritarian Personality* (Adorno et al., 1950), and many critiques of rootless mass society and inauthentic mass culture, had achieved the status of popular literature in intellectual circles. They were widely known among the reading public and prominent in college curricula. Courses that compared the competing interpretations of American society developed by leading scholars and social critics were popular with undergraduates. Discussion of the insights developed by David Riesman, Erich Fromm, C. Wright Mills, Dwight McDonald, and others were a major interest of the nation's intellectuals, filling the pages of several journals and magazines.

Parsons, however, was highly ambivalent about this development. At one level he welcomed the new attention to the varied materials of the contemporary social sciences. Moreover, many of the popular works had an interdisciplinary spirit similar to his own. Yet, at another level, he was sceptical about how deeply the new discussions were rooted in commitments to disciplined social scientific reasoning. He suspected that many of the old ideological posturings of journalists and literary intellectuals were simply being reasserted under the guise of innovative social science. He began to devote time and energy to studying a number of these popular works, characteristically giving particular attention to their conceptual frameworks. He employed the same critical judgement that he had previously used to assess the writings of Weber, Durkheim, Pareto, and Freud (Parsons, 1937; 1952). In these newer works, however, Parsons did not find carefully systematized theories pointing toward fresh empirical insights, but arbitrary premises and poorly developed theoretical structures.

After identifying these conceptual shortcomings, Parsons tried to uncover their consequences for empirical generalization about and explanatory modelling of American society. At this level, too, he found most of the studies he examined to be wanting. In his view they displayed a tendency to injudicious over-generalization of factual materials. Sceptical examination of their conclusions turned up large gaps in the supporting empirical interpretations and arguments. Partial insights into the nature of American society were being presented as comprehensive portraits of the nation. Aspects of American social organization – 'capitalism', 'democracy', and 'mass relationships' – were, by a sort of theoretical synecdoche, being invoked to characterize the whole of society. Changes in specialized domains of culture and social structure were being interpreted as harbingers of sweeping change that might leave the entire society rootless. In short, Parsons concluded, the elements of social science were often being distorted in the service of ideological purposes.

Parsons published several of his critiques of popular writings on American society. Amongst these were 'The Distribution of Power in American Society' (Parsons, 1957), a discussion of C. Wright Mills's treatment of the concentration of power in the hands of a small elite; 'Commentary on *The Mass Media and the Structure of American Society*' (Parsons and White, 1960), a response to several analysts of mass culture who seemed intolerant of its part in the expressive life of middle-class citizens; and 'The Link between Character and Society' (Parsons and White, 1961), a careful analysis of the shortcomings of David Riesman's account of the rise of other-directed actors. Few readers of these articles grasped their import as preliminaries to Parsons's own interpretation of American society, but they represented only a small part of his critical efforts. In his teaching Parsons presented carefully developed criticisms of a number of other authors as well. The objects of these critiques ranged from his friend and colleague Clyde Kluckhohn, who had suggested that

American values were undergoing massive change, to W. Lloyd Warner, who in his 'Yankee City' studies had generalized the rigid class lines of Newburyport, Massachusetts, to American society as a whole, and Maurice Stein and other authors who decried a putative, nearly complete loss of communality in American life (Stein, 1960). Parsons was using critiques of a wide variety of conceptual schemes to define his own perspective on American society by a sort of triangulation among possible orientations.

Parsons finally felt prepared for intensive research on American society only as the end of the 1950s approached. By this time the American society project had taken on several sorts of meaning for him. It remained an effort to counter the ideologies of an older style of literary intellectual with solid social-scientific reasoning. It also represented a means for attacking the ideological distortions in many works of a rising genre of social criticism that was gaining wide acceptance as sociology. At another level, it was a vehicle for challenging well-established orientations in the social sciences against which he had long defined one or another aspect of his own theoretical work. In this context, his targets ranged from utilitarian economics, to 'culture and personality' anthropology, macrosocial applications of psychoanalysis, and theories over-emphasizing 'power structures'. Parsons also continued to hope that his research on American society would constitute a public service by helping to reorient discussion of social conditions in the nation at large. But, at its core, the project was a test for the macrosocial theory that Parsons and his collaborators had developed so rapidly in the course of the 1950s. It was planned to become the first full-scale application of the theory. The capacity of the theory to capture the complexity of modern social life, its ability to integrate many kinds of social-scientific information, its analytical precision, the value of its empirical insights, its originality – all were to be placed on the line.

The perspective on American society

In renewing his work on American society, Parsons wrote a series of long working papers dealing with such matters as the institutional complexity of the American social structure, the American economy, the American polity, and the American value system (Parsons Papers). One of the working papers on American values – probably the first paper and certainly a key one in the development of his thought on the topic – was the 'Tentative Outline', which is reprinted in this volume. The entire set of papers explored interpretive and explanatory themes for the understanding of American society, but was also designed to consolidate and test out the analytical scheme that had emerged from the previous decade's theorizing. It was clear that Parsons was now planning a very large volume on American society. Pleased with his new working papers, he began to write his book and then invited Winston White, a recent doctoral student, to collaborate with him. Together, Parsons and White wrote a new set of working papers and then six or seven chapters of their book. When White suddenly decided to leave the academic profession in the summer of 1962, however, Parsons again turned to other work. The result was to leave major, albeit unfinished, writing unpublished.

When his collaboration with Parsons began, White was about to publish *Beyond Conformity* (White, 1961), a revision of his dissertation that, using social strain theory, analysed ideological themes embedded in the critiques of American society developed by the intellectuals of the 1950s. Thus he shared Parsons's concern to separate an analytically sophisticated treatment of American society from the judgemental attitudes of most intellectuals. He also brought to the enterprise a solid understanding of the macrosocial theory developed during the 1950s, a strong interest in American social life, and a special talent for expressing theoretically shaped ideas in clear prose suitable to the arenas of general intellectual discussion.

Given their shared interests in distinguishing sociological analysis from the ideology of intellectuals, Parsons and White planned the interpretive stance of their volume with great care. The planning took them deeply into the sorts of question that Max Weber designated the 'relevance to values' of social science. Most popular interpretations had depicted American society as profoundly perturbed by the rapid changes of the previous few generations and threatened with the loss of key structural properties as well as connection with valued traditions. The ethic of devotion to hard and productive work, a national character capable of autonomous, responsible conduct, democracy in personal relationships among citizens as well as in general political institutions, communal qualities of connection among persons in social life, and serious, authentic culture were all claimed by one interpreter or another to be verging on extinction. Then, as now, proclamations that the nation is facing unparalleled new threats or challenges seemed to have a special ability to capture the popular imagination. *American Society*, however, was to be a more sober and balanced work. Designed to show up the simplicity of such cries of alarm, it would emphasize the continuing sources of strength and effective functioning in American society.

In this respect, the functionalism of *American Society* represented a deepening of Durkheim's method. Where Durkheim had emphasized the 'facticity' of social things, Parsons and White stressed the durability of complex societies as highly organized and persistent systems. Beneath the many apparent problems of modern social life, whose importance they did not deny, were systemic forces maintaining continuities in social life. In a similar fashion, Parsons and White also planned to challenge studies suggesting that a society as complicated as the United States could be dominated by specific groups or institutional complexes, however strategically placed, whether Wall Street capitalists, a military-industrial complex, an established upper class, or a manipulative industry of advertisers, public relations experts, and broadcasters.

The interpretation offered by Parsons and White was not defensive or part of the complacency generally characteristic of American society during the Eisenhower era. That complacency was in many respects only a surface characteristic of an ideology that, underneath, was struggling with fears over the consequences of rapid social change already experienced. Although not reactionary in the sense of rejecting past change, it was preoccupied with the social consequences of the Second World War and the Cold War, continued industrialization, demographic concentration and bureaucratization, religious and ethnic pluralism, the growth of impersonal forms of relationships, and so forth. It worried that the progressive changes of the preceding decades had been gained at great cost in terms of older, distinctively American traditions and institutional patterns. Thus, encouragement of further progress – in race relations and civil liberties, for example – was viewed with a wary eye in many circles. Even among liberals and progressives there was little confidence that structural changes in economic and political institutions would continue to be beneficial. Fear of the military-industrial complex or the newly concentrated merchants of mass culture in the television and advertising industries was often overriding. Against this widespread social anxiety, *American Society* was planned as a dispassionate effort to restore confidence. It was to highlight in positive terms the challenges for American civilization of increased religious, ethnic, and racial integration, of increased pluralism and democracy in class and status hierarchies, of the rapidly changing structure of local communities in urban and metropolitan areas, of growing political mobilization and formal organization, and of increased economic productivity and material well-being. Moreover, in a fashion that made it quite distinctive, it emphasized the interdependences of these many dimensions of social change and the practical complexities they produced.

In recent years Parsons has widely been portrayed as a scholar who pretended to place his writings outside the domain of socio-political values while surreptitiously maintaining a conservative outlook (Buxton, 1985; Gouldner, 1971). Against a background of such interpretations, the value-laden design of *American Society* may seem quite surprising. But, despite what many critics have alleged, Parsons's methodological writings never suggested that, by cultivating the objectivity of his theory, he hoped to place his interpretations beyond partisan or problematic values. For a period of several years, though not longer, he participated in the movement in American sociology that sought to bring about an 'end of ideology'. However, in Parsons's understanding, this phrase stood for no more than a firm commitment to the principles of a strong 'schema of proof', to use a Weberian phrase. It stood for the effort to extirpate ideological distortions from the orientation of research and the assessment of research findings. It entailed an effort to orient public discussion of social and political conditions to undistorted research findings. However, it did not imply that research should (or even could) be conducted or knowledge synthesized without the guidance of specific value-orientations (Parsons, 1959).

Parsons understood that knowledge could not be created, organized, or used without reference to values. Thus, during the years in which he sought to extirpate 'ideology' from social science, he developed the conception of a 'value-science integrate' (Parsons, 1959). By this awkward term he recognized the importance of practical values in guiding the creation of knowledge even as he tried to underscore the importance of preventing those values from distorting scholarly or scientific procedures. He did not envision knowledge unrelated to practical values, but only sufficiently independent of them to permit the principles of scholarship, codified as a 'schema of proof', to provide effective tests of validity. Entirely consistent with this methodological position, he placed his own practical writings on the ground of a personal liberalism. He was confident that the rootedness of liberal values in the tradition of inner-worldly asceticism or, as he preferred to call it, instrumental activism, made them intrinsically salient to American social experience.

Parsons wrote as a middle-class American proud of his society, its ascetic Protestant and democratic heritages, and its capacity for progressive change. There was undoubtedly an 'Americanocentric' quality to his thought, based on a strong confidence in the long-term worth of American institutional forms and perhaps an overly generous estimate of their future impact on other societies. But Parsons was also sensitive to a number of the limitations and shortcomings of the American variant of Western civilization – its race relations, its proclivity for sacrificing other kinds of social good for economic advancement, its anti-intellectual qualities, and its tendency to react simplistically, hastily, and aggressively to poorly understood problems, perhaps especially in the domain of foreign relations, to cite only some examples. Parsons also had a deep appreciation for the worth of other societies and their contributions to human culture generally. Even during the Second World War, for example, when an intense fear and hatred of everything German swept through the USA, Parsons maintained his esteem for German civilization and his respect for its distinctive contributions to many spheres of modern culture, not least to scholarship (Parsons Papers). Although many qualities of his own thought were rooted in pragmatism, he had an appreciation for German scholarship and culture more generally that contrasted clearly with the distrust of everything 'metaphysical' that predominated in the evaluation of German idealistic thought among American social scientists of his generation.

The analysis of value-systems

However deliberately Parsons and White included a liberal outlook in their design for *American Society*, the leading characteristic of the work was to be its use of technical sociological theory. The principal ambition was to analyse the overall organization and social processes of American society in terms that were more comprehensive and yet also more specific and more precise than those used in any previous study. The book was to be a critical test-application of the theory that Parsons had developed in the course of his whole career, but which had gained important technical elaboration in the previous decade.

The analytical perspective was accordingly rooted in the four-function treatment of major societal subsystems and in the double interchange model of the dynamic relations among subsystems. Thus, separate treatment was to be given to each of the four primary subsystems of society, their major institutional structures and their characteristic social processes. Moreover, each of the societal subsystems was to be analysed in terms of its functional relations with the others. Parsons and White planned to make sure that no one societal subsystem was given disproportionate emphasis or treated as a predominant centre of social causation. Theoretical reductionism of all kinds was to be avoided. Societal process was to be conceptualized in multidimensional, multifactorial terms at every point. But to give shape to such a complicated theoretical project remained, even after the work of the previous decade, a daunting task.

As the 'Tentative Outline' shows, Parsons approached this task by relying on what for him was a firm theoretical reference point: Max Weber's analysis of the Protestant ethic and its social consequences (Weber, 1930). The power of this analysis had played a role, starting with Parsons's student days in Germany, in drawing him toward the field of sociology. At every stage in his career it remained the starting point of his efforts to understand the distinctive qualities of American social institutions. When he renewed his intensive studies of American society during the late 1950s, he sought to refine it as a starting point for understanding the main developmental tendencies of American society. Thus a major theme of his analysis was to underscore the importance of inner-worldly asceticism or, in the more general term he favoured, instrumental activism, as a force in shaping the American experience.

Parsons emphasized the constancy of instrumental activism as a dynamic entity affecting all periods of American history and all institutional spheres of American society. This emphasis set him apart from many other analysts of American culture of the same period. Most scholars – Clyde Kluckhohn (1958) prominent among them – were arguing that American values, or at least key elements of them, were in a stage of rapid decline, perhaps even disintegration. The decline of the 'work ethic' in favour of a new emphasis on consumer values figured prominently in many discussions. So did a loss of values of respect for achievement, for participation in neighbourhood and community affairs, for religious and ethnic commitments, for decency in personal relationships, and for experiences of serious cultural events. Applying a Weberian perspective, however, Parsons doubted that sweeping changes in the value system were occurring. There was no evidence of the intense charismatic movements that would be needed to generate them. Nor was there evidence that American society was falling into the sort of comprehensive anomie which might eventuate in a general slipping away or washing out of values in the absence of a dramatic social movement. Parsons did not deny that American values were changing, but did maintain that they were unlikely to be changing in the inclusive fashion suggested by others.

What separated Parsons from most other interpreters of American values was, he realized, something deeper than a disagreement over empirical conditions. It was also a matter of how values were to be conceptualized. While many anthropologists and sociologists held values to be important determinants of social behaviour, Parsons was emphasizing that values of a specific sort actually *constitute* a central category of social structure. Following the guidance of both Weber and Durkheim, he treated values as the most deeply set and slowly changing of the categories of social structure. He also proposed that values be understood as extending into every domain of the structuring of society. Thus, the Weberian theme of legitimation and the Durkheimian theme of moral authority concerned the relation of values to other categories of social structure in every sphere of continuously organized social life. The stabilization of social relationships was a phenomenon that could not be grasped, he suggested, in any of its many dimensions without reference to values.

To spell out and properly qualify this analytical perspective proved an intricate task. Drawing on the resources of Parsons's already long career, Parsons and White took two years to accomplish it. Their book had a very comprehensive chapter outline, but only the treatment of the American value system in relation to the complicated exigencies of pattern maintenance functioning ever approached completion. The draft materials on the economy and the polity were less fully realized, and the treatment of integrative functioning remained fragmentary. But the discussion of the American value system ran to 300 typewritten pages (Parsons Papers). It encompassed a long historical chapter demonstrating the relation between American instrumental activism and the values of Western civilization generally as well as the continuities in American values from the colonial era to modern times. It also included a lengthy discussion of variations in the American value system, as indicated by cultural differences among regional, social class, ethnic, and religious groups. But the preponderant analytical exercise was to demonstrate the unity of a value system that incorporates functionally differentiated and specialized components legitimating every significant institutional complex in the society. Showing how a value system of such complexity could itself remain ordered over time was a formidable theoretical achievement.

Parsons and White were quite aware that, in beginning the substantive analysis of their book with a treatment of the value system, they left themselves open to a charge of idealism. Of course this is a charge that has often been directed at Max Weber, and Parsons himself had once levelled a similar criticism at Durkheim (Parsons, 1937). One might suggest that they had not chosen bad company. White was not averse to speaking of the conceptual theme that Parsons was then beginning to label 'cybernetic' as establishing a 'neo-idealism'. In this he perhaps foreshadowed the more recent criticisms of Jeffrey Alexander (1983). However, Parsons and White took care to qualify the idealistic/cybernetic theme. They did not attribute special causal force to values. They insisted that social action results from a value-added process that *combines* evaluative with other components. Practical and material interests, situational and environmental conditions, relational ties, normative rules, holdings of wealth, power, and other resources, and a variety of additional components all play their part in shaping social action. The importance of values is tied to the long-term stabilizing effect of legitimation as a mode of relation between values and other components – and to the destabilizing effects of breakdowns in legitimation.

Conclusion

'A Tentative Outline of American Values', though only a working paper and long buried in Parsons's files, marks an important turning point in the development of action theory. Parsons wrote it in 1959 or 1960 to pull together his ideas on the concept of a value system, preliminary to drafting his book on American society. It was later superseded by substantially longer and more refined treatments, especially by four draft chapters on the American value system that Parsons wrote with White as a section of their collaborative book. Nevertheless, the 'Tentative Outline' is more explicit on a number of points than anything that Parsons published on his conception of value systems. It expresses clearly his dissatisfactions with the ways in which value systems had previously been treated in anthropology and sociology. It also points the way towards the better elaborated scheme for analysing values that Parsons and White developed jointly.

In the early 1960s Parsons regarded his theoretical treatment of values as one of his major achievements. Yet he reserved publication of a full account of that treatment for a book that he never completed. When *American Society* was abandoned, an important part of Parsons's macro-sociology was withheld from the profession. In retrospect, it appears likely that significant misunderstandings of his work might have been avoided had he chosen to publish his more refined writings on value systems, even if only in the form of working papers. For example, the specificity of his conception of values as distinct from either personal attitudes or normative standards of conduct might have been made clear to the profession. That he was not a 'value determinist' or 'neo-idealist' who attributed all causation in social life to values should also have become clear. It should have been made clear that, when he did treat values as important causal factors, he had in mind institutions that are structural to society, not just the personal value judgements of individuals. Finally, his conception of a highly differentiated value system ramifying into each of the major institutional sectors of society might have been clarified.

Nearly thirty years after it represented a cutting edge of sociological theory, publication of the 'Tentative Outline' may belatedly inaugurate a process of clarification. Other draft materials on value systems also deserve to be published. To be sure, like the 'Tentative Outline', they too will appear to be flawed works now that we have the benefit of twenty-five years and more of hindsight. But the fundamental project of developing a comprehensive and detailed analysis of value systems remains important. It is an essential task for sociological theory that has yet to be carried out. The essay published here may serve to underscore the importance of Parsons's little-known intention of accomplishing that job in a technical fashion.

To conclude the present discussion, it may satisfy the reader's curiosity if I outline the subsequent history of Parsons's efforts to write a major book on American society. The *American Society* project ended abruptly when White decided to leave academic life during the summer of 1962. Parsons saw no way of completing a book that would have the broad impact he desired without White's collaboration. Once again he interrupted his writing on American society and turned to other research. The famous essays 'On the Concept of Political Power' (1963a) and 'On the Concept of Influence' (1963b) soon appeared. He began work on the theory of social evolution that resulted in *Societies: Evolutionary and Comparative Perspectives* (1966) and *The System of Modern Societies* (1971). Research was also soon begun on the academic profession and on faculty roles in American colleges and universities, research that eventuated in a series of essays and, a decade later, *The American University*, co-authored with Gerald M. Platt (Parsons and Platt, 1973).

A few years later Parsons accepted a Guggenheim fellowship to write on American society. By that time he had become conscious of the fact that he had never synthesized his thought on social integration, even though he had made many substantial contributions in that field over the years. This oversight or shortcoming had begun to seem quite acute to him because he had come to define sociology as the scholarly discipline specializing in the study of integrative institutions and relationships. A volume focused on the integration of American society would accordingly respond to two matters on his intellectual agenda. It would offer many elements of a general interpretation of American society and it would enable him to develop his thought on societal integration. He therefore designated the drafting of a book on integration in American society as his project for the fellowship year. Because of other commitments, however, including his involvement in the faculty roles project, the work on social evolution that was proving far more time-consuming than anticipated, and the writing of several essays for *The International Encyclopedia of the Social Sciences*, he was able to draft only a couple of introductory chapters (Parsons Papers).

Indeed, the new chapters were hastily drafted toward the end of the academic year simply to provide evidence of progress on his designated project. Parsons did not become strongly engaged in his project on American society before once again being distracted by rising interests in other work. At the theoretical level, there were new developments in what he called 'general action theory', that is, the theory treating the overall relationships among cultural, social, and psychological systems. At the empirical level, the student disturbances of the late 1960s and the sometimes ill-planned reactions to them on the part of college and university authorities led him to believe that his studies of institutions of higher education and research held national importance. He (and his collaborator Gerald M. Platt) responded energetically to a request from the Assembly on University Goals and Governance to write a general volume on the organization and functioning of American research universities.

After *The American University* was completed, however, Parsons returned to writing a book on the integrative institutions of American society. With chapters being composed in between the many essays that he wrote during the 1970s, the manuscript took nearly seven years to finish. Entitled *The American Societal Community*, it deals with the functionally defined integrative subsystem of society and its structural and dynamic relations with the economic, political, and pattern maintenance subsystems (Parsons Papers). It provides a final statement of Parsons's understanding of topics central to the sociology of American life, including the transformative nature of instrumental activism, the democratic patterns of civil institutions, the integrative capacities of law and social control, and the ways in which social stratification establishes both consensus and cleavage. It fulfilled his ambition of applying a refined and technical version of his theory to macrosocial analysis of his own society, a society with which he identified deeply. Like *The American University*, it is a book with a highly complicated conceptual scheme. Because Parsons's thought continued to evolve as he wrote, however, the conceptualization is not consistent throughout. In editing the work for future publication, the present author has been introducing notes to explain the most important changes in the theory. But, even with annotation, the inconsistencies are likely to pose difficulties in understanding for many readers.

In *The American Societal Community*, Parsons wrote a subtle combination of a theoretical study and a very personal book about American society. He did not attempt extensive commentary on and response to intellectual interpretations of the American experience, as he had once planned to do in *American Society*. He was not writing a book for the educated citizenry at large, but a more specifically focused treatise in sociology. His assessments of the writings of other scholars were largely confined to the discipline of sociology and to a select body of pertinent historical works. However, he did include a substantial amount of commentary on his own experience and personal relation to American society, including much that would ordinarily be considered inappropriate in scholarly writing. He permitted himself to express a sense of communal belonging in American society, illustrating his argument as well as developing it analytically.

Note

1. This was a frequently stated theme in Parsons's course on American society, taught collaboratively with Winston White, when I took it in the spring semester of 1961.

References

Adorno, T.W., Frenkel-Brunswik, E., Levinson, D.J. and Sanford, R.N. (1950) *The Authoritarian Personality*. New York: Harper.

Alexander, J.C. (1983) *Theoretical Logic in Sociology*, vol. 4, *The Modern Reconstruction of Classical Thought: Talcott Parsons*. Berkeley and Los Angeles: University of California Press.

Buxton, W. (1985) *Talcott Parsons and the Capitalist Nation-State: Political Sociology as a Strategic Vocation*. Toronto: University of Toronto Press.

Fromm, E. (1956) *The Sane Society*. London: Routledge & Kegan Paul.

Gouldner, A.W. (1971) *The Coming Crisis of Western Sociology*. New York: Equinox.

Kluckhohn, C. (1958) 'Have There Been Discernible Shifts in American Values during the Last Generation?', in E.E. Morison (ed.), *The American Style*. New York: Harper.

Lerner, M. (1957) *America as a Civilization*. 2 vols, New York: Simon & Schuster.

Mills, C.W. (1956) *The Power Elite*. New York: Oxford University Press.

Parsons, T. (1937) *The Structure of Social Action*. New York: McGraw-Hill.

Parsons, T. (1951) *The Social System*. New York: Free Press.

Parsons, T. (1952) 'The Superego and the Theory of Social Systems', repr. in Parsons (1964).

Parsons, T. (1953) 'A Revised Analytical Approach to the Theory of Social Stratification', repr. in Parsons (1969).

Parsons, T. (1955) 'Social Strains in America', repr. in Parsons (1969).

Parsons, T. (1957) 'The Distribution of Power in American Society', repr. in Parsons (1969).

Parsons, T. (1959) 'An Approach to the Sociology of Knowledge in Terms of the Theory of Action', repr. in Parsons (1967).

Parsons, T. (1963a) 'On the Concept of Political Power', *Proceedings of the American Philosophical Society*, 107 (3): 232–61.

Parsons, T. (1963b) 'On the Concept of Influence', *Public Opinion Quarterly*, 27 (Spring): 37–62.

Parsons, T. (1964) *Social Structure and Personality*. New York: Free Press.

Parsons, T. (1966) *Societies: Evolutionary and Comparative Perspectives*. Englewood Cliffs, NJ: Prentice-Hall.

Parsons, T. (1967) *Sociological Theory and Modern Society*. New York: Free Press.

Parsons, T. (1969) *Politics and Social Structure*. New York: Free Press.

Parsons, T. (1971) *The System of Modern Societies*. Englewood Cliffs, NJ: Prentice-Hall.

Parsons, T. (1986) 'Social Science: a Basic National Resource', in S.Z. Klausner and V. Lidz (eds), *The Nationalization of the Social Sciences*. Philadelphia: University of Pennsylvania Press. (Originally written in 1948.)

Parsons Papers, Collection in the Harvard University Archives, Nathan M. Pusey Library,

Cambridge, MA. All papers mentioned in this article are readily identified in the catalogue compiled by Dr Clark Elliott of the Harvard University Archives.

Parsons, T. and Bales, R.F. (1955) *Family, Socialization and Interaction Process*. New York: Free Press.

Parsons, T., Bales, R.F. and Shils, E.A. (1953) *Working Papers in the Theory of Action*. New York: Free Press.

Parsons, T. and Fox, R.C. (1953) 'Illness, Therapy, and the Modern Urban American Family', *Journal of Social Issues*, 8: 31–44.

Parsons, T. and Platt, G.M. (1973) *The American University*. Cambridge, MA: Harvard University Press.

Parsons, T. and Shils, E.A. (eds) (1951) *Toward a General Theory of Action*. Cambridge, MA: Harvard University Press.

Parsons, T. and Smelser, N.J. (1956) *Economy and Society, a Study in the Integration of Economic and Social Theory*. New York: Free Press.

Parsons, T. and White, W. (1960) 'Commentary on *The Mass Media and the Structure of American Society*', *Journal of Social Issues*, 16 (3): 67–77.

Parsons, T. and White, W. (1961) 'The Link between Character and Society', in S.M. Lipset and L. Lowenthal (eds), *Culture and Social Character*. New York: Free Press.

Riesman, D. (1950) *The Lonely Crowd*. New Haven, CT: Yale University Press.

Stein, M. (1960) *The Eclipse of Community*. Princeton, NJ: Princeton University Press.

Warner, W.L. (1963) *Yankee City*. 1 vol., abridged. New Haven, CT: Yale University Press.

Weber, M. (1930) *The Protestant Ethic and the Spirit of Capitalism* (tr. Talcott Parsons). New York: Scribner's.

White, W. (1961) *Beyond Conformity*. New York: Free Press.

3

A TENTATIVE OUTLINE
OF AMERICAN VALUES

Talcott Parsons

The main purpose of this brief working paper[1] is to present a tentative outline of the content of the current American value system and its major points of articulation in the structure of the society. Preliminary to that, however, it seems necessary to give a brief account of my own approach to the analysis of values and their place in social systems, hence a few highlights of the theoretical frame of reference in terms of which I shall attempt to approach American values as an empirical phenomenon.

Theoretical background

Some general considerations about social values

I do not wish to present a carefully considered formal definition of values – for most general purposes I subscribe to that of Clyde Kluckhohn in *Toward a General Theory of Action*. A little further specification is, however, necessary for my purposes. I shall be dealing here with social systems, and in that context social values must be considered normative conceptions of the *desirable* as applied to states of the social system of reference as such, not with respect to other subject-matters, however important these may be in other connections. A social value system then consists in a complex of normative cultural patterns which define desirable states, including directions of change, of the social system in question.

Another essential preliminary is to make clear that I conceive the concept of value within the action frame of reference. This is to say that it involves an actor or system acting, a situation and a set of relations between them, which is sometimes called 'orientation' (as seen from the point of view of the actor). Value, in this sense, I treat as a category of the *relations* between actor or system and situation, and hence not as a property or attribute of either, taken independently of each other. (This, I think, goes a step beyond Kluckhohn.) Thus, to refer to the history of the more sociological part of the subject, Weber tended to locate values in the acting unit, hence when the latter was an individual to treat them as 'subjective'; Thomas and Znaniecki, on the other hand, located them in the object or situation in their famous distinction between attitudes and values. In my terminology an object is not a value; it is a property of the process of *evaluation*, which is the establishment of a relation to an actor or set of actors.

A value-orientation[2] is, however, always stated from the point of view of an actor oriented in a situation and to the objects composing that situation which may include the organism or personality of the actor of reference himself as, under certain conditions, constituting situational objects. The actor is always a human individual, but the relevant reference of his values may be to any one of the different subsystems of the general system of action. In the case of interest here, that of social system values, there is always a *role* reference implicit in the statement of the value-pattern. This is not, however, a simple case of the relativity of values, so popular a few years ago, or relativity because of the element of sharing of *common* values in the social system, to be noted presently.

The situation by definition consists of objects, which again may include any of the categories of objects relevant to the analysis of action: social objects, cultural objects, personalities and their subsystem, organisms and the physical environment. For present purposes the most important category of objects is social. Social values, of course, include evaluations of all categories of objects, but it is only the evaluations involved in social objects which in a direct sense become constitutive elements of the structure of the social system itself. It is as components of systems of social interaction that they function in this way. It is above all because of this relation to social interaction that the relational aspect of values as such is so important for their sociological use. What is from one reference perspective actor in a given social system is from the alternative reference perspective object. The concept value, to avoid an unacceptable implication of relativity, must be formulated in such a way as to fit *either* perspective; it is the same value whether held by ego or by alter, to use the familiar convention.

To return, then, to values as normative patterns defining desirable states of the system in relation to its situation. Four further points need to be noted.

1   Values I conceive to be normative components of *culture*. Whatever their relation to the existential or expressive components of the relevant cultural complexes, the component of primary concern in the present context is the *normative* one. Values in this sense are grounded in and justified by existential ideas, and they themselves and attitudes toward them are expressed 'symbolically' in various ways, but neither of these aspects of cultural systems is itself a value. From the point of view of the actor in a system, values are aspects of the definition of the expectations, in the normative, not the predictive sense, governing action, but are not exhaustive of expectations. The questions of whose action, in what circumstances, raise further problems.

2   Not every normative component of a total cultural complex is, how-

ever, a value. I should like to reserve this term for those normative patterns which are on the *highest level of generality* which is relevant to the orientation of action in the social system of reference at all. Values are the *principles* from which less general norms and expectations can be derived. They stand on a level of generality which is independent of any *specific* situational object-structure, external to the social system of reference or internal to it. They involve, therefore, only the exigencies which are *generic* to the category of social system in question. In the case under consideration, that of a society, these include the fact that it is a social system at all, that there are problems of the cognitive grounding and symbolic expression of its values, and that, as a system it is subject to the basic exigencies of any such system, exigencies which will here be analysed in terms of the general paradigm of basic functions of a system of action with which I have been working.[3] It is only at this point that we can speak of the differentiation of a system of values as such. With further specification we come to the level of *norms*, the most important of which for a social system I call institutions. I wish here to distinguish carefully between the social system-value level and the institutional level in the normative aspects of the structure of a social system. Institutions will be differentiated according to much more specific exigencies and according to the level of complexity of structural differentiation of the system itself. It is above all essential to define values as independent of any specific level of structural differentiation of the system in which they are held. On any given level, however, each subsystem of a larger social system will have its own pattern of values but these must be treated as derived from the more general value system, with differing modes of selectivity and degrees of emphasis according to the structure of the concrete system.

3   A value system of a social system is therefore by definition a *common* or shared value system as between the units of the system whether they be individual personalities in roles, or collectivities at various levels of the structure of the system. The primary reference for considering the *cultural* integration of a social system is the degree of commonness or sharedness of its values in *all* parts of its structure, e.g., 'classes' of its population. Empirically of course this degree varies greatly, but other sorts of malintegration are very often mistaken for lack of value-consensus. This is notably perhaps, but by no means exclusively, true of ideological differences. By ideology I mean an 'evaluative', i.e. 'value-loaded' existential statement about the actual or prospective state of a given social system or type or category of social system. An ideological statement therefore differs from an assertion of value in two respects. First it contains an explicit or implicit existential reference at a lower level of generality than simply the generic characteristics of the most general category of system, and secondly, by virtue of these existential references its normative implications apply to a lower level of generality than do the corresponding values. It is thus possible to share values and at the same time differ ideologically. Put a little differently, ideologies may define the values of subtypes and/or

subsystems of the main system of reference, but not of the system itself.

There is, thus, a value-component in an ideology, but it is a derivative and more specific value than the primary system value. At the societal level the existential grounding of a value-system must be treated as religious or philosophical, not ideological. (I would not hesitate to say that there is a philosophical if not religious component in militantly anti-religious thought systems like Marxism – the 'dialectic' is not an empirical entity.)

The above considerations emphasize the importance of careful attention being paid to the level of system to which reference is made in any analysis involving values. Values are always a component of the normative orientation of any system. But in a lower-order subsystem such normative orientation will also include some specification of the order of actors to which such values are relevant. It is this additional specification that characterizes norms, as noted above. Therefore the value-system of a lower-order system can be 'derived' from the *norms* of a higher-order system, but not directly from the latter's value-system without reference to its situational specifications. From the point of reference of the individual as actor, each social value in his total personal value system will, at a given level of generality, refer to a different *role* through which he participates in a different system of social interaction, from his 'membership' in the total society, to each unique diadic relation in which he is involved.

4   From the point of view of the units of a system, hence at some level of the motivation of individuals, values imply what may be called *commitment*. This it is which relates the normative aspect of expectations to the interplay of performances and sanctions. A set of values are 'conceptions of the desirable' to the implementation of which, within limits of objective possibility, the relevant unit of an action system, or the system itself, may be regarded as committed. This aspect of the problem defines the dimension of 'conformity and deviance' in the structure of action systems. It is inherent in the frame of reference that there should be a problem of conformity, and variations in degree of conformity; level of commitment is empirically problematical and favourableness of circumstances is also problematical.

Looked at in social system terms, the level of commitment is what I have often referred to as 'institutionalization'; the cognate conception in personality terms is 'internalization'. The relation between the two is the primary focus of the problem of integration of social systems. Of course not only values but all other components of culture systems are both institutionalized in social systems and internalized in personalities.

Let me now say a few words about the use of a social value system in social system analysis. I use it as the primary point of reference for the analysis of structure and process. On theoretical grounds I take the view that, in addition to level of differentiation, type of value system is the primary basis of differentiating types of social system of any given category, in the presently relevant case, of society.

This involves two substantive working assumptions which I will make in my analysis of American society. The first of these is that for any given social system which is to be subjected to technical analysis, there is a presumption in favour of the existence and importance of a single unified value system at the requisite level of generality. Tolerance of difference is itself a value, not the absence of common values, and at the very least *this* must be institutionalized in a highly pluralistic society. This of course is not to say that the 'integration' of such a paramount value system in the culture pattern sense is ever perfect or complete, or that cases of very considerable malintegration do not exist – these are empirical questions for the particular case, and it is essential not to beg them *either* way. But it seems clear that the bias of most sociological tradition has been against recognizing the importance of the existence of a single value system.

The second working assumption is that the value system of a society tends to remain stable over time. At the very least it is essential to make a clear distinction between changes in the society which constitute or involve changes in its fundamental values and those which do not. Above all, steps in structural differentiation of the system can and do occur without altering the paramount values though they necessarily alter the values of sub-systems, notably those which have been the points of departure for the differentiation of new subsystems. Thus there is no doubt that the values of the American family today are different from what they were even a century ago, because the structural position of the family within the society has changed. Also ideological changes are often confused with changes in fundamental values. Empirically I wish to argue for a basic stability of American values from colonial times to the present, a view which I know runs counter to much opinion in the field, but which I think I can defend.[4]

The derivation, classification and differentiation of value systems

It is my intention to treat American values in as rigorously empirical a manner as is possible in this type of subject-matter. However, I will attempt to do this within the framework of a generalized theoretical scheme. From this point of view it is not sufficient merely to 'look at' American society and observe what its values are and have been. It is necessary to define the empirical problem in theoretical terms. This means essentially developing a classification so that it is possible not only to assert that such and such value-commitments exist in the society but that these are, in determinate ways, selections as between a set of meaningful alternatives. It will not be possible here to develop such a scheme fully, but I shall try to outline briefly, without full grounding, the principal approach and the main conceptual elements which go into my analysis.

The first aspect is a conception of five categories of organized 'reality' which are involved in the system-reference problem, namely culture, social systems, personalities or psychological systems, organisms, and the physical world apart from organic life. These system-types are arranged in a hierarchical order; that in which they were just named being the 'descending' order. From one point of view this is an order of control; the opposite order is one of sets of 'conditions'. Of course in any given empirical situation the degree to which these system references may need to be treated as differentiated from each other may vary.

From the point of view of existential references the total system must be treated as 'open-ended' at both ends. At the 'lower' end is the world of 'physical' reality which in terms of the present scheme does not 'act' whatever may be its properties in another reference scheme. It is, to put it another way, treated only as a category of objects, thus 'conditioning' action. At the 'upper' end the existential reference of some cultural categories must, if it is not to physical, organic, psychological or social systems, be to some 'nonempirical' entity which for present purposes is treated as a residual category.

Whatever may be the philosophical status of this nonempirical category an essential empirically given aspect of culture itself is the normative reference. Norms and values have the structural property of constituting a 'nesting' series such that the 'premises' on which they are based progress from the specific to the more general. Presumably this series must be treated as in some sense open-ended. At least there are normative components which are held to 'govern' action in society and which cannot be derived from lower-order norms or from existential imperatives either of the existence of a society itself or of its dependence on lower-order empirical reality systems in the series. It is these highest normative components of the culture which I call the *cultural* 'values' of the society. This level, as will be noted later, must be distinguished from *social* system values.

I naturally wish to avoid philosophical assumptions as far as possible, but certain propositions about this 'upper' boundary of systems of action at the highest normative level seem to be essential.[5] Whatever one's philosophical views may be about the more general bases of the meaningfulness of normative judgements, there seem to be certain basic alternatives which have to be faced and with reference to which value-orientations can be distinguished and classified. The most essential can, I think, be stated in terms of three dichotomous choices.

The first of these concerns what may be called the 'religious' problem, namely whether the primary source of moral authority is conceived to reside *within* the world of empirical experience, including its cultural components, or in cognate terms to lie in a transcendental reality or entity of some sort.[6] The latter choice may be called the 'religious' alternative, the former the 'secular' one. This basic choice may be called 'precultural' in the sense that it provides the major premise on which the cultural level of value-choices then has to be made.

The second and third choices, then, concern the primacies to be accorded among the functional exigencies to which systems of action in the most general terms are subject. These choices must be made, whether the first one falls to the religious or to the secular side, for whatever the basis of a person's commitments, while he is biologically alive he must act, as a human personality in relation to his fellows in some sort of society, to a physical environment and to a system of cultural meanings. He is thus part of an empirical system of action which must be 'structured'.

These two basic choices may be said to be (1) the choice between 'internal' and 'external' emphases for the system of reference and (2) the choice between 'instrumental' and 'expressive', or 'consummatory', emphases. Let us elucidate each a little.

Every system of action functions within an empirical situation. With reference to the evaluation of its actions the greater emphasis may be placed on the consequences of the action for the relation of the system to the external situation, to the management of those relations, or it may be placed on their consequences for the internal state of the system.

In the case of the empirically 'ultimate' cultural orientations, the system next below this cultural orientation system in the series is the social system. Therefore from the cultural value point of view the most immediate focus of the meaning of 'situation' is the social system. Hence I may interpret the 'external', situation-oriented emphasis to mean the placing of the primary value-accent on the state of the social system and the relation of the actor to it. The internal reference on the other hand is to treat the social system as a set of conditions which provide both opportunities and obstacles to value-realization but the state of which is not the primary focus of evaluative concern.

It is essential to realize that the choice between external and internal emphases in this sense is *independent* of that between religious and secular emphases. The first concerns the *source* of moral authority, while the second concerns the *field* in which moral action is primarily to take place. Above all it is possible for the first choice to fall on the religious side and the second on the external, as indeed is the case with the ascetic Protestant orientation of 'worldly asceticism'.

The second of these functional choices (third in the total series) concerns the instrumental-consummatory problem. Here the alternative is between a state of the system which, from the point of view of the value-emphasis, is a definitive 'realization' (consummatory) of the value-expectation and one which is not definitive, but is a 'way-station' (instrumental) to something else, is a 'contribution' to a state of affairs which is perceived to be not definitively attainable within the relevant value-universe. To what system the orientation in question will apply in what ways, will be a matter for a lower-order specification and will depend on further considerations to be discussed presently. Here the question concerns the 'meaningfulness' of ultimate attainment and hence whether valued activity is to be oriented to such a consummatory state, or whether this is not in the same sense meaningful, and activity is to be oriented to instrumental contributions without either hope of or responsibility for the ultimately consummatory state.

This choice again is logically independent of the religious–secular one

and of course of the external–internal one as well. There may be ultimately valued consummatory states of the individual soul – 'salvation'
in the Christian sense is a conception of such a state – or there may in
secular terms be conceptions of the fully attained 'ideal society' or of
complete individual 'happiness'. On the other hand there may be religiously oriented instrumental value systems enjoining contributions to the
building of the Kingdom of God but with man completely denied both
understanding of what its final attainment would mean, and prospective
participation in it.

The above three dichotomous choices would yield a manifold of eight
possibilities of primacy of value-emphasis. For purely illustrative purposes
in a highly tentative way I present the tabulation in Table 3.1.

From the above it becomes clear that, theoretically, the task of deriving
a particular value-orientation presupposes the working out of a *classification* of possible value-orientation types. This is simply because derivation
means allocation between a determinate number of defined alternative
possibilities at each step of the derivation.

A further general point about this scheme needs to be mentioned. This is
that primacy of value-emphasis need not mean exclusion of some level of
positive valuation of an alternative. The ultimate basis of the general
paradigm I have used is 'functional' with the presumption that all functions
find a place somewhere in a going system of action. This is not to say that
on some occasions certain functions may not be treated so overwhelmingly
as foci of threat to the important values that on the belief level it is often
advocated that they be eliminated altogether. Thus extremes of religious
asceticism have sometimes implied the desirability of race suicide, since
biological reproduction is possible only through the apparently absolutely
unacceptable process of sexual intercourse. Such an extreme could, however, obviously never be fully institutionalized in a going society over a
long period, except of course for special subgroups within it.

Next it is essential to note that what has been under discussion here is the
cultural level of values and not at all a social value system, nor indeed that
of personalities as such. To arrive at either social or personal value systems
it is necessary to take further steps of *application* of the principles involved
in the cultural value system. This is to say it is necessary to enter specifications defining the *problem* which action will encounter in 'actualizing' the
value in empirical fact in the *type* of system in question.

The first order of specification concerns the definition of the category of
system in which the value-commitment is relevant, for which the relevant
action is conceived. In terms of our basic classification the system reference
may be to social systems, personalities and organisms. A social value
system then must define a desirable state or direction for a society or a
subsystem of a society. A personal or psychological value system defines a
desirable state or direction or change for an individual person or subsystem of it, and so on.

These value systems are to be derived by specifying the categories of

Table 3.1 *A tentative typology of cultural-level values*

	The 'nonempirical' reference					
	Religious emphasis			Secular emphasis		
	Ascetic	Mystic		Instrumental	Teleological	
'Worldly'	Worldly asceticism	'Salvationalism' (individual or collective)	**External emphasis**	'Progressism'	Empirical finalism (individual or collective)	'Empirical'
'Other-worldly'	Other-worldly ascetism	'Mysticism' (individual or collective)	**Internal emphasis**	Idealistic essentialism	'Humanism' (individual or collective)	'Idealistic'
	Instrumental	Consummatory		Instrumental	Consummatory	

system-type itself, units of system, situation, etc., in the terms appropriate
for the particular category of system. A social system is thus a system
of interaction of two or more individual actor-persons. Its units are, at
different levels of organization, the *roles* of individuals (not total personalities), collectivities and institutionalized norm-complexes. The focal
category of situation is *other* social systems with which the system of
reference interacts on cognate levels. In a certain type of context I think
the personalities of individuals may also legitimately be treated as situation
for a social system. Only in a carefully qualified sense can organism and
physical environment be so treated, since it may be argued that their
influence on social systems is not 'direct' but *through* the personalities
of individuals. A social value system then should speak in terms of the
orientation of units of social systems and of such systems as a whole to
situations appropriately defined as the situations of social systems, or
components of them. These specifications *should be incorporated into the
formulation of the value-patterns themselves*; it is only this incorporation
which justifies calling the value system social rather than cultural. Cognate
considerations apply to the value systems of personalities. I also believe it
makes sense to speak of the values of organisms in this way, but will not
enter into that question here.

These considerations perhaps make it somewhat clearer why I confined
reference to the *differentiation* of value systems to the next step beyond the
above specification of category of value system within the general framework. The basis of that differentiation is, then, the types of functional
exigency encountered by the type of system to which the value-pattern in
question is relevant. There will then be a conception, generalized at the
social level, of the desirable kind of social system, in the presently relevant
case, the society. This general conception will, however, be differentiated
with reference to the primary functional exigencies of the system other
than the maintenance of its own patterns. Thus there will be a value-
complex concerning desirable types of goals for the system and attitudes
toward goals of the system. There will be conceptions of desirable modes
of adaptation of the system to its situation and finally there will be conceptions of desirable modes of integration of the system, of the relations
of the units to each other in the perspective of this integration.

These more differentiated aspects of the general value system constitute
value-references for the main institutional complexes of the society, the
cluster of norms which in turn 'govern' in the sense of 'applying to' the
behaviour of collectivities and of individuals in roles. It is this 'institutionalization' which is the focus of the relation between values and what
sociologists ordinarily call the 'social structure'.

The American value system

In approaching the main task of this paper after the above rather extensive
preliminaries, my central concern is with the *social* value system in the

sense outlined earlier. My delineation of this will, however, be more comprehensible if I preface it with an outline of the *cultural* premises which underlie it, and supplement it with an account of the personality values which are cognate with it and derive from the same cultural premises. These personality values of course articulate with the social structure through the concept of role; the values of specific role types are the meeting ground of subsystem social values and the values of the appropriate subsystems of the personality.

The cultural premises

In terms of the classification outlined earlier, the American value system belongs, in its earlier historical origins at least, clearly in the category that I have called religious. There is some question of whether there has not been considerable secularization, with consequences which will need discussing. But there is no doubt (1) that its early primacy was clearly religious and (2) of where within the general religious classification it should be placed. In outlining the pattern and its consequences I shall, in both respects, lean rather heavily on Max Weber.

The essential basis of the importance of the early religious emphasis is that, combined with other elements, it provides a basis for exerting powerful leverage on the empirical world, in the first instance the society itself. It is therefore a major factor in the background of what I wish to call the *activism* of American values at the social level, and the *achievement* orientation at the personal. The other components which I shall discuss give the system a 'worldly' and an instrumental emphasis. The value system stimulates 'practical' action in secular rather than traditionally religious, for example devotional, spheres. Hence the question is raised as to the basis of leverage for a stress on active change in the state of the society itself.

Here Weber's analysis is most illuminating. It comes to a climax in his dramatic comparison between Puritanism and Confucianism (*The Religion of China*, final chapter). There Weber speaks of Confucianism being a 'doctrine of rational *adaptation to* the world' whereas Puritanism was a 'doctrine of rational *mastery over* the world'. Apart from the connotations of Weber's particular usage of the term adaptation, the essential point about Puritanism is that what in religious terms is defined as 'the world', i.e. the whole realm of empirical social action in relation to its environment, is not something either to be 'accepted' and adjusted to, or to be escaped from, but to be mastered and controlled in the name of an ideal which, in these terms, is defined as transcendental.

In its purest Calvinist version this took the form that true believers were entrusted with a divinely ordained mission, the building of the Kingdom of God *on Earth*. This is to say a divinely sanctioned 'ideal society'. For various reasons this was an unstable religious definition of the situation. Before entering into some of these reasons and the case for a trend to secularization, it would be well to outline the other components of the cultural orientation in its religious version.

With respect to what I earlier called the second basic alternative, between external and internal orientations, there can be no doubt that the main American trend has been to the external type. This is to say that from the cultural point of view, it has been active orientation to the situation as the primarily valued field of activity, and for the reasons outlined earlier this is in the first instance operative in and on the social system as field of activity. In its application to the society as system this means that the society should not be passively adjusted to *its* external situation, whether this be defined in terms of physical environment or of 'human nature', but should be actively oriented to mastery over this environment; it should be the kind of society which 'gets things done'. On the personality level this leads to one major aspect of the achievement complex.

Religiously and culturally speaking this is what I have been calling the 'worldly' alternative, not in the sense that the standards derived from 'the world' should govern action, but in the sense that what man does in this world as a field of activity is the basis of his moral standing *by religious standards*. This rules out other-worldly asceticism and the type of mysticism which involves seeking religious benefits through absorption in an 'absolute' which is by definition analytically separate from 'the world'.

The third of our main alternatives concerns the instrumental-consummatory basis of selection. Here the relevant choice is clearly on the instrumental side. In religious terms this means that human action is treated, not as destined for some type of ultimate fulfilment, but instrumentally to some interest or task imposed from outside its own sphere of interest. Here again historically Calvinism is the purest type of this kind of orientation. The doctrine of predestination removed the traditional Christian concern for the salvation of the individual altogether from the field of relevance; this had been determined from eternity on grounds altogether irrelevant to the standards governing behaviour and could not in any way be influenced by events in temporal life. The duty of the individual was not to serve his own interests, even on the highest religious plane, but to *contribute* to the realization of the Divine plan.

Though individual salvationism (obviously a consummatory choice) was thus clearly ruled out, it might be argued that ascetic Protestantism did make for a 'social salvationism' in the sense that it advocated a religiously 'ideal society' to be set up under theocratic dominance of its religious leadership. The establishment of this society could be considered the ultimate consummatory attainment of the religious goal set for man, the establishment of the Kingdom.

Historically there have been brief theocratic episodes of this type, in Calvin's Geneva, in the Scotland of John Knox, very briefly in Cromwell's Commonwealth, and in early New England. In all these cases the pattern rapidly broke down, it may be surmised for cultural reasons among others;

it is these which are of interest here. The central cultural difficulty, I should say, was that the radical transcendentalism of the Calvinistic conception of God and of the grounding of Divine decrees ruled out the possibility of any socially and psychologically adequate definition of the nature of the obligations imposed upon men at the requisite level of specification necessary for the definition of institutional patterns and role-expectations. To fill this gap resort had to be had to the direct authority of the religious and political leaders. But there was no religious basis for the institutionalization of such authority since these were mere men with no better right to interpret the divine will than that of anybody else. The social individualism which was implicitly involved in repudiation of the sacramental authority of the Catholic church was too strong to be resisted. This essentially meant that the test of fulfilment of Divine will was not the organizational establishment of a theocratic order, but the *type of conduct* manifested by individuals and groups in the society. To be a 'righteous man' was to be socially responsible and to contribute through high performance in secular 'callings'. The immediate goal of conduct was to attain the maximum of 'righteousness' in this sense; but this could not be identified with a definitive religious goal for the structure of the society.

In religious terms, then, the American system clearly belongs in the category earlier called 'worldly asceticism'. Its 'worldly' orientation is, properly understood, beyond question. It is the farthest antithesis to the type of religious other-worldliness which puts escape from human society (and of course personality and organism) and its obligations as the highest religious goal. Once the theocratic version had been abandoned, there can equally be no doubt that it falls on the instrumental side and not the consummatory. There is essentially no end to the striving for higher levels of 'righteousness', for the expenditure of greater effort and the motivation to remove or minimize defects of character. Moreover the exclusion of individual salvationism meant that the *field* of this striving had to be secular social activity. Given these choices, the strong religious anchorage could not but mean a powerful impetus to activism, thus accounting for the sharp antithesis to any orientations which are predominantly 'adjustive' in the sense Weber attributed to Confucianism.

In interpreting the significance of this religious component of American cultural values, it is important to keep in mind that we are speaking of value-orientations and not religious belief systems. The same order of value-orientation is clearly compatible with considerable variation of theological belief, and such variation has existed in the history of ascetic Protestantism, as Weber explicitly set forth. Thus not only strict Calvinism, but Congregationalism, Quakerism, the Baptist movement, Methodism and the 'evangelical' wing of Anglicanism–Episcopalianism clearly belong in the broad tradition of value-orientation of worldly asceticism. As playing anything like a spearhead role, much of the Anglican influence, Lutheranism and of course Catholicism are excluded. The problem of the influence of Judaism, which does not become important until too late to affect the main tone, raises special issues which would lead too far afield here.

The main problem on the cultural level does not concern which among the main alternatives of orientation under religious primacy is the most important, but the balance between religious and secular primacy. Here there is a case for a shift toward the primacy of secular-oriented values. My present view is that there has been a partial shift, but that it is not so complete or unequivocal as most current social science opinion would hold. It is quite possible for the value-commitments associated with a primarily religious orientation to survive for a considerable time, if possibly not indefinitely, in the absence of widespread explicit commitment to their religious grounding in terms of beliefs.

What then would be the implications of widespread 'secularization' in this special sense? I think it is clear that the principal implication would be the weakening of the stress on 'activism' as I have used that concept and will develop it further later because it would undermine the religious basis of 'leverage'. It would be a change in the direction of an 'adjustive' orientation, of accepting the main conditions of life as 'given' and adjusting to them rather than attempting to 'master' them.[7]

It is clear that secularization in this sense does not touch the other two main components of value-orientation at the cultural level. Clearly the sphere of activity is the 'world' with first-order primacy from the human society; the apparent paradox of 'worldliness' in the religious case disappears in this one. Clearly also the orientation can remain primarily instrumental rather than consummatory. The general tendency then would be towards a 'utilitarian' type of 'worldly' instrumentalism with the society tending to be judged in terms of the effectiveness with which it 'satisfies' the independently given 'wants' of individuals.

Not in the present sketch, but in the relevant parts of the book, I shall try to mobilize evidence that this secularization has not gone as far as seems evident on the surface. This would involve the thesis that much of the current 'utilitarianism' in our belief system (in the sense in which this has been involved in economic thought) is of ideological significance rather than a direct expression or grounding of our values. All I wish at present is to keep the possibility of this direction of analysis open, and not to close the door to it by any flat assertion that our dominant value-orientation is clearly secular, in the above technical sense.

One further consideration which is highly relevant to this problem may be stated. This is that the adjustive version of 'worldly' orientation will result in different *empirical* consequences according to the nature of the empirical reality to which adjustment is called for. But the kind of society which exists is not a given independently of the history of its values. In so far as 'activistic' values have become institutionalized, the orientations 'back of' them come to be built into empirical reality and change in them could not be accounted for by any simple version of the process of secular adjustment. The same is true of course of the 'want-systems' of individuals, because these originate in the institutionalized culture of the society in which the individual is socialized. This argument points strongly to the importance of historical background in judging the character of a value system and to a possible relativity in the religious–secular distinction. In turn it therefore strengthened the case for religious primacy and the importance of the activistic strain. For this set of reasons I shall continue to emphasize the pattern of 'worldly asceticism' as the primary, if not exclusive, cultural base of the American value system at the societal level.

The societal value system

As has been noted in the theoretical introduction, a societal value system is composed of the direct implications of the cultural premises, plus the specifications which are appropriate to the category of empirical system to which the values apply. In cultural terms the American system is clearly 'worldly', instrumental and on the whole predominantly religious in orientation, though with some secular strains.

The social implications of the cultural values   The primary implication of the religious component is clearly what I have called 'activism'. In whatever, on other grounds, may be valued fields of action, the tendency is to avoid 'taking things lying down', to attempt to master the situation. Above all, this activistic orientation may apply both to the society as a system, and to the individual personality. It will be necessary to enquire in what ways it works out for both, but this cannot be done on the basis of the religious component alone.

The 'worldly' component implies that the primarily valued field of activity is 'this world'. Here we have the further specification that in the hierarchy of system-references the social system stands next in order to the cultural system. Cultural values are always *in the first instance* institutionalized in a society and its subsystems; of course they are also internalized in personalities, but this in the nature of the case cannot be independent of their institutionalization in the society.[8] Subject, then, to the kind and importance of the 'individualism' implied in the value system, the first-order 'field of activity' concerns the society. Hence social values specify the *desirable kind of society*, and this has primary significance where the value-orientation is 'worldly' in our sense.

It follows from the activistic element that this kind of society cannot be one which as a society is primarily 'adjustively' oriented to *its* situation. It must seek to master situational exigencies in the interest of its conception of the desirable. 'Fatalism' both at the societal and at the individual level is totally unacceptable. What the principal exigencies which have to be mastered are depends on further specifications which will be taken up presently.

Finally what, in religious terms, is the 'ascetic' component has the implication at the societal level that the society cannot serve primarily 'consummatory' interests. In the first instance it cannot do this in religious terms either in the sense of promoting individual salvation or a theocratic religious goal. But equally it cannot do this at the societal consummatory level, in setting up a definitive goal-state for the society as a system to aim at. It is conceivable that, with full secularization, instrumentalism for the society would imply consummatory primacy for the personality in the utilitarian sense. The difficulty with this implication has been suggested earlier, and I shall not pursue it further here. In any case the process of social change cannot meaningfully have a definitive consummatory goal, the final achievement of the 'ideal society'.

The general formula for the American societal value system, then, would be 'worldly instrumental activism'. The worldly emphasis stands in contrast to much of Christian tradition, notably in the contemporary situation of the Catholic church. The instrumental element stands in contrast to 'eschatological' and 'utopian' value systems and the activistic element stands in contrast to those with adjustive secular emphases.

The transition from cultural to social levels Within this general framework, what are the major areas of emphasis in the functioning of a social system? Linking the cultural and the social levels we may speak of a special emphasis on two of the 'pattern variable' components with which I have worked a good deal in the past. These are *performance* and *universalism*. That performance should receive a heavy accent in evaluative terms follows from the activism element of the value system. The question is, what kind of performance? The field of the performance is then given by what I have called the 'worldly' component of the cultural value system, namely that it should not be in direct devotional communication with a source of religious support or authority, but in the 'world' of empirical reality, that is, as Weber put it, primarily in secular 'callings'. Finally the instrumental component excludes a definitive societal goal as the measure of adequate performance, forcing application of the value of activism to a more pluralistic level. It prescribes of general direction of performance, but performances of many different kinds by many different orders of unit in systems of action are indicated. There is, for instance, no clear-cut preference between individual and collective performance. Performance must be judged by the 'worthwhileness' of its outcome. Sometimes the 'product' can be meaningfully attributed to the efforts and capacities of an individual, for example a handicraft product or an intellectual achievement. But very often, in such a case as an automobile, or the completion of a complex research programme, the individual can be credited only with a 'contribution' to a collective achievement, however important this contribution may have been.

The valuation of performance, then, implies a valuation of the necessary conditions of such performance. These conditions in turn may be broken down into the effective capacity of the performing unit, and the situational factors impinging on it, the level of 'opportunity' for effective performance. If the unit in question is a collectivity, for example a business firm, the proximate focus of this capacity is 'effective organization' which of course in turn depends on the capacities of individuals. In the case of the individual, a possible breakdown is into 'motivation' or 'commitment', ability and training.

The way in which universalism comes in may first be put negatively. A single definitive system-goal is ruled out. Performances or achievements must be pluralistically evaluated, they cannot be evaluated simply as contributions to one given goal of the system. If there is to be an acceptable standard this must involve a reference *outside* the system to a higher-order reference-base. This means essentially a *cultural* standard which applies 'impartially' and 'objectively' to all units competing in the evaluative field. In principle it applies to units of other cognate systems besides the system of reference. Universalism and particularism are respective cases. The universalistic case is that of the higher order of cultural generality which makes possible a standard above and outside the system of reference and its 'welfare'. Universalism is thus implicit in what I have called the instrumental emphasis.

It can thus be seen that the pattern variable concepts of performance and universalism serve to mediate the transition from the cultural level to that of a concrete system of action, the social system. They are essentially cultural concepts, but unlike those used to characterize what I earlier called the cultural value system they are 'pointed towards' the regulation of concrete action in society. Such concepts as 'worldly', 'ascetic' and 'religious' on the other hand are oriented toward what Weber called the 'problem of meaning'. Furthermore the pattern variable concepts are meant to be sufficiently general to cover the value systems not only of the society but of its subsystems, of personalities and even of organisms.

The social specification of American societal values   What, then, are the *fields of application* of these two paramount evaluative standards, namely that units in the system will be evaluated by their worthwhile performances and in universalistic terms? From the answer to this question will be derived the answers to the questions of the content of worthwhile performance and the relevant types of universalistic standards. The problem is to state the specifications which must be added to the direct implications of the cultural values.

Let us remember that our system is oriented to 'this world' and there is no specific definitive system-goal. Then changes in the *society* in a desirable direction must be those which contribute to the generalized achievement or performance *potential* of the system as a whole and of its units taken distributively. If we use the term *capacity* to refer to all the equalities of a unit which bear on its potential performance, and the term *opportunity* to refer to the situational factors which facilitate or impede his or its effective performance, then we can say that performance potential in the system is a direct function of the level of capacity of units and of the level of opportunity open to them. Anything then which contributes to raise the level of capacity of important units, or to improve the level of opportunities open to them, will tend to be positively valued.

For the society as a whole this is equivalent to saying that the value system tends to focus on or give primacy to adaptive functions. The higher the adaptive level, the greater the capacity to get *anything* considered desirable done, in and by the system as a whole. It is crucial to the argument that the accent is on *generalized* performance capacity of the *system*, which for units is the *combination* of capacity and opportunity.

Both the capacity complex and the opportunity complex as they may be called are thus conceived to be of primarily adaptive significance to the society as a system. But since, as just noted, the values give primacy to adaptation, for the society as a whole their valuation of adaptation constitutes the primary content of the central value-pattern itself. This must be distinguished from the ways in which the problem of the stress on the adaptive *subsystem* of the society, which will be defined as the economy, raises further problems of the lines of the *differentiation* of the value system, which will be taken up later. Furthermore it must be kept in mind that the concepts of capacity and opportunity apply to units of the system, *both* individual and collective. It is *not* correct to speak only and directly of valuation of the capacities and opportunities of individuals. The place of the individual must be considered problematical.

It is these two complexes which should form the primary content of the main central value system itself, that is of the 'latent pattern system' which is expected to be maintained. This is to say that the 'goodness' of the society is evaluated in terms of the level of universalistically judged capacity and of opportunity which it provides to its units. It follows from this that there are two orders of performances which are legitimized, i.e. judged to be 'worthwhile'. In the first place there is a 'liberal' permissiveness for units to engage in activities which in their judgement seem to be worth doing; this liberalism derives from the absence of a clear-cut system goal and of a collective authority permitted to enforce contributions toward it. But, secondly, a higher order of legitimation is accorded to activities which can be understood to contribute positively to improve the general level of capacity and/or opportunity. Such contributions may also be relatively direct, for example to economic productivity as such, or indirect, as to institutional stability which favours productivity.

A subclassification of valued factors in capacities and opportunities   It is inherent in the structure of action systems that there are three central foci of performance capacity in a general system of action. These are the organisms of the constituent members, their personalities and the social organization of significant subsystems of the society. Organisms constitute the first focus of one complex of more specific valuations, namely, in the organic sense above all the *health* complex. I shall argue that American society tends to value health very highly indeed, and that its conception of health is heavily oriented to treating it as a condition of performance capacity. The sick person is above all 'incapacitated'.

The second focus is the personality of the individual and here it is again his performance capacity and of course actual achievement which is the focus of evaluative judgement. Naturally there is a base for such capacity in biological heredity which is unalterable by influences playing upon the individual; but this on occasion we would like to improve by eugenic measures and things of that sort. But it is the area of environmental influence, particularly the processes of learning, which has tended to be the main focus. The goodness of the society is then a function of the education or training it can provide its members, but judged primarily in terms of its bearing on performance capacity. In a broad sense education (which of course includes socialization at the family level as well as formal education) breaks down into the ability component on the one hand, and that of 'moral commitment' or 'character' on the other. In recent times still a third focus has been coming to the fore, namely that now usually called 'mental health'. A primary aspect of the definition of mental illness is the insight that a person can both have the values of achievement, and the 'abilities (including the learned component)', and still not be able to perform up to his capacities as evaluated in these terms.

Finally the third focus is social organization, the importance of which derives from the fact that many 'worthwhile' performances are beyond the reach of independent individuals and require organized cooperation of many. Thus the creation and successful operation of organizations through which worthwhile performances can be achieved becomes an eminently worthwhile contribution. This, it seems to me, is the primary basis of the extremely high valuation of the executive role within our occupational system. The most obvious case of valued organization is at the collectivity level. The general strains of individualism and pragmatism in our values tend to make it easy to overlook the dependence of the system on higher-level institutional conditions; concrete individuals and concrete collectivities are much more tangible. But some awareness of this dependence is evident on ideological levels in heavy emphasis on certain (often distorted) features of 'the system' in which we live.

The second major complex of evaluative focus then is the opportunity complex. In general usage there is a conceptual overlap between this and the capacity complex in that we speak of an individual's opportunity for the training which can increase his capacities. But on the present general level I wish to ignore these complications and speak essentially of opportunity for units whose capacities are given. There is, however, inherently a 'wheels-within-wheels' structure to the problem. Parallel to the capacity complex, that of opportunity may be broken down by categories of objects.

First is the physical aspect of action. Here the basic value-orientation being activistic, it is what is done with the physical resources of the environment which is the focus of valuation. And modifications in the physical environment are above all valued which improve the facilities base for further valued performance. What is involved is thus not primarily a consummatory consumption-orientation but rather one emphasizing 'usefulness' at the level of facilities. There are of course many complications and this must not be too naively interpreted to imply the devaluation of consumption in the sense of current economic discussion. Generally speaking, 'mastery' of the physical environment is valued as broadening the range of opportunity in the present technical sense.

Persons are of course an essential aspect of the environment or situation in which any given social unit acts; hence the performance capacities of persons become an essential aspect of opportunity, and their availability for utilization must be included. This, however, is a case of what I just called the wheels within wheels. The same cannot, however, be said of certain aspects of social organization and of culture.

The essential point about social organization is that over and above the particularized and detailed availability of modifications of the physical environment, a society includes an *economy* which is a set of organized facilities for securing command of more specific facilities; i.e. consists of facilities at 'second remove'. This of course involves institutional patterning in areas such as contract and property, the existence, characteristics and extent of markets, the monetary mechanisms, and so on. Perhaps most important of all is the 'labour market' and its relation to the occupational system, namely, the set of arrangements by which human services can be mobilized for the most multifarious functions and goals. The polity, which is the cognate structural focus of governmental process, has similar though less crucial significance.

Culture, so far as it is institutionalized and internalized in performing units, may be assigned to the capacity complex. But it may also be treated in certain respects as situational. Here it involves such categories as technology, science and various others. Here again the primary positive valuation is likely to fall on 'usefulness' of the various cultural components. This is most obvious for technology. Once this usefulness has been demonstrated, it is not far to seek for some areas of science, notably in the cases of physical and biological sciences, the contributions of which become indispensable. Its extension to other areas of culture, such as law as a system, involves higher levels of sophistication but is 'on the cards'. There are various other cases as well.

The problem of the significance of the reward-value of situational objects as distinguished from their facilities-value should be mentioned. Here it may be noted that the 'ascetic' component of the cultural value system does not necessarily imply that offering of rewards should be condemned as such, i.e. that there should not be lower-level 'consummatory' emphases. The criterion is rather the effectiveness of the rewards. If rewards 'stimulate' to high performance, by all means use them, but the value-accent is on the performance and its worthwhileness, not on the more proximate consummatory meaning of the rewards. Rewards thus become an instrumentality for stimulating performance, and command of reward-objects a component of opportunity for contribution through stimulating the performance of other units. There are various strains and difficulties involved in maintaining this valuational attitude in practice, but I think it is clearly the primary focus of *valuation*, however seriously it may be shaken on the level of *motivation*.

The differentiation of the value system relative to the primary functional exigencies of the society   If the above are the primary patterns and foci of valuation, the next question concerns the relation of these general patterns to the functional exigencies and hence bases of differentiation of the society as a system. This concerns mainly the question of the primary structural *location* of the different foci of evaluation. This cannot be completely uniform wherever a given value system applies, because it depends on the level of structural differentiation of the system. The following discussion will assume a high degree of differentiation, that approximately of recent American history. Application to early historical periods would have to be modified because of the lower degree of differentiation of the society of the time.

Very broadly indeed, it may be said that the capacity complex focuses more than anywhere else in the pattern-maintenance system and the opportunity complex focuses mainly in the economy; but this is only a very first approximation. There is obviously a most important set of mutual feedback relations between them and also highly significant relations to the other two primary subsystems.

The location of the capacity complex in the pattern-maintenance system applies most clearly to the case of the personality focus. These are three primary subdivisions: religion, family and formal education. We can say that religion and family are above all the agencies involved in internalization of values, and also in specific ways in 'tension-management'. Formal education also involves internalization of values but above all the knowledge and skill components of performance capacity. The health focus, both organic and mental, may be said to lie on the borderline between pattern-maintenance and integrative subsystems, the more so the more it shades over into mental health. The rise in the significance and public awareness of the mental health problem in the last generation may be said to be a function not only of increased knowledge of intrapsychic processes, but also of salience of certain aspects of the integrative problems of the society.

The social organization aspect of the capacity complex on the other hand is more difficult to place. Its focus in recent history has been more at the level of the operative collectivity than at the institutional level and this involves mainly a combination of 'political' (in an analytical sense) and economic considerations, but these are political considerations relatively dissociated from the governmental structure of the society. It has been very closely connected with the concrete development of technology and economic production.

Turning to the opportunity side, we may say that increasingly, with structural differentiation of the society, this has come to focus on the economy and the processes of economic production. This is so much the case that it can be said that increase in the level of productivity in the economic sense is perhaps the most unequivocally primary focus of positive evaluation in the society. This does not imply depreciation of technology, since technological efficiency is one primary factor in economic productivity, though there are circumstances where conflicts can arise.

It is extremely important to be clear that this accent on the productivity of the economy is not necessarily the manifestation of utilitarian values if by this is meant the valuation of 'material welfare' in its *consummatory* sense, above all if this is extended to the interpretation that material welfare is important because man is in the last analysis guided by hedonistic motivations in a simple psychological sense – or at least *homo americanus*, who allegedly lacks 'spiritual' values, is so guided. This is a gross misinterpretation, however widely held. The accent on the economy is not this, but the consequence of worldly asceticism, hence of *instrumental* activism of the importance of facilities as an indispensable condition of effective performance, and of their generalization as contributing to *any* valued performance.

The cultural component of the opportunity complex raises somewhat different problems, which constitute a very important area of conflict. There is, within the cultural realm, as noted, a strong accent on usefulness, which naturally approves technological know-how and its scientific base. But the higher the level of generalization in a scientific (hence cultural) sense of the cultural component, the less easy is it to grasp how important it is to production and productivity. But even further, scientific knowledge clearly cannot be produced under the same type of economic or business controls (at least at present) which have been so effective in relation to many of its technological applications, and perhaps above all scientists cannot be so produced. Science focuses on the pattern-maintenance system of a society, not on the economy, and just at much on the training of scientists. Hence a strong pressure to value economic productivity as such tends to result in a relative depreciation of the cultural component, and the population elements involved with it – they are 'eggheads'. But this is a depreciation shot through with ambivalence, not an unequivocal evaluation.

Summing up it may be said that the primary valuational emphases tend to fall on the pattern-maintenance subsystem of the society, which includes the main cultural interests and the primary mechanisms of socialization and of stabilization of values, and on the adaptive subsystem which centres on the economy. The former is very broadly the principal locus of the capacity complex, especially so far as it concerns the personality as unit, while the latter is the focus of the generalized facility aspect of the opportunity complex. Since opportunity for the individual is such an important condition of achievement, this is one of the main points at which the universalistic principle leads to the ideal of '*equality* of opportunity'. The other main one is with respect to the training element of capacity. This issue is one of the most important meanings of *individualism* in our society.

It concerns the right of the individual to a fair chance to show what he can do in effective achievement rather than a simple freedom to 'do what he pleases' so long as he respects the corresponding rights of others. His freedoms are necessary conditions of acting *responsibly* in terms of the values.

Let us turn now to the political aspect of the society. Here there can be no doubt of the relatively low priority of political function in the value-scale. The central basis of this is the impossibility of focusing general valuation on a definitive goal for the system as a whole. This would be, given the 'worldly' component of the cultural value system, a very real possibility and would be strongly reinforced by the activist element. But it is blocked by the instrumental emphasis. Hence we may say that the positively valued goals are generally the goals of *units* (both individual and collective). There is, moreover, a 'liberal' aspect of the orientation to such goals which derives from the fact that there can be no human social agency which can legitimately assume authority to *prescribe* the goals of units, to 'tell people what to do'. We can say such prescription is institutionally valid only in cases of collective goal-orientation where the individual has voluntarily agreed, usually by accepting employment in it, to cooperate in achieving the goal of the organization. Hence the unit must be allowed a range of freedom in choice of goals; that is, any objector has the burden of proof on him that what a unit is trying to do is outside the bounds of legitimacy. This is of course not to say that there are no criteria of differential evaluation within these limits; these have already been indicated.

There is, however, one fundamental type of exception to this pattern. Situational exigencies may arise where either there is a general threat to the security of the system, or where an eminently worthwhile particular goal for the system can only be achieved by collective action on the societal level. External threats to security through war are the type case of the first, and mobilization in war emergency is relatively fully legitimized and readily accepted, though there is understandable reluctance to recognize the reality of such threats. In principle the same is true of internal threats to integration or to the security of fundamentally valued features of the society. It is understandable that the negative cases lead more easily to legitimated action than the positive, but it is not possible to draw a rigid line.[9]

Generally speaking, the American attitude toward political functions has approached the view that government is a necessary evil and should not be allowed more scope than absolutely necessary. (Some ideological formulations are quite explicit on this point.) And the political system has been notably 'pluralistic' with wide scope for the interplay of diverse 'interest groups'. But at the same time it has had a certain stability and level of integration, as witness a relatively stable two-party system. A place in the positive evaluative universe is necessary to account for this. Of course there has been an immense increase of pressure to political action in the last generation or two, which is another story. We may sum up the situation by saying that the dominant political subvalues are *pluralistic*. This is an important focus of 'liberalism' in our society.

The last major functional context of social evaluation is the integrative. It may perhaps be said that under 'normal' circumstances this tends to rank lowest of all. Our integrative impetus tends, like our politics, to be pluralistic. It is very intensive for highly valued subsystems like firms, schools, families, but much more problematical at the higher system levels. Highly intensive patriotism apart from in genuine national emergency often smacks of projective processes. We certainly value 'good citizenship' and 'social responsibility', but both the pluralistic and the universalistic strains militate against too great an accent on the societal collectivity and its solidarity *as such*. Social integration is a 'good thing' so far as it is a condition for the development and maintenance of a good society in the sense outlined. There clearly can be too little integration, since this might threaten a whole series of the other conditions of effective performance. But at the same time there can be too tight integration. Group loyalties can interfere with effective performance and with opportunity, can narrow ranges of freedom too much. Hence the tendency is to try to arrive at an optimum degree of integration by referring the case to standards of effectiveness, independence, and so on.

We may be said in a relative sense to be a fairly 'law-abiding people'. But at the same time we tend to be rather lenient in our judgements of those who 'cut corners' if it seems to be necessary in order to 'get things done'. We are jealous of any integrative demands which might interfere with the drive for achievement. Among the highly sensitive areas in this respect are what may be called 'dependency' and authority. By dependency I mean persons (and of course collectivities) becoming so firmly attached to the interests of specific others that responsible independence and freedom to be guided by performance values and universalistic principles is threatened. This may occur in the field of essentially personal relations but also in that of group loyalties. The objective task should, over a very wide area, take precedence.

Somewhat similar considerations apply in the field of authority. It is not correct to say that the American pattern is in any generalized sense 'anti-authoritarian'. There is on the contrary a marked readiness to accept authority when it is understood that it is necessary to attainment of ap-proved collective goals, particularly at the level of subsystem collectivities, for example business firms, and other organizations. On the other hand the type of authority which is associated with presumptions of generalized superiority of the kind so commonly found in other societies tends to be strongly opposed. And there is a general watchfulness lest persons exer-cising authority presume too much. Authority in general seems to work best in the specific function collectivity, the more so the clearer it is that the authority is functionally necessary.[10] The attitude toward authority may thus be called 'pragmatic'. It is clearly accepted, but the burden of proof is on him who would exercise authority that his right is validated by functional necessity. This is connected with certain 'informalities' of life by which people is authority seek to demonstrate that apart from the specific functional contexts they are 'just like everybody else'. In situations of strain of course the element of suspicion can easily get out of hand and interfere seriously with effectiveness. Foreigners rather generally, however, find it difficult to understand how Americans can be organizationally effective at all without a more generalized bolstering of authority and tend to be biased toward thinking American society is anarchistic.

It seems probable that strains are not so acutely felt in the integrative area of economic institutions, contract and property in particular. At least by contrast with Europe the 'rights of property' have not seemed to become such a difficult focus of enduring social conflict; even the labour movement has not made a general attack on ownership. This difference is certainly related to certain specific structural features of American society as well as to its values, but the generally high valuation of economic production creates a presumption that the integrative framework of such activities will not be so great a source of strain as is true of areas where the value-accent is not so strong.

Within the economic area of institutionalization the greatest strains seem to be associated with the competitive aspects of occupational structure. It is here that the greatest departures from ideal patterns are probably to be found, for example labour union 'featherbedding', rigid seniority rules, various types of nepotism and the like. This type of phenomenon may be related in the first instance to the severe strains involved in the subjections of a population to the high levels of occupational discipline, risk and responsibility which our more general type of social organization entails.

The conception of integrative or organizational pragmatism may, I think, be generalized beyond the field of authority. It provides a general characterization of our value-attitudes toward integration. The general trend of an attitude of instrumental activism is away from treating solidarity as an end in itself; any firm integrative pressure has continually to be tested by reference to some standard of usefulness, of 'what does it get you' not simply in the self-interest sense, but of what does it contribute to a worthwhile goal? 'Rocking the boat' is not in principle bad, because the boat may not be getting anywhere. It is this integrative pragmatism which underlines susceptibility to exaggerated fears of expectations of 'conformity'.

To sum up: this main section of the paper has been meant to show how the cultural premises outlined in the preceding section could be articulated with the conditions under which a social value system had to function in a concrete society.

First I tried to work out the *implications* of the cultural values for the social value system, arriving at the formula *worldly instrumental activism*. I then tried to work out the implications of this orientation for the application of the pattern-variable components of performance and universalism to the problem of specifying the relevant areas of value-emphasis in the concrete society.

The outcome of this analysis was to show that the cultural values would imply a primarily *adaptive* emphasis for the society as a whole in relation to its situation. The element of worldly activism precluded primary concern with internal value-realization, and the element of universalism precluded the primary reference to a specific overall goal for the system as a whole. The accent on valuation of performance then fell on the units of the system with no distinction in principle between the valuation of individual or collective achievements. Performance levels for units could then be treated as dependent on two major categories of factors, their *capacities* and the *opportunities* open to them.

These concepts of capacities and opportunities were then used to identify the main foci of evaluation of units as the bearers of the primary values of performance by universalistic standards. These break down according to the categories of objects involved, in the case of capacities the organism, the personality and social organization, in that of opportunity the physical environment, social organization and cultural components (personality is a field of wheels-within-wheels overlap).

From this vantage point the problem was then approached of identifying the main structural locations, relative to functional differentiation of the society, of the implications of the value system, and the priority scale of relative primacy among them. In one sense every social system must give priority to the maintenance of its value-patterns and react strongly to any threat to their stability. This is the case here, but particularly with respect to the personality component of the capacity complex centring structurally on religion, family and education. But operatively the general adaptive emphasis throws particularly strong stress on the function of economic production, particularly the increase in the level of *productivity* of the economy. Because of the instrumental emphasis, these two taken together are the primary focus of the American version of *individualism*, and because of universalistic principles, of stress on equality. Above all this is expressed in the ideal of *equality of opportunity*, where opportunity is taken to include education and training. Another main aspect is the implication of the value system that only the individual himself can decide what performance goals he wishes to devote himself to. Opportunity is valued mainly as opportunity to *achieve*, not simply do 'do what one pleases'.

The political or system-goal-attainment area of social function ranks definitely lower than the first two, mainly because of the way in which instrumentalism blocks the primacy of such an overall goal. The consequence is valuation of considerable political *pluralism* with, however, a residual openness for societally collective action under stress of sufficient urgencies. The element of permissiveness for the pursuit of unit-goals without prescription from above underlines the general strain of *liberalism* in the society.

Finally, the area of integrative function normally probably ranks lowest of the four. Here the main orientation has been called that of *organizational pragmatism*. This is above all a consequence of universalism, but also of the performance emphasis. The integration or solidarity of the society as a collectivity cannot be treated as an end in itself and overstress on it may be 'too much of a good thing'. There is a general wariness of overpresumption of authority or of excessive claims to impose loyalty.

Understood in the above sense we may then speak of American social values as characterized by 'instrumentalism', 'activism', 'individualism', 'liberalism' and 'pragmatism'. But taken out of the context in which this analysis has attempted to place them, these terms may well prove misleading.

Finally it should be emphasized that the lines between the elements especially valued in the different functional contexts of value-relevance are by no means sharp, and may change with structural changes in the society. Nor is their order of evaluative priority a rigidly fixed one. There are important relations of mutual feedback between all four. Moreover there is sensitivity to changes in the external situation of the society, and to internal changes in its structure and states of balance. Therefore one would expect shifts of emphasis from time to time, and that for short periods the low-order foci would assume high rank. If this were permanent, however, it would probably indicate a change in fundamental values. The burden of proof is on him who claims that in a given instance this has taken place.

The valuation of personality in American society

Finally a few words may be said about the specification of the general value system with respect to the personalities of individuals. It is perhaps convenient to use the term *achievement* in this context as cognate with performance in the social one. It seems clear then that the American value system places primary emphasis on achievement as judged by universalistic standards. The societal and the personal value-complexes come together in the valuation of the achievements of individuals in socially institutionalized roles. But it must not be forgotten that the role is a unit or subsystem of the social system and *also a subsystem* of the personality. Hence the values which govern a particular role must not be confused with the overall values of the personality, since the same individual necessarily acts in a plurality of roles.

We may say then that in evaluating persons primacy will be given to universalistically judged achievement. We may also assume that the relevant achievements are socially speaking performances in roles, since the worldly component of the value system puts a premium on participation in 'the world' which is in the first instance the social world.

One fundamental difference from the societal case is that there we were talking about *one* society but here we are talking about a large number of persons who are members of that society. Hence the formula must be particularized in terms of differing categories of persons, who will not all perform in the same roles. The kind of breakdown which was attempted earlier for functions in the societal system has to be applied to role types and role bundles for the personality. Also it will be noted that opportunity is not a relevant basis for the evaluation of a person, but only of a social system involving many persons.

It is, however, quite clear that the standard for evaluation of personal achievement has to be contribution to the implementation of societal values. It is therefore to be judged by the participation of the individual in and his contribution to socially valued performances. Hence the primary point of reference for analysing the stratification of the society is the rank-ordering of significant units, and eventually persons, by differential evaluation of performances and achievements.

In terms of their anchorage in social structure, different role types will have different primary 'locations' in the subsystems of the society. According then to the order of primacy of different roles for the individual, the 'person' can be partly located in the social structure. This can be illustrated by the case of sex role. If the proposition be accepted that the feminine role is anchored primarily in the family, then feminine contributions belong more in the pattern-maintenance system than any other. The masculine role on the other hand is anchored primarily in occupations. More of these have primary significance for economic and technological production than any other functions at the societal level. The evaluation of the achievements of the individual then will be a function of two sets of variables: (1) the place of the 'functions' to which he contributes relative to the societal value system and (2) the 'level' of his achievement within the appropriate functional category.

Strictly speaking this is true of the evaluation of role performance. To arrive at an overall evaluation of the total person it is necessary somehow to synthesize the evaluations of his achievements (actual or potential) in all of his different roles.

Finally it should be remembered that not all valued properties of individuals can legitimately be treated as achievements, or achievement capacities. Thus the beauty of a woman, so far as it is not 'synthetic', need not be an achievement but is certainly valued. What can be suggested is that even such things tend to be 'skewed' in the direction of the *effect* they can have in achievement contexts. Beauty may then be valued as instrumental to the control of men rather than mainly 'for its own sake'. But there is clearly a limit to how far such skewing can be pushed.

Notes

1. I am particularly grateful to Winston White and Ethel M. Albert for helpful critical comments. Without them even this first 'working paper' stage of an attempted analysis would have been far less satisfactory.

2. The term 'value-orientation' is used here as almost exactly equivalent to the 'value-

premise' assumed by Dr Albert elsewhere. Indeed I have, below, without realizing it slipped into this terminology. More technically I would like to speak of value-orientations at the high cultural level, and of values qualified by adjectives like social as at the level constitutive of the appropriate class of action systems.

3. These are the four 'system problems' originally formulated by Bales and stated by R.F. Bales, E.A. Shils and myself in *Working Papers in the Theory of Action* (New York: Free Press, 1953), and used in a number of subsequent publications.

4. There is a serious tendency in some quarters for the concept of value to become a 'depreciated conceptual currency' in social science discussion in a way similar to what happened to the concept of instinct a generation ago. Given an empirical uniformity of behaviour, it tends to be asserted that this expresses the values of those who behave in this way, without treating the behaviour as a function of values *and* one or more *other* variables. Then the category of values in question becomes simply a label for the type of behaviour and the reasoning becomes patently circular – people are said to act the way they do because they have certain values, which is simply saying that they do in fact act that way. The connection of this logic with the tendency to assert that any marked change of behaviour or attitude indicates a change of values, is patent.

5. Dr Albert rightly picks up this statement and asks for elucidation. What I wish to do is to *minimize* philosophical assumptions, and avoid those unnecessary for my immediate purposes and which might stimulate controversy on matters extraneous to these purposes. I do not, however, see how it is possible to contend that we can discuss what, in terms of the empirical system of action, are 'ultimate' value-orientations, without there being any assumptions at all necessary about the nature of the 'boundary' implied by the term 'ultimate' and of what might lie on the other side of it. Such phrases as the 'general conditions of human life' are not sufficiently precise. The assumption that 'nonempirical reality' is not a meaningless category is, however, self-consciously a philosophical assumption, and it is quite deliberately made.

6. This formulation presupposes the breakthrough of the 'natural world view' discussed by Robert N. Bellah (see Bellah, 'Religious Evolution', in his *Beyond Belief*, New York: Harper & Row, 1970: Ch. 2).

7. I use this term adjustment rather than adaptation, which Weber used, because I do not wish to imply passivity by the term adaptation. In biological theory it can mean either adjustment or mastery or any level of shading on this range of variation, and I think it is useful to retain this openness in sociological usage.

8. This is essentially because the source of personal values is always socialization in a social system. Individual 'variance' is of course possible and common, but a single individual cannot create a totally independent basic value-framework any more than he can create a totally new language without ever having learned the language current in his society.

9. A good example of such a case is the problem of providing educational facilities. There is a strong tendency, as at present, to allow the situation to reach a state of serious deficit before large-scale collective political action can be brought about. In other words by neglecting a positive opportunity seriously enough it can be turned into an emergency where *unless* strong action is taken consequences will be patently serious, comparable to defeat in a war.

10. A striking example of this may be taken from S.A. Stouffer, E.A. Suchman, L.C. De Vinney, S.A. Star and R.M. Williams Jr, *The American Soldier* (3 vols, Princeton, NJ: Princeton University Press, 1949). The authority of officers was readily accepted by enlisted men in the combat situation. But in rear areas, and in the more diffuse fields of social privileges and the like, the so-called 'caste system' was fiercely resented. The officers' club in the situation where little functional activity was going on was a symbol of objectionable generalized superiority and privilege.

4

PRACTICE AGAINST THEORY IN AMERICAN SOCIOLOGY: AN EXERCISE IN THE SOCIOLOGY OF KNOWLEDGE

Harold J. Bershady

German sociology, Mannheim said almost sixty years ago, produces ideas that have broad significance, although no one knows whether they are empirically true. American sociology, on the other hand, produces carefully validated observations, although no one knows whether or to what extent they are significant.

Chief among the reasons for the difference between the two, in Mannheim's view, was that American sociology took its problems from the immediate, practical necessities of everyday life, whereas German sociology endeavored to conceive the larger whole within which the smaller part was located. Juvenile delinquency, juvenile gangs, immigration policy, race relations, ghettos, slums were the sorts of subjects with which much of American sociology was occupied in the early 1930s when Mannheim made his commentary.[1] A social policy orientation aimed at bettering one or another social problem inspired the larger part of the American effort. For this reason, the scope of the questions raised in American sociology was narrow, but the methodological apparatus for gathering precise, reliable data was elaborate. General ideas such as those of the German, for which there are no direct, empirical indicators, were thus dismissed as 'mere philosophy', unscientific and useless.

The methodological asceticism of the Americans, Mannheim believed, had bred a fear of general ideas so great that uncontrolled speculation (for which the Germans were also well known) was indiscriminately lumped with careful, constructive efforts to outline a comprehensive understanding of social and historical phenomena. The most valuable specimens of American empirical sociology showed to Mannheim 'a curious lack of ambition to excel in the quality of theoretical insight into phenomenal structures. They reveal a greater anxiety not to violate a certain, very one-sided, ideal of exactness' (Mannheim, 1953: 189).

American sociologists have an 'exactitude complex', Mannheim observed, that is not due simply to their zeal to ameliorate each detail of the social problems they studied. The importance attached to numerical certitude and to the gathering of ever more 'facts' was also due, he believed, to the American fascination with, and desire to imitate, natural science. This fascination, which has led to the canonization of a specific ideal of exactness, does not discriminate among fields of phenomena for which the ideal is inappropriate. Historical, philological and interpretive materials require different, but also precise, standards of assessment. Although American sociology, in Mannheim's judgment, had made genuine progress in perfecting methods of observation and achieving objectivity, it remained lacking in reflective self-control.

As Mannheim was discussing the mainstream of American sociology in the 1930s, it was appropriate that he ignored certain peripheral contributions, such as the work of Cooley and Mead. Perhaps he would have found, particularly in Mead's writings, in which religious, ontological, epistemological, social, normative, perceptual and situational elements were interwoven, an example of the rapprochement between the emphases of German and American social science that he believed would be desirable.[2] In any case, Mannheim's discussion, brief as it was, opened several issues for reflection. In the years since he wrote, German and American scholars of all kinds have had much more contact, and we are better able to see that the distinction he drew between the thought-ways of the two nations was not applicable solely to sociology or the social sciences, as he seemed to suggest.[3] His implicit notion that natural science is the same thing wherever it is pursued is historically inaccurate. Moreover, the terms 'practical' and 'social problem', as he used them, were ambiguous and misleading. Above all, although Mannheim was able fleetingly to characterize certain features of American sociology, he ventured little in the way of understanding their meaning, and therefore did not tap the strength with which they were clung to and would persevere, as I believe they have, to the present day. I will briefly discuss each of these points.

Natural science in the United States, late nineteenth to early twentieth centuries

According to Richard Shryock (1962), American natural scientists were, by and large, indifferent to basic research questions throughout the nineteenth century. Natural science in the United States during this period was technological in nature and overwhelmingly directed to practical, tangible ends.[4] Building houses, cities and roads, transforming means of communication, manufacturing consumer goods, improving crop yields – these were the aims that prompted the American natural science effort. Training in basic science, in the principles of physics, chemistry, biology, botany, was for many decades to be had in Europe, chiefly in Germany. In Europe, a moneyed bourgeois class, with the leisure to pursue abstract knowledge, dominated the universities and undoubtedly established training in pure science as a tradition.[5] But even in the 'republic of the common man', some Americans sought such training. However, only after basic research could be justified as yielding solutions to practical problems was this kind of research and the training which underlay it given support. Charles Rosenberg's studies of the growth of the Agricultural Stations in the United States in the latter part of the nineteenth century document this pattern. Attached to the newly formed land-grant colleges and staffed by young chemists and biologists recently returned from their training in Europe, the experimental work undertaken in these stations was funded by state legislators solely for its practical promise (Rosenberg, 1976). The fulfillment of this promise, in turn, was used in the lobbying efforts of American scientists to develop their own departments of chemistry, biology, plant physiology and so on – departments which have since risen to prominence in the state universities of the USA.

The story of the practical successes of these and kindred scientific efforts became part of the lore of early twentieth-century America, told by teachers to their young pupils, recounted in newspapers and magazines, and popularized in biographies and novels (Rosenberg, 1976). For the lay public, the controlled experiment was dramatized as an ally in man's war against disease, but one that sometimes involved grave risks to the scientist, for example, in finding the agents of yellow fever which later permitted this disease to be brought under control. The devising of precise measures was cast in terms which extolled the benefits brought, for example, in calculating electric charge – with all the attendant dangers – thus permitting the development of an endless stream of inventions and vast electrical and communicational networks. These portraits, as well as more fantastical accounts, produced frequently in the 1920s and 1930s, endowed science and scientists with magical potency, a disciplined ability to manipulate things with numbers, and not least, a romantic quality in which daring, mastery and occasional martyrdom were combined (LaFollette, 1979; Burnham, 1987; Krieghbaum, 1967).

Such characterizations of science were carried after the Second World War in the waves of stories, fictional as well as factual, proclaiming fresh American victories in each field of scientific endeavor. Spurred on by the many actual scientific successes and by increasing public support, the federal government quickly established the Atomic Energy Commission, the National Science Foundation and the National Institute of Health as chief agencies for funding scientific research (Dupree, 1965). In the rapidly burgeoning literature of science fiction, in weekly Sunday supplement features, daily newspaper articles, television programs and movies, American triumphs in applied physics, chemistry, biology and psychology were acclaimed, and visions projected of scientific conquests that would plumb the depths of the human mind and body as well as reach into the farthest regions of the universe.[6]

But this glowing conception of science has not been the only one. The darker, Frankensteinian view, of machines and men running amok, of powerful discoveries impossible to control, of the planet, society, the family, human life itself being imperiled, has also been held since the nineteeth century. Three Mile Island and Chernobyl have provided recent confirmations of these fears. Yet the mistrust of science, while occasionally reaching feverish proportions and never fully subsiding, has remained by and large secondary. Scientists continue to be called upon to solve every kind of problem, including the problems they are presumed to have created. Americans' faith in the human capacity to govern nature, and their enthusiasm for scientific advances, have never remained dampened for long. (Indeed, more than twenty-five years after the program ended *Star Trek* continues to be replayed. And at the height of the recent nuclear alarm, 'Trekkies' from each part of the country were joyfully gathering for their yearly convention.)

In depicting science as an instrument that requires little theoretical contemplation, but will tame the world and bring it closer to human aspirations, Americans recognized themselves, their own ideals and sense of mission.[7] American sociology was in Mannheim's day – and I believe has never ceased to be – of a piece with this, an instance of a broader pattern of American life and culture.

The influx of theory in American sociology

In 1937, four years after Mannheim's essay appeared, Talcott Parsons published *The Structure of Social Action*. Although this book established Parsons as America's premier theorist, American reviews of the book were lukewarm at best and the first edition of a thousand copies was not sold out for a decade.[8] However, the Second World War brought to the United States a great many European scholars and scientists, and the natural as well as the social sciences were stirred by strong, new currents. In sociology alone such figures as Erich Fromm, Theodore Adorno, Herbert Marcuse, Alfred Schutz, and not least Mannheim (who had settled in England), had become eminent by the late 1940s. Through commentaries and translations by Louis Wirth and Edward A. Shils, Mannheim's writings were introduced to an American audience and soon became the subject of doctoral dissertations as well as studies by established scholars. One of the most discussed books of the time among the educated public was, for obvious reasons, Fromm's *Escape from Freedom* (1941). *The Authoritarian Personality*, by Adorno and associates (1950), was hailed in academic quarters as a landmark empirical study of important theoretical and practical issues. Even Marcuse's *Reason and Revolution* (1941), read perhaps by no more than a handful of cognoscenti, became known as the work of a philosopher with a different, powerful viewpoint. Through the works of these scholars and their students, certain of the writings of an older generation of Europeans, notably Weber, Durkheim, Freud and, slightly later, Marx, gained greater currency among American sociologists. Parsons's *Structure*, which dealt with many of the European thinkers, was brought out in a second, more successfully received edition – although readers' interest lay more in finding a shorter account of the Europeans than in grasping Parsons's own theoretical project. Work of the sort that Mannheim considered particularly German, namely the attempt to construct a comprehensive understanding of society, its parts and their relations, was pursued in the United States after the Second World War – by the émigré scholars and also by native American sociologists – with vigor. Translations of books hitherto inaccessible to most Americans, of older as well as contemporary French and German social scientists, appeared. Indeed, by the early 1960s there was not a major university in the United States without one or two sociologists on its faculty who identified themselves as theorists. There were also centers – Harvard, Chicago, the New School for Social Research, Columbia, the Carnegie Institute of Technology, Berkeley, San Diego, UCLA – where challenging, new theoretical work was being produced – in action theory, symbolic interactionism, phenomenological sociology, functionalism, exchange theory, ethnomethodology, neo-Marxism.

Such theoretical ferment was new in American sociology. But this novelty should not obscure the far greater – indeed immense and unprecedented – scale of the research (much of it funded) undertaken to solve the 'practical' problems of the day. Thousands of empirical studies were done in the post-Second World War decades on aspects of political, business and military leadership, bureaucracies, industrial and service organizations, vocational selection, job satisfaction, coalition formation, unions, medical and legal practice, craft organizations, higher education, social mobility, occupational prestige, value, attitude and opinion formation, religious affiliation, small group processes, prejudice, ethnic assimilation, racial conflict, conflict resolution, residential location, suburbs, neighborhood composition, white-collar and juvenile crime, mate selection, family dynamics, voting patterns, class relations, socialization, demographic shifts – and this is just a partial list. A full enumeration of the major topics would take several pages.

The torrent of American sociological research, to which there was nothing comparable in Europe, was as notable for the great numbers of subjects investigated as for its limited theoretical grasp. When taken together the studies appeared as little more than an *ad hoc* aggregate, an assemblage of diverse items lacking internal coherence. However, two assumptions supported these studies, I believe, and made of them a distinctive cultural, if not always intellectually consistent, entity. The first was the common moral imperative, often implicit, that underlay each problem examined *as well as the effort to resolve it*. (This is not simply a matter of value-relevance, as I will explain shortly.) The second was the endeavor, made by many sociologists, but not all, to press rigorous, aggregative instruments – themselves invested with moral significance – upon the subject studied.

The morality of the practical

Despite differences in emphasis and in substantive interests, the American philosophers of pragmatism were in broad agreement that human life was charged by the effort to resolve the 'problematics' of the situation in which it was embedded. For these thinkers, human life was framed by the tension between the pull of 'conditions' and the thrust of aspirations, the two coordinates, one circumstantial, the other ideational that defined a situation. Each situation was thus inherently problematic. However, resolution of the tension in one situation did not mean an end to problems as a new situation would seamlessly take its place. Circumstances and aspirations change. Human beings are ever in new situations and confront new problems. The struggle to bring circumstances into closer conformity with human intentions remains constant.[9] To give up this struggle would thus be virtually to give up human life, to sink into conditions.[10]

Tacit in the pragmatists' view, therefore, was a moral injunction to act. For if to act was to affirm one of the fundaments of being human, then action was a human obligation. And although morality may be, as James put it, 'action in the line of greatest resistance', any action, simply because it resists conditions, whether of physical, economic, psychological, political, social or cultural circumstances, has fulfilled an obligation. Thus any action has a moral aspect. But to act, to resist conditions, implies that human life is not bound solely by conditions. The capacity to act, therefore, further implies that human life is in some respects free. To set about resolving a problem, any problem, is a sign of our freedom.

In this relentlessly activist conception echoes of the Kantian moral philosophy can be heard. But echoes of Calvinist religious ethics are not far behind. For if to act is a *duty*, as I believe the pragmatists assumed, then this proposition is an intellectualized version of the stipulation that the work *ethic*, as Weber's well-worn analysis has made clear, places upon American, and by now a good part of Western, conduct.[11] The emphasis upon being practical that is common among Americans, sociologists no less than ordinary citizens, is not merely a matter of tinkering with things to improve the efficacy with which they work, an effort to ameliorate social conditions, or the pursuit of self-interest – although there are plentiful occurrences of each. To be practical in the American setting one *must* act in such a way that a problem will be solved, a situation altered.

But which situation, which problem? America is a nation of diverse people with diverse interests, and new unanticipated problems and situations constantly arise. Many of these are in competition, vying for greater attention and a larger share of resources for their pursuit. Yet any problem, any interest, any situation, so long as it falls within legal limits, is permissible for Americans. Is it any wonder, then, that Americans have little affinity or appreciation for theoretical work 'of the German kind'? Where is the scheme so comprehensive and finely spun that it will be able to anticipate any situation that may occur? In such schemes many problems are conceptually defined, generated from the inner workings of the theory. In American thought, problems are situationally defined, generated from evaluations of the circumstances of life.

Of instruments and action

To construct a rigorous, comprehensive theory requires sustained reflection. But sustained reflection, whatever its other products, may not yield a practical outcome. This is as true of mathematics and the physical sciences as it is of the social sciences. (Did anyone foresee when they were being invented that the non-Euclidean geometries would become essential for post-Newtonian physics and that this new physics would have astonishing applications?) To act purposefully to no apparent practical end must often appear to Americans tantamount to not acting. The contemplative work of the theorist, seemingly so quiescent, must therefore be seen as passive, something that hardly qualifies as work. And to be passive in the American setting is to arouse suspicion of moral laxness and possibly worse. (Senator Proxmire continues to award his 'golden fleece' each year to government-funded research that is often basic in nature, but that has no apparent application.) Perhaps this is a reason that theories of society in which culture figures prominently are not to the taste of most American sociologists. For culture – religious conceptions, normative orders, moral systems, esthetic standards, values, ideas – is 'mentalistic', as it were. Its elements consist of signs, symbols and language, and these are closely related in substance to the materials the theorist employs. Culture operates on and through the mind and is commonly held to be 'subjective'. Far more important to the sociologist who is concerned with such things, culture also operates on and through conduct, and in this sense is 'objective', but this requires interpretations and reflection to grasp. However, it is not only unsupported cultural interpretations that are dismissed. Also distasteful are cultural interpretations whose validity and scope have been properly assessed.[12] For the mentalistic-subjective associations of culture are likely to stamp it as something passive.

In American sociology, for instance, the work of Durkheim held up most often as an exemplary early scientific study is his *Suicide* (1951). Its scientific status resides in the fact that for this work Durkheim collected data and subjected them to statistical analysis. Not often is it mentioned that the data on suicide rates are unreliable and the statistical operations therefore pointless; it is enough to show that the data are manipulated. The analyses in *Suicide* thus take on an instrumental and potentially active cast. Durkheim's theory of social pathology, of which suicide was for him an indicator, involved the postulation of an imbalance, perhaps impossible precisely to measure – in any case not measured – among four things, freedom versus obligation and commitment to the self versus commitment to the group. In most American discussions the broader theory is virtually ignored, trimmed down to a few words, an occasional article, a typology, even a quantitative scale, merely of anomie. And although (or perhaps because) it has the status of a 'classic', Durkheim's masterwork, *The Elementary Forms of the Religious Life* (1947), in which he accomplished one of the most subtle, rigorous and far-reaching analyses of religious and moral culture, is given, in comparison, scant attention.[13]

With few exceptions, I believe, the treatment of Durkheim's work by American sociologists has been anti-intellectualist in character.[14] And this is also true of the treatment of the work of Weber, Simmel, Schutz, Tönnies, Freud, Parsons, Lévi-Strauss, Mead (whose *Philosophy of the Act* has been largely ignored by the symbolic interactionists) and many others. No doubt, the volumes in The Heritage of Sociology Series, published by the University of Chicago Press, and in similar series of other publishers, have helped keep these thinkers 'alive'. There has also grown in the past decade a small-scale industry devoted to the manufacture of books on Max Weber. But given past experiences, is it not reasonable to suspect that these books, or at least parts of them, serve the majority of their readers primarily as brief substitutes, 'trots', for the actual writings of the theorists they discuss? Then would this not mean that theoretical work, for Americans, becomes more remote with each new commentary published (an irony surely not intended by author or publisher)? In the anti-intellectual attitude there likely has been less an active opposition to intellectual matters than a moral aversion to them, a distancing of oneself from the questionable object, the theory, which has led to difficulty in seeing it (Hofstadter, 1963). Once this attitude became entrenched it was but a small step automatically to dismiss theoretical work of the cultural kind as 'arm-chair speculation' or 'wheel spinning' – self-indulgent, idle pursuits that are unscientific and useless, as Mannheim observed. The proponents of the various behavioralisms that abound in American sociology take this position. The one kind of 'mentalistic' theory not subject to these criticisms is cognitive theory, psychological or sociological, in which calculation – for example, measuring costs and benefits – is viewed as ancillary to action. This operation of the mind, many of whose features have been well known for decades, was not taken for a theory of thinking by such European theorists of mental life as Freud (1950), Scheler (1963: 77ff; 1973: 98ff) and Merleau-Ponty (1962), who held that in thinking passion, imagination, memory and desire were integral parts.

The gender of theories

Americans are problem solvers. They want the strongest, most effective instruments for this purpose. Statistical procedures for the analysis of data, widely approved in American sociology, are not so much an adoring imitation of science as an effort to bend something akin to the powerful instrumentality of science to sociological ends. The statistical shaping and transforming of data is at least a metaphor of action, a numerical expression of what is assumed to be possible and desirable in the social world. To statistical analysis has been transferred some part of the morality of action. But statistical analysis as employed in American sociology has other meanings. The sexual imagery implicit in the passive versus active distinction – interior, conceptual and soft, thus feminine; objective, instrumental and hard (as in data), thus masculine – may well be involved in the discomfort, sometimes antagonism, with which many American sociologists, regardless of gender, respond to theories in which culture is given a large part. This attitude is not limited to sociologists. To call persons of learning 'egg-heads' is to belittle their cultivation and learning by characterizing them as impractical, fragile and, as the term implies, feminine in outlook. The older, derisive term for intellectuals and artists which has gone out of fashion, 'long-hair', was clearly feminine in attribution.

However, not merely in Germany but in all of Europe, to be a theorist and to do intellectual work, regardless of one's gender, is considered a preeminently 'masculine' occupation. Europeans tend more to lionize their intellectuals, Americans their scientists. The immensely long intellectual tradition in Europe has been, with only relatively recent exceptions, an exclusive activity of men. The authors of the Old and the New Testaments (*the* book), the law givers, commentators, philosophers have all been men. Social theory has emerged from philosophy, but philosophy is an offshoot of theology. And both philosophy and theology have been pursuits of men in positions of authority (priests, aristocrats), or of men deemed exemplary by others in authority. Augustine dubbing Aristotle 'the' philosopher is an instance of one exemplary intellectual, a Catholic, esteeming another, who was a pagan. Intellectual endeavor thus is associatively bound to masculinity, authority and honor. Theoretical work in Europe and America is now a largely secular undertaking. However, in Europe, charismatic fragments of the older tradition likely continue to endow the theorist with an authoritative, masculine, and sometimes – as, for example, in the case of Marx – even prophetic, cast.[15]

In America, by contrast, it is as though cultural theories, although feminine and presumably weak, nevertheless possessed the dangerous potentiality of feminizing and thus weakening their bearers. There is in this, of course, the implied seductiveness of 'soft' theories which must be avoided. For the lure of such theories is to give up the struggle and sink into inaction. And to sink into inaction is to fall into a kind of death. Statistical analysis, in comparison, is masculine and active *par excellence*. However, the fact is that, although statistical analysis may be a trope of action, it is commonly (if perhaps mistakenly) believed that sociologists have not been nearly as able to alter the social world as physicists and biologists the natural world. If there is indeed a sexual loading of these different approaches in sociology, as I believe there is, this would help to clarify an aspect of the frequent obduracy, seemingly irrational and defensive, with which statistical procedures are adhered to and cultural analysis rejected. But there are meanings other than fear and denial of weakness in this response.

The religious connection – preachers and teachers

The thought of many American social thinkers in late nineteenth century, most of whom were trained in the ministry and taught in colleges and universities, was under the sway of the Social Gospel Movement. These thinkers sought to improve social problems and to grasp the meaning of the unprecedented, momentous changes reshaping the nation. Their aim was to guide the nation more surely and swiftly towards an advent they believed certain, the coming kingdom of God *on earth*. This was the mission for which America was created, the monument the nation was striving to become. A broad eschatological strand was woven into each of their analyses – of the nature of the new methods of machine production, working arrangements, class relationships, population, cities, bureaucracy, government, family life, child-rearing, authority, and finance capitalism, among many others (Haskell, 1982: 17).

In Herbert Spencer's account of social evolution, society was described as moving ceaselessly, inexorably to an ever higher plane. Propounders of the Social Gospel seized upon the Spencerian scheme, for they saw in it a powerful secular parallel to, and fresh warrant of, their own convictions (Miller, 1954: introduction). They never doubted the kingdom of God would first occur in America, the most highly evolved nation on earth, and that the American mission was to herald and extend this kingdom to all mankind (Niebuhr, 1959). Even among those not trained in the ministry, such as Charles H. Cooley and Lester Ward, the evolving, organic view of social life was adopted and a realizable ideal put forth of a future society as a perfected, all-embracing Christian commonwealth (Haskell, 1982; Barnes, 1948).

The transformation of social thought to social science in America, begun in late nineteenth century, culminated in a thoroughly professional and secular set of social science disciplines by the end of the First World War. The more insistently the call to become scientific was made, the more determinedly were the religious, if not the melioristic, constituents of American social thought cast out.[16] Religion dealt with meanings of things, science with 'facts'. The concern with religion and meanings was perhaps appropriate to the past which the historian studied, or to the 'primitive' peoples in whom the anthropologist was interested, but for the sociologist this concern betrayed at least a pre-scientific, even retrograde passion; at worst it was anti-scientific.[17]

In a resolutely secular and anti-clerical age, the interpretive sociological effort that dwells upon culture must strike a discordant note. For even on its surface the word 'culture' displays its religious roots: *cultus*, to cultivate, to worship. No one may any longer read Spencer, but American social theory, in its endeavor to understand the meanings of social life , bears the mark of its religious and metaphysical paternity; it is descended from the Social Gospel Movement.[18] These very nearly taboo associations, I believe, contribute to the discomfort and irritation with which cultural theories are usually received.

The leisure of the theory class

Before the Second World War, a junior faculty member in German universities, a *Privatdozent*, lectured without salary. Income from sources other than the university was, thus, a necessity for an aspirant to a German university career. Most of the nineteenth- and twentieth-century German founders of sociology, as well as European intellectuals generally, were born into moderately successful, urban, bourgeois families – the kind Americans now refer to as upper middle class. These men were, for the most part, not rich, but of independent means. Engels was an exception, for his family were wealthy textile manufacturers and he went 'riding to hounds' as a young man. But Marx was subsidized by his businessman father, his wife's family who were minor nobility, his maternal uncle, and by Engels for many years after he moved to England. Weber relied upon the patrimony of his Prussian bourgeois father not only to help launch his academic career but to sustain him during several years of illness and, after his recovery, for nearly two decades as an independent scholar. Simmel drew from his inheritance which permitted him to teach without pay for decades at the University of Berlin. Practically all the members of the Frankfurt School were supported, in their early careers in Germany and later in America, by their businessmen or banker fathers. A great many other well-known sociologists – Tönnies, Troeltsch, Sombart, Stein, von Weise, Scheler, Mannheim, among others – were financed similarly.[19]

Only rarely in the Germanic countries, as in the case of Sigmund Freud and Franz Oppenheimer, was someone with poor economic means able to support himself and yet have enough energy and time to produce scholarly work. Freud's income during his years as lecturer at the University of Vienna was from his medical practice (as was Oppenheimer's in Germany), an occupation that proved to be felicitous to his intellectual interests (Jones, 1953). The German situation was, and is, virtually the exact opposite of the American one. Although there continue to be men and women of inherited wealth among American scholars, most faculty at all levels in American universities have depended entirely on university salaries for financial support. Weber was struck, when he visited the United States in 1904, with the modest circumstances of American professors, their small, doll-like houses, their lack of servants.[20] These circumstances have not drastically changed. Indeed, to become a professor in the United States has been for many a rise in social and economic status into the middle class.

Whatever may be the reasons for the German penchant for 'general theory', which is found in many disciplines, to do theoretical work in German universities was perforce *also* a mark of one's privilege. How else could one have afforded the unsalaried 'leisure', the long, hard devotion free from financial responsibilities, that theoretical work required? In Germany, some of the prestige of the social class of the men who produced theory was likely transferred to their work. But in America, it is exactly its foreign associations with hierarchy that spark suspicion of general theory. American sociologists, as is true of Americans generally, win status largely through occupational achievements and often disapprove of ascription of status, high or low, to class membership. Indeed, Americans are at least as much occupied in renouncing the privileged as in elevating the poor. To renounce general theory, therefore, is by metaphorical extension to renounce the elite class that has produced such theory.

Consider, for example, the rhetorical point made in calling general theory 'grand theory'. This is hardly to describe, but to castigate general theory, to treat general theory with contempt and condemn it for elitist pretensions (Mills, 1959). The barely veiled antagonism of such a rhetorical maneuver has given way at times to murderous verbal attacks against the presumed elitism, either of outlook, class origins, or academic affiliation, of general theorists (Gouldner, 1971). Talcott Parsons, the foremost American sociological theorist of the twentieth century, was a favorite subject of such verbal assaults.

Consider, on the other hand, the rhetorical tactic – aside from the logical merits of the case – of offering 'middle range' theory as an alternative to general theory (Merton, 1957). Is this not perfectly suited to the American temper? This kind of theory, the name intimates, is not too high, not too low, but, like the modest accomplishments of the middle class, accessible to everyone. There is nothing comparable to this view of theory in Germany.

Differences of university systems, academic recruitment patterns, occupational structures and class conceptions in Germany and the United States have contributed to opposite judgments of general theory in the two countries. This is true for sociology and likely also for other disciplines. In the United States, the association of general sociological theories with the privileged status of their European or American authors has, I believe, encouraged the disfavor in which such theories are held.

Equality, individuality and statistics

Americans uphold the principles of individuality and equality, although they do not always observe them. But because of this disjunction such principles play a vital role in American life. It is in these terms that the civil rights and women's movements were launched and gained legitimacy. These principles serve as standards of fairness, and their violation, sooner or later, causes protest. Social inequalities are offensive to Americans, and much research has been directed to exposing and, if possible, correcting their harmful effects. For this purpose, American sociologists (and social scientists generally) have developed measures to gauge inequalities. They have assumed that although some people may have more and some less (of schooling, money, power, intelligence, and so on) all people are nevertheless 'fundamentally equal', and that the *same* measures may be used to compare them. (Although the meaning of equality has never been unequivocally decided, one or another meaning is for a time agreed upon. Like 'democracy', to which it is related, equality is an essentially contested term [Gallie, 1968].) Furthermore, American sociologists are acutely aware that there are vast differences in the arrangements of social life – between huge, corporate bureaucracies, which they have studied with care, and small, primary friendship or family groups. But because of their individualistic and action premises, American sociologists have tended to understand differences among groups as a function of two things, variations in the numbers and characteristics of their members and variations in their goals. The aggregation of individual characteristics through demographic surveys – age, sex, ethnicity, attitudes, political affiliation, education and the like – has become the major, although not the only, way of representing group life. This is consistent with the widely held American view that groups are themselves 'instruments', to be shaped and reshaped for certain objectives, and to be entered and left voluntarily by individuals in pursuit of their own goals.

However, the assumptions and procedures of mainstream American sociology are inimical to much of the understanding of social life that theoretical reflection has gained over the past century. Virtually each such theoretical effort (with the possible exception of Mead's) has, for example, viewed the social world as consisting of various hierarchies. To understand the significance of groups upon which honor is bestowed – doctors, lawyers, jurists, scribes, or in some contexts, scientists, ministers, Brahmans or priests – was a prominent concern. The outlook and training of members of such groups were examined. Also examined were rules, formal or informal, regulating entry into one or another group, constraints placed upon conduct of members, grounds of expulsion, relations to governmental bodies and to the larger society, and so on. Durkheim's (1958) analysis of professional ethics, Weber's analysis of functionaries in China (1951) and India (1958) and of scientists in the West (1946), Parsons's analysis of the medical profession in the United States (1951) are among the chief examples. These analyses portrayed each group as a distinctive entity which imposed upon its members unique, demanding sets of duties. The honor accorded such groups signified that the activities of their members, the duties they performed and the manner in which they performed them, were prized by the larger community. To prize something is to elevate that thing above others. But American sociologists, with notable exceptions, have found it difficult to accommodate to this non-egalitarian view.[21] The members of such groups – their training, language, outlook, duties, work – are not different from the members of other groups solely in matters of degree. It is not merely that they have more schooling, say, than bus drivers, but schooling of a different kind, not more responsibilities than house painters, but responsibilities of a different kind. They may have more or less money, power and prestige, more or fewer children, cars, houses, suits, shoes – all of which are obviously measurable, but have little, if anything, to do with the honor they receive. For the honor they receive is a function of the group to which they belong and the moral standards they represent. The ethical nature and responsibility of the lives of priests or scientists are of a different order, not simply of magnitude, but of quality, from that of parishioners or laymen. Aggregative measures cannot capture such differences. The cohesion, solidarity or integrity of such groups – as various of the theoretical sociologists put it – is not a matter of their size and objectives alone. A common moral outlook among members, acceptance of discipline, respect for authority, shared faith in the ultimate value of the group – these are the principles which theoretical reflection upon several historical instances has discovered to bind a group together. However, these are general, theoretical principles, whereas there are many different kinds of concrete, real groups. In any given empirical case, therefore, methods should allow us to discern the particular embodiment such principles have taken. To these research issues the aggregative methods preferred by Americans, themselves expressive of powerful moral sentiments, are silent.

Theoretical work of the sort Mannheim extolled is dubious on five grounds in the American setting: for a pretension to comprehensiveness shattered by the appearance of a fresh situation, for a passivity repellent to the activist mentality that dominates the American outlook, for a concern with understanding meaning associated with an unscientific, religious orientation, for an identification with a leisured, privileged class inimical to American values, and for conceptions of the social world intractable to the research methods Americans favor.

Coda

The great burst of theoretical enthusiasm that enlightened the American sociological landscape for more than three decades is now over. The generation of European scholars is gone, dead or no longer productive. The demise of action theory in the United States coincided with the demise of its principal author, Talcott Parsons, although European, largely German, commentary on his work is occasionally still made. Phenomenological sociology continues to linger in its rechristened state as ethnomethodology, not yet moribund, but no longer robust – perhaps new sources of vitality will soon appear. Neo-Marxism, although widespread, has been too diluted with American premises to retain the concentrated

vigor of its earlier, European versions. There is, in any event, no American
Marxist theory. To whatever place 'grand theory' may be returning, it is
not to the United States – at least not in the foreseeable future (Skinner,
1985).

American sociologists do not need much theory. To claim that theory is
at the heart of sociology is to voice a theorist's conceit. The love of system
characteristic of German thinkers, the binding together of many ideas into
a single community of ideas, has rarely been attractive to Americans who
perhaps suspect their individuality and freedom will be lost in the toils of
such schemes. (Parallel investigations to the one this essay has undertaken
would explore the cultural, social, political and economic promptings and
supports that have given rise to the distinctive sociologies of France and
Germany.) American sociologists will continue to solve problems, try to
change disturbing circumstances in social life, strengthen their
methodological tools, and generally strive to be more effective. For much
of this, little more than a handful of concepts is needed.

Indeed, few American sociologists are presently willing to identify
themselves as theorists. For perhaps a decade or two at the most, from the
mid-1950s to the mid-1970s, many younger sociologists were eager to be
considered theorists of some sort. But although never pursued seriously by
the majority of students, theory had sufficient cachet to be recognized as a
specialty in several leading graduate departments. Courses and seminars
were offered in theoretical subjects and often a required doctoral examination. Little of this now remains. There is the obligatory one-semester
course in 'History of Theory' and perhaps a seminar – for example, on the
Frankfurt School, or Weber, or Durkheim – given every few years. As in
the past, the theorist is occasionally called upon by colleagues to help
clarify a proposition for empirical test. But the theorist's main function has
become that of teacher of a wide range of courses at the undergraduate
level. For although the theorist is 'the generalist', theory has become an
adjunct and is thus peripheral. Theorists are, accordingly, learning to
develop other subspecialties to gain professional identity – deviance, the
professions, occupations and work, politics, stratification, and doubtless
for the next several years, gender.

But American sociology will, I think, continue to produce scholars who
endeavor a 'comprehensive understanding of social life'. Their place in
sociology will be in the future, as it has been in the past, marginal yet
necessary, somewhat analogous to Emerson's place in philosophy. They
will express in their thinking a complementary side of the American activist
ethos. For if American sociologists should ever achieve all the things the
activist outlook aims for, conquer all social conditions and subdue their
own yearnings for rest, they will lose the need to act. Theorists provide a
counter to the dominant trend, an opposition and therefore a spur. However, the work of theorists will doubtless never be fully assimilated by
the reigning orthodoxies.

Notes

This chapter is a revised version of an address delivered at the conference, 'History of the Human Sciences' in Durham, England, 1986. I am grateful to Stuart Bogom, Charles Bosk, Christine Bowditch, Laura Farmelo, Richard Farnum, Renee Fox, Victor Lidz, Charles E. Rosenberg, Pamela Spritzer, Robin Wagner-Pacifici, Karen Walker, Adam Weisberger, Marcia Westcott and R. Jackson Wilson for stimulating and helpful comments. I am solely responsible for the views expressed.

1. See Mannheim (1953).

2. Cf. Mead (1938), Parts I–IV, for the extraordinary scope of the issues Mead formulated, and the discussion, in ch. XXXIII, of the categories involved in an 'act'.

3. Cf. Ben-David and Zloczower (1965). Several other essays in this volume, especially in section III, are instructive of such differences.

4. Shryock's portrait has been voluminously amplified by Robert V. Bruce (1987).

5. There is a large literature on these points. See the comments and bibliography in Ben-David and Zloczower (1965).

6. Analysis of portraits of scientists and science in science fiction remains meager. Cf. Burnham (1987): 216–17.

7. Cf. Miller (1953) and Bercovitch (1978).

8. See Parsons's (1968) Introduction to the paperback edition of *The Structure of Social Action*.

9. In his *Logic* (1938), John Dewey argued that even such logical principles as excluded middle, non-contradiction, etc., are at best ideal canons that guide research, but are only approximated at the conclusion of the research endeavor. Since, in his view, the effort to resolve problems never halts, the principles are never finally achieved.

10. Cf. Peirce (1931: 329ff, 429ff); James (1890; 1938); Dewey (1958; 1922).

11. Cf. the analysis of Calvinist strains in pragmatist thought in the recent study by Bruce Kuklick (1986).

12. Many members of an older generation of sociologists were forthright in condemning *any* cultural interpretation, irresponsible or validated, on the grounds of its subjectivity; cf. Lundberg (1939): 41–2. Cf. also Parsons's report (1977) of the prevalence of anti-subjectivist views and the strength of behavioralism in the 1920s. Essays which center on analysis of cultural phenomena continue to be largely ignored in mainstream sociological journals.

13. There have been notable commentaries on this work by sociologists in the past twenty years; see Lukes (1973). And some sociologists of religion utilize insights of *The Elementary Forms* in their own work, for example, Bellah and Glock (1976), and Bellah and Hammond (1980). But these and similar efforts do not remotely approximate the volume of American sociological literature on 'anomie'.

14. Even during the heyday of theory in American sociology, the main exceptions were, I believe, Parsons himself, Bellah (1973) and – although I disagree with his interpretation – Nisbet (1965).

15. See Max Scheler's (1963) comments on Weber's failure to tap the subterranean spiritual and philosophical currents of the professional vocations.

16. Or at least were believed to have been cast out. Religious, specifically Protestant, themes continued to appear unwittingly in numerous sociological publications. See Mills (1963), Miller (1954) and Higham (1954).

17. This language is of course reminiscent of Comte's. But an affined view of intellectual evolution was in vogue in the philosophy of science literature of the 1940s, 1950s and 1960s. It was held that because historical explanations did not include statements of invariance they were not 'scientific', but mere 'explanation sketches', inferior to the fully-fledged explanations found in the physical sciences. See Hempel and Oppenheim (1953).

18. The reference to Spencer is in Parsons's opening remarks in *The Structure of Social Action* (1937). Parsons noted that his decision to go into social science was associated with his

father who was active in the Social Gospel Movement, which 'had much to do with the origins of sociology in this country'. See Parsons (1977: 33, n. 24); cf. Wearne (1986).

19. See Marcus (1985): 67ff; Mehring (1962); McLellan (1971); Marianne Weber (1975); Honigsheim (1959); Arendt (1968). See the essays on the German sociologists in Barnes (1948). For Scheler, see Staude (1967). See also Kettler et al. (1984) for Mannheim.

20. See Marianne Weber's discussion (1975: 277ff).

21. See Barnard (1938). This book is genuinely an exception to the prevailing pattern and is often cited in the literature of organizations, but apparently not often read.

References

Adorno, T.W., Frenkel-Brunswik, E., Levinson, D.J. and Sanford, R.N. (1950) *The Authoritarian Personality*. New York: Harper.

Arendt, H. (1968) Introduction to Walter Benjamin, *Illuminations*. New York: Harcourt, Brace World.

Barber, B. and Hirsch, W. (eds) (1962) *The Sociology of Science*. New York: Free Press.

Barnard, C. (1938) *The Functions of the Executive*. Cambridge, Mass.: Harvard University Press.

Barnes, H.E. (ed.) (1948) *An Introduction to the History of Sociology*. Chicago: University of Chicago Press.

Bellah, R. (1973) *Emile Durkheim on Morality and Society*. Chicago: University of Chicago Press.

Bellah, R.N. and Glock, C.Y. (1976) *The New Religious Consciousness*. Berkeley, CA: University of California Press.

Bellah, R.N. and Hammond, P.E. (1980) *Varieties of Civil Religion*. San Francisco: Harper & Row.

Ben-David, J. and Zloczower, A. (1965) 'Universities and Academic Systems in Modern Societies', pp. 62–85 in N. Kaplan (ed.), *Science and Society*. Chicago: Rand McNally.

Bercovitch, S. (1978) *The American Jeremiad*. Madison: University of Wisconsin Press.

Bruce, R.V. (1987) *The Launching of Modern American Science*. New York: Knopf.

Burnham, J.C. (1987) *How Superstition Won and Science Lost*. New Brunswick: Rutgers University Press.

Dewey, J. (1922) *Human Nature and Conduct*. New York: Henry Holt.

Dewey, J. (1938) *Logic*. New York: Henry Holt.

Dewey, J. (1958) *Experience and Nature*. New York: Dover.

Dupree, A.H. (1965) 'Central Scientific Organization in the United States', pp. 261–77 in N. Kaplan (ed.), *Science and Society*. Chicago: Rand McNally.

Durkheim, E. (1947) *The Elementary Forms of the Religious Life*. Glencoe, IL: Free Press.

Durkheim, E. (1951) *Suicide*. New York: Free Press.

Durkheim, E. (1958) *Professional Ethics and Civic Morals*. New York: Free Press.

Freud, S. (1950) *The Ego and the Id*. London: Hogarth Press.

Freud, S. (1959) *Group Psychology and the Analysis of the Ego*. New York: W.W. Norton.

Fromm, E. (1941) *Escape from Freedom*. New York: Rinehart.

Gallie, W.B. (1968) *Philosophy and the Historical Understanding*. New York: Schocken.

Gouldner, A.W. (1971) *The Coming Crisis of Western Sociology*. New York: Equinox.

Haskell, T. (1982) *The Emergence of Professional Social Science: the American Social Science Association*. New York: Basic Books.

Hempel, C.G. and Oppenheim, P. (1953) 'The Logic of Explanation', pp. 319–52 in Herbert Feigl and May Brodbeck (eds), *Readings in the Philosophy of Science*. New York: Appleton Crofts.

Higham, J. (1954) 'The Reorientation of American Culture in the 1890s', in *Writing American History: Essays in Modern Scholarship* (1970). Bloomington: Indiana University Press.

Hofstadter, R. (1963) *Anti-Intellectualism in American Life*. New York: Vintage.

Honigsheim, P. (1959) 'The Time and Thought of the Young Simmel', pp. 167–74 in Kurt

Wolff (ed.), *Essays on Sociology, Philosophy and Aesthetics by Georg Simmel, et al.* New York: Harper Torchbooks.

James, W. (1890) *The Principles of Psychology.* 2 vols, New York: Henry Holt.

James, W. (1938) *Pragmatism.* New York: Longmans Green.

James, W. (1949) *Essays on Faith and Morals.* New York: Longmans Green.

Jones, E. (1953) *The Life and Work of Sigmund Freud.* New York: Basic Books.

Kaplan, N. (ed.) (1965) *Science and Society.* Chicago: Rand McNally.

Kettler, D., Meja, V. and Stehr, N. (1984) *Karl Mannheim.* New York: Tavistock/Ellis Horwood.

Krieghbaum, H. (1967) *Science and the Mass Media.* New York: New York University Press.

Kuklick, B. (1986) *Churchmen and Philosophers.* New Haven: Yale University Press.

LaFollette, M.E.C. (1979) 'Authority, Promise and Expectation: the Images of Science and Scientists in American Popular Magazines, 1910–1955'. PhD thesis, Indiana University, Ann Arbor, Michigan, University Microfilm International.

Lassman, P. and Velody, I. with Martins, H. (eds) (1989) *Max Weber's 'Science as a Vocation'.* London: Unwin Hyman.

Lukes, S. (1973) *Emile Durkheim, his Life and Work.* New York: Harper & Row.

Lundberg, G. (1939) *The Foundations of Sociology.* New York: Macmillan.

McLellan, D. (1971) *Marx Before Marxism.* New York: Harper Torchbooks.

Mannheim, K. (1953) 'American Sociology', Ch. 4 in Paul Kecskemeti (ed.), *Essays on Sociology and Social Psychology.* London: Routledge & Kegan Paul.

Marcus, S. (1985) *Engels, Manchester and the Working Class.* New York: W.W. Norton.

Marcuse, H. (1941) *Reason and Revolution.* New York: Oxford University Press.

Mead, G.H. (1938) *The Philosophy of the Act.* Chicago: University of Chicago Press.

Mehring, F. (1962) *Karl Marx.* Ann Arbor: University of Michigan Press.

Merleau-Ponty, M. (1962) *Phenomenology of Perception.* London: Routledge & Kegan Paul.

Merton, R.K. (1957) *Social Theory and Social Structure.* Glencoe, IL: Free Press.

Miller, P. (1953) *Errand into the Wilderness,* Cambridge, MA: Harvard University Press.

Miller, P. (1954) *American Thought: Civil War to World War I.* New York: Holt Rinehart & Winston.

Mills, C.W. (1959) *The Sociological Imagination.* New York: Oxford University Press.

Mills, C.W. (1963) *Power, Politics and People.* New York: Ballantine.

Niebuhr, H.R. (1959) *The Kingdom of God in America.* New York: Harper Torchbooks.

Nisbet, R.K. (1965) *Emile Durkheim.* Englewood Cliffs, NJ: Prentice-Hall.

Parsons, T. (1937) *The Structure of Social Action.* New York: McGraw Hill.

Parsons, T. (1951) *The Social System.* London: Routledge & Kegan Paul.

Parsons, T. (1968) Introduction to the paperback edition, *The Structure of Social Action.* New York: Free Press.

Parsons, T. (1977) 'On Building Social System Theory: a Personal History,' pp. 22–6 in *Social Systems and the Evolution of Action Theory.* New York: Free Press.

Peirce, C.S. (1931) *Collected Papers* (ed. C. Hartshorne and P. Weiss). Cambridge, MA: Harvard University Press.

Rosenberg, C. (1976) *No Other Gods.* Baltimore: Johns Hopkins University Press.

Scheler, M. (1963) 'Liebe und Erkenntnis', *Gesammelte Werke,* vol. 6, p. 77. Bern/Munich: Francke Verlag.

Scheler, M. (1973) 'Ordo Amoris', pp. 98–135 in D.R. Lachterman (ed.), *Max Scheler: Selected Philosophical Essays.* Evanston, IL: Northwestern University Press.

Shryock, R. (1962) 'American Indifference to Basic Science during the 19th Century, repr. pp. 98–110 in B. Barber and W. Hirsch (eds), *The Sociology of Science,* New York: Free Press.

Skinner, Q. (1985) *The Return of Grand Theory in the Human Sciences.* Cambridge: Cambridge University Press.

Staude, J.R. (1967) *Max Scheler.* New York: Free Press.

Wearne, B. (1986) 'The Theory and Scholarship of Talcott Parsons to 1951'. PhD thesis, La Trobe University, Bundoora, Victoria, Australia.

Weber, Marianne (1975) *Max Weber, a Biography*. New York: John Wiley.
Weber, M. (1946) *From Max Weber: Essays in Sociology*, ed. C.W. Mills and H. Gerth. New York: Oxford University Press.
Weber, M. (1951) *The Religion of China*. Glencoe, IL: Free Press.
Weber, M (1958) *The Religion of India*. New York: Free Press.

5

THE STRUCTURE OF SOCIAL ACTION: AT LEAST SIXTY YEARS AHEAD OF ITS TIME

Mark Gould

> But as Nero Wolfe says, a nurse that pushes the perambulator in the park without putting the baby in it has missed the point. (Stout, 1963: 156)

1987 marked the fiftieth anniversary of the publication of Talcott Parsons's *The Structure of Social Action* (hereafter *SSA*). Charles Camic spotlighted the occasion with the publication of two essays examining the 'Early Parsons' (1987; 1989). The first argued that 'The position that Parsons occupied at Harvard, moving from the high-status field of economics to the low-status field of sociology, led him to accept the basic methodological argument of neoclassical economists – and to shape from it an equivalent method for sociology' (1987: 421). The second argued that *SSA* was intended as a charter for sociology as a discipline. Camic's argument identified 'Parsons's disciplinary concerns and struggles as constitutive of the basic design and shape of *Structure*' (1989: 46; see also p. 94, and *passim*).[1] According to Camic, Parsons's defence of sociology against behaviorism and neoclassicism resulted in a lamentable consequence: Parsons converted an historically specific argument, drawn out of a particular set of polemics, into one that he falsely contended was of universal validity (Camic, 1989).

Camic's two essays have generated considerable attention and many sociologists appear to accept their arguments as valid (for example, Coleman, 1990a: 338). In contrast to this assessment, in an essay published prior to the appearance of Camic's 1989 piece I argued that his claim that Parsons adopted the method of neoclassical economics is superficial and misleading. By focusing only on those attributes of science common across all scientific disciplines (from physics to the social sciences), Camic failed to understand that *SSA* is a polemic against utilitarian economics, and he seemingly failed to grasp that Parsons's goal was to demonstrate the (methodological and theoretical) limitations inherent in any utilitarian (or idealist) theory. In fact, Parsons argues that a viable social theory must be constituted as a voluntaristic theory of action, a form of theory he viewed as antithetical to utilitarianism (Gould, 1989).

The crux of Camic's argument in his second essay is that Parsons thought in terms of simple dichotomies, including, most importantly, the 'great dichotomy' between norms and the biological conditions of heredity and environment. He contends that 'some of the terminological mist over *Structure* dissolves when one appreciates that its "definitions" often work less to assign precise meanings than to associate key concepts with one *or* the other side of the book's "great dichotomy"' (1989: 50). In consequence, Camic would have us believe that *SSA* 'holds its greatest present-day utility only when its original meaning is benignly overlooked' (1989: 40). This conclusion is meaningful only insofar as Camic has correctly understood what Parsons was arguing in his text. I believe that he misunderstands the argument of *SSA* in several key respects.

In this chapter I emphasize the necessity of a correct understanding of the nature and logic of sociological theory for an accurate comprehension of Parsons's mission in *SSA*. I argue this point in an examination of a number of the controversies in the interpretation of Parsons's early (and later) work that are raised by Camic: (a) What were Parsons's goals in *SSA* and how do they relate to his understanding of 'voluntarism'? Camic misunderstands what Parsons hoped to accomplish in contrasting voluntarism, as a theoretical problematic, with utilitarianism and idealism. (b) What role do 'norms' and 'conditions' play in Parsons's argument? I show that Camic reifies the distinction between norms and conditions and attributes an erroneous meaning to conditions within voluntaristic theory. This misunderstanding is the linchpin of his critique; many of the critical comments he makes fall apart with a correct understanding of the relationship between norms and conditions. (c) What is the nature of functional theory and what is its relationship to empirical research? When we grasp the character of functional theory it will be seen that Camic misunderstands the difference between a theoretical argument and an empirical claim. (d) What are the objectives of general sociological theory and how does such a theory analyze the multifaceted complexities inherent in social activities? Camic's critique argues for an historicism incapable of formulating general, explanatory propositions. He criticizes Parsons's text from a position foreign to the social sciences.

In this chapter I examine a number of the issues Camic discusses in his second paper (1989). While I make no attempt to discuss each of the points he raises in his lengthy essay, my argument suggests that he fails to understand the nature of the project that constituted *SSA* and that in consequence his critique of Parsons is fundamentally misplaced; even his valid criticisms of particular arguments are misleading owing to their context within his essay. I believe that Camic misunderstands the nature and the logic of sociological theory and of the sociological theory Parsons constructed; in consequence he seriously misconstrues Parsons's aim in *SSA*. In addition to refuting a number of Camic's central contentions, I hope to dispel the impression that *SSA* is of interest only as an historical artifact.[2]

The argument of *The Structure of Social Action*

The Structure of Social Action is a theoretical examination of a body of empirical material. The essential conceptual framework within which the theory is articulated is the unit act; the empirical materials analyzed are also theoretical-conceptual systems, theories of social action. Parsons's goal in this analysis is twofold. He wants to demonstrate the near convergence of a variety of seminal thinkers within the voluntaristic theory of action. More importantly, he argues that an analysis of how different theories of action implicitly or explicitly conceptualize the unit act will allow him to differentiate between modes of theory that are potentially viable (voluntaristic theories) and those that are fundamentally flawed (positivistic and idealist theories).

Parsons believes that any voluntaristic theory of action, while it may contain erroneous arguments, is articulated within a fundamentally sound structure. An idealist or positivist theory is, according to Parsons, bound to lead to theoretical errors, however brilliant its insights. Any consequential conceptual framework used to categorize Parsons's own position must clearly and unequivocally differentiate between it and both positivism and idealism (see my criticisms of Camic, 1987, in Gould, 1989).

It is the second of his two goals – separating the wheat from the chaff – that is crucial. It is this objective that motivates Parsons to reconstruct Weber's and Durkheim's arguments, focusing on their immanent development. Parsons wanted his work to be judged in light of the systematic theory he constructed, a voluntarist theory, not on the veracity of his characterizations of Weber and Durkheim. Thus, perhaps paradoxically, the relevance of the central arguments in *SSA* is best evaluated in an examination of Parsons's own theoretical work in the years that followed its publication. At the same time, Parsons felt that his capacity to transcend Weber's and Durkheim's theories was indicative of his fundamentally correct understanding of their work.

The essential point might be better understood if we imagine Parsons as a student attempting to select a body of social science theory within which to articulate his work. Like our current students, he had a wide variety to select from, each assuming a respectable position within a legitimate academic discipline, yet each in serious contradiction, at one or another level of analysis, with the others. Parsons conceptualized the elements of the unit act and their relationships with one another, along with the way unit acts were themselves related, as the conceptual tools allowing him to categorize the various types of action theory. Within this context, the utility of his conceptual schema is to be judged in terms of its capacity to discriminate between 'good' and 'bad' theory.

The unit act is an analytical tool. It must not be reified.[3] For example, the distinction between the means and conditions of action is not conceptualizable at the level of a single unit act, unless that act is analytically abstracted from a system of interaction. A Porsche is a means of transportation in some situations; in others it is the functional equivalent of a large rock, a condition of action. The difference is not explicable in focusing on a concrete unit act.

More clearly, a shared normative orientation may be specified to an isolated unit act, but it is not conceptualizable in terms of that act. The attempt to do so is an indication of the type of theoretical error encountered in atomistic, positivistic utilitarianism. For Parsons, the unit act was an abstraction allowing for the categorization of action theories. It should not be understood as a theoretically isolable element either of action or of any viable, nonatomistic theory of action.

Nonetheless, at times Parsons falls into a Weberian trap. For Weber, action was prior to social action (1964: 88). In his methodological reflections Weber sometimes failed to recognize that *all action* is socially and culturally constituted.[4] The meaning of an action is always adduced from the cultural, social and personality *systems* within which the action is placed. Perhaps in consequence of the priority Parsons accorded to 'action' he was ambiguous about the status of the unit act. The structure of his argument generally led him to treat it, correctly, as a conceptual tool for analyzing theories of action. An analysis of its construction in different theories provided a coordinate schema in terms of which theories of social action might be categorized and evaluated.

Unfortunately, there is an undercurrent of a different usage for the unit act (Parsons, 1949: 731ff; 745), one which came to a stillbirth in the unpublished essay 'Action, Situation, and Normative Pattern'.[5] In this essay Parsons tried to use the unit act to analyze social action directly. Here the danger of treating individual acts as prior to their social and cultural system context is all too manifest. He misses, until his writings in the 1970s, the absolute conceptual priority of social action.[6]

In Camic's discussion there is a conflation between the unit act and 'action theory'. He implies that Parsons's belief that social relationships may be conceptualized within an action frame of reference entails a reduction of the social to the means–ends relationship of discrete unit acts (1989: 74–5). Generally, however, Parsons recognizes that the unit act is not analytically adequate to discuss systems of social relationships (e.g. 1949: 743; cf. 745); nonetheless, such relationships may be conceptualized within a voluntaristic theory of action. The latter conceptualization, as is clear even from his earliest work (Parsons, 1990 [written in 1934–5]), focused on action *systems*, which incorporated, but were not reducible to, shared normative orientations.[7]

After describing the elements of the unit act (an agent, an end, a situation consisting of means and conditions and a normative orientation), Chapter 2 of *SSA* continues with a characterization of utilitarianism in terms of the unit act. It then analyzes two ways that utilitarianism may disintegrate, while still remaining within the more general positivist framework (conceptualizing only one positively-stated normative orientation). Most of the remainder of the book is taken up with Parsons teasing the logic of the voluntaristic alternative to positivism and idealism from an examination of four figures: Marshall and Pareto and, much more importantly, Durkheim and Weber. He concludes that the work of Weber and Durkheim is paradigmatic for the further construction of social theory; they provide the framework within which Parsons will build. (Later he included Freud and Mead in this pantheon.) Others, like Marx, might have been brilliant theorists, but their work is deemed fatally flawed.

The main focus of Parsons's attack is the utilitarian tradition, deriving from Hobbes, passing through Locke and manifest in neoclassical economics.[8] His central argument concerns the limitations of utilitarian thought. He is at pains to demonstrate why a viable social theory cannot be atomistic (reducing all theoretical propositions to statements about individual unit acts), positivistic (treating instrumental rationality as the sole positively-stated normative orientation), and empiricist (banning constructs and reducing all concepts to directly observable phenomena); nor can it maintain the independence and exogenism of ends.[9] Voluntaristic theory contradicts utilitarianism on all of these points and they are the four attributes of utilitarianism that Parsons explicates. His analysis throughout the book is an attempt to lay the foundation for a systematic construction of the voluntarist alternative to utilitarianism.[10] While utilitarianism is caught up within a reified image of the unit act, including, as a form of positivism, a sharp dichotomy between norms and conditions, we will see that voluntaristic theory, contrary to Camic's arguments, transcended these sharp divisions.

Voluntarism and theoretical convergence

Camic writes that *SSA*'s 'most serious shortcoming [is] its denial that the sociological tradition was rooted in a variety of theoretical approaches, which developed diverging perspectives *despite* agreement on the importance of normative and non-normative elements' (1989: 58). One consequence of this purported error is 'that *Structure*'s "reconstruction of the sociological tradition must be judged erroneous on every fundamental point"' (Camic, 1989: 56, quoting Levine, 1980: xxv).[11]

The importance of these contentions is simple: 'in the few cases where the action schema has been carefully compared with others, what has emerged is that there are fundamental aspects of social phenomena that elude reduction to the schema's terms' (Camic, 1989: 77). Most of the examples that Camic gives involve a focus on a conception of social structure that appears to escape formulation from within a theory of social action (including modes of production, class structures, state apparatuses, exchange, conflict, super- and subordination, interpersonal communication, networks and population ecology) (Camic, 1989: 73; 77).[12] For Camic, this claim provides warrant not for the reconstruction of Parsonian theory, nor for the construction of an alternative sociology, but rather for a reassertion of the importance of theoretical pluralism (Camic, 1989: 77, citing Merton, 1981: v). 'Approaches that attempt, following the example of *Structure*, to embrace not only action modes but also institutions, social relations, and the rest with a single theoretical vocabulary impair, as Blau (1987) suggests, the analysis of each domain at an appropriate level and in terms suited to that level – terms that take different forms and work for some societies but not all' (Camic, 1989: 77).[13]

I think that these criticisms are misplaced. The crucial question to answer is not whether Parsons discussed all forms of social organization in his early work, nor even in his subsequent work. The pivotal questions are (1) whether his theoretical conceptualization allows for the inclusion of such discussions when they are deemed important, and (2) whether it is consistent with the various structural conceptualizations of social organization we find it necessary to articulate. No theory is exhaustive; this is the grain of truth in pleas for pluralism. Good theory is compatible with other types of good theory and allows for their systematic integration into a coherent theoretical framework. To say that Parsons's theory is limited ought to be a plea for a better theory, not for chaos.[14] To understand its limits, what Parsons's theory includes and what it excludes, we need to characterize the nature of the voluntaristic theory of action, and to do this we must discuss in a bit more detail the conceptual framework within which Parsons analyzed its foundations.

As I have noted above, the unit act is a set of theoretical concepts. As such it both illuminates and blinds. Like all concepts it is selective. Like all concepts it is neither true nor false; it is useful or not for a particular task. The task for which Parsons uses the unit act is his attempt to discriminate between good and bad theory. The convergence argument in *SSA* is not a claim that Weber and Durkheim were the same; it is the contention that *when analyzed in terms of the attributes of the unit act* their theories were consistent and fell within an emerging voluntaristic theory of social action.

Voluntarism is a type of theoretical problematic. In *SSA* it is delineated from within the unit act. It entails an analysis that incorporates a discussion of the situation of action (means and conditions) and multiple normative orientations. Thus it allows for the normative regulation of the choice of ends as well as for conditional constraints on their selection and attainment. It incorporates concepts that are not directly reducible to observable phenomena, including constructs like a societal value system and the logic of meaning within a particular cultural system. In consequence it need not reduce social action to the attributes of discrete unit acts and it need not reduce actors to the aggregation of the unit acts they perform.

Camic's discussion of these points is marred by his misunderstanding of voluntarism. He sometimes seems to believe that a determination of action by conditions as well as norms is incompatible with voluntarism (1989: 90; cf. 58). Thus he follows Alexander in defining voluntarism as 'freedom vis-à-vis the conditions of action' (Camic, 1989: 91, quoting Alexander, 1983: 35). But this is not the same as what Parsons contends in arguing for the *independence* of ends and norms from the conditions of action. The former, in Camic's characterization, entails a determination of action that excludes conditions and is better equated with Parsons's notion of idealism; the latter, Parsons's actual position, recognizes that the autonomy of normative and conditional variables entails their independence (see Parsons, 1949: 25, n. 2) *and* their interpenetration.[15]

Voluntarism is not a description of any particular theory; it is an enunciation of the attributes of a type of sociological theory that includes many variants. For example, I have argued, contrary to Parsons, that Marxian theory falls within the rubric of the voluntaristic theory of action (1981). In making this contention I claim that it has certain affinities with the theories articulated by Weber and Durkheim, in contrast, for example, to the theories articulated by Paul Samuelson and Alfred Schutz. These common attributes are manifest in the way the elements of the unit act are organized; within other conceptual frameworks the groupings would be different. To take a trivial example, if I am concerned with the accessibility of theoretical texts for a group of community college freshmen, I might use a computer to examine the complexity of the text's sentence structure. Here I might group Samuelson with Durkheim and Marx with Weber. Using sentence complexity as a conceptual tool is useful insofar as it allows me to determine what texts will be accessible to a particular group of students. This categorization is not wrong, even though it obviously misses essential aspects of the texts in question. It would be absurd, for example, to suggest that it is relevant to the truth of the theories.

Camic contends that Parsons's convergence argument is meaningless, because of a 'simple methodological point – which bears not only on Parsons but also on those who counter his interpretation with other convergence arguments – that with flexible enough interpretative standards, it is relatively easy, as Mulkay has observed, to prove assorted convergences "among virtually any group of theorists"' (Camic, 1989: 62, quoting Mulkay, 1971: 69). The contention that convergence arguments are meaningless is absurd. While it is true that within some set of standards any texts can be made to converge (or any units be included as members of one set), the relevant questions concern one's goal in carrying out the analysis and utility of the conceptual framework in attaining that goal. It may well seem foolish to contend that there is a convergence between Samuelson and Parsons because they both wrote in English, but if one's goal in establishing this 'convergence' is to determine the accessibility of their original texts for United States college students, it is crucial. Once again, the utility of the unit act (the relevant 'interpretative standard') depends on whether it enabled Parsons to accomplish his goal, separating theoretical wheat from chaff, and providing the foundation on which a viable body of sociological theory might be constructed.

This point should not be misinterpreted. Parsons sought to transcend the theoretical positions he rejected, not to discard them. Camic is correct in believing that Parsons sought to incorporate what was valid from utilitarianism and idealism into the voluntaristic theory of action (1989: 62). It was Parsons's belief that when the empirical predictions and explanations of a utilitarian theory were valid they would be generated from within a voluntaristic theory. It was also his belief, however, that there were circumstances in which a voluntaristic theory would generate valid empirical predictions and explanations, whereas those emerging from within a utilitarian or idealist theory would be false.[16] These points will become clearer as we consider the role 'norms' and 'conditions' play in Parsons's argument.[17]

Norms and conditions

It is difficult to discuss Camic's analysis of Parsons's treatment of the relationship between norms and conditions, as Camic's treatment is based on a misreading of what Parsons actually says. Repeatedly in his essays Camic associates statements that Parsons makes as characterizations of the work of others with Parsons's own point of view (for an example from Camic, 1987, see Gould, 1989: 647). It is as if a discussion of Lutheranism made one a Lutheran.

Camic's discussion of the conditions of action reduces them to the biological categories of heredity and environment (1989: 65).[18] This misconstrues Parsons's analysis. Parsons's point is that departures from utilitarianism, insofar as they remain within the positivistic framework (radical rationalistic positivism and radical anti-intellectualistic positivism), result in an

> explanation of action in terms of the ultimate nonsubjective conditions, conveniently designated as heredity and environment. . . . In so far as the utilitarian position is abandoned in either of its two major tenets [regarding the status of ends or the status of the norm of rationality], the only alternative on a positivistic basis in the explanation of action lies in the conditions of the situation of action objectively rather than subjectively considered, which for most practical purposes may be taken to mean in the factors of heredity and environment in the analytical sense of biological theory. (Parsons, 1949: 67)

But this is not the only conceptualization of the conditions of action, as will become clear if we compare Parsons's discussion of Marx with Camic's reconstruction of that discussion.

Camic criticizes Alexander's understanding of Parsons's use of the notion of 'conditions'. He writes that

> one must beware of anachronistic projections, especially regarding the term 'conditions'. Alexander, for instance, equates the concept with material social conditions in a sense similar to material conditions in Marxism (see [Alexander,] 1978: 1979 [sic]; 1983: 12–37; 1987: 24). But Structure expressly rejects this view, dissociating Marxist materialism from 'the prevailing Western sense of the same term', which refers to 'the nonhuman environment, as natural resources, or [to – C.C.] biological heredity' (S [Parsons, 1949], pp. 490–1). (Camic 1989: 64–5)[19]

This Western sense of 'material conditions' is the view Camic attributes to Parsons. In contrast, Parsons writes that 'Marx did not use the word materialism in the familiar *positivistic* sense of reducing social phenomena causally to terms of the nonhuman environment, as natural resources, or of biological heredity or some combination of both' (1949: 490; my italics). Contrary to Camic, Parsons does not contrast Marx's usage of 'conditions' with his own usage; he contrasts Marx's usage with the positivistic usage.

Parsons goes on to say that 'This [positivistic] interpretation [of materialism as reducing social phenomena causally to the nonhuman environment, and therefore of Marx's conceptualization of the conditions of action] is definitely precluded by the historical features of the Marxian theory. . . . Marxism is a social doctrine' (1949: 490). According to Parsons, 'Marx, through his doctrine of interests, elevated not only competition but the whole structure of the economic order into a great control mechanism, a compulsive system. . . . On the one hand, the system itself is the resultant of the myriad of individual acts but, on the other, it creates for each acting individual a specific situation which compels him to act in certain ways if he is not to go contrary to his interest. . . . The peculiar forms of compulsion found in the capitalistic system are not universal, but are limited to its particular conditions, to its specific combination of the "conditions of production"' (491–2). Parsons emphasizes that Marxism was an advance over utilitarianism because it recognized the historical variability and the social construction of the conditions of action; his, in my opinion (Gould, 1981), misplaced criticism was that Marxism did not transcend the logic of utilitarian thought.

Whatever the validity of Parsons's critique of Marxism, there is no question that Parsons recognized that for Marx and for voluntarist theories, the conditions of action, subjectively conceived, were largely social. This was even true for utilitarianism, in contrast to the radical forms of positivism, as utilitarianism maintained a subjective frame of reference. Parsons recognized that even in an atomistic theory 'the potential acts of one may be relevant as means and conditions to the situation of action of another' (1949: 52). Interaction from within a utilitarian framework consists of one action affecting the situation (conditions and/or means) of another action and therefore affecting the nature of the responding action. For voluntarism, there was the added recognition that these relationships might be socially patterned, and thus might well be normatively regulated. Normatively regulated social relationships could very well be aspects of a situation limiting (as conditions) or facilitating (as means) the attainment of a (socially regulated) goal. The notion that Parsons excluded social actions and relationships from a discussion of the 'conditions' of action is a figment of Camic's imagination.[20] This bears on a number of the criticisms that Camic makes of Parsons's arguments.

Some of the most significant criticisms that Camic levels at Parsons stem from Camic's belief that a voluntaristic framework cannot 'make room theoretically for socially constituted interests that are not resolvable into common normative factors, or, indeed, for any aspect of the means–end relationship that is not to be fitted into the polemical categories of heredity-environment versus common norms' (1989: 67).[21] If the only alternatives available to Parsons were common norms and biologically constituted conditions, he would not be able to deal with the non-normative aspects of structural relationships, including 'complex modes of involvement in bounded arenas of social and material objects – that is, historically changing *practices*, economic, political, scientific, legal, artistic, moral, familial, and so on' (Camic, 1989: 68–9). Nor would Parsons be able to analyze the structure of divergent personalities; apart from commonalties explicable in terms of universal norms, they would be reduced to biologically constituted appetites.

Parsons's actual problem is quite different. It is his tendency to reduce external social constraints to conditions of action. For example, he argues that Marx not only reintroduced power into social theory, but that Marx recognized that the power of capitalists over employees within the employment relationship 'was the result of a power relation within a determinate institutional framework, involving a definite social organization' (Parsons, 1949: 110). The fact that this situation was socially constituted and included the sanctions that enforced institutionalized norms was downplayed. Parsons tended to reduce the explicitly social to its normative elements, to those normative controls internalized by actors. In consequence, he conceptualized the Marxian actor as rationally adapting to his or her socially constituted situation. Thus Marx was erroneously reduced to a utilitarian and Parsons was able to downplay the importance of social structural constraints. The problem was not that Parsons viewed the conditions of action as biologically constituted; the problem was almost the opposite, that Parsons included too much of the structure of social systems as components of the conditions of action and this enabled him to over-emphasize the normative aspects of social structure as the most suitable object of sociological analysis.

Camic's parallel misunderstanding of what Parsons says about power and wealth stems from his misreading of what Parsons says about actors. Camic treats Parsons's discussion of random ends in Hobbes as if this characterization represented Parsons's own orientation. He suggests that Parsons adopts a bipolar image of the personality, where untamed desires meet externally constituted and constraining normative controls. '[T]he model [Parsons constructs] knows only the antithesis of the normative and conditional [here biological] elements; it nowhere allows for personality attributes not resolvable into this highly particular dichotomy' (Camic, 1989: 80). In consequence, Camic can argue that 'for Parsons, power and wealth are instantiations of the broader factor of interest, which, when not a manifestation of value elements, itself derives from the conditional factors of unlimited appetite and desire' (1989: 84). Thus according to Camic, there is no room for an institutional analysis in Parsons's discussion of social relations (Camic, 1989: 84). What Camic has done is reify a distinction Parsons finds in Hobbes (and somewhat differently in Pareto and Durkheim). He has then constructed an analysis of Parsons's arguments as if it was Parsons who reified the distinction.

This disjunction between biologically constituted appetites and external normative controls is in fact the image that Parsons suggests is found in the early Durkheim. It is not, as Camic sometimes indicates, Parsons's image. For Parsons normative controls may be internalized by the actor and they may constitute the very desires that actors pursue. (See the quotation from Parsons, 1949: 385–6 that Camic, 1989, quotes at p. 79; cf. Parsons, 1954, Ch. 1.) There is no absolute dichotomy between biologically constituted conditions and normatively constituted controls. The internalization of values requires their integration into a structured personality system, including, as Parsons later argued, a recognition that the id itself was, in part, socio-culturally constituted (Parsons, 1964). While it is correct that the motivational and affectual components of a personality were ill-developed in *SSA* (as Parsons recognized; see the citations in Camic, 1989: 80), this is not to say that a more adequate formulation of their role in the personality was incompatible with a voluntaristic theory. (See Parsons, 1959; 1964. These essays include sensitive discussions of affect and an insightful reconstruction of the developmental basis of Freud's theory of character types.)

Camic is correct in suggesting that an adequate analysis of structures like a mode of production (1989: 73, where he cites two of my essays, Gould, 1981 and 1989) or a particular type of personality system requires extensions in Parsons's theory. Unfortunately, Camic confuses two different issues: what Parsons does and *does not* accomplish in *SSA* (and in his later work) and what he can and *cannot* accomplish within the context of his theory. A brief discussion of functional theory will make clear the nature of this confusion.

Functional theory and empirical research

Much of Camic's confusion stems from a misunderstanding of the type of theory Parsons sought to formulate. In the next section I will discuss Parsons's understanding of 'general theory' and its relationship to the great variety of empirical cases it seeks to account for. In the current section I briefly explicate the nature of functional theory, focusing on the way it interrelates variables relevant in an explanation of social order.

Camic states what he takes to be the three presuppositions of Parsons's claim that order is a consequence of 'the effective functioning of [common – C.C.] normative elements' (Camic, 1989: 85, quoting Parsons, 1949: 92). These include the presumption 'that, (i) in significant measure, common normative elements exist' (Camic, 1989: 85).[22] Camic questions this presumption: 'Regarding (i), empirical research disconfirms the significant presence of common normative factors not only in certain modern societies, characterized by divergent class, regional, ethnic, and religious subcultures rarely reconciled through higher values, but also in traditional societies, like the Christian Middle Ages – the prototype, for Parsons, of a situation of shared values (see [Parsons], 1935: 296; *S* [1949]: 248)' (Camic, 1989: 85).

Such a comment indicates a fundamental misunderstanding of what it is that Parsons is arguing. Parsons is not claiming that shared value orientations are well institutionalized in all societies. He is claiming that there will be determinate consequences for societies when such values are absent. We can see this on the very pages that Camic cites:

> Of course it is clearly understood that 'integration' in this complete sense applies only to the abstract society; in this as in other respects it is a limiting case. Certainly neither Pareto [whose work is under discussion in the passage I am quoting – M.G.] nor the present author means to imply that concrete societies are in general even approximately perfectly integrated in this sense . . . whether integration be closely or only very distantly approached, does not affect the theoretical importance of this theorem [about the significance of common values as one determinant of order within a society] . . . (Parsons, 1949: 248–9)[23]

The point is that Parsons is not making an empirical claim about the presence of institutionalized common values in any society. He is making a theoretical argument about the consequences of the presence or absence of these values for one type of order (mechanical solidarity) within a society. Parsons is arguing that order is a function of various variables, including an institutionalized value system. The presence of one of these variables increases the probability that social order will be manifest.[24]

A similar point can be made about the third presupposition that Camic articulates: '(iii) that actors uphold ends and rules "for their own sake" and out of moral obligation' (1989: 85). Camic suggests the contrary, that 'the message of scholarship has been that "the extent to which [actors experience and affirm the – C.C.] oughtness [of normative elements] is an empirical issue, not" – as is often true in *Structure* – a matter "to be decided a priori" (Warner, 1978: 1341)' (Camic, 1989: 86). This comment once again indicates an elementary misunderstanding of Parsons's argument. Parsons does not claim that values are always institutionalized in a society and thus internalized by a significant portion of its members. With Weber, he claims that the probability of conformity to norms increases when those norms are viewed as morally binding, when they are legitimated by institutionalized values. This is a functional argument, emphasizing the consequences for social order of the presence or absence of binding moral obligations, not suggesting that such obligations are always present. While their presence or absence is an 'empirical question', Parsons is interested in the theoretical question: what are the consequences of their presence or absence for order within a society?

In the other text that Camic cites in this connection, and at the page he cites, Parsons writes that 'It is advisable, though it should scarcely be necessary, to point out once more that we are merely arguing for the necessity of assuming that a common system of ends plays a significant part in social life. We are not arguing that the concrete reality may be understood completely, or even predominantly in such terms' (1935: 296).[25] In other words, Parsons does not argue that common values are always present; nor does he contend that they are the only factor leading to social order.

If we use the simple dichotomy that dominates Camic's essay, Parsons argues that social order is a product of *both* normative and conditional variables. He writes that 'In one main aspect the integration of the society is to be measured in terms of the degrees to which . . . rules [embodying common values] are lived up to from motives of moral obligation. But besides this there is always the motive of "interest" which, looking upon the rules as essentially conditions of action, acts in terms of the comparative personal advantage of obedience or disobedience and acceptance of the sanctions which will have to be suffered' (1949: 404). This is true, *a fortiori*, of conditions that are not normatively constructed.[26]

Camic admits that a factual order, but not a normative order, is a product of both normative and conditional factors (1989: 89, where he cites Adriaansens, 1980: 50). He misunderstands the dependence of a normative order on conditional factors because he draws a false distinction between a factual and a normative order. Parsons argues that the factual order that is sometimes found in societies is, in part, a product of normative regulation. 'The factual order of concrete human society is partly due to the normative order of its institutional system' (Parsons, 1990: 332, n. 26; see also 1949: 92). In other words the statistical regularity that constitutes a factual order is partially explained by normative regulation. Parsons insists that it is also partly explained by conditional factors, encompassing economic constraints, interests and situational sanctions, including those constituted by and supporting a system of institutionalized norms. While it is true that Parsons believed that 'the ultimate source of the power behind sanctions is the common sense of moral attachment to norms' (1949: 404), and while it is true that he too often tended to reduce social structural controls to their normative elements, it is also true that the logic of his theory demands the inclusion of (social) conditions in the explanation of social order.[27]

The reified dichotomy between norms and conditions leads Camic to believe that for Parsons norms produce order and conditions produce disorder (Camic, 1989: 89). The problem with Camic's analysis is that for Parsons both norms and conditions can produce order or disorder. We saw an example of a situation where norms produce disorder in a passage that Camic quotes, where Parsons writes of the irreconcilable value conflicts in the post-Reformation religious wars (see n. 23, below). The key task is to provide a theory explicating the interrelationships between variables that produce order, or disorder, as an outcome.

Camic writes that 'As Parsons sees it, to include economic and political (or other nonsociological) factors in the solution to the problem of order is to minimize the general necessity of the normative element, the cornerstone of sociology, and to merge order with phenomena largely anchored in the conditional' (1989: 89). *SSA* did emphasize normative variables, the variables that Parsons then saw as exemplarily sociological. But even in *SSA* (and more clearly in 'Prolegomena to a Theory of Social Institutions', 1990) Parsons was beginning to outline a functional theory of social systems, where a formal theory of the resources necessary for the stable reproduction of any social system was to be articulated, where propositions detailing the consequences of the withdrawal of, for example, economic resources from the polity, would be articulated. This was to become the systems analysis paradigm. While it is fair to criticize *SSA* for the incomplete and sometimes stilted development of this theory (cf. Parsons, 1990: 331), it is likewise fair to admit that this theory occupied a considerable portion of Parsons's life after the completion of *SSA* and that its outline is clearly present in his early work.[28]

General theory and the complexities of empirical data

This section does not primarily focus on Camic's misunderstanding of a position argued by Parsons. Instead it emphasizes Camic's misunderstanding of what a sociological (or any) theory attempts to do.

Camic understands the basics of Parsons's attitude toward social theory. For example, in his 1987 essay he quotes Parsons as follows: '"*all* concrete phenomena" – including the particulars that fell to the historian – are capable of description and explanation "only in terms of a [law governed – C.C.] combination of the values of analytical elements"' (Camic, 1987: 435, quoting Parsons, 1949: 621 and 628, Camic's italics; there is a similar quotation in Camic, 1989: 54). In contrast, Camic sees the explanation of social order (or any other phenomena?) as '"a concrete historical problem whose terms are defined by . . . the society in which it arises"' (Camic, 1989: 85, quoting Clarke, 1982: 4). Camic argues that in analyzing variation in terms of the same, transhistorical analytical elements, Parsons 'elevates the specific method most useful for chartering sociology in the 1930s as *the* method of the field; alternative approaches are foreclosed' (Camic, 1989: 54). Such a comment indicates a fundamental misunderstanding of the nature and task of sociological theory. It is the ultimate grounding for Camic's criticism of Parsons, that he, Parsons, sought to formulate a general, functional, theory of society.

In his 1987 paper Camic asserts that differences in the social world are 'so ineffably multivalent as to defy reduction to a delimited set of variables and explanation by uniform laws' (1987: 435). We never learn in that paper, nor in the more recent one, how these social patterns are to be explained.[29]

Camic bases his contention on a quotation from Weber (Camic, 1987: 435, quoting Weber, 1949). In contrast, Parsons's position was that of Weber in *Economy and Society*:

We have taken it for granted that sociology seeks to formulate type concepts and generalized uniformities of empirical process. This distinguishes it from history, which is oriented to the causal analysis and explanation of individual actions, structures, and personalities possessing cultural significance. The empirical material which underlies the concepts of sociology consists to a very large extent, though by no means exclusively, of the same concrete processes of action which are dealt with by historians. (Weber, 1968: 19 [my italics]; cf. Camic, 1987: 434)[30]

This issue may be made clearer if we return to Camic's discussion of voluntarism. Camic argues that Parsons 'presents voluntarism as (in Alexander's words [1978: 184]) "a universal property of all action abstracted from time and space", not as a trait that sometimes accompanies action and sometimes does not. . . . For him, "nonvoluntaristic action" is a violation of the very definition of action, not a point of departure for an analysis of the historical conditions that release or restrict the "voluntaristic character of action". . . . At all events, the idea of historicizing voluntarism . . . by embedding it in a changing matrix of personality forms, social practices and action modes, social relations, interactional patterns, and institutions is an idea that his book simply is theoretically unequipped to pursue' (1989: 93–4).

These statements are, to be charitable, misguided. Firstly, Parsons characterizes voluntarism as a type of social theory, not as a type of action. As I noted above, voluntarism is examined from within the unit act. Unlike the radical forms of positivism, it does not reduce the explanation of action to nonsubjective components of a situation, although it incorporates these into its frame of reference (cf. Camic, 1989: 93, with Parsons, 1949: 465, n. 2). Unlike utilitarianism, it allows for the conceptualization of innumerable positively-stated normative orientations.[31] It conceptualizes ends as both normatively regulated and conditionally constrained. It incorporates nonempiricist constructs, including concepts like the collective conscience and Freud's unconscious. In consequence it does not reduce social action to the attributes of discrete unit acts and it does not reduce actors to the sum of the unit acts they perform (for example, to a reinforcement schedule).

As such a voluntaristic theory is universal only in that it purports to be able to explain human action in the widest variety of historical settings. It does not presume that actors act in any particular way; it does not even presume that actors 'act'. It is capable of conceptualizing human behavior as a limiting case of action, explicable in terms of the 'ultimate conditions' of action. Voluntaristic theories, unlike their positivist counterparts, have the analytical resources, Camic to the contrary notwithstanding, to explain when an individual will act and when he or she will 'behave', when his or her action requires a psychological and social and cultural explanation instead of a 'biological' explanation. They can also conceptualize action constrained by social (or nonsocial) conditions and at the same time steered by various levels of social and cultural controls. To suggest that a voluntaristic theory cannot conceptualize a changing matrix of personality forms, embedded in concrete social practices, is to profoundly misunderstand the nature of the theory. The voluntaristic theory that Parsons began to formulate in *SSA* either had, or had space for, the conceptual resources necessary to conceptualize, and to explain, an incredibly wide variety of types and forms of social activity. When Camic suggests that Parsons does not acknowledge sociological variations in the underlying form of the human personality (1989: 81), one wonders what he makes of Parsons's discussion of innerworldly asceticism in his introduction to Weber's *The Protestant Ethic and the Spirit of Capitalism* (even ignoring Parsons's own contributions in the 1950s and 1960s). Parsons constructed a general theory of action; he wanted it to be universally applicable, capable of explaining the multitudinous states and varieties of personality, social and cultural systems.

We can surely differ about the nature of the appropriate explanatory theory. We can all agree that Parsons's theory is in many respects ill-developed; no one would claim that his theory was, in Heisenberg's sense, complete. It is full of problems (see Gould, 1989: 648–50), but to generate explanatory theory and to evaluate it in attempting to explain concrete social processes is surely the primary task of the sociologist (see Gould, 1990). This can only be accomplished with the formulation of a general analytical theory capable of encompassing and explaining a wide variety of empirical particularity. A failure of resolve here entails a regress into (usually an idealist) empiricism.

Conclusion

Camic presents a utilitarian analysis of *SSA*. He postulates Parsons's end, chartering sociology as a discipline, and subject to this end, he reduced *SSA* to a rational, calculating adaptation to the conditions within which it emerged. Fortunately such an analysis is inadequate. *SSA* manifests the creativity of language; while it surely emerged from within both a social context and the linguistic and cultural codes that regulated its creation, it cannot be reduced to an epiphenomenon of a particular social setting. Parsons provided a pathbreaking analysis of the voluntaristic theory of action. It requires a voluntaristic theory to adequately come to grips with his text.

Instead Camic reifies the categories that framed Parsons's discussion of the various theories of action, and he seeks to embed these reified categories – most especially a radical disjunction between norms and conditions, where the latter are reduced to biological categories – within the voluntarist framework. In so doing, he misses a central point of Parsons's analysis, that a viable sociological theory must transcend this very dichotomy. Parsons is explicit concerned to understand the interdependence of conditional and normative variables in forming a social system. While it may be legitimate to refer to heredity and environment as the 'ultimate conditions of action', it is only within radical positivist theories that conditions are reduced to these biological categories. In a voluntaristic theory the conditions of action are largely social. In other words, Parsons draws on those theories that transcend the categories that Camic reifies and holds static (cf. Parsons, 1949: 449).

It was Parsons's goal throughout his career to formulate a functionalist theory of social systems, a theory that constructed societal universals, propositions intended to be valid for all societies. As such he slighted the importance of structural theories, theories valid only for a particular type of social system. This is, in my opinion, a limitation to the comprehensiveness of Parsons's theoretical project. But it is by no means the case that a viable structural theory is incompatible with a functional theory of the sort Parsons constructed. Here the proof of the pudding is in the eating, and I believe that I have demonstrated the compatibility of the two varieties of theory in successfully integrating them in a macrotheoretical analysis of a complex historical situation (Gould, 1987). While I certainly recognize weaknesses in my work, in terms of the problematic of a voluntaristic theory there is no reason why any theory must exclude a structural dimension.[32]

SSA is by no means perfect. Nor is the remainder of Parsons's work. But he provided us with the most sophisticated theory of the interrelationships between the elements of a social system that we have today; he also made great progress in the analysis of the interrelationships between personality, social and cultural systems. In addition, he furnished us with a powerful critique of utilitarian theory, one that is more important today than when it was written. Contrary to Camic, Parsons's work (for example in *SSA*) is not an historical artifact, valuable in 1937 in constituting the discipline, but out-of-date today. *Today* James Coleman mistakenly calls on Parsons's early writings to legitimize his utilitarian project (Coleman, 1990a). More appropriately, Jack Goldstone writes that Coleman's *Foundations of Social Theory* is a reply to *SSA* (Coleman, 1990b, jacket blurb). If I may be so presumptuous as to respond for Parsons: fifty-three years ago he published a book that provided a groundbreaking critique of utilitarianism. This critique is as correct today as it was fifty years ago, and it is crucial for sociologists to reaffirm it in the face of the colonization of sociology by neoclassical (utilitarian) theory (as manifest in Coleman's recent work).

The central problem with Parsons's work in this regard is that the position he staked out in *SSA* was not maintained with comparable vigor in his later work dealing with economics. But that is another story, one that includes an explanation of why his criticism did not come to dominate the social sciences (a story partially told in Gould, forthcoming). Parsons hoped that the 'charter' he constructed for the discipline would become an historical antiquity, of interest as a brilliant historical artifact, but out of date as social science. Perhaps someday, but not now. Today sociologists still need it as the foundation upon which to build a viable social science, as a vehicle (a 'charter') in an attempt to sociologically reconstruct the logic of neoclassical, utilitarian theory, before it reconstructs us (Gould, 1991). *The Structure of Social Action* is at least fifty-three years ahead of its time.

Notes

1. Parsons did not slight the importance of intellectual context in constructing his interpretation of the texts he analyzed. For example, he made the following comment in reference to his discussion of Marx: 'The experience of this study has certainly been that it is always helpful to attempt to understand a writer in terms of the polemical oppositions of the thought of his time' (1949: 490).

2. This essay was originally intended as a minor revision of Gould, 1989, taking into account Camic's more recent contribution. This simple revision proved to be too limited if I was to provide a meaningful criticism of Camic, 1989. As written, Gould, 1989, and the current essay should be read independently. However, it has been necessary in this essay to repeat certain of the points made in the earlier and there is, in consequence, some repetition between them. This is especially true of the following section.

3. Habermas tends to reify the unit act in his analysis of Parsons's work (Habermas, 1987: 205ff; cf. Camic, 1989: 71ff).

4. In *SSA* Parsons adopts a Weberian definition of social action ('Involving a plurality of actors mutually oriented to each other's action', Parsons, 1949: 768, n. 1), while suggesting that sociology seeks to explain 'social action systems in so far as these systems can be understood in terms of the property of common-value integration' (Parsons, 1949: 768). Here as elsewhere he does not fully grasp that a single actor's understanding of his or her own activities is always socio-culturally composed; meaning is always a socio-cultural construct (cf. Camic, 1989: 75).

It is worth nothing that Weber did not fall into the 'Weberian trap' in carrying out his actual research (cf. Wuthnow, 1987, Ch. 2).

5. 'Action, Situation, and Normative Pattern' was written shorly after *SSA* was published and Parsons used it in his teaching. It has recently appeared in a German translation and Victor Lidz is preparing an edition of the original English version.

6. It is this ambiguity that gives some small warrant for Coleman's interpretation of Parsons's early work (1986; 1990a).

7. For Parsons's image of a system and the relationship between norm and condition in social action, see below.

8. In this essay I slight Parsons's parallel analysis of idealism.

9. A more detailed characterization of utilitarianism, correcting Parsons's picture in some particulars, is found in Gould, 1981; cf. Camic, 1979.

10. The word 'foundation' is crucial. Parsons's primary goal in *SSA* is not to construct his own theory of social action; this was his life-long project after the completion of *SSA*. In *SSA* he sought to define the problematic within which such a theory might be successfully constructed.

11. Camic's criticism of Parsons's reconstruction of the figures discussed in *SSA* is an argument by authority. He quotes and/or cites the conclusions, with very little substantiation, of a number of critical discussions (including his own, Camic, 1979) that support one or another aspect of his negative assessment. In this context I do not have the space to dispute Camic's assertions (Camic, 1989: 56ff). Their point is to convey the erroneous message that the scholarly community has reached a consensus concerning Parsons's reconstructions; this is done by citing selectively within the literature, ignoring those arguments that tend to refute Camic's assertions. It is also accomplished by accepting casual comments as adequate characterizations of an author's position (e.g., erroneously assuming that Knight's utilitarian economics could structurally assimilate 'norms having an imperative quality', Camic, 1989:

56) and by a seemingly calculated misunderstanding of the nature of certain comments (e.g., failing to recognize that when a utilitarian theory conceptualizes economic activities within 'strongly enforced rules', this means that the rules are reduced to the situational sanctions that support them, i.e., to conditions of action, Camic, 1989: 56–7). Since I am primarily concerned with the import of Parsons's arguments for the construction of social theory, I move in the next paragraph of the text to what I think is the central point at issue.

My own position with regard to the veracity of Parsons's reconstructions is that there are significant errors in his reading of the figures he discusses, and most importantly in his analyses of Weber and Durkheim. I nonetheless would be prepared to argue that his assessment of both was fundamentally correct and enabled him to make his point about their convergence. What we must understand, and what Camic sometimes forgets, is that this convergence was analyzed within one of innumerable possible points of view, focusing on the continuing viability of the underlying logic of their theories. From other perspectives there was no convergence.

12. There are other comments in the essay that refer to Parsons's conceptualization of the actor and to the more overtly methodological point of how he conceptualizes varieties of normative orientation. These also relate to the importance of structure. In the next section I briefly discuss the conceptualization of social and personality structures within Parsons's theory.

13. In Gould, 1990, I have attempted to demolish Merton's argument in favor of plural theories of the middle range, showing that his actual analyses are weakened by the absence of a general sociological theory. I will not repeat this demonstration in this context.

14. In a later section I will amplify these comments as I articulate more systematically my understanding of the nature of theoretical sociology.

The desirability of theoretical pluralism is manifest in the importance of accepting a wide variety of strategies for constructing arguments within a discipline. In sociology, where no theoretical or methodological school has any justification to claim a monopoly of wisdom, we must be capable of evaluating a wide range of work in terms of its excellence, not in terms of its allegiance to any particular coda.

15. When Parsons wrote *SSA* the notion of a cybernetic hierarchy was not yet available to him. Nonetheless, his argument assumes an implicit cybernetic hierarchy between norms and conditions. Norms control action within the context of limits defined by conditions.

16. The problem with this contention is that utilitarian theory is inherently vacuous, or perhaps more precisely, tautologous. It is always capable of providing a *post hoc* explanation of any social action.

17. I return to Camic's discussion of voluntarism below when I discuss the nature of sociological theory.

18. It is frequently very difficult to follow Camic's discussion as he often quotes isolated passages from a number of places in *SSA* and puts them together in a construction of his own, one that sometimes misrepresents Parsons's argument. For example, Camic writes that 'According to Parsons, the conditions of action are not "the concrete conditions of a particular act" or the actor's actual "social environment", "but the ultimate analytical conditions of action in general", that is, the nonsubjective categories of "heredity and environment in the biological sense"' (Camic, 1989: 65, quoting Parsons, 1949: 364 (although I cannot locate the exact phrase), 364, 700, 83 [not 82], where the fourth quotation occurs). The penultimate quotation refers, in Parsons's actual discussion, to a characterization of the limits of utilitarianism, as a positivistic theory (p. 700 and also p. 71), while the last refers to non-action theoretical conceptualizations, not of the conditions of action, but of 'elements of action that are capable of nonsubjective formulation' (Parsons, 1949: 83). The other references for this passage cite a discussion of Pareto (Parsons, 1949: 252, 267) and a, to my mind, misleading discussion of Durkheim as sociologistic positivist (Parsons, 1949: 364), where Parsons misconstrues Durkheim as reducing 'the social environment' to conditions external to an actor. Contrary to Camic's analysis, none is relevant to Parsons's understanding of the conditions of action as they appear within a voluntaristic theory, where conditions include elements requiring a subjective formulation. (Camic makes similar mistakes in his discussion

of the 'great dichotomy' between norms and the biological conditions of heredity and environment [Camic, 1989: 50]).

19. The quotation from Camic (1989: 65) that appears in n. 18 above directly follows the passage quoted in the text.

20. The closest Parsons comes to Camic's analysis is in comments referring to the 'ultimate conditions of action', i.e., 'to either of the two great categories of nonhuman environment or of "human nature" in so far as it is determined by the mechanisms of biological heredity' (Parsons, 1990: 322). Unlike Camic, Parsons adds the following comment: 'That [the nonhuman environment and human nature] is what forms conditions or means only, in terms of the *general* analysis of the elements of action. For a concrete individual acting in a social environment . . . the laws and customs of the society may constitute *conditions*. The distinction is vital' (Parsons, 1990: 322, n. 10). The reduction of conditions to the nonhuman environment and heredity treats one type of condition as if it were the only variety available within a voluntaristic theory. While Parsons argues that this reduction is exhibited in radical positivism, he never suggests that it is manifest in voluntarism.

21. Surprisingly in the light of the above comments, Camic does recognize a structural schema in *SSA* residing between the conceptualization of ultimate values and ultimate ends (1989: 70–3). He discounts this type of analysis because it is of secondary importance in Parsons's theory (75). In Parsons's discussion the characterization of social relationships as secondary stems from his granting priority to action instead of social action, an error rectified in his later work (see Parsons, 1949: 745).

22. I am emphasizing the first and third of the three presumptions in this discussion. Similar points could be made about the second.

23. One of the reasons that Camic's essays are difficult to criticize is that he grants points and then takes them away. On pp. 83–4 (1989), just a bit before the contention under analysis, Camic writes as follows: 'According to Parsons, "the integration [of society through – C.C.] a common system of ultimate ends . . . is not a generalized description of the usual concrete state of affairs but formulates only one extreme limiting type" of case (S [1949], 248, 263; also 238, 254–5). This is so "because there is room for wide variation both in the degree of integration and in the kind of [common-value – C.C.] system" – a circumstance that allows for the "struggle[s – C.C.] between different individuals and groups of power and wealth" *and* for those "irreconcilable [value – C.C.] divisions in the social body [that appeared in – C.C.] the religious wars of the post-Reformation period" (S [1949]: 263–4, 434, 643–5; 1934: 231; 1935c: 15).' 1935c is the manuscript version of Parsons, 1990.

24. It is worth mentioning that Parsons seeks to explain the presence of social order; analytically this entails a presumption of disorder as the baseline for his explanation. It is also worth mentioning, although strictly speaking it is not relevant to the criticism I have made, that the claim that 'empirical research disconfirms the significant presence of common normative factors' is contentious at best, and arguably wrong. Camic often makes assertions like this as if his position on a question was definitively supported by the weight of the evidence.

25. Parsons does claim, on this page, that the values clustering around the church in the Middle Ages constituted a set of common values for some unspecified social system. I am not concerned with the veracity of this empirical claim (especially since Parsons does not indicate for whom they were common). The relevant question is whether the concept of common values has explanatory power, their presence a force for order, their absence one variable explaining the increased probability of disorder (cf. Parsons's similar comments, 1935: 296).

26. It is easy to see that the distinction between conditions and norms cannot be locked in stone if we look at the relationship between norms and the situational sanctions that support them. As we have seen and as is clear from the quotation in the text, the conditions of action may well be normatively constructed. In addition norms are themselves supported by the force of situational sanctions. These sanctions, i.e. conditions of action, are themselves dependent on moral values, 'since the strength of sanctions and the willingness to apply them is to a large, though not exclusive, extent an expression of moral attitudes' (Parsons, 1990: 327). The willingness to implement sanctions is also a consequence of the situational sanctions faced by the persons deciding whether or not to wield a sanction. The boundaries of moral

values are constituted by sanctioning their public violation. And so on.

27. These points are clear in an unpublished paper from 1934 or 1935 (Parsons, 1990). The discussion in *SSA* (404) reads like a paraphrase of 1990: 326–7.

28. While Parsons never succeeded in formulating a set of formal propositions within the systems analysis model (see the criticisms in Gould, 1991), I have endeavored to do so in Gould, 1987, Ch. 2; Gould, 1976: 470–8, reconstructs the systems analysis paradigm to facilitate this task. In Chapter 1 of Gould, 1987, I outline the interrelationships between functional, structural and developmental theory (see also Gould, 1985; Gould, 1987, Chs 2, 3, 4).

29. It is important to note that Camic is not arguing for the inclusion of structural propositions. Parsons emphasized the development of functional theory, societal universals intended to be valid for all societies. In contrast, structural theory is meant to be valid only for a specific stage in the development of a society. Camic's criticisms are applicable to both, to any general explanations that are not descriptively particularistic. His position is historicistic, ultimately refusing to acknowledge any role for theory at all. He fails to grasp that concepts must be abstract, not to eliminate particularity, but in recognition of the almost infinite variety of concrete detail.

30. A bit later in the same text Weber wrote that 'Within the realm of social action certain empirical uniformities can be observed, that is, courses of action that are repeated by the actor or (simultaneously) occur among numerous actors since the subjective meaning is meant to be the same. Sociological investigation is concerned with these typical modes of action. Thereby it differs from history, the subject of which is rather the causal explanation of important individual events . . . ' (Weber, 1968: 29; cf. Parsons, 1949: 597–9; 760).

31. When Parsons suggests that 'if a theory of action is to have the status of an independent analytical system at all, it must, in the nature of the case, be a voluntaristic theory' (1949: 762, n. 1), he is mistaken. Even if we exclude idealist theories, unlike radical positivist theories, utilitarian theory does not eliminate a subjective frame of reference as it maintains the autonomy of the ends of action. Thus its explanations cannot be reduced to adaptations to the situation of action (cf. Camic, 1989: 93).

32. The same is true of hermeneutic analyses. It is the case that Parsons provided an inadequately textured understanding of the symbolic mediation of social and cultural action, especially in *SSA* (cf. Camic, 1989: 54, 68). The point is that the voluntaristic framework demands this amplification; its absence is a lacuna *within* a voluntaristic framework. Interpretations of Parsons's voluntarism that suggest its reduction to the conceptualization of a single positively stated normative orientation (Coleman, 1986; 1990a) completely miss the point.

References

Adriaansens, H.P.M. (1980) *Talcott Parsons and the Conceptual Dilemma*. London: Routledge & Kegan Paul.

Alexander, J.C. (1978) 'Formal and Substantive Voluntarism in the Work of Talcott Parsons', *American Sociological Review*, 43 (2): 177–98.

Alexander, J.C. (1983) *Theoretical Logic in Sociology*, vol. 4, *The Modern Reconstruction of Classical Thought: Talcott Parsons*. Berkeley and Los Angeles: University of California Press.

Alexander, J.C. (1987) *Twenty Lectures: Sociological Theory since World War II*. New York: Columbia University Press.

Blau, P. (1987) 'Contrasting Theoretical Perspectives', pp. 71–85 in J. Alexander et al. (eds), *The Micro-Macro Link*. Berkeley and Los Angeles: University of California Press.

Camic, C. (1979) 'The Utilitarians Revisited', *American Journal of Sociology*, 85 (3): 516–50.

Camic, C. (1987) 'The Making of a Method: a Historical Reinterpretation of the Early Parsons', *American Sociological Review*, 52 (4): 421–39.

Camic, C. (1989) 'Structure after 50 Years: the Anatomy of a Charter', American Journal of Sociology, 95 (1): 38–107.

Clarke, S. (1982) Marx, Marginalism and Modern Sociology. London: Macmillan.

Coleman, J. (1986) 'Social Theory, Social Research, and a Theory of Action', American Journal of Sociology, 91 (6): 1309–45.

Coleman, J. (1990a) 'Commentary: Social Institutions and Social Theory', American Sociological Review, 55 (3): 333–9.

Coleman, J. (1990b) Foundations of Social Theory. Cambridge, Mass: Harvard University Press.

Gould, M. (1976) 'Systems Analysis, Macrosociology, and the Generalized Media of Action', pp. 470–506 in J. Loubser et al. (eds), Explorations in General Theory in Social Science, vol. 2. New York: Free Press.

Gould, M. (1981) 'Parsons versus Marx: "An earnest warning . . . "', Sociological Inquiry, 51 (3/4): 197–218.

Gould, M. (1985) 'Prolegomena to Any Future Theory of Societal Crisis', pp. 51–72 in J.C. Alexander (ed.), Neofunctionalism. Beverly Hills: Sage.

Gould, M. (1987) Revolution in the Development of Capitalism: the Coming of the English Revolution. Berkeley and Los Angeles: University of California Press.

Gould, M. (1989) 'Voluntarism versus Utilitarianism: a Critique of Camic's History of Ideas', Theory, Culture & Society, 6 (4): 637–54.

Gould, M. (1990) 'The Interplay of General Sociological Theory and Empirical Research: "In Order Thereby to Arrive at a Causal Explanation of its Course and Effects"', pp. 399–416 in Jon Clark, Sohan Modgil and Celia Modgil (eds), Robert Merton: Consensus and Controversy. London and New York: Falmer Press.

Gould, M. (1991) 'Parsons's Economic Sociology: a Failure of Will', Sociological Inquiry, 64 (1): 89–101.

Gould, M. (forthcoming) 'The Problem of Order in Perfect and Imperfect Information Theories'. Presented at the 1990 meeting of the American Economics Association, Washington, DC.

Habermas, J. (1987) The Theory of Communicative Action, vol. 2, Lifeworld and System: a Critique of Functionalist Reason, tr. T. McCarthy. Boston: Beacon Press. (Original work published in 1981.)

Levine, D. (1980) Introduction to Simmel and Parsons: Two Approaches to the Study of Society. New York: Arno Press.

Merton, R.K. (1981) 'Forward: Remarks on Theoretical Pluralism', pp. i–viii in P. Blau and R.K. Merton (eds), Continuities in Structural Inquiry. Beverly Hills: Sage.

Mulkay, M.J. (1971) Functionalism, Exchange and Theoretical Sociology. London: Routledge & Kegan Paul.

Parsons, T. (1935) 'The Place of Ultimate Values in Sociological Theory', International Journal of Ethics, 45 (3): 282–316.

Parsons, T. (1949) The Structure of Social Action. New York: Free Press. (Original work published in 1937.)

Parsons, T. (1954) Essays in Sociological Theory, 2nd edn. New York: Free Press.

Parsons, T. (1959) 'An Approach to Psychological Theory in Terms of the Theory of Action', pp. 612–711 in S. Koch (ed.), Psychology: a Study of a Science, vol. 3, Formulations of the Person and the Social Context. New York: McGraw-Hill.

Parsons, T. (1964) Social Structure and Personality. New York: Free Press.

Parsons, T. (1990) 'Prolegomena to a Theory of Social Institutions', American Sociological Review, 55 (3): 319–33. (Originally written in 1934–5.)

Stout, R. (1963) The League of Frightened Men. New York: Pyramid Books. (Original work published in 1935.)

Warner, R.S. (1978) 'Toward a Redefinition of Action Theory: Paying the Cognitive Element its Due', American Journal of Sociology, 83: 1317–49.

Weber, M. (1930) The Protestant Ethic and the Spirit of Capitalism, tr. T. Parsons. London: Allen & Unwin.

Weber, M. (1949) '"Objectivity" in Social Science and Social Policy', pp. 49–112 in M. Weber, *The Methodology of the Social Sciences*, ed. and tr. E.A. Shils and H.A. Finch. New York: Free Press. (Original work published in 1904.)

Weber, M. (1964) *The Theory of Social and Economic Organization*, tr. A.M. Henderson and T. Parsons. New York: Free Press. (Original work published in 1925.)

Weber, M. (1968) *Economy and Society*, ed. G. Roth and G. Wittich, tr. various hands. New York: Bedminster. (Original work published in 1925.)

Wuthnow, R. (1987) *Meaning and Moral Order: Explorations in Cultural Analysis*. Berkeley and Los Angeles: University of California Press.

6

INFLUENCE AND SOLIDARITY: DEFINING A CONCEPTUAL CORE FOR SOCIOLOGY

Victor Lidz

The frame of reference

Talcott Parsons wrote his theoretical works under the ambitious title of 'the general theory of action'. In his use of this title, two bold claims were implicit. The first concerns the scope of the object world to which the theory applies. Parsons designed his theoretical framework to provide concepts for analyzing every empirical field within the domain of social action, vast as that is. The theory is intended to be general in the sense of encompassing everything that is constituted by meaningful human conduct. The second claim concerns the range of intellectual orientations toward the world of social action that the theory incorporates. Parsons hoped to unify in a coherent, logically consistent framework the validated elements of all previously established conceptual schemes for studying social action. The theory was to be general in the sense of providing essential theoretical means for the entire community of social scientists, excluding no necessary schools or styles of thought. It was to protect social scientists from building a new Tower of Babel, where commitments to logically incommensurable theories would predestine scholars to talk past one another and hence fail to resolve their disputes.[1]

To be sure, Parsons held these twin ambitions for his general theory of action with qualifications. He understood, for example, that parts of his theory remained in the form of preliminary concepts. These parts figured in the overall frame of reference, but their value could not be fully established until they were complemented by more precise analytical categories and more specific causal propositions. Until a large number of empirical areas had been analyzed in terms of more precise categories and explanatory hypotheses, the claim of general validity remained provisional and largely formal. This is hardly to say that the importance of the general framework was negligible, but simply to acknowledge its limits. Parsons also understood that determining the theory's logical relations with independent conceptual schemes, for example, symbolic interactionism, ethnomethodology, psychoanalysis, or some variants of Marxism, involved complicated issues.[2]

Being aware of these difficulties, Parsons worked on developing his general theory in a flexible manner. As he elaborated the technical formulations that might give analytical precision to specific parts of the theory, he frequently revised more general concepts. He also subjected competing theories to critical study, often identifying additional concepts for incorporation in the theory of action. His ambition to achieve generality thus resulted not in a claim about a fixed corpus of theory, but in a set of values guiding the construction of better theory.

Throughout his career, Parsons gave special attention to the problem of defining the place of sociological theory within the larger, multidisciplinary body of the theory of action. He tried to establish core concepts and hypotheses within the larger theory specifically for orienting sociological thought. To summarize his treatment of this problem, we can identify three distinct approaches that he followed at different times in his career. The first was developed in *The Structure of Social Action*. It assigned to sociology the task of developing a comprehensive understanding of how systems of social action are integrated through common values (1937: Ch. XIX). Parsons's main concern was to demonstrate that this proposal codified the traditions of comparative macroinstitutional analysis established by Weber and Durkheim. The second approach, presented in *The Social System*, is closely related, but cast in somewhat broader terms. Sociology is to be focused on analysis of how normative orders are institutionalized (1951: Ch. XII). Parsons argued that this proposal would unify the dynamic study of interaction and interpersonal relationships with macrosociological and institutional analysis, as emphasized in his early work.

The third approach emerged during the late 1950s and early 1960s along with the four-function paradigm and the notion of functionally differentiated subsystems of society. In this schema, social systems are conceived as organized along four conceptually distinct but interrelated dimensions, the adaptive, goal attaining, integrative and pattern maintaining.[3] Sociology is identified with study of the integrative dimension of social systems, including its mutual dependencies with the other three dimensions. Sociological research should focus on all structures and processes of social life that affect (or are affected by) the solidarity or social coherence of whatever empirical relationships of interaction may be in question. At the macro-social level of research, legal institutions, the mechanisms of social control, and relations among social classes and status groups were treated as major factors shaping integration. They were said to constitute the integrative subsystem of society, that is, the set of social relationships specialized about generating solidarity for society as a whole.[4] The present essay is concerned with this third approach to devising a central theoretical scheme for sociology, and the notion of an integrative subsystem of society will play a large role in the discussion.

Parsons adhered to this third conception of the core tasks of sociology for the last twenty years or so of his life. During this period, he wrote with characteristic insight on many aspects of societal integration, including various processes of social control, legal institutions, social stratification, civil rights, and the solidarity of societal community.[5] He also developed a dynamic conception of integrative processes around the notion of influence as a generalized medium of persuasion (1969c). Despite these important contributions, however, Parsons failed to establish the issues of societal integration as the basis of a conceptually unified research program for sociology. Besides the essentially false issues of a 'harmonist' view of society and an inability to analyze social conflict, which were hardly of negligible import in the profession at large, two real difficulties undermined his efforts.

Parsons was himself quite aware of the first difficulty. His treatments of integrative institutions and dynamics lacked the analytic force to attract professional attention as a compelling program of research. As he acknowledged, his writings on influence as a generalized medium were far less satisfactory than his essays on political power.[6] They did not convey the same sense of a dynamic unity of the empirical processes to which they were addressed, nor did they impress readers as comparably fresh and enlightening. As a number of critics commented, those essays lacked the conceptual precision of his celebrated essay 'On the Concept of Political Power' (1969d) or his discussions of money as the prototypal generalized medium. Parsons also knew that he had not explained the connections among the major complexes of integrative institutions – law and other mechanisms of social control, social stratification, and societal community – in terms that conveyed the functional coherence of a societal subsystem. The notion that the study of societal integration constitutes a distinct and unitary field of investigation accordingly did not withstand skeptical examination. The book for which Parsons had nearly completed a draft when he died, *The American Societal Community*,[7] was intended in part to establish the cohesiveness of this research field. That his own thinking on societal integration, including the four-function paradigms he used to formalize relationships among theoretical propositions, continued to change while he was writing this manuscript, a period of roughly seven years, does not promote confidence in his claims of conceptual consistency.

The second difficulty concerns the overall theory of action and its standing in the discipline. The years during which Parsons hoped to establish the project of understanding social integration as a core research program were just the years during which he lost a general following in sociology. In retrospect, it is clear that the rapid development of his thought after the mid-1950s, especially the proliferation of levels of analysis, four-function paradigms, and hypotheses about various generalized media, overwhelmed the great majority of sociologists. His early writings may have been formidable, but they gave readers a clear message about the focus of sociological analysis. By contrast, the later writings required mastery of a highly technical system of theory before a reader could grasp in precise terms the frame of analysis that Parsons proposed to place at the center of sociology. Following the design of specific hypotheses within this frame of reference posed additional problems before a particular study could be planned. The vast majority of sociologists lost patience and sought theoretical guidance elsewhere, often citing the familiar allegations – harmonism, structural bias, inattention to change, and failure to treat conflict – in justification. These charges seemed especially fitting as reasons for rejecting a theory that purported to focus on societal integration.

The present essay addresses both of the basic difficulties. Given space limitations, it must be largely programmatic. The key will be to outline a way of reformulating the theory of influence: the conception of influence as a generalized medium facilitating integrative processes will be joined to a dynamic conception of solidarity drawn from Durkheim. By reviving ideas from Durkheim's early writings on solidarity, a clearer, more parsimonious statement of the core interests of sociological theory is gained. A central research paradigm in Kuhn's (1970) sense should be established. However, it is not my intent to reduce either the general theory of action or the intellectual interests of sociology to a spare core. Rather, the dynamic theory of influence and solidarity is intended merely as a start. It should lead research from central issues about relationships that generate solidarity to an array of other problems concerning major integrative institutions, the connections between influence/solidarity and other dynamic mechanisms in society (money and markets, power and authority, commitments and value-structures), and the 'social psychological' (that is, more technically, general action system) questions of how solidary relationships, as realities in social experience, are tied in with processes of culture, personality, and mind.[8] The core paradigm is intended to provide a flexible means of entry to the analytical riches of the action schema.

The theory of influence and its problems

Some highlights of Parsons's treatment of influence should be noted, even though this cannot be the occasion for a general critique. Parsons wrote his key essay on influence shortly after his innovative paper on political power. The treatment of influence (1969c) was intended to capitalize on a major theme of the essay on power, namely, that money as a generalized symbolic medium is not a unique phenomenon but only a prominent member of a 'family' of media. Parsons's discussion of political process (1969d; 1969e) had highlighted the strategic importance of leadership as a source of flexibility in the functioning of political institutions. But it had also emphasized that leadership, in its essence, was not a form of power or binding decision-making, but a more supple means of mobilizing constituencies to back policy initiatives. Leadership was a mode of popular appeal to the public at large. Parsons treated it as an effort to wield influence over the public and suggested that the public (the members of society considering issues of the common weal in their roles as citizens and constituents of their leaders) should be viewed as an institution of societal integration rather than of directly political action (1969d; 1969e). Thus, his writings on power and the polity had led him to posit the independent importance of influence as a medium of social integration.

Parsons's underlying hypothesis was that each of the primary subsystems of society provides a 'home' for a medium of its own, the economy for money, the polity for power, the integrative system (or societal community) for influence, and the pattern maintenance (or fiduciary) system for value-commitments.[9] To be sure, each medium circulates throughout all four of the subsystems. Parsons analyzed at length the processes by which actors interchange quantities of media from institutionally defined, reciprocal role-positions in two different subsystems. For example, the phenomena of leadership in relation to public support were treated as an interchange between polity and societal community, one with interesting parallels to the relationship between business firms in the economy and households in the fiduciary system.[10] The term interchange was used to underscore the systemic implications of aggregate flows of media between subsystems of society as well as specific exchanges of media between pairs of individuals or collectivities. Here, Parsons was extending the model of economic analysis of the 'circular flow' between firm and household to a larger set of interchanges. He developed specific hypotheses about the consequences of imbalances in aggregate flows of media, suggesting, for example, that the inability of political leadership to attract sufficient support from the public could result in the political analogue of a depression. In *The American Societal Community*, the aftermath of 'Watergate' is treated as a political depression produced by a weakening of influence relations between high officials and constituents.

Despite the emphasis on circulation of the media, the notion of a medium's home was also important in Parsons's model. Just as money provides the measure of value for all economic goods that enter exchange, so power was conceived as defining the generalized value of political resources and influence was treated as indexing integrative value (Parsons, 1969c; 1969d). Of course, neither power nor influence can be quantified on a numerical scale in the fashion of money. But in common-sense terms members of society comfortably make judgments about which actors have greater power or greater influence and which actors have less power or less influence. People routinely make decisions about how much power or influence they are willing to expend in given social situations. People also make routine judgments about gains or losses of power and influence experienced by other actors who have succeeded or failed in changing their positions and modes of participation in networks of social relationships. More deeply, power and influence as measures of value serve to define the kinds or qualities of social resources that are pertinent, respectively, to political and integrative contexts of relationship. For example, the civic principle that a wealthy person whose conduct has affected the public welfare ought not to be able to buy protection from criticism in the mass media constitutes a normative boundary between money and influence. The inhibitions, firmer in some societies and in some social settings than in others, against buying public offices or bribing public officials similarly affect the boundary between wealth and power. The limits on the capacity of a public official to determine by command how he or she will be discussed in the public press is a factor in the boundary between polity and integrative subsystem. All of these boundary elements rest partly on quantitative notions of the media.

In developing his conception of influence, Parsons made a special effort to forge links with previous empirical and theoretical research. The 'Columbia School' studies by Merton, Lazarsfeld and their colleagues on reference groups, personal influence and change in opinions provided the main background.[11] Parsons (1969e) had re-analyzed the data in *Voting* (Berelson et al., 1954) in a major essay on the polity. He then concentrated on the careful review of the field of 'opinion research' contained in *Personal Influence*.[12] Parsons followed the lead of Lazarsfeld and others at Columbia, but also his Harvard colleague Samuel A. Stouffer,[13] in using the concept of 'opinion' to designate the category of dependent variables in influence theory. That is, the objects of study were conceptualized as the opinions that dispose individuals to act in specific ways. Reference group theory, concepts such as cross-pressures, and hypotheses, such as the 'two step flow of influence', that relate public leaders or mass media sources to individual members of society through primary groups could be used to explain changes in opinions.[14]

To this conceptual apparatus, Parsons added the idea that influence circulates in society in the form of a generalized medium. Influence, he argued (1969c), can be viewed as a generalized capacity to persuade or change opinions. An actor who holds a quantity of influence commands an expendable resource for advancing specific interests by leading others to accept his or her opinions. In encouraging others to change their opinions, an influential typically affects the grounds of their subsequent conduct as well. The influential generally holds an advantage in gaining the co-operation of the others or perhaps in denying it to third parties. Given these practical advantages that accrue to influentials, sociologists should examine the overall distributions of influence among individuals, groups, associations, and communities within society. Sociologists should also examine the relationships through which influence is exercised and the processes that may change distributions of influence. Systemic and macro-social constraints on the allocations and uses of influence came more directly into view from Parsons's perspective. For example, patterns of allocation of influence can be related to the structure of status groups and uses of influence can be related to operations of social control. An impetus to integrate the study of influence with general research on social stratification was a clear product of Parsons's emphasis on influence as a generalized medium.

Briefly, we may note several difficulties with Parsons's effort to treat influence as a generalized medium of social integration. First, the concept of opinion is rather diffuse and tended to take on psychological or social psychological meanings that deflect theoretical attention from directly social relationships. In this respect, the concept of opinion poses difficulties similar to the concept of 'attitude' in the tradition of work deriving from G.H. Mead. The problem is essentially one of levels of analysis, for there can be little doubt that opinions and attitudes exist and that changes in them require social psychological explanations. However, as it became easier to see in later years when Parsons drew a distinction between the social system media and the general action media,[15] changes in opinion or attitude are not the empirical processes on which societal integration rests most directly. Rather, it is changes in solidary social relationships, and they should be treated as the primary objects for explanation in influence theory.

Second, a parallel difficulty applies to the concept of 'persuasion'. Too many things are capable of exercising a persuasive effect in social life. Thus, the term connotes a diffuse process with a wide range of factors playing a part. Coercion may be said to change opinions, but also various cultural processes, including scientific demonstrations, rhetorical flourishes, and artistic performances. If research is extended to the whole field of persuasion, the focus on integrative relationships and processes will be lost.

A third difficulty emerged when Parsons connected the theory of influence to his own studies of the medical profession and, later, academic professionals.[16] The analysis of professional settings brought the generalization of influence sharply into focus. Generalization can be seen in situations where a patient accepts a doctor's recommendations about treatment without having the medical knowledge to evaluate them or where a student accepts the teachings of a professor without commanding the scholarly information needed to assess them. In both cases, influence is tied to the professional status (and credentials) of the influential figure. The exercise of influence bridges what Parsons called a competence or information gap. Professional influence, Parsons argued, is rooted in competence and consists in a generalized capacity to 'persuade' across gaps of information (see also Parsons, 1968). Although insightful, this formulation leaves aside important considerations. For example, the roles of physician and professor involve responsibilities for the welfare of patients or students in addition to a command of greater technical knowledge. Other sorts of influence, for example, that of political or community leaders, rest on responsibilities to which greater knowledge may be tangential. That President Reagan's public influence was so slightly diminished by his displays of ignorance on major social issues may stand as proof of this point. The notion of competence or information gaps accordingly captures only part of the generalization of influence. Parsons tended to draw overly broad conclusions from what are actually specialized features of professional relationships.

Finally, Parsons missed an opportunity to shape the concept of influence more directly on the model of money. Economists have emphasized, as Parsons himself often recounted, that a quantity of money represents a share of the productivity of an entire economy. On this model, influence should be related not simply to ability to persuade, but to a conception of the capacity for producing solidary social relationships in a society. Parsons's writings on societal integration show that he did have this conception. Far from presuming that society exists in a condition of natural harmony, as other scholars have so often alleged, Parsons knew that societies are filled with tensions and conflicts which only active institutions of social integration can offset.[17]

The premise of the following discussion is that influence represents a generalized capacity to take part in the difficult processes, fallible at every stage, of creating or producing solidarity. Recourse to Durkheim's formulations about the cohesion of modern societies and their social pathologies will enable us to conceptualize the social conditions that shape the production of solidarity. But a Parsonian notion of influence as a generalized medium of social integration will constitute a basic ingredient of the discussion as well, albeit one that requires refinement.

The rational actor in integrative settings

Economic theory is based on a model of the rational actor seeking to maximize his or her utilities or control of means for satisfying wants. As Weber argued years ago, this model sets up an ideal-type of an actor with rational motives in order to make certain commonly observed courses of conduct understandable in theoretical terms (Weber, 1968). It does not determine that actual people necessarily follow rational courses of conduct under the particular circumstances of their lives. Parsons, too, warned repeatedly against the dangers of reifying utilitarian premises concerning the rational actor into unquestioned conceptual frameworks. Utilitarian conceptions, he emphasized, raise blinders that often hide from view the institutional factors shaping economic life (Parsons, 1937; Parsons and Smelser, 1956). He insisted that efforts to place sociology on utilitarian foundations were doomed to failure, not least when he opposed the new political economy of the 1960s and 1970s[18] and the new economic sociology of the 1970s.[19] These latter movements struck him as products of intellectual imperialism on the part of economic utilitarians. He thought them no less narrow-minded in their understanding of human purposes than they are ambitious and clever. Yet, despite his reservations about its scope, Parsons fully acknowledged that the model of the economic actor ('economic man') is a useful starting point for economic theory *per se*.[20] It provides a clear-cut statement of basic premises for systematizing a complicated body of theory.

In the spirit of that judgment, I will outline elements of a model of the integrative or solidarizing actor. This model should be regarded as, at best,

an introductory statement of premises about how actors maximize their
interests within integrative relationships and institutions insofar as they act
rationally.[21] No assumption is intended about its adequacy as a foundation
for full explanation of solidarizing conduct or integrative processes. It
requires the same sort of complementary institutional analysis that Parsons
identified for the foundations of neoclassical economics (Parsons and
Smelser, 1956). Nor should we assume that social actors involved in ties of
solidarity necesarily act on the basis of rational motives. However, the
model provides a basis for developing hypotheses about the dynamics or
workings of integrative mechanisms in society, just as the model of the
economic actor leads to hypotheses about economic markets. It also
establishes some reference points for introducing propositions about how
integrative relationships and mechanisms differ from economic ones. In
highlighting differences from economic theory, it is designed to contrast
with utilitarian theories in sociology while yet adhering to comparable
premises concerning the rationality of human conduct.

If economic actors maximize utilities, solidarizing actors maximize advantages to be gained through their relatedness with other members of
society. Insofar as they engage with other actors in ties of social solidarity,
they should be able to place the other actors in obligations to themselves.
When they have need of social support from others, they can then activate
those obligations. Influence may be regarded as a generalized medium for
activating obligations that are rooted in underlying relationships of solidarity. Influence also serves as a means for measuring approximate quantities
of the social capacity to activate obligations, much as money provides a
measure of wealth as well as a way of demanding utilities. Actors will
accordingly seek influence much as, through different relational mechanisms, they are apt to seek money. Holding influence provides some
generalized advantages in managing one's social life. An influential person
is one who commands the human good of being able to activate the duties
or obligations of other actors. We often think of such social obligations as
owed to particular individuals. But influence is always held within and
usually on behalf of groups, associations, or communities. Thus, it is
important to think of influence as rooted in solidary relationships and as
measuring or at least indicating the strength of their solidarity. We should
not regard influence merely as a possession of individuals.

Solidary relationships are intrinsically reciprocal. They bind actors to
one another, and hence locate each in a complex of duties to the other or
others.[22] Accordingly, individuals involved in solidary relationships gain
influence over one another. Typically, however, the influence contains
asymmetries. Not only do some actors have greater influence than others,
but their levels of influence are integrated into differences in the social
roles they perform (compare Parsons, 1954). Particular individuals will
have influence to activate only certain kinds of obligations acknowledged
by others. For example, the influence that a spouse can exercise over a
physician is different in kind from the sorts of influence exercised by

patients or colleagues, and vice versa. Due to the reciprocal nature of solidary ties, actors tend to be aware that they live in a complicated and differentiated environment of potential influences.

It is a part of common sense for an actor to be conscious of the respects in which he or she is the object of influence of many kinds which can be exercised by others. For this reason, actors are likely to be aware that influence is a scarce resource. They are also likely to be sensitive to the kinds and levels of influence they lack. Rationality will lead them to be purposeful in acquiring influence and careful in expending it. All members of society have experience with influence they failed to acquire but subsequently wished they had acquired as well as with influence they squandered needlessly and perhaps purposelessly. The cultures of all societies contain maxims about how to acquire and use influence rationally.

The actor who uses influence and then benefits from the performance of obligations by others receives a special sort of good. This type of good is distinct from an economic good. Above and beyond practical concomitants that may include empowerment and economic gain, the actor receives social support. This is recognition or, better, confirmation of his or her position in a network of solidary ties. It represents a response of others to his or her capacity to activate processes of the collective coordination of conduct. It is in some degree an affirmation of personal judgment. It is acceptance of his or her participation within the solidary whole. It is an experience of membership and community.[23] Within the on-going life of a solidary entity, the responses to uses of influence, as members make claims on one another, reveal the evolving qualities of the collectivity as a reality *sui generis*. Trust or distrust, decency or manipulativeness, kindness or cruelty, expansive optimism or restrictive pessimism, and so forth, emerge as features of collective relationships. What uses of influence bring to individuals, therefore, should be viewed as shares of a collective good. To be sure, we must recognize that in some settings – for example a repressive prison, an anomic community, a conflict-ridden factory, a rivalrous academic department – this 'good' may have palpably oppressive or painful qualities at the same time that it constitutes a sought-after advantage of supportive recognition by others. Indeed, particular qualities of the 'good' sought by some members may be closely connected with what is experienced as painful by the group or community as a whole. Insight into such phenomena lies at the core of Durkheim's theory of social pathologies, as we will see.

Although individual actors will on some occasions experience social support as an end in itself and on other occasions as a means to further ends, performances of obligations are not reducible to utilities. Their significance in on-going systems of social action transcends whatever import they may have to various individuals as means of satisfying wants, because they are constitutive of essentially collective relationships and rest on the reciprocal obligations of the members to one another. The fundamental entity is not the want of an individual, but the obligation of a group member. As Durkheim (1950) insisted, solidary obligations make up a reality of a different order from the satisfactions of individuals. That they are usually well integrated with personal want-satisfactions does not detract from the validity of this Durkheimian principle. Indeed, the seeking of influence and, with it, the capacity to have one's judgment and personality recognized by others should be regarded as a universal social activity independent of the economic effort to gain means for satisfying wants.

The performance of obligations is a burden. People may say that they are pleased to do something for a friend or associate and that no effort will be involved. However, such remarks are simply expressions of positive sentiment for another person. Performance of a duty ordinarily consumes scarce time and effort. It may also prevent one from fulfilling other duties. Where obligations are being fulfilled in complicated settings, conflicting expectations or sources of influence are regularly encountered.[24] This is the kind of situation familiar to sociologists under the heading of latent or not-so-latent cross-pressures. In such cases, the decisions entailed in fulfilling a particular duty will involve obstructing actual or potential efforts, whether on the part of oneself or associates, to discharge other obligations.

From the standpoint of a theory of solidarity concerned with large-scale social integration, performance of duties in the face of cross-pressures should be taken as typical. The burden of fulfilling obligations in the manner desired by one actor who exercises influence is generally that one must frustrate others who also hold influence and expect that one act differently. One's course of conduct must be calculated in terms that encompass one's duties to a variety of others and extend into the future of those relationships. Responding to the influence of one person typically involves a fortitude to resist the influence of others and, in some degree, place one's relationship with the others at risk. Acting on the basis of solidarity with one actor, and presumably reinforcing that relationship, generally comes at a cost in terms of the strength of other relationships. Unless one can justify one's conduct well, one may lose influence with the people one has frustrated and perhaps still others over whom they have influence.

A use of influence amounts to a 'demand' for another actor or actors to enter a new solidary relation or fulfill a duty based on a continuing association or relationship of solidarity. It represents a claim that a solidary tie, loyalty, duty, or relation of obligation should be activated. It is a means of using one's judgment to start integrative or solidarizing processes in motion. It is an expenditure in the sense that in seeking co-operation one expects to turn over part of one's influence to others in reciprocation for their support. For the sake of convenience, I will use the term 'associative performance' for the category of conduct carried out in response to uses of influence. An associative performance differs from various other types of conduct through its connections with ties of solidarity, not by any observable characteristics of the concrete behavior it may involve. Just as an economic good derives its value from its place in a complicated 'world' of utilities and relations to culturally legitimated wants, not simply from its intrinsic properties, so an associative performance derives its significance from an entire 'world' of solidary ties. A particular associative performance is undertaken to fulfill the duties of a solidary relation or to confirm the establishment of a new relationship by acting on the responsibilities it creates. The performer must expend the effort of will entailed in meeting his or her obligations. Often the chief problem in fulfilling an obligation is to rearrange priorities among the duties one is expected to perform in connection with a variety of solidary attachments. Responding to the influence of one person or group may require a delay in meeting expectations established in other settings or, given conflicts, even outright refusal to meet them. Rearranging priorities in this sense poses intrinsic difficulties for actors who are engaged in a number of social roles and who plan to sustain a variety of solidary ties – which is to say nearly everyone. When a value is set upon an associative performance, it typically rests upon the importance of changed priorities in the planning of future courses of conduct. The value cannot be estimated simply in terms of the immediate utility or efficacy of concrete services, although practical benefits to an association may be important, because its essence is a willingness to act in ways that will sustain a particular solidary relationship into the future despite the competing demands of other relationships. As a general category, then, associative performance consists in the uses of judgment that preserve solidarity as an on-going quality of social relationships.

Where expenditures of influence are rationalized, they rest on a set of underlying judgments that can be represented by a schedule roughly in the manner of economic theory. An influence schedule tends to slope downward to the right where the quantity of influence is plotted on the vertical axis and the quantity or value of associative performances is plotted on the horizontal axis. That is, at lesser costs in terms of quantities of influence that must be expended, there will be an increase in demand for associative performances of given kinds.

Obversely, associative performance is also subject to rational judgment on the part of the actors who supply it. It will be offered along a schedule that slopes upward to the right, with the quantity or value offered increasing with the amount of influence that can be gained. Particular flows of influence, that is, particular exchanges of influence for associative performance, occur where the expectational schedules of the users of influence and the performers intersect. To analyze the quantities of influence that circulate, one must attend to the underlying phenomena of the influence and performance schedules. Costs of performance, for example the difficulties facing the performer who must sustain solidary relations, affect the quantity of influence expended as much as an actor's holdings or funds of available influence.

Figure 6.1 presents a downward sloping influence schedule intersecting with an upward sloping associative performance schedule at point E.[25]

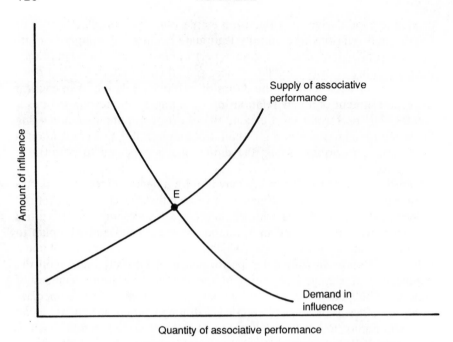

Figure 6.1   *'Normal' schedules for influence and associative performance*

Point E represents the hypothetical condition of equilibrium. It will be reached on the aggregate insofar as members of the solidary system in question enjoy freedom of association. As Parsons himself emphasized, freedom of association constitutes, for integrative relationships, the analogue of market freedom as a complex of institutions shaping the economy.[26] However, freedom of association does not arise simply from an absence of normative constraints on solidary relationships. Just as freedom of the market rests on such institutions as property and contract, freedom of association requires positive regulation of integrative ties. Institutions such as the freedoms of citizenship must protect the capacity of individuals to exercise judgment free of coercion and with reasonable expectation that others will make good on promises to fulfill obligations.

In fact, a complex society contains myriads of independent arenas for the formation of associational ties. Local communities, kinship networks, professional associations, industrial interest groups, civic organizations, charitable associations, and so forth present independent settings for the exchange of influence and solidary performances, as do the settings in which ties may develop among such groups. Separated from one another by differentiation and by segmentation, these arenas for solidarity are all formed under particular social conditions.[27] Only some of these conditions permit an approximation to the ideal-type of freedom of association. Many settings contain social forces that distort associational processes away from the ideal of freedom. Citizens of slum neighborhoods who experience the oppressions of poverty or fear the coercion of street criminals cannot associate with one another freely. Military and intelligence organizations restrict the associational freedoms of their staffs. Family life ordinarily involves limitations on the freedom of marital partners to enter confidential and especially intimate relationships with others and on the freedom of children to act independently of the fiduciary judgments of their parents. In the political process, wealthy lobbyists may establish oligopolies of influence that obstruct the efforts of competing associations to gain audiences for their opinions at the centers of power and policy-deliberation.

Tocqueville's *Democracy in America* is the classic study of freedom of association's fateful role in the development of modern civilization. Tocqueville compared the democratic and aristocratic conditions of society essentially in terms of associational freedom.[28] In the aristocratic condition, members of society are tied ascriptively into the social blocs through which their principal duties in society are defined. If they are aristocrats, they are obligated to provide leadership for their blocs and to represent the interests of these ascriptive communities in the society at large. If they are commoners, they can exercise their influence only locally and within traditionally established channels. In order to affect larger political bodies, they must deferentially approach their aristocratic leader and attempt to influence him to act on their behalf. By contrast, the democratic condition places members of society in the role of independent and equal citizens. Tocqueville emphasized that, without ascriptive ties to rely upon, the citizens of a democracy are intrinsically weak and lonely. They have no durable channels of influence through which to mobilize social support or exert their wills. In order to compensate for this weakness, they are driven to participate in many associational arenas with energy and creativity. They must forge ever anew the solidary relationships through which they can assert and protect their social interests. The numbers of associations proliferate and influence circulates far more rapidly and widely. Although Tocqueville's models of the aristocratic and democratic conditions may be crude, they correctly depict the essential difference between the restricted 'markets' for influence in pre-modern Europe and the extremely active 'markets' of contemporary equalitarian societies. The transition from the aristocratic to the democratic condition constituted a fundamental change in systems of solidarity, one that elaborated greatly the pluralism of role relations and the energy devoted to associational ties.

Durkheim formulated a similar idea in terms that can be interpreted as concentrating on the aggregate balances of influence and associative performance. In Book Two of *The Division of Labor in Society*, Durkheim argued that the shift to greater reliance on organic relationships and the division of labor in modern times has been stimulated by prior increases in moral or dynamic density.[29] By dynamic density, he meant the direct involvement of groups and individuals in unified arenas of interaction where, under the regulation of a common normative framework, they will enjoy opportunities to develop solidary ties with one another. Dynamic density increases when, through the development of more abstract and generalized conceptions of moral identity, the institutional boundaries dividing a society into a number of narrower segmental communities are dissolved and then supplanted by cultural frameworks establishing more inclusive grounds of solidarity.

Durkheim saw this process at work in a number of phases of history, ranging from the consolidation of the *poleis* in ancient Greece, to the incorporation of many 'peoples' in the Roman Empire of late antiquity, to the formation of supra-regional nations in modern times. In each case, Durkheim argued, social life had been rearranged less by an extension in the volume or population of society than by an increase in dynamic density. Some traditional societies, such as China or India before modern times, attained large volumes while remaining attached to a pattern of segmental, village-centered, dispersed solidarities. Yet, other societies small in volume but dense in structure – we can cite the Netherlands or Belgium, for example – have developed modern forms of solidarity based on a broad freedom of association. Thus, the fateful changes of modern times have been associated specifically with growth in dynamic density. Only dynamic density brings the members of society into more direct contact and dependence upon one another. The economic consequence is that competition is heightened and producers have greater need to differentiate themselves from one another. The division of labor is accordingly extended. The integrative consequence is that individuals and groups are tied into a common set of 'markets' for influence and associative performance. A richer and more supple set of associational ties must then be developed for members of society to feel effectively supported and adequately related to one another in their everyday social lives.

Durkheim wrote of this enrichment of the division of labor and associational life as the increasing intensity of civilization.[30] At the end of Book Two and in Book Three of *The Division of Labor in Society* (1933), he argued that growing intensity is a response to heightened density, one that best emerges with the sort of spontaneity that Adam Smith observed in the adjustment of the division of labor to prior increases in the extent of the market. As represented in Figure 6.2, increased density causes an outward shift of the influence curve while increased intensity causes an outward shift of the associative performance curve. Together, the outward shifts in the influence and associative performance curves move the point of equilibrium to E'. The new equilibrium is reached at a point representing a higher level of integrative or solidarizing operations. It indicates growth in the integrative system.

Influence and social integration

The concept of influence as a generalized medium may be clarified if we make some brief comparisons with money. We will see that in some

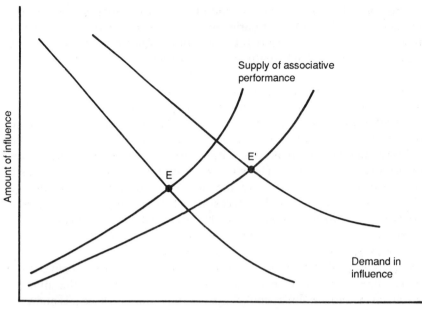

Figure 6.2 *Outward shifts in the schedules for influence and associative
performance, representing growth in the system of solidary relationships*

respects influence is similar to money while in others it is different due
to its integrative specialization.

Like exchanges of money for goods and service, exchanges of influence
for associative performances have an essentially contractual quality. The
rationality implicit in exchanges of influence for associative performance,
as discussed in the previous section, presumes and depends on this contractual quality. An actor who becomes the object of another's efforts to exert
influence retains the right to accept or reject the proffered relationship.
The amount of influence that is offered may be deemed insufficient. Or
possibly the expected associative performance involves conduct the actor
cannot or will not undertake. Just as one can refuse to sell an object of
economic value, one can reject the claim of a solidary relationship asserted
by an influential person. This contractual or voluntary nature of influence
relationships differs sharply from relationships based on power.[31] When
power is used to issue a command, obligations are imposed on people
without respect to their agreement. To be sure, they retain a choice
between obedience and suffering punishment for disobedience, and in that
sense they act voluntarily. Typically, however, the obligations become
formally incumbent on them regardless of their wills. They do not have a
choice about accepting the obligations, short of disobedience or leaving
the power structure in question.

As we have already noted in a couple of connections, influence is ordinarily used against a background of actually or potentially competing influences. Like money, but perhaps unlike power, influence is a medium that adjusts flexibly to competitive situations. The competitive nature of influence as a medium points to the importance of the reference group structuring of social situations. Both in making and in accepting offers of influence, actors typically reach judgments about how to secure the most advantageous relationships from arrays of opportunities presented by their respective reference group structures. Thus, latent or underlying reference group structures sensitize actors to the alternative relationships that may be foregone or placed at risk with every 'contract' for influence and associative performance. The stronger a reference group is in terms of previously established solidarity, the more certainly an actor will attend to the social support he or she places at risk by favoring a competing or conflicting tie with another group. Notions similar to opportunity costs accordingly enter into the formation of specific solidary relationships.

In one key respect, however, the formation of solidary relationships contrasts sharply with the *quid pro quo* form of economic contracts. A dampening of the competitive and conflictual potentials of the influence mechanism, and a stabilization of cross-cutting, pluralistic ties, is bound up with this difference. In economic contexts, the actor who sells given property rights may properly contract to convey them only to one other party. Attempts to sell the same rights in the same resources to more than one party are fraudulent. If a plurality of actors must control the same 'community' resources, such complex legal forms as condominiums or joint stock ownership must be used to sort out the rights. Where solidary relationships are in question, however, 'contracts' between parties are not necessarily exclusive. Unlike money, influence does not necessarily require actors to choose among the offers of solidary relationship to which they are responding. An adept associate performance can be a positive response to a plurality of competing influences at the same time. Every big city politician who promises to expand police services to give middle-class homeowners additional security while offering new jobs to poor minorities has a common-sense grasp of the principle. Solidarity can be enhanced by finding a measure that responds to competing influences and bypasses conflict or potential conflict.

When complex collectivities or communities are developing policy, new proposals are often designed to mediate among the interests of a variety of groups that have exerted their influence in prior discussions. The capacity of associative performances to create new ties of solidarity by promoting common interests among previously competing groups is a mark of their integrative specialization in social life. Insofar as this capacity constitutes an important means for limiting social competition, sociologists have perhaps underestimated the extent to which acting under cross-pressures is a positive feature of associational life. The situation of acting under cross-pressures, though it involves conflicting expectations and social tension, cannot generally be as paralyzing of creative and resolute conduct as sociologists often suggest. The leader of a community who devises a means of acting in response to diverse sources of influence stands to gain a large quantity of influence. Where the policies are important and the groups truly diverse, the influence can be so vast as to give a leader – a Franklin Roosevelt after the political successes of the New Deal, for example – a nearly unassailable position in the hearts of the citizenry. Thus, the stakes to be gained in public life by creative design of associative performances are large, and they derive from the possibility of concluding policy 'contracts' with a wide range of groups.

Ever since Tocqueville, comment on the reluctance of leaders to alienate any notable source of influence among the public has been a hackneyed observation about American politics. Nevertheless, rejections of influence do occur and sometimes play a large part in politics. Groups are at times removed from effective participation in public discussion when their needs and influence appear difficult to satisfy without alienating other groups whose influence has already gained them control over public policy. Such disenfranchisement seems especially common when newly articulated needs and influences also challenge the customary normative frameworks of middle-class styles of using influence. In recent years, American authorities have found it easier to ignore the homeless, the mentally ill, welfare families, and drug-users from poor neighborhoods than to abandon the middle-class moralisms underpinning public policy and respond to their needs.

Influence also seems to differ from money by circulating in differentiated forms that cannot readily be converted to one another. Given the nature of money and accounting procedures in a modern economy, cash, checks, bank deposits, and even credit lines are formally equivalent. If it is convenient for Actor A to give Actor B a check for $100 and for Actor B to return $100 in cash, equivalent amounts have been exchanged so long as no interest accrues through a delay in the return payment. Moreover, the equivalence stands without regard to differences between the social roles of A and B. Money in a like amount is formally equivalent regardless of who owns it or spends it, whether business corporation, government agency, non-profit foundation or household. All holdings of money are formally interchangeable regardless of the industry in which it is earned or expended. In the case of influence, however, there tends to be a difference predicated precisely upon the different roles played by A and B.[32] If A is a physician and B is a politician, the forms of influence they use in their occupational roles will be different and not interchangeable. If B receives influence from A, he is not thereby enabled to advise patients. If A receives influence from B, he cannot thereby exercise public leadership. However, there are specialized uses for which once-circulated influence may be recirculated. The political leader may be able to re-use the physician's influence – invoking his or her name, titles, statuses, prestige etc. – if public discussion involves a matter of health policy. Or if, as a private citizen, he or she claims the cooperation of family and friends in order to adhere to a medical regimen, the physician's influence might also be invoked. Similarly, the physician might recirculate the politician's influence in soliciting the cooperation of colleagues on a matter of public policy affecting the conditions of medical practice.

In cases such as these, recirculated influence must be brought to bear in the social settings engaged by the second or derivative user. The new situations are often regulated by very different standards for assessing uses of influence. For example, the influential physician who wishes to shape policies on public health and the politician who would cite that physician's views must deal with the procedures for deliberating on policy, not the procedures for making decisions on patient care. Moreover, practical features of the new setting may differ along with normative standards. Physicians usually exercise influence in settings characterized by mutual support among colleagues and the comparatively clear-cut hierarchies of medical decision-making. Politicians typically act in more competitive and less tightly constraining situations. As compared with physicians using influence in a hospital, politicians must anticipate opposition from spokesmen who can be far more freewheeling in their pronouncements and challenges. Making the transition from one style and setting for exercising influence to the other often proves difficult, as many medical scientists have learned when giving legislative testimony.

The conditions of recirculating influence thus appear to be subject to additive constraints concerning the specialized statuses of the actors involved. If a politician receives medical influence, he properly re-uses it only when a politician (a first set of status-linked constraints) can appropriately invoke influence bearing on medical matters (a second set of status-linked constraints). It follows that the receipt or acceptance of influence is not quite the same as depositing a check in a general-purpose bank account, for the various forms of influence that one 'deposits' do not mingle. This circumstance places important integrative pressures on actors who attempt to speak with influence on behalf of solidary groups. They must hold stocks of a variety of forms of influence on hand to be recirculated when necessary. In order to do this productively, they must sustain solidary ties with a range of groups holding influence in the particular social settings of importance to them. But in securing their own influence in this particularistic fashion, they also tend, by reciprocation, to protect the efficacy of other figures who are influential in the same networks of solidary relationships.

The specialization among forms of influence should not be regarded as a restriction in its generalization. Influence seems to be generalized in relation to the inclusiveness of the communities in which it is accepted. The specialization of a form of influence does not diminish its generalization. If the professional influence of a prestigious physician is respected throughout the national medical community or, when health matters are at stake, the entire society, it is highly generalized, however specialized. Thus, the late physician, Dr Paul Dudley White, who played a key role in establishing exercise as part of recuperation after heart attacks and as a measure to prevent heart attacks, commanded highly generalized influence even though it centered on the field of cardiology. Moreover, a crucial aspect of the generalization of influence concerns the reciprocal acceptability of its various forms among reference groups that are set off from one another by lines of differentiation and segmentation. Professional and political forms of influence may not be mutually convertible, but if they both circulate through a wide variety of solidary relationships they are both highly generalized.

Normal equilibrium and social pathologies

In developing his notion of a spontaneous equilibrium of solidarity between the moral density and the intensity of social ties in a society, Durkheim recognized the importance of many disturbing factors. He argued that a truly spontaneous equilibrium, in which members of society act freely yet responsibly, autonomously yet with loyalty to others, was a difficult condition to protect. Spontaneous equilibrium could be threatened by a variety of conditions, especially in times of rapid social change and dislocation of major institutions.[33] In continuing his analysis of these conditions and revising his earlier formulations, he categorized, in *Suicide* (1951), the factors disturbing equilibria of solidarity under four headings.[34] These four categories constitute the general types of 'social pathology', egoism and altruism, anomie and fatalism.

Many scholars, not least Parsons himself,[35] have interpreted the scheme of social pathologies as resting essentially on Durkheim's personal value judgments. They have suggested that the social conditions labelled pathological are not intrinsically better or worse than other conditions, but were simply made to appear so by the force of Durkheim's ideology. People who participate in cultures different from the one with which Durkheim identified may accordingly value one or another of the pathological conditions over the condition of normal, spontaneous equilibrium. Americans may actually favor a degree of egoism and perhaps anomie as well. Soviets, by contrast, may favor degrees of altruism and fatalism. On this view, it is not possible to justify in sociological terms the attribution of 'normality' to the conditions of spontaneous equilibrium favored by Durkheim.

Against this established interpretation, I wish to pose a different account of Durkheim's analysis. Durkheim drew a careful analogy between normal solidarity, the result of spontaneous equilibrium, and the economists' notion of the equilibrium reached by a free and competitive market. In the economic model, any force that disturbs the processes of supply, of demand, or of market integration, will produce an equilibrium that is less efficient in satisfying the wants of members of society. Durkheim intended his categories of pathology simply as a classification of forces that drive the equilibrium in solidary relationships away from its theoretically optimum point. A social pathology is thus an analogue of an economic force that prevents a market from clearing at the point of optimum efficiency. A social pathology distorts the processes of reaching equilibrium in a particular field of social relationships and reduces the actual solidarity that will be generated.

However difficult it may be to realize in specific empirical studies, the basic idea of pathology is both precise and nonjudgmental on a plane of general theory. Durkheim himself recognized that pathological conditions in society are closely bound up with positive social values. In arguing that social ethics favoring progress are a major source of anomie, Durkheim hardly intended to attack them. Rather, he intended to underscore the perplexities of social life by highlighting the human costs of values that stood at the core of his own belief system.[36]

We must also recognize that Durkheim's idea of normal equilibrium does not imply that every community, every arena of social relationships and every society should institute the same pattern of solidarity. Two considerations bearing on this problem should be acknowledged. First, in Durkheim's conception, normal equilibrium is a spontaneous, hence constantly changing, balance between a state of density and a state of intensity. Factors deeply rooted in the moral culture of a society affect its state of density. Established patterns of solidary relationship shape the conditions of intensity. Thus, the point of normal equilibrium will always be a momentary adjustment to well-institutionalized but evolving characteristics of a specific society. Second, various institutional domains of any given society will have their own states of density and intensity, hence, their own needs for an equilibrium of solidarity. Military and academic institutions, families and business firms, local communities and far-flung industries, regions of the nation, social classes and status groups will all adopt somewhat different patterns of solidarity. An overall societal equilibrium will be a complicated aggregation of many different forms of solidarity. Deviations from the point of normal equilibrium will be strongly valued in many settings. Often the deviations will be firmly rooted in the 'functional' requisites of specific kinds of institutions – the military's need for discipline, a nursing staff's need for devotion to others, a stock brokerage's need for individualism in seeking profit.

Figure 6.3 uses the influence and associative performance schedules to interpret Durkheim's four types of social pathology in a more precise fashion. Two of the pathologies, egoism and altruism, are treated as conditions that alter the shape of the influence schedule. Anomie and fatalism are treated as conditions altering the associative performance schedule. Egoism and altruism are pathologies that affect the conditions of demand for solidary relationships, while anomie and fatalism affect conditions of the genesis and supply of solidarity.

Egoism is a condition in which actors need not be strongly identified with one another in a collective entity in order to associate, but may act on a basis of enlightened self-interest in forming their mutual ties. In egoistic

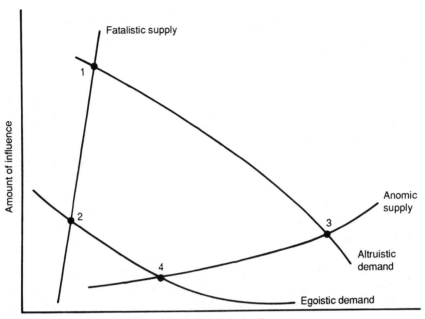

Figure 6.3 *'Pathological' schedules for influence and associative performance*

settings, institutional conditions cause the influence curve to fall more sharply or rapidly as it slopes down to the right. Influence is exercised through appeals to the self-interest, or perhaps enlightened self-interest, of the performer. It does not operate on a basis of firm integration of social units into a collectivity or community, and the weakness of the resulting solidarity comprises a pathology for people who may need to rely upon their associates. Only if the quantity of associative performance gained in exchange for influence is very large will egoistic actors expend influence which in the future may be used to activate duties they must perform. In American society, egoism is often found in the world of small, independent businesses where the animating spirit of most conduct is a firm sense of self-interest.

By contrast, altruism is a condition in which strong mutual identification is a necessary condition of association. The premise of conduct is that one will act in the collective interest. Altruism addresses conditions in which the influence curve is deflected upwards and falls off slowly, such that the activated solidary relations imply strong communal ties. More influence will be expended in order to gain performances. The performer will receive in return for fulfilling his obligations far greater capacity to activate the reciprocal solidary ties in the future. Altruistic uses of influence stress the need to perform in the collective or communal welfare, implying a stronger point of leverage for activation of reciprocal obligations. But altruism can be experienced as a pathology by people who, constrained always to act in the collective interest, lose a capacity for autonomous judgment and action. Altruism in a moderate form is a common element in what Parsons, late in his career, called the fiduciary character of parental roles in the family. In caring for and socializing their children, parents have a duty to subordinate their own immediate interests to the welfare of the family and the long-term well-being of its next generation.

Anomie arises when the social constraints regulating the ties of reciprocal obligations between actors are weakened. In formal terms, anomie may be conceptualized as the deflection of the performance curve downward to the right, so that it rises only slowly from the horizontal axis. It expresses the schedule that emerges when performances can be gained readily and cheaply in terms of the collective obligations represented by influence, when solidary 'costs' of supply are low due to a weakening of the underlying conditions of solidarity. Although associations are readily formed under anomic conditions, and as Durkheim recognized anomie can encourage innovation in social life, actors are likely to experience the relative weakness and incalculability of constraints as a pathology. Whether others will acknowledge their duties when one attempts to influence them remains frequently in doubt. As Durkheim emphasized, anomie is often found in rapidly changing industries and sciences where standards of work are open to rapid, disorienting mutation.

Fatalism consists in a great strengthening of social constraints. It characterizes situations in which the performance curve rises sharply, nearly parallel to the vertical axis. Solidary ties and obligations are strong and the consequences of any associative performance are determinate and burdensome, hence 'costs' are very high. Specific performances can be gained only through the expenditure of large amounts of influence, that is, great capacity for the performer subsequently to activate the reciprocal solidary ties. If the dilemma facing the actor in anomic situations is whether his or her conduct will have any determinate or determinable consequences in the field of solidary relationships, the dilemma facing the actor in fatalistic situations is whether he or she can dare to act knowing the weight of consequences that may attach to the course of action. When the burdens of exercising one's judgment are so heavy that one hardly dares to act, a pathology is experienced. Among the institutional settings of social life in contemporary societies, high security prisons are perhaps the most fatalistic.

Figure 6.3 shows four points of equilibrium at intersections of pathologically deflected influence and associative performance schedules. The schedules have been drawn to highlight the hypothetical differences among four distinct patterns of social pathology:

1   Fatalistic-altruistic solidarity. Military life and life in monastic orders may be examples. The quantity of solidarity is restricted, but the

component ties are firm and reliable, though requiring a strong discipline from participants.

2 Fatalistic-egoistic solidarity. This may be a common pattern among participants in organized crime, whose relations with one another may be supported by firm, indeed forceful, constraints yet also rest on giving free play to self-interest.

3 Anomic-altruistic solidarity. The practice of social work in settings within the American welfare system appear to involve this pattern. The meaning of the professional role rests on an altruism, but in fulfilling their duties social workers must participate in relationships that involve the manipulation of rules and social constraints by many different parties.

4 Anomic-egoistic solidarity. The efforts of interest groups and voluntary associations to wield influence over public policy occur under this pattern of solidarity in most American communities. The competition is open and free, with a great variety of interests receiving a voice, but levels of responsibility are low.

The sociological interest in identifying general patterns of solidarity is partly to develop hypotheses about differences in the dynamic and experiential qualities of solidarity under varying conditions. For example, the quantity of solidarity generated in a fatalistic-altruistic system will be much less than in an anomic-egoistic system. However, for individual participants in specific relationships, the solidarity will have far greater strength in a fatalistic-altruistic system. The influence and associative performance schedules, with their pathological deflections, should serve as a guide to forming and interpreting hypotheses.

Discussion

The purpose of the present theoretical exercise has been to introduce in direct and spare terms a conceptual apparatus that can serve as a core theory for sociology. By contrast with other rational actor theories, however, the present scheme is intended to provide connection to the conceptual riches of the general theory of action and the tradition of institutional analysis in sociology. To gain the benefit of these riches, to be sure, a great deal of further work will be necessary. It may be helpful to conclude by simply listing some chief items on the research agenda:

1 Studies must be made of the institutional forces that shape the influence and associative performance schedules for relationships in various sectors of society.

2 Research must be undertaken on the interplay between the mechanisms of solidarity and the market system of the economy, the power structure of the polity, and the value-commitment mechanisms of the fiduciary system. These are complicated matters involving many of the

basic structural elements of the society, for example, legal structures, class systems, and so forth. A dynamic theory of solidarity should enable sociologists to analyze these matters more effectively than heretofore.

3   The patterns of social pathology and related deflections of the influence and associative performance schedules should be used in comparative studies of integrative institutions. For example, American society appears to be characterized by a pattern of egoistic-anomic integration. Japanese society is more altruistic and fatalistic in its mode of integration. France is more altruistic than America and probably more anomic than Germany. Studies of Ireland suggest that it may be egoistic and fatalistic (Scheper-Hughes, 1979).

4   Following the lead of Baum (1975), solidary relationships must be analyzed at the general action level as well as the social system level. It then becomes possible to treat the affective and sentimental qualities of involvement in solidary or communal ties more directly than has been suggested in this essay.

5   The writings of Simmel, Tönnies and other figures in the phenomenological tradition should be studied for help in analyzing the formal and essential qualities of solidary relationships of various kinds.

Notes

This chapter previously appeared in French under the title 'Influence et solidarité, définir un fondement théorique à la sociologie', *Sociologie et sociétés*, 21 (1), April 1989, pp. 117–42. It is republished with the permission of Professor Guy Rocher and the editors.

1. On Parsons's methodology of theory development, see Lidz (1986), Bershady (1973).

2. Parsons's understanding of these problems was based throughout his career on the method of convergence developed in his first book, *The Structure of Social Action* (1937).

3. See Parsons (1961) for an introduction to the four-function paradigm.

4. See, for example, the focus on integrative categories in the presentation of action theory in Parsons (1966; 1971). The integrative focus is most firmly pronounced in the manuscript on which Parsons was working at his death, *The American Societal Community* (forthcoming).

5. See Parsons (1954; 1964; 1967b; 1969a; 1969d; 1969e); also 'Some Reflections on the Institutional Framework of Economic Development' and 'The Principal Structures of Community' in Parsons (1960); 'Some Comments on the Sociology of Karl Marx' in Parsons (1967a); and 'The Mass Media and the Structure of American Society' (with W. White) in Parsons (1969a).

6. Thus, his original essay on influence (1969c) was followed by intensive discussions of its difficulties with graduate students, research assistants and collaborators. I was privileged to participate in a number of these sessions. Parsons introduced several reformulations into his theory of influence in the succeeding years. See 'Postscript to Chapter 15', appended to the original essay on influence when it was republished in Parsons (1969a), 'Polity and Society: Some General Considerations', the concluding chapter of Parsons (1969a), and the discussion of influence in Parsons and Platt (1973). The treatment of influence in *The American Societal Community* (forthcoming) shows further reformulation, but did not settle Parsons's own sense of uncertainty over a number of problems.

7. The manuscript of this work may be examined in the Talcott Parsons Papers at the Harvard University Archives. It is currently being edited by the present author for eventual publication.

8. On this last aspect of the study of solidarity, a classic essay is Baum (1975).

9. An elementary overview of the theory of media was presented in Parsons (1961).

10. Parsons (1969d; 1969e). For treatment of the business firm–household relationship, see also Parsons and Smelser (1956). For the economic theory in the background of this analysis, see Keynes (1936) and Knight (1951).

11. For example, Merton, 'Continuities in the Theory of Reference Groups and Social Structure' and 'Patterns of Influence: Local and Cosmopolitan Influentials', Chs IX and X in Merton (1957); Lazarsfeld et al. (1948); and Berelson et al. (1954).

12. Katz and Lazarsfeld (1955). Oddly, this work is not cited in Parsons's essay on influence. But in his teaching and in personal discussions about influence, Parsons made quite clear that it had been a major source for his own theoretical efforts in the late 1950s and early 1960s.

13. The work of more immediate influence was Stouffer (1955), but *The American Soldier* (Stouffer et al., 1949) had been an early and large source of research on influence and opinion change.

14. Katz and Lazarsfeld (1955). Another key source for Parsons on the importance of primary groups in social integration was Shils (1951).

15. See 'Some Problems of General Theory in Sociology', in Parsons (1977); also Ch. 2, 'The Cognitive Complex: Knowledge, Rationality, Learning, Competence, Intelligence', in Parsons and Platt (1973); and Lidz (1976; 1981).

16. 'The Sick Role and the Role of the Physician Reconsidered', 'Research with Human Subjects and the "Professional Complex"' and 'Health and Disease: a Sociological and Action Perspective', in Parsons (1978); also Parsons and Platt (1973).

17. This point is a major burden of Parsons's (1937) discussion of Durkheim's work in *The Structure of Social Action* and in Parsons (1967b). It can also be identified as a theme in Parsons (1954; 1964; 1969b).

18. For example, Parsons examined and critiqued for his own purposes such works as Dahl (1956), Downs (1957) and Buchanan and Tullock (1965).

19. For example, Becker (1976) was a work that Parsons believed profoundly misguided although he acknowledged its brilliance and creativity.

20. Mark Gould (pers. comm.) has recently argued that Parsons conceded too much to neoclassical economics in admitting this point. Basing his argument on recent critiques of the neoclassical framework within economics itself as well as on his own critique using Parsonian and Marxian perspectives in sociology, Gould now suggests that a more radical judgment of utilitarian economics is necessary. This view will be presented in a series of forthcoming essays. I am presenting my theory of solidarity in terms that are consistent with the older Parsonian evaluation of the premises of economic theory. I reserve judgment on what changes in the formulation of the theory of solidarity may be required by Gould's critique of economics. It may prove to be the case that recognizing solidarity to be problematic along with questions of utility in every concrete economic relationship is an alternate way of making *part* of Gould's argument.

21. My formulations may be compared with the utilitarian theory developed by Hechter (1987). Hechter's formulations have an engaging precision, but are subject to all of the limitations that Parsons identified in utilitarianism. Hechter's criticisms of 'normativists', which would include action theorists, are directed at a crude parody. They do not actually engage the major arguments of *The Structure of Social Action* (1937) or the other selected works of Parsons that Hechter cites. Hechter does not cite or indicate familiarity with Parsons's major writings on influence, solidarity, or integrative institutions.

22. I draw here on the conception of solidarity developed by Emile Durkheim in *The Division of Labor in Society* (1933, tr. Simpson, and 1984, tr. Halls), first published in French in 1893. See especially Ch. II on Mechanical Solidarity and Ch. III on Organic Solidarity.

23. Compare Georg Simmel's discussions of membership and participation in social circles, in Wolff (1950).

24. Compare Parsons (1951), esp. Ch. VII, 'Deviant Behavior and the Mechanisms of Social Control'. Unfortunately, Parsons never attempted a close re-analysis of this material in the context of the theory of influence as a generalized medium.

25. In designing the figures presented in this chapter I have enjoyed the assistance of my son, Larry Lidz, who first ventured to draw them on a computer screen.

26. See Parsons (1969b). The theme is developed far more fully in Parsons (forthcoming).

27. Simmel's writings on the formation of social circles in modern societies constitute the major classic resource in sociology for examining the interconnections among independent arenas of influence. See Wolff (1950) and Simmel, 'Group Expansion and the Development of Individuality', in Levine (1971).

28. Tocqueville (1945). See esp. Ch. III for the initial presentation of the concepts of social condition of democracy and social condition of aristocracy.

29. The interpretation of Durkheim's concept of moral or dynamic density has involved a great deal of confusion. The present interpretation is based on a rejection of Parsons's idea that Durkheim's explanation of the growth of the division of labor and organic solidarity ultimately pointed to population pressure and hence was 'biological' (Parsons, 1937: 323), and also the view developed by Traugott (1978: introduction) and elaborated by Alexander (1982) that Durkheim propounded a 'material' explanation. In my understanding, which cannot be fully justified here, Durkheim emphasized that the key causative factor is 'moral' density, which consists in the bonds of solidarity that hold the members of society into a unified network of relationships. This explanation is entirely consistent with the emphasis placed on moral culture and social institutions in the most basic concept of Durkheim's early works, the collective conscience. Durkheim emphasizes 'material' density because it is more accessible to observation and measurement than 'moral' density, and appears to provide an approximate index of states of the underlying dynamic factor. Consistent with this scheme of interpretation, Durkheim uses 'dynamic' density as an alternative term for moral density, not material density.

30. See especially Durkheim (1933), Book 2, Ch. IV and V.

31. I address in these terms the differences between money and influence, on the one hand, and power and value commitments, on the other hand, that Parsons (1969c; 1969d) addressed in terms of the positive and negative sanctions on which generalization of the respective symbolic media rests.

32. Parsons anticipated parts of the following discussion. In his initial paper on influence as a generalized medium, he emphasized the differentiation of influence into a plurality of forms. He tended to identify these forms with subsystems of the societal community, however. See Parsons (1969: 419ff) Later, he tended to treat specific kinds of influence as bound to the functioning of given institutional complexes, such as academia. See Parsons and Platt (1973). Obscured in his discussions was the question of how specialization among forms of influence should be related theoretically to the basic idea of the generalization of the medium.

33. This is the general argument of Book 3 of Durkheim (1933).

34. Durkheim (1951). The concept of fatalistic suicide, although logically integral to Durkheim's scheme of analysis, is mentioned only in passing in one footnote (1951: 276).

35. Compare Parsons (1937: 371ff). Parsons never changed his mind regarding this tough criticism of Durkheim's concept of pathologies.

36. See Durkheim (1951), esp. Book 3, Ch. III, 'Practical Consequences'.

References

Alexander, J.C. (1982) *Theoretical Logic in Sociology*, vol. 2, *The Antinomies of Classical Thought: Marx and Durkheim*. London: Routledge & Kegan Paul.

Baum, R.C. (1975) 'The System of Solidarities', *Indian Journal of Social Research*, 16 (1 and 2): 305–53 (special issue in honour of Talcott Parsons).

Becker, G. (1976) *The Economic Approach to Human Behavior*. Chicago: University of Chicago Press.

Berelson, B.R., Lazarsfeld, P.F. and McPhee, W.N. (1954) *Voting*. Chicago: University of Chicago Press.

Bershady, H.J. (1973) *Ideology and Social Knowledge*. Oxford: Blackwell.

Buchanan, J.M. and Tullock, G. (1965) *The Calculus of Consent*. Ann Arbor, Michigan: University of Michigan Press.

Dahl, R.A. (1956) *A Preface to Democracy*. Chicago: University of Chicago Press.

Downs, A. (1957) *An Economic Theory of Democracy*. New York: Harper.

Durkheim, E. (1933) *The Division of Labor in Society*, tr. G. Simpson. New York: Free Press. Also tr. W.D. Halls (1984). First published in French, 1893.

Durkheim, E. (1950) *The Rules of Sociological Method*, tr. G.E.G. Cathin. New York: Free Press. Also tr. W.D. Halls (1982). First published in French, 1895.

Durkheim, E. (1951) *Suicide*. New York: Free Press. First published in French, 1897.

Hechter, M. (1987) *Principles of Group Solidarity*. Berkeley and Los Angeles: University of California Press.

Katz, E. and Lazarsfeld, P.F. (1955) *Personal Influence*. New York: Free Press.

Keynes, J.M. (1936) *The General Theory of Employment, Interest and Money*. London: Macmillan.

Knight, F. (1951) *The Economic Organization*. New York: Harper.

Kuhn, T.S. (1970) *The Structure of Scientific Revolutions*, rev. edn. Chicago: University of Chicago Press.

Lazarsfeld, P.F., Berelson, B.R. and Gaudet, H. (1948) *The People's Choice*. New York: Columbia University Press.

Levine, D.N. (ed.) (1971) *Georg Simmel on Individuality and Social Forms*. Chicago: University of Chicago Press.

Lidz, V. (1976) 'Introduction to General Action Analysis', pp. 124–50 in J.J. Loubser, A. Effrat, R.C. Baum and V. Lidz (eds), *Explorations in General Theory in Social Science*. New York: Free Press.

Lidz, V. (1981) 'Transformational Theory and the Internal Environment of Action Systems', pp. 205–33 in K. Knorr-Cetina and A.V. Cicourel (eds), *Advances in Social Theory and Methodology: Toward an Integration of Micro- and Macro-sociologies*. London: Routledge & Kegan Paul.

Lidz, V. (1986) 'Parsons and Empirical Sociology', pp. 141–82 in S.Z. Klausner and V. Lidz, *The Nationalization of the Social Sciences*. Philadelphia: University of Pennsylvania Press.

Merton, R.K. (1957) *Social Theory and Social Structure*, rev. edn. New York: Free Press.

Parsons, T. (1937) *The Structure of Social Action*. New York: McGraw-Hill.

Parsons, T. (1951) *The Social System*. New York: Free Press.

Parsons, T. (1954) 'A Revised Analytical Approach to the Theory of Social Stratification', pp. 386–439 in T. Parsons, *Essays in Sociological Theory*, rev. edn. New York: Free Press.

Parsons, T. (1960) *Structure and Process in Modern Societies*. New York: Free Press.

Parsons, T. (1961) 'An Outline of the Social System', pp. 30–79 in T. Parsons, E.A. Shils, K.D. Naegele and J.R. Pitts (eds), *Theories of Society*. New York: Free Press.

Parsons, T. (1964) 'Social Strains in America', pp. 209–29 in D. Bell (ed.), *The Radical Right*. Garden City, NY: Anchor Books.

Parsons, T. (1966) *Societies: Evolutionary and Comparative Perspectives*. Englewood Cliffs, NJ: Prentice-Hall.

Parsons, T. (1967a) *Sociological Theory and Modern Society*. New York: Free Press.

Parsons, T. (1967b) 'Durkheim's Contribution to the Theory of Integration of Social Systems', pp. 3–34 in Parsons (1967a).

Parsons, T. (1968) 'Professions', *International Encyclopedia of the Social Sciences*. New York: Free Press/Macmillan.

Parsons, T. (1969a) *Politics and Social Structure*. New York: Free Press.

Parsons, T. (1969b) 'Full Citizenship for the Negro American?', pp. 422–65 in Parsons (1967a).

Parsons, T. (1969c) 'On the Concept of Influence', pp. 405–38 in Parsons (1969a).

Parsons, T. (1969d) 'On the Concept of Political Power', pp. 352–404 in Parsons (1969a).

Parsons, T. (1969e) '"Voting" and the Equilibrium of the American Political System', pp. 204–40 in Parsons (1969a).

Parsons, T. (1971) *The System of Modern Societies*. Englewood Cliffs, NJ: Prentice-Hall.

Parsons, T. (1977) *Social Systems and the Evolution of Action Theory*. New York: Free Press.

Parsons, T. (1978) *Action Theory and the Human Condition*. New York: Free Press.

Parsons, T. (forthcoming) *The American Societal Community*.

Parsons, T. and Platt, G.M. (1973) *The American University*. Cambridge, Mass: Harvard University Press.

Parsons, T. and Smelser, N.J. (1956) *Economy and Society*. New York: Free Press.

Scheper-Hughes, N. (1979) *Saints, Scholars and Schizophrenics*. Berkeley, Calif.: University of California Press.

Shils, E.A. (1951) 'The Study of the Primary Group', pp. 44–69 in D. Lerner and H.D. Lasswell (eds), *The Policy Sciences*, Stanford, Calif.: Stanford University Press.

Stouffer, S.A. (1955) *Communism, Conformity and Civil Liberties*. New York: Doubleday.

Stouffer, S.A., Suchman, E.A., De Vinney, L.C., Star, S.A. and Williams, R.M. Jr (1949) *The American Soldier*, 3 vols. Princeton, NJ: Princeton University Press.

Tocqueville, A. de (1945) *Democracy in America*. New York: Knopf. First published in French, 1835.

Traugott, M. (1978) *Emile Durkheim on Morality and Society*. Chicago: University of Chicago Press.

Weber, M. (1968) *Economy and Society*. New York: Bedminster.

Wolff, K. (ed.) (1950) *The Sociology of Georg Simmel*. New York: Free Press.

7

THE CENTRAL SIGNIFICANCE OF 'RELIGION' IN SOCIAL THEORY: PARSONS AS AN EPICAL THEORIST

Roland Robertson

Interpreting Parsons now

Talcott Parsons has typically been discussed in two major frames of reference. He has been viewed as a formal sociological theorist, with considerable attention to the technicalities of his schemata; while, on the other hand, his work has been inspected in metatheoretical and ideological terms. Some have attempted to combine these two perspectives, but there have been few who have been concerned directly with Parsons as an interpreter of trends in and dilemmas of the human condition. More specifically, while there have been those who have sought to explicate, often in very negative terms, what Parsons was 'really saying', there is no tradition which deals directly with Parsons's own attempts to 'be interpretive'. I argue that the greatest problem in coming to terms with the writings of Talcott Parsons hinges upon this lacuna.

While Parsons was certainly constrained and indeed restricted by his desire to professionalize sociology and advance it as an 'objective science', it is clear to me that he was also driven by a concern to comprehend and display, both theoretically and empirically, the contours of global sociocultural change. The most exciting thing to me about Parsons's writings is that he was always keen to understand the significance both of the major existential predicaments of the human condition – sexuality, sickness, death, alienation, exploitation, inequality, gender differences, prejudice and so on – and of the shifting terms in which the world has been defined and politically contested along religious, ideological and other grounds.

Parsons did not live to see either the full rise to global prominence of contemporary Japan and East Asia (although he certainly was conscious of the probability of that development) or the return of Germany to a central position on the world scene. Nor did he live long enough to witness either the resurgence of Islam or the retreat of communism. Yet he wrote a great deal about matters which have a strong bearing upon these, and other, globally significant circumstances. The often tedious discussions of his architectonic endeavors, on the one hand, and diagnoses of his position on the conventional ideological, Left–Right continuum, on the other, have obscured what he had to say about such central issues.

Much of what Parsons had to say along interpretive, world-historical lines was expressed in his writings about religion. However, most specialists in the sociology of religion have apparently found Parsons too wide-ranging and burdened to incorporate his work into the confines of their carefully circumscribed studies, while – at the other extreme – more fashionable, 'secular' writers have apparently ignored his work on religion precisely because he dared to proclaim that religion is still relevant to the contemporary world. In contrast, I consider the writings of Talcott Parsons on religion as the major entry to crucial themes in the series consisting of *theory*, *America* and *the world*; arguing that it is in his work on religion that one finds encapsulated most of the crucial questions concerning his social theory, his philosophy, his methodology, his image of world history and his own value-commitments. That is an empirical claim. In other words I am arguing that Parsons did in fact use 'religion' as a vehicle for the expression of many of his most significant thoughts. Whether he, at the same time, demonstrated the ongoing centrality of religion is, in principle, a separate matter.[1]

I address both of these issues in this discussion, claiming that Parsons was in large part engaged in 'epical' theorizing (Wolin, 1969; Wolin, 1970; Lassman and Velody, 1989a: 170–89). As stated by Sheldon Wolin (1970: 4), epical theory involves the fusion of 'concepts, symbols, and language ... into a great political gesture towards the world, a thought-deed inspired by the hope that now or some day action will be joined to theory and become the means for making a great theoretical statement in the world'. In their interesting exploration of the meaning and significance of Weber's (1948c) 'Science as a Vocation', Peter Lassman and Irving Velody (1989a) discuss, *inter re*, the tensions in Max Weber's work between 'pure' scientific work and the search for large-scale historical meaning, in the process indicting Parsons for having presented a sanitized version of Weber as a value-neutral, 'pure' social scientist (Lassman and Velody, 1989b). My own claim is, however, that Parsons's work itself exhibits similar tensions – although in less agonistic and 'tortured' form. Parsons's writings, taken as a whole, should be regarded as epical in roughly the same way that Lassman and Velody ascribe that characteristic to Max Weber. On top of that, I argue that Parsons was a global theorist – a 'calling' which Weber definitely disavowed.

The general significance of Parsons's writings on religion

As I have said, little sustained attention has been given to Parsons's analyses of religion. This is particularly disturbing in view of the fact that the topic of religion thoroughly permeates his *œuvre*, to the extent that it would be plausible to maintain that religion became increasingly central in his overall action theory. From even before his translation of Weber's

Protestant Ethic and the Spirit of Capitalism (Weber, 1930) to his very last writings, Parsons never relinquished his deep interest in religion. Indeed, concern with religion and related issues was particularly explicit during the last fifteen years of his life, when Parsons produced his analyses of the evolution of action systems and the structure of the global system, culminating in the specification of the analytic dimensions of 'the human condition', most notably what he called the telic aspect thereof (Parsons, 1978: 352–433).

My most specific aim is to highlight a central theme of Parsons's approach to religion; namely, his location of the United States of America within the context of the historical-evolutionary significance of Christianity and, more loosely, within the frame of world history. It has, then, to be understood that I do not intend to discuss Parsons's sociology and philosophy of religion as a whole, although some important aspects of his general approach to religion will necessarily receive attention. The nature of my general task provides a rationale for the interest which I will display in the relationship between some aspects of Max Weber's writings and those of Parsons, on the one hand, and the relative paucity of explicit references by Parsons to Durkheim, on the other. As far as Parsons's sociological interest in the evolutionary and universal-historical significance of Christianity – more particularly, American Christianity – is concerned, Weber's work was clearly the touchstone. Parsons's writings on this topic were indeed influenced by Durkheim – notably with respect to the latter's ideas concerning the moral and communal aspects of religion and, even more basically, Durkheim's insistence that religion is 'the serious life'. However, Durkheim was a diffuse, often a corrective, presence; while Parsons's interest in Weber (more generally, Germany) was specific and, ultimately, more ambivalent.

Parsons was unshakeable in his belief that America – for all of its times of trouble, its scars and its transparent deficiencies – represents the highest point yet reached in the evolution of systems of human action. In brief, Parsons argued sociologically that it is in America that one finds the greatest development of both challenges, primarily in the form of complexity, and the cultural resources for engagement with those challenges. Nothing better illustrates Parsons's faith in that respect than the story of his deep disappointment upon the occasion of Robert Bellah's announcement that the American Covenant had been broken (Bellah, 1975) via the war in Indochina and the Watergate scandal. That such a claim could be made at all was apparently saddening enough. That one who had worked influentially in what Parsons called the inner circle of action theorists – indeed had made a major contribution to the study of 'religious evolution' (Bellah, 1964) – should have made the, rather widely applauded, announcement was all the more disturbing. What Parsons might have said with respect to current debate about 'American decline' is thus of no small interest.

As with all great social thinkers, Parsons was driven by both passion and intellectual curiosity. I argue that in his work on religion in the USA and the West the two came together in a form which is poignant, analytically powerful and profoundly – even embarrassingly – optimistic. The claim that the USA is a new kind of Christian, but also more-than-Christian, society constituted the core of Parsons's sociological attitude toward his own society.

If one is forced to characterize his theological stance, Parsons was – to put it simply – a liberal Calvinist, of a somewhat secular kind, having once described himself as an *un-* rather than a *dis*believer. He stated that his early rejection of positivism was closely related to his concern with religion, which was a focus of a continuing attempt to understand the balance of the roles of rational and nonrational components in human action (Parsons, 1978: 233–63). But even though one cannot deny the fact of his objective and subjective location in the mainstream American, liberal-Calvinist tradition – which has placed so much emphasis upon the historical extension of the original Puritan, New England-based, notion of a community of individuals striving to enhance the God-given worldly domain as instruments of God's will – I have little doubt that Parsons's 'religious' identity was sustained and nourished by his scientific work, rather than the latter being simply an outcome or a projection of his personal convictions (although there probably was an element of that).[2]

Like both Durkheim and Weber, Parsons spent the larger part of his life's work struggling with utilitarian individualism and economism – and, perhaps, also eroticism. Like both of his main 'heroes' Parsons saw religion as an historical constrainer and channeler of economic wants, although he departed from Weber's insistence on the modern autonomy of the monetary-economic realm. For Parsons, going beyond both Durkheim and Weber, the shaping of 'the economic factor', in historical-evolutionary terms, was of such importance that 'absolutist' conceptions of it – such as those of communistic Marxism and 'establishment' economism – should be seen as having quasi-religious significance (Parsons, 1979), an argument which is particularly relevant at a time when the 'market economy' and economic individualism are being zealously promoted by both outsiders and insiders as a solution to most of the problems of postcommunist societies. For while Parsons (1964a) clearly predicted the evolution of communism in the direction of political democracy he would surely have found the shrill economism which has followed the collapse of communism in Eastern Europe and elsewhere alarming, not to say ironic.

There was, according to Parsons, no escape – only mediated distancing – from the constitutive dimensions, the 'productive forces', of human society. The constitutive significance of human societies was manifested particularly in the struggle to deal with – to both tame and infuse with meaning – the economic and the erotic appetites in relation to the 'reality beyond' society. Religion was the core of the struggle in this regard. In essence, that is what Parsons's hierarchy of cybernetic controls and conditions is all about (Parsons, 1979). In this regard it has to be emphasized that Parsons became increasingly explicit about the erotic-sexual aspect of religion. Inspired partly by Freud, Parsons eschewed the scholarly reticence of Weber and, particularly, Durkheim as far as sexual matters are concerned – at least during his later years. Weber did, of course, attend to the relationship between religion and sexuality, even to the point of suggesting that religion is always bound up with eroticism. However, he did not in his public work directly discuss sexual symbolism in the manner that Parsons was eventually to do.[3] Inspired as he clearly was by Freud, Parsons (1964b: 34–56) was nonetheless critical of him for the failure to recognize the cultural significance of symbolism and its non-referential significance.

The major basis of the imbalance with respect to Weber and Durkheim is that, beginning with *The Structure of Social Action* (Parsons, 1937), Parsons frequently expressed reservations about what he called the positivistic elements in Durkheim's theory of religion – most notably with respect to the significance of religious symbolism, which Parsons invariably insisted should not be seen as having direct empirical referents. However, he was to make his peace with Durkheim on this point, relinquishing much of his view of Durkheim as a reductionist in his essay of 1973 on Durkheim's mature sociology of religion (Parsons, 1978: 2213–32). Another reason is that Durkheim's empirical writing on religion was largely confined to the indigenous Australian context (Durkheim, 1961).[4] Parsons, on the other hand, did not argue that his own writings on religion and on societies generally in an evolutionary context were straightforwardly 'Weberian'. They differed analytically from Weber, first, in respect of Parsons's rejection of what he called Weber's 'type atomism', and second, in Parsons's concern to construct evolutionary sequences as 'a *first* order of business' with respect to an explicitly evolutionary approach (Parsons, 1966b: 111). In one sense these are two sides of the same coin. The rejection of 'type atomism' in favor of an approach which emphasizes how 'variability can . . . be analyzed as a function of different combinations of the same analytically defined elements' (Parsons, 1966b: 112) pushes the analyst toward a concern with synchronicity and with sequences in the mode of diachronic order. In spite of the implication that a *second* 'order of business' would be to provide a more dynamic element to evolutionary theory – in the form of the analysis of processes of change as such – Parsons was clearly not himself much interested in causality (in the sense that Weber sometimes claimed to be). Moreover, Parsons's comparative-evolutionary work was more culturally orientated than was that of Weber. It should also be stressed that Parsons did not subscribe to Weber's disenchantment thesis, at least not in any simple form. Rather than thinking in terms of secularization Parsons followed Durkheim in talking about modern religious change and generalization (Pickering, 1984: 452–6).

Classical sociologists tended to see British and American societies as the major sites upon which utilitarianism had developed, both intellectually and actually. Parsons, on the other hand, analytically used the USA and, to a lesser extent, Britain as vehicles for displaying how societies could be both conspicuously utilitarian and religious. In so doing he argued not merely against utilitarian but also against directly moral-religious characterizations of America. He did this mainly in terms of the notion of institutionalized individualism, a concept inspired by Durkheim and which involved the idea of the interpenetration of what Weber had called material and ideal interests. Although often invoking Weber, Parsons certainly did not agree with Weber's claim that in America 'the mutual supplementarity' of proving oneself before God and before other men had been transformed into a secular mutuality of concern with personal well-being and other-directed peer approval (Weber, 1948a: 321). For Parsons, Weber's characterization of early twentieth-century America as a major example of secularity had only limited validity. His reservation took two, closely related, forms. First, Parsons regarded what Weber called world-images and nonrational presuppositions so seriously that he refused to see any rupture between the clearly religious Judeo-Christian world-image and the modern circumstance, which Weber tended to approach in terms of its resting on nonrational presuppositions concerning the central reality of the money economy. Second, from Durkheim Parsons took explicitly the notion of the sacred, transforming that idea into a differentiated conception of constitutive symbolism at the level of culture and civil religion at the level of the social system.

In sum, Parsons tried to cut through the thorny issue which lies at the center of the early development of sociology: Is religion being replaced? If it is, is it being replaced along the historical-evolutionary tracts honed across many hundreds of years of world history? Marx, Durkheim and Weber, among others, had answered the basic question in different degrees of the affirmative – Durkheim being the most ambiguous, and leaning, as I have said, toward the idea of transformation of religion rather than clear-cut secularization. Parsons, on the other hand – often inspired by German philosophical and theological views crystallized by Paul Tillich (Scharlemann, 1987) – insisted throughout his career that societies and persons are perpetually exposed to 'ultimate' questions.

In that connection it should be emphasized that Parsons's conception of religion as having to do with 'ultimate concern' apparently predated his becoming familiar with the work of Tillich. In fact, he began talking about ultimate values in the mid-1930s, while his first major statement on the sociology of religion as a subdiscipline in 1944 (Parsons, 1954: 197–211) invoked the notion of ultimacy without reference to Tillich. Nonetheless, in my judgment Parsons's eventual invocation of the Tillichian conception of ultimate concern often appears as a definitional 'trick'. Tillich's notion is not easily reconcilable with Parsons's covenantalism, while the stress on ultimacy also exposes Parsons to the charge of religious reductionism – reducing life *to* religion. (Tillich had, after all, tended to see life itself as pivotally religious.) From a different angle Jürgen Habermas (1987: 254) has gone so far as to suggest that in his 'late philosophy', like Saint-Simon and Comte before him, Parsons's 'theoretical development lands him in the attempt to create a social-theoretical substitute for the socially integrating functions of a religion whose very substance has been snapped.' Nonetheless I am persuaded that in his later years Parsons made a powerful argument concerning religious continuity up to and beyond the present era.

Whereas Parsons's statements on religion up to the early 1960s tended to be abstract, unhistorical and highly nominalistic, his subsequent work involved detailed and comparative attention to the history of religion.[5] Moreover, in his very latest years Parsons veered toward a statement on the grounding of religion. By this I mean that, rather than stipulating by definitional fiat that religion has to do with matters of ultimate concern – giving the impression that the latter needs no specification, that it is existentially obvious – Parsons (1978: 352–432) attempted to connect the cultural dimension of religion at the action system level to what he called the telic aspect of the human condition as a whole. As usual, profoundly in tune with the trends of the modern world – I think here of the present, near-global thematization of concern with the fate of the human species and of 'planet earth' – Parsons (with particular assistance from Robert Bellah) centered the telic system upon the idea of 'the ends of humankind'. Such a perspective has the general effect of placing religions within a metareligious, from another perspective, an ecumenical (Parsons, 1978: 233; 63) human context. Certainly there are indications that Parsons himself thought that the evolutionary process involved in our time the subsumption of societies by a higher-order, universal 'religious' concern with the human circumstance (Parsons 1978: 264–433).[6]

With some reservation, in view of my own previously expressed skepticism about Parsons's highly inclusive definitions of religion (Robertson, 1970: 34–51; 1978: 258–76), I am close to being convinced by his insistence on the ubiquity and evolutionary generalization of religion, particularly in view of the contemporary political thematization of what Parsons called issues relating to 'the ends of man'. Nevertheless there is bound to be some unease for the foreseeable future about the very open-ended nature of Parsons's conception of religion, not least because the apparatus of contemporary sociological research centers upon more exclusive, substantive definitions of religion. Moreover, and much more significantly, Habermas (1987: 248–56) has raised serious questions concerning the relationship between Parsons's work on 'the action system' (containing cultural, social, psychological and behavioral-cognitive components) and his elaboration of a nonactional, suprahuman 'telic system'. Where 'religion' – as opposed to 'a divine being' (Habermas, 1987: 253) – is to be placed in what Habermas calls Parsons's 'late philosophy' is certainly less than clear. That being readily conceded I would, however, still insist that vital sociological issues arise from Parsons's observations upon the major themes raised during the history of the world religions and their contemporary relevance.

American social theory and the evolution of Christianity

There has been a persisting image of Parsons as having been concerned to provide merely a functional account of religion, interwoven with a declared principle of value-neutrality. Ironically, particularly in view of Parsons's early critique of Durkheim, he was attacked for being anti-religious or at least reductionist during the 1950s and early 1960s (Kolb, 1961; Pemberton, 1956; O'Dea, 1954). Parsons's (1961c) reply to William Kolb in that respect was, in fact, one of the earliest occasions upon which he addressed the theme of institutionalized individualism. Normative patterning, argued Parsons, enables the individual to be free from arbitrariness and thus to act as a free agent. In sum, voluntariness rests upon the interpenetration of normative factors on the one hand and 'low-order' wants and desires on the other. (Parsons used the notion of interpenetration with reference to religion in another essay [1960] of the same period, Parsons, 1964b: 292–324). More specifically, institutionalized individualism refers to the ideal of 'the self-fulfillment of the individual in a social setting in which the aspect of solidarity . . . figures at least as prominently as does that of self-interest in the utilitarian sense' (Parsons, 1978: 321).

Parsons has also been accused of presenting an image of limited religious freedom in his theory as a whole. For example, Rudolph Siebert (1980) has argued that Parsons in functionalizing religion subverted it. On the other hand, Siebert concedes that Parsons's notion of ultimate reality enjoys what might be called a metafunctional status. Nevertheless Parsons's ultimate reality 'constitutes an explicit ontological and theological residual in the allegedly non-metaphysical logic of functionalism' (Siebert, 1980: 33), which opened the way, claims Siebert, for Niklas Luhmann's functionalization of meaning and ultimate concern – religion being then seen as constituting one among a series of ways of reducing complexity and coping with contingency (Luhmann, 1977; Beyer, 1984). What Siebert fails to confront is, first, that Parsons insisted on something like the metareligious grounding of the relationship between the sacred and the secular (a point emphasized particularly in relation to America), and second, that the notion of contingency itself has a theological history within Christian thought (Troeltsch, 1911–12; 1914–15).

In any case, only in the 1950s, during his most notoriously abstract phase, did Parsons come close to discussing religion in straightforwardly functional terms. It was only when he was writing in a very circumscribed manner about the social system that he spoke facilely of the functions of religion. More specifically, when he was talking exclusively about the patterning of social interaction *per se* (relative to culture and personality) he spoke of the ways in which religious symbols, values and beliefs entered the concrete realm of institutionally structured social relationships and of the significance of religion in the structuring of motivation to participate in the social domain via role performance. Thus in one phase of his work from an exclusively social-systemic (and primarily synchronic) perspective

Parsons did indeed focus upon religion in terms of it being functionally significant in providing the social system with an operative set of *raisons d'être* and foci of integration. Moreover, from that perspective there issued the never-relinquished, but not unambiguous, tendency also to define religion so as to make it the most basic aspect of culture; while on the personality boundary of the social system Parsons did indeed tend to speak of religious commitment as a basic provider of motivation to participate in the social system, an idea which was apparently centered on the paradigm case of Weber's Calvinist, but specified for the analysis of American society in terms of instrumental activism (Parsons and White, in Parsons, 1964b: 183–235). At that stage of his work Parsons still adhered to the idea that culture was a kind of objective template, lacking in directly actional significance. He was yet to move to a position involving culture as a (sub)-system of action (Parsons, 1961a) – yielding, for example, a treatment of Christianity as an actional-cultural system. He was also yet to move fully to the conception of an action complex, which provides the possibility of treating religion intrinsically, in terms of its cultural, its social, its personal and its behavioral-system aspects (Lidz, 1982).

The characterization of Parsons as merely analyzing religion in a crude functional manner is thus extremely misleading. That claim is supported here with particular reference to Parsons's concern with developing a theory of evolution at the level of human action as a whole during the last twenty years of his life, a period marked in its very early stages (the early 1960s) by the articulation of a sociological theory of the history of Christianity. The main feature of that theory, in comparison with Parsons's work prior to that time, was that it was cast in the form of a mixture of universal history, in Weber's sense, and evolutionary theory (inspired by contemporary biology). Parsons began to proclaim at that juncture that Weber had to all intents and purposes adhered to an evolutionary perspective. While I do not wish to involve myself here in that much-disputed issue, there can be no doubt that Parsons's early writing on Christianity, in particular, and the evolution of human action systems, in general, adhered fairly close to what Weber called – following but not precisely in line with, Rickert – the idea of 'the historical center' (Robertson, 1985). Later, Parsons was, in fact, to invoke – without using that precise concept – the notion of historical center: the problematic consisting in the fact that certain characteristics of Western civilization have come to acquire universal significance and value.

It is important to note that in talking directly of 'the universal significance and value' of 'cultural phenomena' which have appeared only in Western civilization, Weber (1930: 13) qualified his perspective with the crucial phrase 'as we like to think'. In other words, and I believe that Parsons departed from this stricture, Weber sought to emphasize that he undertook his studies from within the hermeneutical context (Schluchter, 1981) of an heuristic assumption concerning Western 'superiority' (Robertson, 1985). Weber did not explicitly argue that the West, objectively speaking, manifested cultural phenomena of concrete universal value, in which respect he departed from Rickert's program. Specifically, in addressing the question of the uniqueness and universal significance and value of Western developments, Weber did not attend to the issue of the extent to which one would expect Western developments to assimilate or become fused with, let alone be directly affected by, those in non-Occidental contexts. In other words (notwithstanding Collins, 1980), Weber chose to neglect, or at least had neglected up to his early death, the by-now crucial issue of what Parsons (1971) called 'the system of modern societies', 'the world-system' or, more generally, of the modern world as 'a single place' (Robertson, 1987).

Whatever the circumstance of Weber not addressing that issue, the fact remains that we can characterize his demonstrable position on the meaning of the phrase 'universal significance and value' as a minimalist one, with Parsons appearing as a maximalist. A minimalist in this context is one who takes the view that the attribution of universality is a perspective-bound judgment concerning a shift in one civilizational context markedly 'beyond' that which was known before and/or exists in other civilizational contexts. A maximalist stance, however, involves a claim concerning the empiricity of universality, in the sense that the developments in the relevant context are definitely regarded as affecting the structure and the future of the global circumstance *as a whole*. That, I believe, is how Parsons should be read, one major clue in that respect being his argument that the Western system of societies has been progressively expanded, so as to yield a global 'system of societies'. In other words, Parsons's evolutionism was not directed simply at tracing an evolutionary path along the lines of successive 'seed-societal' and 'lead-societal' complexes. It was, in fact, part of his perspective on 'universal history' that the world, in the specific sense of the global system, was increasingly concretized in the evolutionary process. There are certainly problems in Parsons's theory in this respect. In one sense he seems to have argued that the entire world is being pulled in an American direction. On the other hand, as he became increasingly interested in the contours of the world-as-a-whole, he was analytically constrained to relativize, along loosely functional lines, the evolution and evolutionary significance of the USA.[7]

Weber's interest in 'universal history' involved him in writing extensively about non-Western religions; whereas Parsons's writings on such were relatively sparse. That difference arises partly from the point which I have just made; for whereas Weber emphasized the great differences between East and West, Parsons followed him mainly in concentrating upon the West, pivotally upon Christianity, and speaking only towards the end of his life of the problematic inclusion of other civilizational elements within a system of modern societies created mainly from a West-led evolutionary thrust. In that regard Parsons's end-of-life concern with the human condition was in part responsible for his raising, as I have noted, what amounts to the theme of 'really' universal values – which the evolutionary process increasingly manifests, in the sense of it involving the increasingly global thematization of telic concerns relative to the evolution of the lead-societal sectors. Thus Parsons differed from Weber in somewhat de-emphasizing the East–West historical differential and, in contrast, emphasizing the evolutionary making of a world in which differences would become interdependent, indeed interpenetrative, within a single global system (Parsons, 1971: 122–37). Thus it could well be argued that Parsons was actually much more interested, in a positive sense, than Weber in 'really existing' variety and heterogeneity. Indeed the fact that their respective *œuvres* differ in relation to the degree of published concern with the non-Occident is misleading, for it was only relatively late in *his* life that Max Weber turned comparatively to the East. (Although, as I have argued elsewhere [Robertson, 1985], Weber was from the beginning held in thrall by Hegel's 'universalistic' rejection of the Orient.) The fact that Talcott Parsons did not live long enough to address comprehensively either the global Islamic presence or the centrality of Japan-centered East Asia in the late twentieth century should thus not be held against him, not least because he obviously sought to go well beyond what Benjamin Nelson (1981) called the comparative, historical and differential approach of Weber. Parsons was, towards the end of his life, beginning to engage systematically with the pivotal issues of global society and global history – with the global-human condition in both existential and sociological perspectives.

Parsons was much more elaborate than Weber in pinpointing the trajectories of development of Christianity. This circumstance derives, on the one hand, from his particular interest in specifying the evolutionary significance of American society and, on the other, from his implicit denial that one can sensibly speak, from a sociological point of view, of the disenchantment of societies in the modern world. Those two points, which are very closely related, constitute the nub of the interpretation of American religion (and, indeed, the USA as a whole) in Parsons's work. It would seem that Parsons's contention that he was drawing upon Weber in claiming that American religion constitutes an advanced pattern of the religion–society relationship rested considerably upon the idea that Weber's notion of the disenchantment of the world applies only to certain aspects of action systems. Again it must be emphasized that Parsons did not like such terms as 'disenchantment' and 'iron cage' because of their misleading connotations. Evidence for this can be seen in his critical commentaries on Troeltsch's view that medieval society was the last truly Christian form of society (there being much to suggest that Weber shared that view) and, relatedly, from Parsons's (1961b: 251) claim that Troeltsch's church–sect distinction provides an insufficiently sophisticated image of the range of relationships between 'religion and society'.[8] According to Troeltsch, the church seeks to dominate society, the sect seeks either to withdraw from or to transform society. The denominational pattern, however, involves differentiation of religious from social-systemic roles (but also increasing interdependence between them), and thus, according to Parsons, constitutes an evolutionarily new religion–society circumstance, one to be found in the USA in its most advanced form.

In the denominational pattern – which first crystallized, according to Parsons (1966b: 54–70), in England and, to a lesser extent, Holland – Weber's 'world' is indeed, in one sense, secularized. In particular, there developed in this circumstance a moral sphere – the moral underpinnings of what Parsons calculatedly called the societal community – which is differentiated from (but interdependent with) subscription to particular faiths, the latter becoming in the American situation increasingly 'privatized' (Parsons, 1960: 295–321; 1966a). That moral sphere is itself supported and 'controlled' by the civil religion. (Parsons [1966a] originally called it civic religion.) Civil religion of the American type – the major modern alternative to (now almost dead) institutionalized Marxism (Parsons, 1978: 308) – provides validation of and a basis of trust in relation to the secular realm, a realm (consisting primarily of the economic and political spheres, as far as the social system is concerned) which is an evolutionary extension of the notion of the Kingdom of God on Earth. While this increasingly autonomous, but still contingent, secular sphere is no longer as such governed by religious principles, it 'may still be interpreted as God's work in a sense similar to that in which physical nature has always been so interpreted within [the tradition of ascetic Protestantism]' (Parsons, 1960: 312). In part Parsons was talking in this respect about the institutionalization of Christian values (Parsons, 1963a) from the cultural system to the social system. He was also, however, referring to the differentiation (interdependence-within-reciprocity) of the social system and of the action system (culture, social system, personality systems and behavioral systems) as a whole. Most generally, he was talking about a particular religious mode of acceptance of the world.

Whether it is truly in line with Weber's thought to talk as Parsons, in effect, did about religious acceptance of the modern world is very debatable. (It is, most certainly, in line with the general thinking of Durkheim.) In any case, as I have said, much of Parsons's work – but particularly his work on religion – was directed at refutation of those who believe that we are destined to live in 'the Weberian world' of meaningless bureaucracy and utilitarian individualism. Religion provided, notably in modern America, the basic cultural and psychological resources for dealing morally with the complexity of the modern world; although Parsons was well aware of the ways in which religion could be narrowed in funda-mentalistic ways or at the other, 'liberal', extreme over-generalized so as to make it ineffective in that respect.

In his pivotal essay on religious rejections of the world (the 'Inter-mediary Reflections'), Weber (1948b) talked of Western history in terms of tensions between religion (in the form of 'brotherly love') and other spheres of life: the erotic, the economic, the political, the esthetic and the intellectual. As is by now rather well known, Weber produced three versions of this essay (Schluchter, 1989: Ch. 12) and he may well have been working on a fourth at the time of his death; while Parsons's late, posthumously published essay (1979) was also about such tensions, specifically those involving the erotic, the economic and the intellectual spheres. Parsons saw Christianity as symbolically expressing and concretely guiding the erotic and economic spheres and the tensions between them. On the other hand, he regarded the intellect as a 'risky' resource (an idea derived from Neoplatonic thinkers), notably with respect to the systematization and universalization of dilemmas arising from early Christian experience. The Christian symbol system was above all, argued Parsons, characterized by its capacity to express optimal ambivalence concerning erotic and economic matters. He thus merged, without explicitly saying so, Weberian and Freudian notions of the sublimation of spheres of life, in relation to the constitutive and normative significance of Christian symbolism. In this regard Parsons may be seen as having constructed a research program along what Bellah (1970) called 'symbolic realist' grounds, but not committing himself to the radical version of that stance advocated by Bellah himself. In other words, Parsons did not reify religious symbolism.

Parsons's use of the concept of ambivalence departed from the specific, unhistorical attempt of Robert Merton to extend the notion of ambivalence beyond the psychological realm, so as to speak of sociological ambivalence – that is, ambivalence 'built into the structure of statuses and roles' (Merton and Barber, 1963: 93). Parsons himself had earlier employed the notion of ambivalence in its more-or-less Freudian sense, as in the phrase 'ambivalent motivational structure' (Parsons, 1951: 253). His later historical and comparative enrichment of the concept is, however, bound up with his critique of Freud for not taking into account the relative autonomy of cultural symbolism.[9] Of course we are well aware by now that the break between Jung and Freud developed largely in reference to this kind of problem, notably Jung's objection to the restriction of the significance of symbols to dreams, the free-associational significance of symbols in Freud's work, their basically 'private' significance, and Freud's commitment to the view that all symbols have an erotic significance (Jung, 1964: 18–103). I suggest that – notwithstanding the well-known problems arising from Jung's notion of the objective psyche (often known as the collective unconscious), his concept of archetypes, and so on – there is a potential meeting-point between Parsons and Jung. One important aspect of an encounter of that kind would involve consideration of the idea that Jung's perspective may well be more appropriate to the human-conditional and world-societal themes in Parsons's later thought than those of Freud (Robertson and Chirico, 1985). In any case, as far as ambivalence is concerned, I suggest that we should now talk of *ambiguity* at the cultural level; *multiple involvements* (corresponding to the 'sociological ambivalence' of Merton and Barber) at the social level; *ambivalence* at the personal level; and *indifference* at the behavioral level.

In the history of Christianity, said Parsons (1979), there have been two particularly critical junctures with respect to the crystallization of 'worldly' domains, involving the two most basic conditions of human action systems (sexual and economic production). First, the long passage from ancient Judaism to Constantinian Christianity had involved the releasing of the erotic sphere, in the sense that erotic sentiments and relationships became thematized as relatively autonomous aspects of life. They could thus, in principle, be 'treated' and symbolically expressed in a relatively disciplined manner by the Christian. In the ancient Judaistic perspective the erotic dimension had been, so to say, hidden by laws and rituals concerning family life and in-group/out-group relations. The universalistic and individuating thrust of Christianity – its move away from the pre-Christian conception of the relationship between God and a particular people (concretized in the Jewish mission to the Gentiles) – involved very explicit acknowledgment of both the reality and the danger of erotic sentiments. 'Sex' was increasingly to be directly confronted, a standpoint which reached a crucial stage in the vow of chastity demanded of the priest and the monk. However, the central monastic vows related not merely to eroticism but also to economic gain (the vows of chastity and poverty); and it was thus the gradual emergence of acknowledgment of the reality and the danger, the revelation, of economic preoccupation which Parsons saw as the next crucial step in the unfolding of the Christian, but more diffusely the Western, conception of 'the world'. That step culminated in the universalizing economic aspects of the Industrial Revolution, which Parsons saw as a diachronic-functional equivalent of the mission to the Gentiles. The Industrial Revolution of the eighteenth century, occurring at the same time as the founding of the USA, involved the complete crystallization of the economy as a realm in its own right.

Parsons's general argument was that the distinctiveness of Christianity has centered upon what might be called the human creation of a 'world', or a series of 'worlds', in reference to which the very possibility of being Christian – or indeed, being religious in a modern sense – has arisen.[10] Without 'the world' there can be no possibility of religion, and vice versa. Thus the interdependence between supra-worldliness and worldliness is at the very heart of Parsons's analysis of religion. In effect, what Parsons did in his later work on Christian symbolism, notably in reference to erotic and familial relationships, was to reverse Marx's dictum that the idea of the holy family is an echo of the real, earthly family. (See also Bellah, 1970: 76–97.) In parallel to Weber's treatment of Marx's economism, Parsons tried to show that Christian symbolism concerning erotic and familial relationships was developed in conditional reference to, but mainly in symbolic independence of, concrete forms of those relationships. The strength of Christianity in historical perspective has thus inhered in its capacity to frame and subsume earthly relationships in symbolic terms.

Parsons obviously departed from Weber in emphasizing the religio-cultural grounding of the differentiation of the major spheres of life. Weber's approach to the latter theme (so central to current debates about modernity and postmodernity) was, in contrast to that of Parsons, basically 'secular' in that his major analytical emphasis was upon autonomous processes of *rationalization*. While the inner-worldly, mastery-seeking character of Occidental religion had played a substantial part in getting the will to rationalize in high momentum, instrumental rationalization had long ago become a definitely self-propelling tendency. This crucial difference between Parsons and Weber has been penetratingly discussed by Habermas with particular reference to 'the project of modernity', and it is to Habermas's critique of Parsons that I now briefly turn, not least because Habermas has been one of the small number of prominent contemporary social theorists who have recognized that religion-centered sociological discussions may well have great relevance to central issues of social theory. Certainly Habermas recognizes the centrality of Parsons's later writings on religion, as being pivotal in the general assessment of Parsons's work (Habermas, 1987: 199–299).[11]

The considerable interest which Parsons exhibited in the symbolic, interpretive aspects of Christianity (and, by implication, all religio-cultural traditions) nevertheless flies in the face of much of Habermas's critique. Habermas has continuously found Parsons to be deficient in addressing only the objective, adaptive significance of 'the system' within an evolutionary perspective drawn from a natural-scientific perspective. Allegedly Parsons ignored the relatively autonomous development of cultural traditions, within the frame of 'the lifeworld', via communicative activity. There is certainly something to Habermas's charge that during the course of his writing Parsons moved from an initial concern with subjectivity, but with little attention to interaction *per se*, to a focus on systems which allowed neither for action nor interaction other than in purely systemic terms. However there is more to the problem than Habermas allows for. In particular there are problems in Habermas's critique of Parsons's theory of modernity, upon which much of Parsons's interpretations of religion actually depends. The scene can be set for this brief discussion of Habermas's critique by emphasizing that Parsons insisted that in the European feudal period Christianity was more modern than the primary 'systemic' institutions (in Habermas's sense).

According to Habermas (1987: 204), Parsons 'underestimated the capacity and degree of self-sufficiency of action-theoretical concepts and strategies [and] as a consequence, in constructing his theory of society he joined the system and action models too soon.' Parsons did not dwell long enough on the problem of linking internal with external perspectives. Specifically, as Parsons moved from action to system he 'did not concern himself with hermeneutics, . . . with the problem of gaining access to the object domain of social science through an understanding of meaning' (Habermas, 1987: 205). He did not 'see the methodological point of the question, whether systems theory has to be coordinated with and subordinated to action theory' (Habermas, 1987: 205).

That Parsons did not directly consider hermeneutical matters until very late in his career (as, for example, in his piece with Renée Fox and Victor Lidz (1972) on 'the gift of life') is clear, but it still has to be said that from the early 1960s – that is, after he had established a firm systemic perspective – his work was replete with discussions of symbolic meaning and the relationship between cultural traditions and institutional configurations. Thus the question arises as to the degree to which in his more historical and comparative work Parsons actually adhered to his own principles of theorizing, which can be clearly discerned in his more abstract and better-known writings of the 1950s and early 1960s. Thus it could reasonably be argued that even though Parsons lacked a sophisticated hermeneutical method – at least by the standards of explicitly hermeneutical inquiry – he was in practice much more directly concerned with the construction and reconstruction of meaning in a *macro*hermeneutical sense than even some of his followers, not to speak of his critics, have recognized. Clearly most of the writings of Parsons which I concentrate upon in this chapter are directly concerned with 'the understanding of meaning' – although certainly not along the lines advocated by Habermas.

Much of Habermas's emphasis upon the action/system distinction is based upon empirical, not simply theoretical or metatheoretical, claims. Specifically he claims that it is an historical splitting of the socio-cultural domain of interaction from the systemic domain of 'steering' which has made the problem of the relationship between 'internal' and 'external' analytical perspectives particularly pressing. While still not denying the existence of problems in Parsons's work in this respect, it is very important for us to recognize that Habermas's (1975) invocation of the social/system distinction not merely stands firmly in line with the old German separation of *Gesellschaft* from *Gemeinschaft* but that, from Parsons's perspective, it falls into the Weberian trap of type atomism. In other words, Habermas renders the system/social distinction as a universal phenomenon – or at least a phenomenon of great universal relevance – without either reflexive attention to its historical or socio-cultural sources or making any attempt to compare societies or civilizations with respect to its undoubtedly uneven crystallization. In contrast, from an early stage of his writing Parsons was critical of Tönnies, as well as Weber, for what he saw as an attempt to generalize to social theory as a whole a particularly Germanic (or, at the most, European) intellectual encounter with modernity. In that respect *The Structure of Social Action* was surely driven by a wish to develop a comprehensive social and moral theory of modernity in the face of the encounters with modernity which had been registered in the writings of leading European interpreters, with particular reference to the American experience. In other words, Parsons was not willing to concede to European intellectuals a privileged set of positions from which to make globally-binding judgments about modernity.

In that Parsons involved himself in interpretation of 'the meaning' of Christianity (in the 'American Century') his work can, for certain purposes, be discussed in theological terms. But to those who would then say that his work is primarily theological I would point out that much of theology has become increasingly involved with precisely the kinds of questions which Parsons addressed. In fact I would go so far as to say that much of contemporary theology and 'religious studies theory' is as relevant to the contemporary world as is quite a lot of 'secular' social theory.[12] I think that Parsons's attitudes toward the works of Troeltsch and Weber are illuminating with respect to these considerations. As I have shown, Parsons argued that the American case of denominational pluralism indicates that Ernst Troeltsch was wrong in having claimed that there had been only three versions of a Christian society – namely, medieval Catholicism (what Troeltsch himself called the Medieval Synthesis), Lutheranism and Calvinism; each of them allegedly involving a single established church as the primary agency for the implementation and symbolization of the Christianity of the whole society. Regardless of the minutiae of Troeltsch's orientation there can be no doubt that Troeltsch did claim that in the West religion was fighting for its very existence (Antoni, 1959: 44; Robertson, 1985). However, Troeltsch also argued that it was the task, indeed the calling, of the Christian intellectual to demonstrate the relevance of Christian values and beliefs to the world – in the double sense of modernity and globality. In contrast, Weber, while agreeing that religion was indeed fighting precariously for its existence, maintained not merely that the fight was futile but that the program for 'bringing religion back' was potentially destructive. He argued, instead, for the development of individualistic ethical principles of 'responsibility' – never, however, directly addressing the problem of their institutionalization.

In terms of 'the Tolstoyan lesson', Max Weber insisted that the propagation of 'absolute values' was as threatening to the attempt to stabilize modernity as was purely instrumental rationality. What, however, Parsons saw, beyond Weber's concerns, was that absolution could take a number of forms. It could take the form which Weber worried about the most – namely, substantive-value (ultimately 'decisionist') absolutism. Secondly, it could involve the systematic ideological conflation of instrumental and substantive rationality (the totalitarian route to Auschwitz and the Gulag?). Thirdly, it could center on the one-sided accentuation of one of the increasingly autonomous spheres of life – such as the economic or the erotic. Fourthly, it could involve the attempt to dedifferentiate the spheres of modern societies – that is, collapse the lateral dimension of life into a single bundle. Needless to say, it could also take the form – which runs on a taken-for-granted basis through most of Weber's work – of pure instrumentalism (the steel-hard, or the iron, cage).[13] The crucial consideration here is that in all the canonical anti-Parsons literature virtually no attention has been paid to the multifaceted character of Parsons's reservations about the Troeltsch–Weber debate. (As I have argued elsewhere [Robertson, 1985], Georg Simmel tried to effect a bridge between Troeltsch and Weber, which unfortunately Parsons failed to recognize.)

I have little doubt that Parsons was very conscious of the general thrust of Weber's convictions about the predicaments of the modern world. However, he bypassed explicit discussion of them in favor of a more direct, interpretive emphasis upon the evolutionary 'upgrading' of the relationship between religion and world as depicted in Weber's analysis of early Calvinism. In other words, Parsons calculatedly overlooked much of Weber's writing on the degeneration of inner-worldly asceticism into utilitarian instrumentalism – a strategy which was guided by Parsons's long-held criticism of Weber for not having provided the analytical tools with which to deal with systems of action, as opposed to action *per se.* Ironically, what sustained that 'oversight' in Parsons's own work was a general interpretation of the relationship between religion and world which has much in common with that of Troeltsch. Troeltsch's own interpretation of Christianity (Troeltsch, 1960; 1971; Robertson, 1985) was centered on the claim that the strength (the 'absoluteness') of Christianity was manifested in its *implication* in the world, in the sense that there was within Christianity a distinctive relationship of autonomy-within-reciprocity between the spiritual and the secular (Clayton, 1979). That Christianity was in retreat arose from a lack of recognition of an umbilical connection, an interpenetration, between religion and world. On the other hand, while Troeltsch may well have worried that we will not again see a 'Christian' or even a 'religious' society, he did not believe that any society – let alone the world-as-a-whole – is viable without religio-moral and communal components. In contrast, Weber saw the relevant connections as having been effectively broken. The realm of what had previously been culturally-based individual religiosity was rapidly becoming a realm of conflicting personal values; while the major societal realms themselves had become separated and sublimated in terms of their own, internal dynamics. Mediation between meaning-oriented convictions, on the one hand, and the 'reality' of increasingly autonomous, 'self-legislating' spheres, was now a matter of personal ethics. One can plausibly read Parsons along not dissimilar lines, in the sense that Parsons also maintained that modern societies are increasingly dependent upon voluntaristic 'inputs' from individuals (Bourricaud, 1981). However, Parsons also emphasized the moral-communal, civil-religious and religious-cultural aspects of modern societies which framed and intersected with the individual conscience (Parsons, 1966a).

It can thus be established that with respect to the issue of the relevance of religion (however 'secularized' it may have become), Parsons's position was closer to that of Troeltsch than to that of Weber. This is so because of Parsons's commitment to a 'voluntaristic' theory focusing upon the 'upgrading' of interpenetrative relationships between different spheres of life, a stance which can indeed be called a *critical*-theoretical one (Robertson, 1979: 299–300) in that it is ever-watchful concerning the maximization of the conditions which promote individual freedom and responsibility in relation to the increasingly complex and concrete realization of the global-human condition as a whole.

In this regard the issue again arises of ambivalence. Ambivalence toward 'the world' was for Parsons a central feature of religion. Parsons made that idea central to his last writings, developing in the process an implicit notion of what I have called optimal ambivalence. Optimal ambivalence does not involve full acceptance of the world, for that would involve meaningless-ness and failure to acknowledge complexity. This is where the relationship between individual-centered ambivalence and system-centered inter-penetration comes to the fore. Ambivalence refers to an 'attitudinal' aspect of action (located at the personality level), while interpenetration (as thematized by Richard Münch) is a more objective aspect, referring to the ways in and degrees to which domains of life and levels of action give each other 'energy' or 'control'. This, however, cannot be the place to deal with these general problems of action theory, except to say that Parsons appears not to have distinguished sufficiently between cultural *ambiguity* and *orientational* ambivalence, nor to have thematized sufficiently the rela-tionship between ambivalence and the general idea of interpenetration.

Parsons on the pattern of world history and the problem of globality

I turn now in very schematic form to Parsons's evolutionary image of Christianity, connecting my interpretation to some considerations on the contemporary global circumstance. The primary sociological result of early Christianity was, said Parsons, a generalization beyond the confines of a particular people of the idea of individual salvation relative to a monotheis-tic conception of God – a process which was fed by basically Hellenistic conceptions of religious individualism. In particular, the extension of salvation opportunities beyond the context of a particular collectivity involved, as I have already noted, a thematization of erotic-familial concerns, made manifest in Christian symbolism concerning love and the Holy Family. The relatively autonomous development of early Christianity in relation to wider societal settings made it, in turn, relatively resistant to purely political processes when Christianity was later adopted as the religion of the Roman Empire; besides which the universalistic tendencies of the latter themselves amplified the universalism of Christianity. That, according to Parsons, was the most evolutionarily effective development. In contrast, another, 'nonproductive', strand consisted in eschatological-collectivist (and, presumably, gnostic-mystical) Christian orientations. The split between the West and the East within the Christian Church involved an emphasis in the Eastern Orthodox Church upon monasticism and contemplation on the one hand, and a yielding on the part of the church to the secular political authorities on the other; while in the West there developed a different kind of hierarchal system, structured around the distinction between an elite which lived outside the world and a mass of adherents who lived, under church tutelage, in the world. The Western arrangement facilitated a circumstance whereby the church had legitimating leverage on the secular authorities, the church–state relationship being expressed under the rubric of the Holy Roman Empire.

It is in respect of the Western-Christian church–state relation that Parsons made one of his most consequential claims. He insisted (Parsons, 1963a: 43–4) that the coronation of Charlemagne by Pope Leo III on Christmas Day 800 was not a 'subordination of secular authority to the church', nor was it a compromising of the church by secular authority. Rather it was 'a putting of the seal of religious legitimacy on the differentiation of the two spheres. A true differentiation always involves at the same time an allegiance to common values and norms.' It is worth comparing this interpretation with that of Louis Dumont (1982). Dumont has spoken of Charlemagne's coronation as a 'glaring contradiction' of what he calls 'hierarchical complementarity' – the principle of material subordination of the church and spiritual subordination of the emperor. He views the event on Christmas Day 800 as the foundation of the modern religion–state and individual–society confusions within Western societies. In contrast, Parsons insisted that Charlemagne's coronation not only constituted a religious-normative upgrading of the differentiation of the religious and political spheres, but that it also facilitated the subsequent unfolding of the pattern of denominational pluralism. Clearly, interpretation of this event is of considerable relevance to the debate about the modern world. But this cannot be the occasion for full discussion of its historiographical importance.

Thus, according to Parsons, there must be 'something' other and 'more than' politics ('the state') and religion ('the church') in order for the two to become relatively independent spheres. For Parsons that something else was embryonic civil religion, which was – over evolutionary time – enhanced so as to become the fully-fledged civil religion of modern America, 'serving the function' of patterning the individual–society and religion–politics differentiations. My interpretation here rests in part on the claim that 'in terms of the ultimate trusteeship' of the values involved in a '*true* differentiation . . . the church is the higher authority' (Parsons, 1963a: 44; my emphasis). An alternative view, such as that provided by Dumont, would claim that the question of trusteeship was unresolved and remains so up to the present. In any case, Parsons's interpretation of the Charlemagne aspect of what he called the medieval synthesis is of pivotal significance in the understanding of his work as a whole.

The Reformation, which was prepared for by the humanistic side of the Renaissance, involved, said Parsons, a repetition within the Western Catholic context of the previous split between the Western and Eastern portions of the Christian Church. Specifically, Calvinism repeated – in upgraded, evolutionary terms – the Western solution, whereas Lutheranism repeated, in new circumstances, the Eastern solution. More generally, the Reformation of the sixteenth century involved the extension into 'the world' of the previously church-contained hierarchy. In other words, there was now within the Calvinist orbit a definite distinction in the wider societal setting between elite and mass – between activist 'saints' and 'regular' adherents. Secular life was endowed with a new form of religious legitimation on the Calvinist side. However, Calvinism itself then split into two principal forms. The theocratic, radical type of Calvinism involved formal emphasis upon the control of the masses by the salvational elite (as in Geneva, Prussia, parts of Scotland, early New England and twentieth-century South Africa); while 'ascetic Protestantism', on the other hand, developed a more flexible orientation based on involvement in the world, guided in principle by individual conscience.

In Parsons's perspective the most recent, critical point in the evolution of Christianity, but in a more fundamental sense in the evolution of human-kind in its entirety, has centered on the differentiation and symbolic thematization of the economic realm (Parsons, 1979). It is indeed impor-tant in this connection to note that the impact of the Industrial Revolution of the late eighteenth century should be seen as extending well beyond Western civilization itself. Nevertheless, within the Western and proximate spheres Parsons noted two axes of response to the newly thematized economic factor. On the one hand, there were two, mutually antagonistic, forms of rejection of 'the new world': socialism (of the eventually Marxist type) and what Parsons called '*Gemeinschaft* romanticism'. Both of these 'religious orientations' involved regarding the economic factor as demonic. On the other hand, there was an axis concerning forms of acceptance of the world. Parsons concentrated on utilitarian individualism as that form of world acceptance which constituted a 'counter-absolutism' in relation to the absolutism of socialism. The fully-fledged rivalry in this regard came to take the form of Marxism (most acutely in its communist form) versus 'establishment economism'. The latter is, so to say, an over-worldly variation on ascetic-turned-liberal Protestantism, while communistic Marx-ism stood on a path mapped by theocratic Calvinism. Marxism, however, produced its own 'equivalent' of liberal Protestantism – namely, democra-tic socialism. Liberal Protestantism and democratic socialism – unlike the four extreme positions defined by the axes of socialism-*Gemeinschaft*ism and rejection-acceptance of the autonomy of the economic realm – consti-tute, respectively, more-or-less religious and more-or-less secular re-sponses to the Industrial Revolution, maintaining 'optimal' ambivalence concerning the balance between ideals and the complexity of the structur-ally differentiated world. More specifically, and this is where the theme of the autonomization of the intellectual sphere through the whole course of the post-Hellenic world issues is of crucial modern relevance, it is the crystallization of beliefs about the world in the form of individual con-victions, rather than the organized enforcement of beliefs, which is par-ticularly modern and realistic. That possibility has been the unique contribution of the liberal-Protestant – in a more structural sense, of the denominational-pluralist – form.

Since the late eighteenth century, argued Parsons (1978: 308–20), there have been two main rival modes of civil religion – the socialist (particularly the Marxist-communist) and the denominational-pluralist. The latter has constituted a distinctive evolutionary step, in that it has 'rendered untenable the old coincidence of the individual's concern with personal salvation and the collective concept of the church as a social unity' (Parsons, 1978: 308). The communist form of civil religion, on the other hand, grew out of the secular, anti-church and anti-monarchy orientations of the French Revolution and substituted one form of conflation of individual and society for another. In this sense the Cold War was 'a set of wars which [were] not without their relation to the wars of religion that followed the Reformation' (Parsons, 1978: 311). In fact, Parsons's overall conception of the cultural-human significance of Marxism in its more rigid form involved the idea of communism attempting to retrieve all of the main, 'less productive', steps of the entire post-ancient-Israel evolutionary process. It drew upon – and stood in the present-to-past line of – theocratic Calvinism, Lutheranism, Catholicism, Eastern Orthodoxy and early, eschatological Christianity, each of them being 'drags' upon the passage into modernity. In fact, Marxism's spread during the twentieth century was in areas where all of those tendencies had survived (until 1989) outside the evolutionary mainstream. On the other hand, Parsons insisted that communism had made a crucial contribution to the modern world in its internationalism.

Parsons's conception of the evolution of broad symbolic conceptions and actual patterns of society in the West may be depicted in terms of a continuous line, sloping diagonally across a two-dimensional space and representing the main, productive evolutionary path from the beginnings of the dualistic religious worldview up to denominational-pluralism and liberal Protestantism. Junctures along this line are each marked by two main branches from the extending line, one branch at each juncture going on to form the basis for another bifurcation, the other 'leading nowhere', but remaining as a latent structural feature of the human condition and available for 'fundamentalistic' reactivation in new circumstances. In extension of Parsons, it could then be said that the 'discovery' – or the 'baring' – of the second of the most productive forces of the human condition (the economic, following the previously revealed erotic force) has been met by a range of symbolic responses which involve the attempt to infuse that factor with meaning *on an increasingly global scale*. Thus the human condition comes to fully-fledged thematization at the point where the problem of its infusion-with-meaning and the channeling of both of the main productive forces (plus their immediate 'tamer,' the intellect) become necessarily globe-wide, resulting in conflicts over the definition of the global-human condition, including the problem of the nature, meaning and significance of life itself (Robertson and Chirico, 1985; Robertson, 1987; 1990a). In sum, humanity is, so to say, finally revealed. 'The world' acquires the double meaning of worldliness in Weber's sense and of globality (Robertson, 1991).[14]

Parsons and the reordering of the world

I conclude by offering some suggestions as to why Talcott Parsons was so convinced of the highly modern nature of the religion–society relationship in America and its relevance to the future of the global system. At the same time I register some reservations about his contributions.

Parsons managed to fuse Durkheim's idea that religion is the serious life with Weber's so-called reality principle. He saw both as particularly applicable to American society. The high degree of religiosity in America compared to many other societies makes – on the Durkheimian principle – for modes of discourse, patterns of interaction and of personal reflection which allow for the living and the mutual penetration of both the serious and the 'non-serious' aspects of life. With respect to the Weberian reality principle the 'tough contingencies' of social, economic and political life are nevertheless given their due; particularly in terms of conscience-guided individual actions. These two basic sides of life are, in Parsons's view, held together, often precariously, by the civil religion of the USA, centered upon the idea of One Nation Under God, which itself is an evolutionary expansion of the old Christian theme of the Kingdom of God upon Earth. Thus, to put the matter a little differently, Parsons was both a symbolic realist and a mundane realist, insisting that the connection between the two, vertically related, spheres has itself historically been and 'must' continue to be symbolized even by those who, using parallel notions for different purposes, have tried to overcome the idealism–materialism antinomy.

Clearly Parsons recognized that a society which possesses the 'equipment' with which to be both serious and nonserious about the meaning of life is – perhaps alarmingly – vulnerable to what he called processes of inflation and deflation (in the diffuse, rather than the limited, economic sense of those words). And it is precisely in those terms that Parsons (for example, 1966a) intermittently offered suggestive comments concerning, for example, the extremities of American fundamentalism and liberalism. Toward the end of his life Parsons frequently expressed his fondness for Benjamin Nelson's (1969) conception of the trend from 'tribal brotherhood to universal otherhood'. One of the most suggestive ways in which Parsons invoked Nelson's idea was in his attempt to show that, contrary to much conventional wisdom, Americans were not deniers of death compared to others (Baum, 1982). Rather, the concern with death arose in circumstances both of religiosity and of recognition, in the Weberian sense, of the reality principle. The institutionalized individualism of American society, Parsons's own term for universal otherhood, involves attempts to define and redefine both the beginning of human life and its end.

The view that much of what happens within the USA has a significant impact on virtually all societies is both obvious and highly problematic. That religion is crucially bound up with America's position in this regard is particularly troublesome to non-Americans. Yet, that is how Parsons did argue. If Parsons was right, that does not necessarily mean that other societies have to become 'equally religious' in order to travel a similar path. For from Parsons's point of view 'evolution' itself has become universalized, and thus the reference point should now be the global-human condition as a whole.

At least that is my own reading of the later Parsons. As I read him, Parsons came to the conclusion that the USA has in recent centuries been in the vanguard of an evolutionary process which has increasingly involved the entire world. That is to say it is the global-human condition as a whole which is now being structured, through a mixture of 'voluntarism' and systemic constraint (Robertson, 1990a). The concrete world is the site of the shift beyond the dilemmas posed around the *Gemeinschaft–Gesellschaft* problem, which unfolded in the wake of the Industrial Revolution. The global baring of life itself is the new 'post-Parsonian' problem, if there is one. In other words Parsons saw, even in the 1930s, that the *Gemeinschaft–Gesellschaft* problem would have to be transcended (although *not* in the forms announced by the fascism and the communism of that time).

What would Parsons have thought about the present debate about the decline of the USA, the apparent end of the Cold War, the clear return of Islam to the global scene, and the 'bouncing back' of Germany and Japan (in which regard he played a role as an 'applied sociologist')? In short, what shape does a 'Parsonian' analysis of the late twentieth-century world take? Candidly, I doubt whether Parsons could have dealt convincingly with all of these questions without some reconstruction of his interpretive framework.

Perhaps the greatest problem with Talcott Parsons's work is that he attempted so strenuously to legitimize his work along 'technical' and 'professional' lines. Or, to put it another way, he may have made a strategic error in trying so hard to get a serious audience through the claim to be 'scientific'. I do not, on the other hand, doubt for a moment that he himself thought that the roles of epical theorist and professional scientist were perfectly compatible. His 'faith in America' was at the root of his conviction in that respect. Using his own kind of analysis, it might then be said that he was not able fully to understand his own role and status in American society. He could not differentiate between the scientific and the epical sides of his own project. But the onus is now on those who judge Parsons negatively. Where else does one find such a considered mixture of technical theory and globally relevant speculation?

Parsons did not of course live to participate in the current debate about globalization (Robertson and Chirico, 1985; Robertson, 1990a). However, his *The System of Modern Societies* (Parsons, 1971) clearly anticipated some significant aspects of the debate about contemporary global change; while much of his writing on large-scale, long-term change and the problem of world order is of great relevance to it. Parsons (1978: 366) argued that 'the end' of humankind, in the general sense of the purpose and meaning of humanity, is defined by 'telic considerations', insisting at the same time that the 'end' is not constituted by such considerations. In other words, while the world is not in and of itself religious, the kinds of theme which have been at the core of the great religious (as well as newer ideological) traditions will remain of central significance in the inexorable attempt to define, to provide a sense of meaningful order to, the world as a whole. The compression of the world-as-a-whole which has become much more evident since Talcott Parsons's death at the end of the 1970s is clearly giving rise to new juxtapositions of 'telic considerations', the understanding of which can, at the very least, be greatly assisted by a thorough understanding of the vast number of issues which Talcott Parsons raised under the rubric of 'religion'.

It seems safe to say that Parsons's interpretation of the global circumstance at the end of the twentieth century would not have involved relinquishment of his conviction as to the unique place of the USA in 'world evolution'. On the other hand, it is extremely doubtful if he would have had much, if any, time for the politico-economic terms in which that debate is being largely conducted in the USA itself and elsewhere. Parsons's 'faith in America' had little if anything to do with American power. It centered, rather, upon such themes as voluntarism and the coping with social and cultural complexity – most generally, with pluralism. From his point of view the notion of American decline would have made sense only in reference to general socio-cultural considerations. America was not the 'lead society' directly because of its material resources or its world power, but for other more 'religious' reasons. In any case, with confusion as to the ending of the Cold War and the ensuing uncertainty in world order, quickened by the Iraq-centered crisis of 1990–91, Parsons would probably have been as much interested in dealing with those issues as with America as such – trying, for example, to locate Japan and Asia generally more clearly and positively in the global order in historical-evolutionary perspective.

Notes

1. This chapter is a greatly revised and expanded version of Robertson (1982). (I was the guest editor of that issue of *Sociological Analysis*, which was largely devoted to Parsons's writings on religion.) For a list of Parsons's main publications on religion and related matters, see Robertson and Cavanaugh (1982).

2. For further discussion of this issue see Vidich and Lyman (1986), who take the adamant view that Parsons's sociology issued directly from his Christian orientation and that he presented 'a secular theodicy of salvation through work and evolution' (Vidich and Lyman, 1986: 54). See also Jaworski (1990: 110–11), who appears to agree generally with Parsons's own view that 'the pursuit of the secular disciplines . . . had to become autonomous from – which is not the same thing as dissociated from – theology' (Parsons, 1967: 148).

3. For discussions of Weber and eroticism see Schwentker (1987) and Lichtblau (1989–90). Max Weber's interest in sexual and erotic matters remains a matter of considerable controversy. For a hostile critique of Durkheim's views on gender relations, which has some bearing on the relevant matters, see Roth (1989–90). While more frank than Weber in the sense of being explicit in his published writing about particular kinds of sexual activity,

Parsons clearly had a conventional liberal attitude towards sexual matters (Parsons, 1978: 300–24).

4. Durkheim did, of course, also write extensively about religion in *The Evolution of Educational Thought* (Durkheim, 1977), and indeed saw education as having the 'quasi-religious character of morality' (quoted by Alexander, 1982: 280). Parsons, however, did not attend directly to this significant aspect of Durkheim's writing.

5. Exceptions to this generalization are the discussions of the theories of religion of the classical sociologists in *The Structure of Social Action* (1937). The section on religion in *The Social System* (1951: 362–83) epitomizes the general point which I am trying to make in this part of my discussion.

6. Cf. Smith's (1981) conception of world religion (in the singular) as 'the context of faith'. One of the objections to Parsons's writings on the human condition is that it is a system with no other system(s) at its boundaries. In that regard, it is instructive to compare Parsons's conception of the human condition with the briefly stated ideas on the same theme of Louis Dumont, who insists that the human world as a whole is made finally possible only by the positing of a 'superior entity' (Dumont, 1980a: 223).

7. It should be noted that Parsons (1977b: 315) spoke briefly of a world 'cultural-social system' near the middle of the first millennium BC. Pointing out that Weber did not treat the four mid-millennium movements (Confucianism-Taoism, Brahmanism, the Prophetic movement in Israel and Greek philosophy) together, Parsons attempted to do just that.

8. Although Parsons (1960) interpreted Troeltsch (1960) along these lines, it is not at all clear that this was Troeltsch's final view of the history of Christianity. Troeltsch wrote much after *The Social Teachings of the Christian Churches* (1960) to which Parsons did not directly refer. See Robertson (1978; 1985).

9. It is important to note that it was Eugen Bleuler who actually introduced the term 'ambivalence' (Merton and Barber, 1963: 91 and 117).

10. In other respects, we may speak of the 'creation' of society as a secular entity. Parsons's (1978: 213–32) last interpretation of Durkheim in 1973 was centered on the idea that religion uniting individuals into a moral community made society possible. In that regard it should be said that Parsons spoke much in his overall commentary upon Christianity of its part in the crystallization in the West of the idea of the political domain. However, it has to be emphasized that in his late, major essays on religious symbolism Parsons was particularly concerned with the two most basic aspects of what in another context he (Parsons, 1978: 322) called – with explicit reference to Marx – '"the productive forces" which have created an industrial society'.

11. There is a complex set of issues arising from the relationships among such concepts as rationalization, differentiation and interpenetration which cannot be treated here. These concepts have been central to recent German social theory and German interpretations of Weber and/or Parsons. For an overview of some of the main issues from the point of view of a prominent participant, see Münch (1990). Parsons's major statement on Weber's sociology of religion, which is the real focus of some of the current debates in German theory, was his introduction to Weber's *The Sociology of Religion* (Parsons, 1963b).

12. The ongoing debate about modernity and postmodernity among theologians is particularly relevant to this claim. See, to take a major example, Hans Küng's *Theology for the Third Millennium* (1988).

13. For more on Parsons's conception of absolutism see Parsons (1977a); see also Robertson (1990a; 1990b).

14. I have tried to expand Parsons's treatment of the industrial revolution to an analysis of responses to the challenges of globalization in Robertson (1991).

References

Antoni, C. (1959) *From History to Sociology*. Detroit: Wayne State University Press.

Alexander, J.C. (1982) *Theoretical Logic in Sociology*, vol. 2, *The Antinomies of Classical Thought: Marx and Durkheim*. Berkeley: University of California Press.

Baum, R.C. (1977) 'Beyond the Iron Cage', *Sociological Analysis*, 38 (4): 309–30.

Baum, R.C. (1982) 'A Revised Interpretive Approach to the Religious Significance of Death in Western Societies', *Sociological Analysis*, 43 (4): 327–50.

Bellah, R.N. (1964) 'Religious Evolution', *American Sociological Review*, 29 (3): 358–74.

Bellah, R.N. (1970) *Beyond Belief*. New York: Harper & Row.

Bellah, R.N. (1975) *The Broken Convenant*. New York: Seabury Press.

Beyer, P. (1984) 'Religion in Modern Society', pp. 167–203 in B. Hargrove (ed.), *Religion and the Sociology of Knowledge*. Lewistown, NY: Edwin Mellen Press.

Bourricaud, F. (1981) *The Sociology of Talcott Parsons*. Chicago: University of Chicago Press.

Clayton, J.P. (1979) 'Can Theology be both Cultural and Christian?', pp. 82–111 in B.E. Patterson (ed.), *Science, Faith, and Revelation*. Nashville: Broadman Press.

Collins, R. (1980) 'Weber's Last Theory of Capitalism', *American Sociological Review*, 45 (6): 925–42.

Dumont, L. (1977) *From Mandeville to Marx*. Chicago: University of Chicago Press.

Dumont, L. (1980a) 'On Value', *Proceedings of the British Academy*.

Dumont, L. (1980b) *Homo Hierarchicus*. Chicago: University of Chicago Press.

Dumont, L. (1982) 'A Modified View of our Origins: the Christian Beginnings of Modern Individualism', *Religion* 12 (1): 1–27.

Durkheim, E. (1961) *The Elementary Forms of the Religious Life*. New York: Collier Books.

Durkheim, E. (1977) *The Evolution of Educational Thought*. London: Routledge.

Habermas, J. (1975) *Legitimation Crisis*. Boston: Beacon Press.

Habermas, J. (1987) *The Theory of Communicative Action*, vol. 2, *Lifeworld and System: a Critique of Functionalist Reason*, tr. T. McCarthy. Boston: Beacon Press.

Jaworski, G.D. (1990) 'Simmel's Contribution to Parsons' Action Theory and its Fate', pp. 109–30 in M. Kaern, B.S. Phillips and R.S. Cohen (eds), *Georg Simmel and Contemporary Sociology*. Dordrecht: Kluwer.

Jung, C.G. (1964) *Man and His Symbols*. New York: Doubleday.

Kolb, W. (1961) 'Images of Man and the Sociology of Religion', *Journal for the Scientific Study of Religion*, 1 (October): 5–22.

Küng, H. (1988) *Theology for the Third Millennium*. New York: Anchor.

Lassman, P. and Velody, I. (1989a) 'Max Weber on Science, Disenchantment and the Search for Meaning', pp. 159–204 in P. Lassman and I. Velody with H. Martins (eds), *Max Weber's 'Science as a Vocation'*. London: Unwin Hyman.

Lassman, P. and Velody, I. (1989b) 'Introduction', pp. xiii–xvii in P. Lassman and I. Velody with H. Martins (eds), *Max Weber's 'Science as a Vocation'*. London: Unwin Hyman.

Lichtblau, K. (1989–90) 'Eros and Culture; Gender Theory in Simmel, Tönnies and Weber', *Telos*, 82 (Winter): 89–110.

Lidz, V. (1982) 'Religion and Cybernetic Concepts in the Theory of Action', *Sociological Analysis*, 43 (4): 287–306.

Luhmann, N. (1977) *Funktion der Religion*. Frankfurt: Suhrkamp Verlag.

Merton, R.K. and Barber, E. (1963) 'Sociological Ambivalence', pp. 91–120 in E.A. Tiryakian (ed.), *Sociological Theory, Values and Sociocultural Change*. New York: Free Press.

Münch, R. (1982) 'Talcott Parsons and the Theory of Action II: the Continuity of the Development', *American Journal of Sociology*, 87 (4): 771–826.

Münch, R. (1990) 'Differentiation, Rationalization, Interpenetration: the Emergence of Modern Society', pp. 441–64 in J.C. Alexander and P. Colomy (eds), *Differentiation Theory and Social Change*. New York: Columbia University Press.

Nelson, B. (1969) *The Idea of Usury: from Tribal Brotherhood to Universal Otherhood.* Chicago: University of Chicago Press.

Nelson, B. (1981) *On the Roads to Modernity*, ed. T.E. Huff. Totowa: Rowman & Littlefield.

O'Dea, T. (1954) 'The Sociology of Religion', *American Catholic Sociological Review*, 15: 73–103.

Parsons, T. (1937) *The Structure of Social Action.* New York: McGraw-Hill.

Parsons, T. (1951) *The Social System.* New York: Free Press.

Parsons, T. (1954) *Essays in Sociological Theory*, rev. edn. Glencoe, IL: Free Press.

Parsons, T. (1960) *Structure and Process in Modern Society.* New York: Free Press.

Parsons, T. (1961a) 'Introduction' (to Culture and the Social System), pp. 963–96 in T. Parsons, E. Shils, K.D. Naegele and J.R. Pitts (eds), *Theories of Society.* New York: Free Press.

Parsons, T. (1961b) 'Introduction' (to Differentiation and Variation in Social Structures), pp. 239–66 in T. Parsons, E. Shils, K.D. Naegele and J.R. Pitts (eds), *Theories of Society.* New York: Free Press.

Parsons, T. (1961c) 'Comment' (on William Kolb, 'Images of Man and the Sociology of Religion'), *Journal for the Scientific Study of Religion*, 1: 22–9.

Parsons, T. (1963a) 'Christianity and Modern Industrial Society', pp. 33–70 in E.A. Tiryakian (ed.), *Sociological Theory, Values and Sociocultural Change.* New York: Free Press.

Parsons, T. (1963b) 'Introduction' to M. Weber, *The Sociology of Religion.* Boston: Beacon Press.

Parsons, T. (1964a) 'Communism and the West: the Sociology of Conflict', pp. 390–9 in A. Etzioni and E. Etzioni (eds), *Social Change: Sources, Patterns and Consequences.* New York: Basic Books.

Parsons, T. (1964b) *Social Structure and Personality.* New York: Free Press.

Parsons, T. (1966a) 'Religion in a Modern Pluralistic Society', *Review of Religious Research*, 7 (3): 125–46.

Parsons, T. (1966b) *Societies: Evolutionary and Comparative Perspectives.* Englewood Cliffs, NJ: Prentice-Hall.

Parsons, T. (1967) 'Social Science and Theology', pp. 136–57 in W.A. Beardslee (ed.), *America and the Future of Theology.* Philadelphia: Westminster Press.

Parsons, T. (1971) *The System of Modern Societies.* Englewood Cliffs, NJ: Prentice-Hall.

Parsons, T. (1977a) 'Law as an Intellectual Stepchild', *Sociological Inquiry*, 47 (3–4): 11–58.

Parsons, T. (1977b) *Social Systems and the Evolution of Action Theory.* New York: Free Press.

Parsons, T. (1978) *Action Theory and the Human Condition.* New York: Free Press.

Parsons, T. (1979) 'Religious and Economic Symbolism in the Western World', *Sociological Inquiry*, 49 (1): 1–48.

Parsons, T., Fox, R.C. and Lidz, V.M. (1972) 'The "Gift of Life" and its Reciprocation', *Social Research*, 39 (3): 367–415.

Parsons, T. and Platt, G.M. (1973) *The American University.* Cambridge, MA: Harvard University Press.

Pemberton, P.L. (1956) 'An Examination of Some Criticism of Talcott Parsons's Sociology of Religion', *Journal of Religion*, 36: 241–56.

Pickering, W.S.F. (1984) *Durkheim's Sociology of Religion.* London: Routledge.

Robertson, R. (1970) *The Sociological Interpretation of Religion.* New York: Schocken.

Robertson, R. (1978) *Meaning and Change.* New York: New York University Press.

Robertson, R. (1979) 'Talcott Parsons', pp. 284–300 in T. Raison (ed.), *The Founding Fathers of Social Science.* London: Scolar.

Robertson, R. (1982) 'Parsons on the Evolutionary Significance of American Religion', *Sociological Analysis*, 43 (4): 307–26.

Robertson, R. (1985) 'Max Weber and German Sociology of Religion', pp. 263–304 in N. Smart, J. Clayton, P. Sherry and S.T. Katz (eds), *Nineteenth Century Religious Thought in the West*, vol. 3. London: Cambridge University Press.

Robertson, R. (1987) 'Globalization Theory and Civilization Analysis', *Comparative Civilizations Review*, 17 (Fall): 20–30.

Robertson, R. (1990a) 'Mapping the Global Condition: Globalization as the Central Concept', pp. 15–30 in M. Featherstone (ed.), *Global Culture*. London: Sage.

Robertson, R. (1990b) 'After Nostalgia? Wilful Nostalgia and the Phases of Globalization', pp. 45–61 in B.S. Turner, (ed.), *Theories of Modernity and Postmodernity*. London: Sage.

Robertson, R. (1991) 'Globality, Global Culture and Images of World Order', in H. Haferkamp and N.J. Smelser (eds), *Social Change and Modernity*. Berkeley, CA: University of California Press.

Robertson, R. and Cavanaugh, M. (1982) 'Bibliography of Talcott Parsons' Writings on Religion', *Sociological Analysis*, 43 (4): 369–73.

Robertson, R. and Chirico, J. (1985) 'Humanity, Globalization and Worldwide Religious Resurgence: a Theoretical Exploration', *Sociological Analysis*, 46 (3): 219–42.

Roth, G. (1989–90) 'Durkheim and the Principles of 1789: the Issue of Gender Equality', *Telos*, 82 (Winter): 71–88.

Scharlemann, R.P. (1987) 'Tillich, Paul', pp. 530–3 in M. Eliade (ed.), *Encyclopedia of Religion*, vol. 14. New York: Macmillan.

Schluchter, W. (1981) *The Rise of Western Rationalism*. Berkeley, CA: University of California Press.

Schluchter, W. (1989) *Rationalism, Religion and Domination: a Weberian Perspective*. Berkeley: University of California Press.

Schwentker, W. (1987) 'Passion as a Mode of Life: Max Weber, the Otto Gross Circle and Eroticism', pp. 483–98 in W.J. Mommsen and J. Osterhammel (eds), *Max Weber and His Contemporaries*. London: Allen & Unwin.

Siebert, R.J. (1980) 'Parsons' Analytical Theory of Religion as Ultimate Reality', pp. 27–55 in G. Baum (ed.), *Sociology and Human Destiny*. New York: Seabury Press.

Smith, W.C. (1981) *Towards a World Theology*. Philadelphia: Westminster Press.

Troeltsch, E. (1911–12) 'Contingency', pp. 87–9 in J. Hastings (ed.), *Encyclopedia of Religion and Ethics*, vol. 4. Edinburgh: Clark.

Troeltsch, E. (1914–15) 'Kant', in J. Hastings (ed.), *Encyclopedia of Religion and Ethics*, vol. 7. Edinburgh: Clark.

Troeltsch, E. (1960) *The Social Teachings of the Christian Churches*. New York: Harper.

Troeltsch, E. (1971) *The Absoluteness of Christianity and the History of Religions*. Richmond: John Knox Press.

Vidich, A.J. and Lyman, S.M. (1986) *American Sociology: Worldly Rejections of Religion and Their Directions*. New Haven: Yale University Press.

Weber, M. (1930) *The Protestant Ethic and the Spirit of Capitalism*, tr. T. Parsons. London: Allen & Unwin.

Weber, M. (1948a) 'The Protestant Sects and the Spirit of Capitalism', pp. 302–22 in H.H. Gerth and C. Wright Mills (eds), *From Max Weber*. London: Routledge.

Weber, M. (1948b) 'Religious Rejections of the World and their Directions,' pp. 323–59 in H.H. Gerth and C. Wright Mills (eds), *From Max Weber*. London: Routledge.

Weber, M. (1948c) 'Science as a Vocation', pp. 129–56 in H.H. Gerth and C. Wright Mills (eds), *From Max Weber*. London: Routledge.

Wolin, S. (1969) 'Political Theory as a Vocation,' *American Political Science Review*, 63: 1062–82.

Wolin, S. (1970) *Hobbes*. Los Angeles: William Andrew Clark Memorial Library, University of California.

8

PARSONS AND MODERNITY: AN INTERPRETATION

Frank J. Lechner

Parsons' sociology is . . . against nostalgia, for the modern world, and unambiguously post-classical. (Holton and Turner, 1986: 234)

How can we now read Parsons? In this chapter I argue that we can plausibly interpret his work in a number of different ways. By itself, this is nothing new; after all, Parsons had been subject to many kinds of critical readings throughout his career. Currently fashionable approaches to the interpretation of texts indeed suggest that in many fields such interpretive pluralism is the rule rather than the exception. From our collective experience in analyzing the classical tradition in sociology we also know that any complex body of work actually invites multiple reconstructions and assessments; openness to such multiplicity now may in fact constitute a mark of classical status. Thus, the fact that Parsons's *œuvre* can be read in several ways is neither surprising nor disconcerting. Insofar as it comes to serve as an interpretive Rorschach test, enabling scholars to define their position by creatively appropriating certain aspects of Parsons's work, its chances of becoming considered 'classic' may well be enhanced.

By emphasizing the 'fact' that different readings can be plausible I first want to make a plea for 'methodological pluralism' in the *interpretation* of theory (cf. Booth, 1979; Levine, 1986; 1989). The pluralistic way of dealing with the current state of interpretive affairs is to argue, first, that divergent, mutually irreconcilable positions can be equally acceptable (cf. Levine, 1989: 165–6), and secondly, that we can nevertheless engage in vigorous, critical examination and comparison of interpretive perspectives, aiming at a form of 'critical understanding'. At least with respect to certain bodies of texts, pluralists thus have to give up the idea that diversity is only a prelude to synthesis, even though among the possibilities they cannot exclude in advance is that of a temporarily satisfying synthesis.

However uncontroversial the recognition of interpretive diversity may seem, by briefly interpreting different lines of interpretation I also want to stress one point that has not been clearly made before: for a project that claimed to demonstrate convergence in an all-encompassing tradition and to provide a comprehensive framework for the study of human action, the plurality of interpretations is especially problematic. It suggests that the grand attempt at generality has failed: action theory may not be the interpretation to end all interpretations, the theory to include all theories. It may not be a center that can hold divergent views in check by controlling the critical discourse about itself. This, too, is not very surprising, since few bodies of theory constitute or create a form of discourse so tightly coherent and all-inclusive that any alternatives become unthinkable. In fact, I suggest that good theories are the ones that provide the tools for their own critical transformation: they force *and* help us to think creatively about alternatives. For all its faults, the so-called voluntaristic theory of action is such a theory, as I will try to show. To use Booth's (1979) terms, the critical interpretation of a largely 'monistic' project can be used to support a 'pluralistic' position.

But what are the different ways in which we can read Parsons? Since my initial goal is only to make a point about interpretation, I shall not exhaustively discuss the whole range of possibilities (cf. Holton and Turner, 1986: 184). Rather, I propose a simple distinction between two types of interpretation, each represented by a number of critics: of Parsons as general theorist and Parsons as grand metaphysician, to use rough but convenient labels. The first kind of interpretation relies on what are taken to be the author's intentions, examines the extent to which these are realized, fills gaps where needed, reconstructs sources, and evaluates the project's accomplishments on its 'own' terms. Quite different from this 'internal' mode of interpretation is the 'external' kind, which focuses on the problematic relationship of the Parsonian texts to the ones from which they claim to be derived, examines the rhetorical and ideological significance of particular discursive moves Parsons makes, and subjects his project to standards alien to it. What I offer, then, is an interpretation of interpretations. I readily concede that it necessarily reduces the complexity of its subject matter and that it is, in turn, subject to critical interpretation. But rather than slide into infinite regress, I want to argue that in spite of the real differences between the types of critique I have outlined, the latter converge in *some* respects on a particular critical diagnosis. That diagnosis might be summarized as: 'Parsons was wrong in all the right ways.' In arguing for partial convergence on this point, I thus reach a 'Parsonian' conclusion by non-Parsonian interpretive means.

Yet this conclusion forces us to ask what remains valuable in the action-theory tradition. That is to say, if internal and external critics are right about some serious deficiencies, what can we still do with the Parsonian corpus once we have read it? Following the lead of others I want to add a third type of reading by viewing the main body of his work as part of a larger discourse of modernity. Parsons's contribution above all was to provide, with the help of general concepts, a certain 'model' of modernity. Part explanatory theory, part 'metaphysics', it remains a coherent and heuristically fruitful set of metaphors. But precisely when we take seriously what Parsons had to say in his interpretation of modernity, we also realize, once again, that we have to go beyond Parsons. To put it a bit too bluntly, if he is right about modernity, he cannot be right about his theory. If we are to come to terms with (differentiated, pluralistic) modernity, we need more than (analytical, monistic) action theory. But not only are its failures and limitations instructive, the theory also helps to point us in the right direction. That is what I shall argue.

Interpretations

All theorists interpret theory, but few have been critically self-reflexive in doing so. Parsons's work is a case in point: proceeding by means of interpretation from the very beginning of his career (1928; 1929; 1937), Parsons rarely examined the problems of interpretation as such. Even in *The Structure of Social Action* he largely overlooked intellectual precursors, such as the continental hermeneutic scholars and American pragmatists, whose work was not only relevant to his convergence thesis but also could have alerted him to such interpretive problems. As I see it, his primary interpretive stance is similar to that of many of his critics: there are older texts that contain an important message we can objectively decode in the form of a valid interpretation. This very approach, a form of 'presentism', is of course problematic in the light of Parsons's own philosophical position. After all, like many others Parsons has argued that the meaning of objects in the world is never 'given', but always has to be interpreted in terms of a conceptual framework. Surprisingly, Parsons never systematically applied this insight to his own interpretive work. But greater reflexiveness is mandated not just by his analytical realism. Indeed, the theory of action readily suggests a rich and multilayered approach to interpretation. If we think of a body of theory as a cultural object or 'system', then action theory itself would require us to consider its cognitive, aesthetic, moral and constitutive qualities, all of which are necessarily linked to larger traditions. Moreover, we would have to think of the ways in which it is embedded in a social system, and break that 'social' environment down into various subcomponents. Of course, we would have to think about the 'personal' motives behind the theory as well, and examine in what ways it provides resources to solve behavioral problems. To determine the 'meaning' of the theory we would also have to analyze the way it treats the environment of action – telic problems and irreducible features of the world. Unfortunately, Parsons never systematically engaged in Parsonian interpretation along these lines. In this chapter I can offer little more than a first approximation of a fully Parsonian interpretation of Parsons. I do so in a critical spirit precisely in order to see where and how we must go beyond Parsons.

Even if we do not wish to frame our interpretation in Parsonian terms, increased reflexiveness is both possible and fruitful. Recent work on the interpretive devices and orientations inherent in different kinds of theory has shown as much (e.g. Brown, 1976; Seidman, 1983; Levine, 1989). At the very least, such work has led to greater recognition of the role of interpretation in theory, not least on the part of scholars influenced by Parsons, such as Robert Bellah and Clifford Geertz. This recognition is strengthened if we view all theory as embedded in discursive traditions, since discourse necessarily involves continual interpretation of signs – a way of viewing theory that itself is gaining support (cf. Alexander, 1988). Of course, there is considerable disagreement about the form interpretation ideally should take. For example, the debate about presentism versus historicism has not been, and perhaps cannot be, resolved. But such disagreement largely reflects the differences between theoretical traditions. For a pluralist this is not inherently disconcerting, if only because a vigorous dialogue between representatives of different discursive traditions can in fact contribute to greater interpretive reflexiveness. If pluralism in theory and interpretation were commonly accepted, we could leave it at that. But unfortunately we cannot, since systematic treatment of interpretation in theory, Parsonian or otherwise, still faces at least two kinds of objections.

First, to sociological theorists interpretation sometimes seems a dangerous temptation. Many would acknowledge that it is a necessary device when it comes to understanding 'the world'. Good theory must have a hermeneutic dimension. The danger presumably lies in turning hermeneutics back on the activity of theorizing itself. Once we focus on the meaning of texts, we might become ensnared in a web of signifiers, a viciously self-referential discourse. Gazing at our textual navels might prevent us from addressing our 'real' problems. For the purposes of substantive theory, so it would seem, interpretation is bound to be fruitless. Now in a discipline aspiring to 'scientific' status such concerns are of course eminently reasonable. The risk of proceeding in interpretive circles is real. As the record of interpretations of the classics attests, there is no guarantee that interpretation will contribute to 'substantive' theory that will tell us more about 'the world'.

Yet interpretation cannot be avoided. Everything is always already interpreted (Fish, 1988), including the tradition within which we work. Texts, however 'objectively' or 'authoritatively' framed, never 'tell' us what they mean. Even dismissing a tradition, in order to get on with the current business of theorizing, involves a complex interpretive judgment. Moreover, interpretation in the form of critically reconsidering the themes inherent in an ongoing tradition is one indispensable aspect of theoretical work; if we try to do without such interpretation, in an effort to 'overcome' our links with a tradition, our theorizing is bound to flounder (Robertson, 1978; Alexander, 1987). Most importantly, interpretation can also serve a 'constructive' purpose, especially if we can show that similar results or problems appear from different interpretive points of view. A simple example of possibly illuminating agreement is the salient aspect of Parsons's own work I mentioned above, namely his way of doing theory-by-interpretation. It would not be difficult to achieve a reasonable consensus

among interpreters with very different axes to grind that this is one
plausible characterization of Parsons, that this feature is indeed 'salient',
and that it is a source of some of the main problems in Parsons's work. I
hasten to add that for a pluralist such 'consensus' is not a necessary goal of
interpretation.

The possibility of constructive convergence also alleviates a second
concern about interpretation in theory. That concern has to do with the
threatening diversity and inconsistency of readings. Once we engage in
reading, as opposed to 'constructing', theory we are faced with many
interpretive options. If the texts do not constrain our readings and if we do
not have a solid interpretive code on which everyone agrees, then we could
end up with a congeries of 'views' rather than cumulative theory. Unless
interpretation is tied to substantive theorizing, anything might go – a
disturbing prospect for a discipline aspiring to produce greater knowledge
by rational means. Now this fear is also understandable. It is indeed the
case that many readings are possible; there is no guarantee that we will
reach agreement; diverse interpretations will not necessarily lead to a
higher-level 'synthesis'. Interpreters with different purposes can come to
radically divergent conclusions. For example, some may assert that
Parsons was a general theorist and *therefore* transcended all 'ideology',
while others may assert that Parsons was a metaphysician and *therefore*
cannot lay claim to any 'theory'. There is no clear-cut (that is, non-
interpretive) way to adjudicate such divergence.

However, the fear of relativist chaos can be allayed to some extent. First
of all, while many things 'go', some things go better than others. Even if
many readings are possible, they can all be evaluated in terms of how well
they live up to their own standards. Different interpretations of the state of
literary interpretation confirm this: interpretive pluralism need not imply
radical deconstruction in which the meaning of any text becomes indeter-
minate; although there are no criteria that guarantee validity in advance, in
interpretive practice 'bad' readings can still be ruled out (Fischer, 1985;
Fish, 1988). Moreover, just as there is no *a priori* guarantee of agreement,
a stand-off between hostile interpretive modes is not inevitable either.
Indeed, few interpretations entail a wholesale rejection of all alternatives –
most allow some sort of recognition of the plausibility of other views. In a
contentious setting, different interpretations can actually be played off
against each other, as a way to examine different dimensions of theoretical
objects. 'Convergence' represents only one possible outcome of such an
interpretive exercise. Yet it carries special meaning: where different perspectives intersect we can expect to find truly 'central' problems and
insights. From a Parsonian point of view, highlighting the possibility of
convergence is again not very surprising. After all, Parsons claimed to
build on a convergence of traditions (see Parsons, 1937). Yet he saw this by
and large as an empirical 'event' he 'discovered', not as itself an act of
interpretation (or better: he viewed his interpretation of materials he had
selected for analysis as the discovery of a given textual reality). We can go

beyond Parsons by being more self-reflexive than he, and thereby show as well that progress in interpretation is actually possible.

Interpreting interpretation, then, is a meaningful part of theorizing. Fears of relativism notwithstanding, it is certainly indispensable if we are to make use of the already-interpreted legacy of Talcott Parsons. To get a clearer view of the very crowded discursive 'field' that now surrounds the Parsonian texts themselves, I want to distinguish between different forms of interpretation. We can view all of them as answers to the Kuhnian question: how was it possible for an intelligent sociologist to hold those views? The question is itself a simple interpretive device. Of course it can be answered in different ways, hence the multiplicity of views I just discussed. Most simply put, we can consider intellectual function, subjective intent, social context and objective structure as interpretive strategies that can help us in formulating answers. Although these are conventions of interpretation in other fields, they roughly correspond to the four main dimensions of the Parsonian general action system (A-G-I-L, respectively). While it is usually fair to say that each interpreter has a definite preference for one of these devices, most interpretations will combine different answers. Thus the distinction I use to group several authors is a deliberate simplification.

On Parsons

Standard 'internal' interpretations of Parsons's work rely above all on the intent of the author and the structure of his work (the 'L' and 'G' dimensions, in Parsonian lingo). They would answer the basic question by saying that Parsons was engaged in building a general theory from elementary premises. In an earlier period readings of this kind would focus mainly on *The Social System* (1951), but for at least a generation or so they usually have started by examining *The Structure of Social Action*, which was treated as the foundation for the edifice to be built later, and as the scaffolding from which to build it. In that book, so many have claimed, Parsons not only argued for convergence in the work of a number of European authors but also issued a manifesto for a new kind of analytical theory. For all its 'empirical' claims about the dominant trend in sociological theory, leading to a consensual framework for the study of social action, the primary significance of *Structure* lay elsewhere. It was masterful above all in advocating a 'voluntaristic' approach to action and a 'general' kind of analytical theory. More clearly than any of his predecessors, Parsons proposed to analyze action as the process of using means to reach ends in a situation, a process governed by a norm as a selective principle. A theory developed around the core element of the unit act would cover all aspects of action, in all domains of human endeavor. In proposing his theory, Parsons also tackled a major problem in the tradition with which he grappled, namely the utilitarian dilemma. That is to say, once he had identified the Hobbesian problem of order, he proceeded to sketch a solution to it by linking the value element in action to other elements. Thus, the *Structure* was far more than an interpretation of other people's works; it also was, by design, a creative extension of a tradition and an exercise in theory construction. In this way, the internal interpretation highlights the significance of the *Structure* for the structure of Parsons's work and does justice to the manifest intent of the author, at least as expressed in his 'retrospective teleologies' (Parsons, 1961; 1977).

Assisted by Parsons's own self-conscious reconstructions of the course of his theoretical activity, this line of interpretation suggests that we should see all the work he did after 1937 as gradual elaboration. His work on the professions and on stratification, for example, can be seen as ways to flesh out the abstract solution to the problem of social order proposed in the *Structure* and as applications of the voluntaristic frame of reference. More important from a theoretical point of view was the publication of *The Social System*, soon followed by general statements on the theory of action and the crystallization of the four-function paradigm. The latter enabled Parsons to deal with problems of institutionalization and the relationships between social system, culture and personality, in a much more systematic fashion. The pattern-variables could then be translated into new terms, supporting a more coherent treatment of action systems. The relationships between these systems, once clarified, presented a special problem, one Parsons addressed by generalizing the concept of 'medium'. Since modern societies constituted a distinctive arrangement of systems and subsystems, the obvious question was how this came about in the first place; a new evolutionary theory evolved to deal with this problem. In striving for generality Parsons not only drew on evolutionary theory, but also (however cursorily) on developments in genetics, linguistics and cybernetics. He turned an initially crude form of structural functionalism into a more sophisticated kind of systems theory. Throughout, he tried his theoretical hand at various applications, ranging from an evolutionary interpretation of Christianity to a comprehensive analysis of the American university. The very familiarity of this brief sketch serves to make the point that the internal account of Parsons's intellectual development has become standard. We have been asked to see his work whole, as one integrated and integrative theory project.

But is it? All but the most sympathetic interpreters have voiced their doubts. For Adriaansens (1980), the four-function scheme of Parsons's late period is a successful realization of his earlier intentions; yet to show this he also argues that Parsons's middle period was essentially an unfortunate aberration in an otherwise continuous project. Münch (1981; 1982; 1987), surely one of the most 'sympathetic' interpreters, reads this same middle period as just another step in the elaboration of Parsons's basic ideas, but he feels forced to reformulate the foundation of the four-function scheme, sacrifice the cybernetic hierarchy, and turn one of Parsons's theoretical tools (namely interpenetration) into an all-important concept. Even a more orthodox attempt ostensibly to continue the Parsonian project (Baum, 1976) finds significant gaps at the very core of the theory (such as the undertheorized 'integrative' box) and introduces extraneous notions (such as a distinction between action and experience) to fill it. Less concerned with refurbishing an incomplete project, other interpretations emphasize simply the strength of the 'multidimensional' foundations while criticizing the shaky edifice as a distorted, idealist rendering (Alexander, 1984). But objective inconsistency may outweigh such 'subjective' failure, as Brownstein (1982) argues; with respect to just one element of Parsons's apparatus, namely the cybernetic hierarchy, others diagnose confusion to the point of incoherence (Baum and Lechner, 1987). Indeed, arguments about one integrated project notwithstanding, many have seen a fundamental discontinuity between the 'action' and 'system' phases in Parsons's work (cf. Habermas, 1981). And even if the project is integrated, it can hardly be integrative if its products are logically and empirically suspect (cf. Black, 1961; Mulkay, 1971, among many others). In short, 'internal' interpreters have come up with widely divergent assessments of Parsons's work, hardly any aspect of which has escaped serious criticism (cf. Alexander, 1984: Appendix). While I do not agree with all these assessments, together they provide interpretive evidence concerning the problematic structure and unrealized ambition of the general theory project.

Without further critical analysis of the various interpretations – which, I plan to argue elsewhere, do not do equal justice to Parsons and are not equally 'vital' (Booth, 1979) – we cannot consider this evidence decisive. My purpose, however, is not to judge the judgments or to draw an edifying consensual lesson from serious intellectual conflicts. I only want to emphasize two points here. First, interpretations of the internal kind usually presuppose that Parsons's work 'has' an intent and structure that can be uncovered by the right interpretation; they find the views of 'others' wrong not by virtue of their different purpose or procedure, but largely because they have failed to do justice to Parsons. Even an advocate of postpositivism in social science like Alexander (1984) is surprisingly 'positivist' in his otherwise probing treatment of alternative interpretations: he sets up an 'objective' standard of evaluation and accuses others of either not meeting this standard or factually distorting 'the' meaning of (parts of) Parsons's work. But the very diversity of critical arguments about Parsons suggests that neither 'intent' nor 'structure' are clear-cut guides to interpretation; indeed, both always are and have to be interpreted. This means that there is no simple way to settle the differences by appealing to 'the' intent or structure presumably manifested in Parsons's work. But are we then left with a multitude of views, none wholly convincing by itself? I do not think so, for the second main point I want to make is that there is a message in the conflicts as such. It is difficult to formulate it in a way that would prove acceptable to all, but my earlier strong statement may come close: Parsons was wrong in all the right ways.

The foundations for his mature scheme may be faulty, but he was right to try and formulate it. His results may not realize the presuppositional mandate, but it was a mandate worth implementing. The structure of action theory may be logically fragile, but Parsons was right to try to erect it at all. The theory may fall short of generality, but at least that was a worthwhile ambition. Or so different 'internal' critics might hold. Interpreting their interpretations, however briefly, thus leads to appreciation combined with serious doubt about the viability of the action theory project as 'it' stands.

About 'external' interpretations we can tell a similar story. In spite of differences between them, they all rely on intellectual function and social context to answer the question of why Parsons wrote what he wrote. Their composite answer might be that Parsons was a sociological entrepreneur engaged in promoting ideology by other means. Pulling together different strands of familiar works on Parsons (such as Mills; Wrong; Gouldner; Camic; Buxton), the story behind it might go as follows: His early work on capitalism already betrayed a deep concern about the viability of this kind of society, a concern he expressed in more general terms when he came to focus on the 'problem of social order' in *The Structure of Social Action*. By reinterpreting the classics and formulating highly general concepts he defended a conservative view of society without being exposed to ideological criticism. The normative element in action was not so much a theoretical innovation as a way of formulating the ideological requirements of an unstable capitalist system. His very concern with norms and values in an open but stable society reflected his own values as a secularized liberal Protestant. At the same time, by articulating his ideas the way he did, he also intervened in the development of social science in the USA. Parsons's purpose was to provide a charter for sociology that would put it on an equal footing with other, established sciences. This he could only do by formulating an analytical, 'scientifically respectable' theory. To succeed, such a theory nevertheless had to take into account some distinctively human dimensions of action that were not yet covered by other disciplines. A general, voluntaristic theory would do precisely that.

The further development of action theory, so externalists might continue, was closely related both to Parsons's position in the discipline and to the broader social context in which he found himself as a professor at Harvard. Playing down the role of power, he first presented a rosy view of the professions. As he saw it, the larger social system was held together by value consensus, smoothly institutionalized. Possibilities of serious conflict were eliminated; the individual was reduced to an 'oversocialized' automaton. With pretentious concepts, easily translated into common-sensical terms, Parsons tried to dominate the theoretical discourse in the discipline. Not only did his work reflect the standard self-congratulatory and consensual view of modern culture, he also wanted to use it to stifle serious disagreement within the discipline by absorbing alternative views in a process of 'convergence'. His theoretical development culminated in an 'interchange' paradigm that curiously generalized utilitarian views of inter-action. Once he addressed change in any sustained manner, the result was not surprising: history could be treated as evolution toward the immanent telos of a differentiated, pluralistic society. America, for this liberal Protestant, was still the city on the hill, one built after centuries of 'pre-paration'. Parsons's work, then, was a project in disciplinary politics as well as a continuation of bourgeois ideology by other means.

Did it work? From their different points of view, many externalists have expressed their doubts. Again a small sampling must suffice. Examining the relationship between Parsons and his intellectual predecessors, some critics have seen more gap than convergence and thus question the legit-imacy of his 'intervention' in the tradition (Pope et al., 1975). Focusing on Parsons's attempt to provide a 'charter' for sociology, Camic (1989) similarly notes that Parsons distorted the tradition he used and criticized; moreover, the charter itself was made up of components that did not fit together very well. Mills (1959) sees more coherence, but thinks it amounts only to dressed-up common sense. Wrong (1961), on the other hand, might not agree that the oversocialized conception of man is indeed common sense. For Gouldner (1970), that conception is only one of Parsons's problems; while he took up significant issues, Parsons was only able to treat them in an ideologically distorted and ultimately untenable way. This in turn is echoed by Buxton (1985), who thinks Parsons's liberal defense of the capitalist nation-state is deeply flawed. Although externalists also judge the work 'itself', this is not the main target of their assessments. Their criticism concerns above all its implications for the discipline and society at large. Overinterpreting for the sake of argument, let me draw their conclusions for them: Parsons's attempt at disciplinary integration has failed and his now-antiquated defense of the American nation-state has had little, if any, impact.

It would be fairly easy to take issue with these external challenges, if only by noting some puzzling features. For example, even a sophisticated interpreter like Camic does not raise the problem of the standards of inter-pretation and leaves us with the puzzle of how an internally inconsistent document like the *Structure* could even be considered a viable charter. Buxton's liberal is not quite the same Parsons as Gouldner's conservative. But as in the case of the 'internal' interpretations my main purpose is to suggest that function and context are selective interpretive devices, which can be used for a variety of purposes in dealing with different parts of Parsons's work. Again, this is not to say that anything goes, or that we can no longer critically examine different interpretations. Indeed, given a cer-tain range of interpretive tools, we can analyze how well these are used – an exercise that would confirm, say, that the diagnoses of Wrong and Gouldner are themselves flawed. Interpretive diversity is no charter for relativism. Yet, as I interpret it, it does contain a message: from the point of view of many if not most external critics, Parsons was also wrong in all (or at least many of) the right ways. His exercise in bourgeois legitimation was bound to fail, but his was more sophisticated than any other. His attempt to create, rather than discover, convergence breaks down, but at least his was a creative reinterpretation of previous work. His charter for sociology was at best temporarily useful, but this was still a masterful attempt to clarify the nature of sociology as an independent discipline.

Stated in this way, it is a message many of the more sympathetic internalists cannot accept. For example, from Münch's (1987) point of view the charter can still work if it is properly reconstructed. For others, the idea that general theory could aid in bourgeois legitimation would seem crude at best. Externalists, for their part, would play down the structural incoherence that vexes some of the internalists. They would interpret the very meaning of intent and structure differently. All this indicates, if only with limited evidence, that there is no full-fledged 'convergence' on the horizon. Nevertheless, considering both kinds of interpretation together, I suggest that there is a pattern to the pluralism. First, each kind of interpretation results in a specific conclusion, but in many cases this takes the form of a negative assessment coupled with appreciation for some important aspect of Parsons's project. Secondly, while interpretive purposes differ and some interpretations are better than others, there is no *a priori* reason for particular interpreters to reject the conclusions of others. Indeed, precisely when these different purposes, and the strategies that go with them, are clearly recognized does it become easier to appreciate and learn from other interpretations, at least in principle. The ability to do that is one of the virtues of the pluralistic position I advocate. For pluralists, convergence does not take the form of substantive agreement but rather of constructive mutual recognition, which involves not only the legitimacy of different interpretations but also awareness of different kinds of serious deficiencies in Parsons. This kind of convergence is further strengthened by a third possible reading of Parsons, which partially draws on the strengths of other interpretations to clarify the meaning of Parsons's work.

On modernity

The third type of interpretation extends a line of argument that has become increasingly prominent in recent years. Robertson (1982) has presented a view of Parsons as an interpretive theorist; Mayhew (1984) has noted Parsons's systematic defense of modernity; Holton and Turner (1986) have argued for a consistently modernist, anti-nostalgic Parsons; Buxton (1985) has noted the 'activist' element in Parsons's theorizing; and Alexander (1988) bolsters such views with his emphasis on interpreting theory as part of a larger discourse. The emerging reading of Parsons is not meant to 'transcend' other views, nor does it claim to be exclusively 'true'. Rather, it is an interpretation that locates Parsons in a particular kind of discourse and argues that his work derives its meaning (or one of its meanings) from

the way it is connected to this discourse. It simply
cumbersome terms, that we can plausibly read Par
constructivist engaged in formulating a model of m
interpret the nature and development of a particular
tion. With this constructive effort Parsons participat
tradition centered on the meaning and viability of mo
goes back at least to the late eighteenth century. In
obviously used 'general' theoretical resources; his ide   ., nad
'ideological' connotations – internalists and externalists boun have a point.
But the distinctive feature of his work was the way in which theoretical
form and intellectual function, generalizing intent and cultural content, fit
together as part of an interpretation of modernity. This interpretive effort
goes 'all the way down'. That is to say, most if not all of Parsons's work can
be read as part of a 'constructive' interpretation of modernity. This interpretation is rich and fruitful: it incorporates elements of many kinds of
modern thought to show that a distinctly modern form of social order is
'possible'. Moreover, it can remain useful even if the general-theoretical
foundations of action theory are found wanting. But it is also problematic:
while its image of modernity is pluralistic, the theory is monistic. My
argument below is that if we accept that image as plausible, Parsons's
theory cannot sustain its claim to theoretical preeminence, since at best
it represents only one possible account of modernity – one that may be
called a form of cognitive reductionism.

What, then, is the image of modernity Parsons constructed? Let me pull
together different components of his work. Most simply put, Parsons
viewed modern societies as relatively autonomous nation-states that are
internally differentiated yet inclusive; such societies achieve a greater
mastery of their environment than any others; and their secular cultures
center on highly generalized values. These societies incorporate certain
'evolutionary universals', such as bureaucratic organization, into their
structure. In their much more complex division of labor, professions play a
special integrative role. On the basis of new form of equality, new kinds
of inequality emerge – not as divisive cleavages but as the outcome of
evaluation of action in terms of common standards. 'Interchange' relations mediate between differentiated subsystems. The economy is only
one such subsystem, embedded in a larger social system, which in turn is
part of a larger action system, itself differentiated. In modernity, action
crystallizes into at least four distinct kinds of systems, which can be
combined into 'complexes' such as that of cognitive rationality, in which
the university plays a special role. But how is such an arrangement
possible? Modernity can be seen as the institutionalization of a pattern of
'modern' values – individualism and rational activism above all – specified
to guide action in different spheres. The specification of such 'controlling'
values, when properly linked with resources for action, makes a modern
order coherent. At the same time, modernity is the outcome of an evolutionary process that leads to a higher level of organized social complexity.

is process actually took place in a particular civilizational context; nce the outcome is possible only as the secularized version of an originally Christian society. While the process has this specific origin, it increasingly encompasses the global system of societies. Of course this is only a simple composite image, but my point is that adding greater detail drawn from various parts of his work would still fit this overall image of modernity.

Parsons was a constructive modernist from the very beginning of his career. As I can sketch only very briefly, he stands in a tradition which he creatively transforms. Recall that he starts out by taking on Sombart and Weber – interpreting their views of capitalism (Parsons, 1928; 1929). This was not so much a study of historical changes in capitalism *per se*, nor a deductive effort in generating new theory, but rather a way to arrive at a meaningful and coherent image of capitalism via a close reading of texts. In *The Structure of Social Action* the very problem of social order, though ostensibly taken from Hobbes, derives it urgency from the specter of an 'atomistic' society. Rather than addressing the problems of that society 'directly' or examining all possible views of action and order, Parsons frames his problems and solution in the (modified) terms of an on-going discourse. The main problem, of course, is interpretively derived from the utilitarian tradition. The elements of the solution, starting with the motto of the book, are themselves taken from a distinctively modern conception of action. The whole enterprise is thoroughly modernist: an attempt to give a general account of the possibility of 'voluntaristic' action within the context of a social 'order'. In this way, the rational autonomy of actors, inadequately treated by other theories, is actually to be vindicated. On this reading, it is also no accident that the philosophical core of this work was indeed Kantian. Above all, this expresses modernist confidence, first, in our rational ability to achieve certain knowledge of the world by giving conceptual form to sense experience, and second, in our rational ability to account for the 'existence' of social order. This confidence is bolstered by interpretation, not by an argument from first premises or an inductive demonstration.

While the early phase of Parsons's career is relatively well known, the very last period has received less attention. Yet for the interpretation I propose this is equally crucial. Parsons's most ambitious paper is clearly that on the human condition (1978: Ch. 15), conceived as a synthesis and ultimate generalization of all his previous work. The theory is itself interpretive: it 'categorizes the world accessible to human experience in terms of the *meanings* to human beings of its various parts and aspects' (p. 361). In treating these meanings Parsons thinks 'it is legitimate to adopt the Kantian account of *knowing* as the prototype' (p. 368). The dimensions of action as well as its 'environments' are all conceived as 'systems', all of which have four subsystems. Systems are related by way of 'interchange' via media. They are held together by a 'cybernetic hierarchy'. To fill in the various boxes Parsons relies on the usual modern suspects – Kant, Freud,

Weber above all. The telic system has a definite Christian cast; to comple-
ment the universal components of the family, Parsons suspects we can find
evidence for the universality of the symbolic components of Christianity.
In such arguments we find a constructivist modernist at work. Creatively
appropriating the resources of distinctively Western, modern thinkers,
Parsons formulates a set of distinctively modern metaphors in terms of
which our lives as human beings can be considered meaningful – and, in
good modernist fashion, presents this as a rationally derived, scientifically
valid picture of *the* human condition.

In his paper on 'Religious and Economic Symbolism in the Western
World' (1979), Parsons claims to focus on the role of symbolic structures in
progressive, evolutionary change. But of course his real interest, as the
title suggests, is in the crystallization of Western civilization, as a process of
universal significance – which could be viewed as the secularization of the
religious conception of a 'Christian society' (p. 1). Accordingly, Parsons
first looks for symbolic roots in the Christian tradition, reinterpreting
Weber above all. Christianity 'contributed' to evolution because of its
ambivalent approach to dangers (erotic, economic, intellectual) inherent
in the human condition. The Reformation added to the ambivalence,
though the moral conflict over worldly concerns did not 'come to a head'
until three centuries after the original Reformation (p. 14). Liberal Protestantism 'has been the framework in which what now seems to have been
the most influential sector of modern society has come to crystallize'
(p. 18). The primary symbolic responses to the new modern 'baring' of the
economic factor after the Industrial Revolution were Marxism and establishment economism of the utilitarian variety. Neither can account for
solidarity and social order, if only because they both ignore the meaning
actors give to economic matters. But these forms of economic absolutism
are being broken by the main trend of Western thought. Thus Parsons uses
selected aspects of the Christian tradition, as filtered by Weber, to present
an image of modern culture; he interprets Marxism and utilitarianism as
'understandable' responses to the problems of this culture, which themselves can only give a partial account of that culture.

As the simple composite sketch above indicates, Parsons added pieces to
the mosaic of modernity between the early and late phases of his work.
What he wrote on the professions, on socialization, on stratification, on
religion, on the media, even on illness and death all contributed to a
particular image of modern society. Over time, his interests shifted, not
least with respect to the problem of social change. In his many publications
we can obviously find many statements that appear to contradict each
other. Without being able to consider the whole record here I suggest that,
conceived as an interpretive construction of modernity, Parsons's work has
great diachronic coherence. For Parsons, living in modernity means being
collectively oriented to certain values, but only some and only of the most
general kind; it means being included on an equal basis into large societal
communities irrespective of ascriptive characteristics; it means having to

cope with differentiation, itself sustained by a complex flow of 'media'; it means having to manage personal autonomy, without the security of faith or community; it means having to contribute to a process of 'adaptive upgrading' or world mastery; it means acting rationally, guided by selective norms; it means being connected to the core components of a Christian civilization, even though these have lost their original force; it means realizing that no one single system or principle or perspective drives all of the modern 'action system'; it means trying to give an abstract, rational account of how this modern condition is possible at all; it means living in one's imperfectly modern (for Parsons himself, American) society without nostalgia.

The added benefit of this reading is that it also helps us to make sense of Parsons's style. Parsons himself appropriately compared the development of his work with that of the common law. Relying on precedent he dealt with particular cases at hand, treating new problems 'as if' they were like old ones. Only occasionally did he codify his concepts and principles; every such codification was tentative. The precedents are primarily the ideas of a select group of modernist intellectuals. The 'cases' are linked by a pervasive concern with describing/constructing/accounting for a modern social order. The continuity of the project is served by many revisits to the same precedents. The rhetorical style is that of constructive interpretation, combined with illocutionary assertion – rather than deductive, empirical or ideological argument. Like a common law judge forming an opinion, Parsons would use previous cases and presumably 'established' principles to make an authoritative claim ('we think').

Does this reading set Parsons apart from mainstream social science? Doesn't this reading veer more toward metaphysics than toward theory? In one sense, yes: If by 'mainstream' we mean formal, deductive, testable theory, then Parsons on my reading is not (or at least in many ways not) 'mainstream' – as many skeptics had already suspected. Yet it would be difficult to show that there is a 'main' stream in sociology today. Moreover, I suggest that all bodies of theoretical work are at least partly 'analytically constructivist', albeit to varying extents. The different types of interpretation I have sketched here can in principle be applied to all kinds of theory, though not every type of interpretation is equally plausible for every type of theory. And unlike sociological 'metaphysics', Parsons's interpretation of modernity can still be held accountable in many respects, ranging from his selective and unreflexive use of previous work to his selective view of the Christian tradition that presumably laid the groundwork for modernity. But however problematic Parsons's view may be in particulars, it is one that creatively captures significant dimensions of our modern condition. It can withstand many kinds of criticism (Holton and Turner, 1986) and it is rich and coherent enough to be used for heuristic purposes – for example, to examine *anti*-modern movements in systematic fashion (Lechner, 1985; 1990). And it tells us what is wrong with the theory as Parsons presented it.

Beyond Parsons

If modernity means what Parsons says it means, then the theory he presented cannot be the only possible account of it.

Consider first Parsons's characterization of modernity in its American version. 'The society as a system tends to be evaluated, not as an end in itself but as *instrumental* to bases of value outside itself. Its desirability is to be judged in terms of its contribution to these *extra*societal grounds of value' (Parsons, 1982). The same applies to theory as a system. It must also be instrumental to other values and evaluated in extratheoretical terms. For Parsons, some of the higher values to be served might be a sense of intellectual clarity, or even the quality of modernity itself. But if theory is instrumental, it must necessarily be superseded. If it must contribute to higher values, there must be other ways to realize such values as well. This theory, then, can only be one among several possible modes of intellectual work. We can reach this conclusion as well by considering the other side of Parsons's view of modern society, namely institutionalized individualism. For Parsons this applied mainly to a differentiated society in which equal citizens contribute in radically different ways, integrated only by some commitment to very general standards (1982: 328–9). But it applies equally well to modern cultural systems: different disciplines, different forms of cultural action perform different cultural functions, at best oriented to some very general cultural ideals. In such a culture, a general theory of action can be only one of many contenders for interpretive primacy. Indeed, the very idea that one theory can do justice to radical cultural diversity comes to seem implausible. The theory describes a condition of 'individualized', differentiated cultural and social action, while it incongruously projects itself as a potentially hegemonic view of that condition.

Parsons called the main modern value-pattern 'instrumental activism'. The activist component consisted of a special concern for 'increasing the sphere of freedom of action within the environment and ultimately control over the environment' (Parsons, 1982: 328). This is of course a persistent theme in Parsons's work, a variation on Weber's treatment of world-mastery. But the theory itself is a project in world-mastery as well, an effort to gain cognitive control over the modern environments of action. The 'morality' of this theory is that of cognitive control – over action, modernity and other accounts of both. Even telic problems beyond the sphere of human action receive their place in a categorical scheme, which has its own peculiar esthetic qualities. The world is made orderly in theory. In this way, Parsonian theory 'reflects' a modern value-orientation. But what is this mastery for? While cognitive mastery may be meaningful in itself, it cannot exhaust the range of human concerns, as Parsons recognized in his discussion of telic problems and by his analysis of the cultural system. Theoretical work, after all, can be only one part of all the cultural work done in a society that tries to give an account of itself and its values.

Moral discourse, modern literature, theological reflection all must 'contribute' to the image of modernity that is collectively produced. The attempt to develop a 'general' theory is appropriate for 'adaptive' cultural
action, but other forms of action can legitimately resist being 'incorporated' into such a voracious cognitive scheme. To claim that general
theory in Parsons's sense is the only or even the main way to give a
plausible account of modernity is to engage in cognitive reductionism.
Parsons's multilayered analysis of action systems and of modern values
enables us to see that such reductionism is implausible.

Another way to arrive at this conclusion is to consider the implications
of Parsons's structural theory of differentiation. He provides a cognitive
account of differentiation as a process by which a more complex desirable
order is institutionalized in a stable manner. Of course this requires all
the usual tools in the Parsonian kit – integrative mechanisms, media,
generalized values and the like. But once roles are differentiated, occu-
pants of such roles are bound to 'see' the world differently. Once systems
are differentiated, they must engage in the symbolic processing of 'environmental inputs' – and they, too, are bound to do so according to their
own requirements. Insofar as modernity becomes institutionally and culturally differentiated, it is bound to generate many different kinds of
accounts of the 'modern' experience. As the environment for any system,
any role, it can be imagined and reconstructed in different ways, from
multiple subsystem perspectives. The (neo)classical economic theory Parsons criticized throughout his career is a case in point: it is a reconstruction
of the modern condition from a specifically 'economic' point of view. As
such, it is only a 'partial' picture, 'insufficient' by itself. Moreover, its
terms can be translated into alternative, more 'comprehensive' theories.
Parsons certainly treated his own theory as a translation scheme and as a
way to show the 'insufficiency' of many other 'partial' points of view. But in
a fully differentiated situation, any translation involves loss, any point of
view is partial. A theory project that is institutionally at home in the
Western academy can 'encompass' the moral perspectives of, say, minorities in a presumably more inclusive society, but it cannot present the world
'from the moral point of view' of such minorities. It can 'go beyond' conventional economics, but not without losing the specificity of the 'economic'
perspective itself. It can conceptualize the process of differentiation and
the condition of pluralism, but it can do so *only* conceptually; for example,
what the theory sees as pluralism is experienced very differently, as a slide
into a cultural abyss, from an orthodox religious point of view. Now of
course the theory is still interesting precisely as a way to think hard about
such pluralism and its implications; yet taking the theory seriously in this
way means having to listen to the 'original languages' as well, not just to
action-theoretical 'translations'. Thinking of Parsonian action theory as
the account of modernity is like thinking that Bauhaus is *the* modern
architectural style. In fact, both are instances of self-undermining, monistic
modernism.

If we approach Parsonian theory in the same spirit in which Parsons himself approached the utilitarian and idealistic traditions, we find that he erred in ways similar to the utilitarians and suffered from different kinds of 'idealism'. Though Parsons challenged the former's reliance on 'given' individual rationality as a basis of social order, he in fact substituted a 'given' social order for their unexamined, bedrock individual. To be sure, Parsons went on to examine many dimensions of 'society', but the existence of that orderly entity was taken for granted; once it was properly described, all kinds of other puzzles could be solved, including the problem of individual autonomy. But what does it mean to say, as Parsons did in the *Structure of Social Action*, that modern 'social order' exists? This presupposes a conception of social order, a way to decide what does and does not exist, and some sort of experiential knowledge prior to the development of any theory. Of course, the assumption formally parallels Kant's assumption that we have 'certain' knowledge. The effort to account for the 'possibility' of modern social order on this basis marks Parsons's project as an exercise in sociological transcendental idealism. Yet Parsons's Kantian assumption can be easily challenged, in the same way he challenged naive assumptions concerning individuals and their rationality. How is such 'knowledge' itself possible? How did it come into being? Without answering such questions directly, we can say that Parsons's starting point is an expression of modernist confidence in the viability of modern society rather than a matter of justified belief. For Parsons, it was 'desirable' to think of the world in this way, and thus his very starting point is a form of modernist idealism. His later work compounded this idealism by presenting a consistently 'biased' version of modernity as the institutionalization of a modern value pattern, maintained by a cybernetic hierarchy of 'control', as Alexander (1984) has demonstrated at some length. But if we take seriously Parsons's intent to develop a 'general' and 'multidimensional' theory, then all these forms of idealism must be called into question. The form of critique practiced by Parsons and at least some of the premises of his early work can thus be turned against the project as he developed it. By Parsonian means we can show, as I have tried to do in only very brief compass, that the Parsonian account of modernity is at best one, partial version – one way to 'make' the modern world among others.

With his rich analysis of action systems and his pluralistic image of modernity Parsons not only attacked various forms of theoretical reductionism, but also what he occasionally called 'absolutism'. His interpretation of modernity was also a defense of modernity against 'anti-modern' views harking back to the security of community or faith. He bolstered his own serenely 'pro-modern' position by treating all forms of nostalgia rather critically, as both undesirable and doomed to fail. Holton and Turner are right to see action theory as aimed 'against nostalgia' – an interpretation I tried to support in the previous section. But did Parsons himself manage to resist the temptation of nostalgia? In one respect, he did not. That is to say, the very attempt to provide one all-encompassing account of modernity, framed in 'general' terms, may be called a form of nostalgic modernism. Parsons still exhibits a desire-for-the-whole; there is a kind of residual nostalgia in his effort to achieve wholeness by other (i.e. 'scientific') means. It is a more sophisticated kind of nostalgia, to be sure, but one that the theory itself forces us to recognize as such. Both the arguments I have presented in this section and the critical interpretations I discussed above suggest that the 'whole' of action theory is not quite as nicely integrated and integrative as Parsons may have wished. They thus confirm in the case of Parsons what Parsons thought about other forms of nostalgia.

Conclusion

This chapter has been an extended plea for interpretive pluralism in theory and in the analysis of modernity. While Parsonian action theory in principle provides good grounds for a 'pluralistic' approach to interpretation, Parsons's own approach to interpretation was largely 'monistic'; thus, as has become quite clear to many sociologists, we have to go 'beyond Parsons' in interpretation. Many 'internal' interpretations of his work actually follow him in his interpretive monism, but the very diversity of critical assessments of Parsons's project casts further doubt on such attempts. Rather than making peaceful coexistence of conflicting views possible, a pluralistic treatment of the current range of Parsons-interpretations does yield a complex critical diagnosis, which I have briefly sketched here. I have tried to bolster that diagnosis by first reading Parsons as an analytically constructive interpreter of modernity, then using the image of modernity Parsons produced to challenge the way in which he went about constructing it. If Parsons is at least partially 'right' about modernity – and I have assumed he is – then his general-theoretical, monistic account of it cannot suffice. On good Parsonian grounds, we have to go 'beyond Parsons' in the interpretation of modernity – as 'we' (that is, all intellectual and practical modernists) have done in any case.

If there are different legitimate ways to read Parsons but all such readings identify important deficiencies in his project, as my discussion of interpretations and my Parsonian critique of Parsons's theoretical approach to modernity have suggested, then why should we now read him? The way I prefer to read Parsons suggests one answer. Parsons remains interesting as perhaps the last of the old-fashioned, self-confident, generalizing modernists – one who drew in subtle fashion on the ongoing discourse of modernity to express the mid-twentieth-century liberal self-understanding. Parsons matters because of his role in a still vital, though now more problematic, kind of discourse. His contribution, read in the way I have sketched here, helps to provide a 'charter' for a pluralistic treatment of interpretation as well as of modernity itself. But from a pluralistic point of view there are some other good reasons for reading Parsons in this post-Parsonian era. One can read him to elaborate on existing internal interpretations and engage in fairly 'orthodox' work, for example following

Münch (1986, 1987); or one can add to the external interpretations by doing more sociology-of-knowledge work on Parsons, for example following Camic (1989); or one can read him to identify, once again, fundamental deficiencies from alternative theoretical points of view, and thus go 'beyond' him in a different way than I have sketched here. It can still be fruitful to use Parsons's model of modernity in heuristic fashion, as I have tried to show elsewhere. And certainly a pluralist cannot exclude the obvious possibility of eclectically 'mining' the riches in Parsons's *œuvre*.

If we continue to read Parsons for such reasons, we will undoubtedly discover even more fundamental difficulties in the action-theory project as Parsons conceived and developed it. If we treat action theory in the pluralistic manner I have advocated here, not least by applying Parsonian ideas to the Parsonian project, I suspect we will also confirm the already widely shared conclusion I have reached here again via a new route – namely, that we need to go 'beyond Parsons' in different ways. This may come to mean the demise of action theory as we know it. When that happens, sociologists may well recall one lesson Parsons taught, and consider that just as there is no need to be nostalgic about the once-tempting alternatives to modernity, there is no need to feel nostalgic about Talcott Parsons either.

Note

I would like to thank my colleagues Alvin Boskoff and Alex Hicks, Emory University graduate students Richard Lee, Jenny Miller-Scher and Joya Misra, and the editors of this volume for their very helpful comments.

References

Adriaansens, H.P.M. (1980) *Talcott Parsons and the Conceptual Dilemma*. London: Routledge & Kegan Paul.

Alexander, J.C. (1984) *Theoretical Logic in Sociology*, vol. 4, *The Modern Reconstruction of Classical Thought: Talcott Parsons*. Berkeley and Los Angeles: University of California Press.

Alexander, J.C. (1987) 'On the Centrality of the Classics', pp. 11–57 in A. Giddens and J. Turner (eds), *Social Theory Today*. London: Macmillan.

Alexander, J.C. (1988) 'The New Theoretical Movement', pp. 77–101 in N. Smelser (ed.), *Handbook of Sociology*. Newbury Park: Sage.

Baum, R.C. (1976) 'The System of Solidarities', *Indian Journal of Sociology*, 16 (1 and 2): 305–53.

Baum, R.C. and Lechner F.J. (1987) 'Zum Begriff der Hierarchie: von Luhmann zu Parsons', pp. 298–332 in D. Baecker et al. (eds), *Theorie als Passion*. Frankfurt: Suhrkamp.

Black, M. (1961) 'Some Questions about Talcott Parsons' Theories', pp. 268–88 in Max Black (ed.), *The Social Theories of Talcott Parsons*. Englewood Cliffs, NJ: Prentice-Hall.

Booth, W.C. (1979) *Critical Understanding*. Chicago: University of Chicago Press.

Brown, R.H. (1976) *A Poetic for Sociology*. Cambridge: Cambridge University Press.

Brownstein, L. (1982) *Talcott Parsons' General Action Scheme*. Cambridge, MA: Schenkman.

Buxton, W. (1985) *Talcott Parsons and the Capitalist Nation-State*. Toronto: University of Toronto Press.

Camic, C. (1989) '*Structure* after 50 Years: the Anatomy of a Charter', *American Journal of Sociology*, 95 (1): 38–107.

Fischer, M. (1985) *Does Deconstruction Make Any Difference? Poststructuralism and the Defense of Poetry in Modern Criticism*. Bloomington: Indiana University Press.

Fish, S. (1988) *Doing What Comes Naturally*. Durham, NC: Duke University Press.

Gouldner, A.W. (1970) *The Coming Crisis of Western Sociology*. New York: Basic Books.

Habermas, J. (1981) *Theorie des Kommunikativen Handelns*. Frankfurt: Suhrkamp.

Holton, R.J., and Turner, B.S. (1986) *Talcott Parsons on Economy and Society*. London and New York: Routledge & Kegan Paul.

Lechner, F.J. (1985) 'Modernity and its Discontents', pp. 157–76 in J.C. Alexander (ed.), *Neofunctionalism*. Beverly Hills: Sage.

Lechner, F.J. (1990) 'Fundamentalism and Sociocultural Revitalization: On the Logic of Dedifferentiation', pp. 88–118 in J.C. Alexander and P. Colomy (eds), *Differentiation Theory and Social Change*. New York: Columbia University Press.

Levine, D.N. (1986) 'The Forms and Functions of Social Knowledge', pp. 271–83 in D.N. Fiske and R.A. Schweder (eds), *Metatheory in Social Science*. Chicago: University of Chicago Press.

Levine, D.N. (1989) 'Simmel as a Resource for Sociological Metatheory', *Sociological Theory*, 7 (2): 161–74.

Mayhew, L. (1984) 'In Defense of Modernity: Talcott Parsons and the Utilitarian Tradition', *American Journal of Sociology*, 89 (6): 1273–1305.

Mills, C.W. (1959) *The Sociological Imagination*. New York: Oxford University Press.

Mulkay, M.J. (1971) *Functionalism, Exchange and Theoretical Strategy*. London: Routledge & Kegan Paul.

Münch, R. (1981) 'Talcott Parsons and the Theory of Action I: the Structure of the Kantian Core', *American Journal of Sociology*, 86 (3): 709–40.

Münch, R. (1982) 'Talcott Parsons and the Theory of Action II: the Continuity of the Development', *American Journal of Sociology*, 8 (4): 771–826.

Münch, R. (1984) *Die Struktur der Moderne*. Frankfurt: Suhrkamp.

Münch, R. (1986) *Die Kultur der Moderne*. Frankfurt: Suhrkamp.

Münch, R. (1987) *Theory of Action: Towards a New Synthesis Going Beyond Parsons*. London and Boston: Routledge & Kegan Paul.

Parsons, T. (1928) '"Capitalism" in Recent German Literature: Sombart and Weber, I', *Journal of Political Economy*, 36: 641–61.

Parsons, T. (1929) '"Capitalism" in Recent German Literature: Sombart and Weber, II', *Journal of Political Economy*, 37: 31–51.

Parsons, T. (1937) *The Structure of Social Action*. New York: McGraw-Hill.

Parsons, T. (1951) *The Social System*. London: Routledge & Kegan Paul.

Parsons, T. (1961) 'The Point of View of the Author', pp. 311–63 in M. Black (ed.), *The Social Theories of Talcott Parsons*. Englewood Cliffs, NJ: Prentice-Hall.

Parsons, T. (1977) *Social Systems and the Evolution of Action Theory*. New York: Free Press.

Parsons, T. (1978) *Action Theory and the Human Condition*. New York: Free Press.

Parsons, T. (1979) 'Religious and Economic Symbolism in the Western World', *Sociological Inquiry*, 49 (1): 1–48.

Parsons, T. (1982) 'American Values and American Society', in L. Mayhew (ed.), *Talcott Parsons on Institutions and Social Evolution*. Chicago: University of Chicago Press.

Pope, W., Cohen, J. and Hazelrigg, L.E. (1975) 'On the Divergence of Weber and Durkheim: a Critique of Parsons' Convergence Thesis', *American Sociological Review*, 40 (4): 417–27.

Robertson, R. (1978) *Meaning and Change*. New York: New York University Press.

Robertson, R. (1982) 'Parsons on the Evolutionary Significance of American Religion', *Sociological Analysis*, 43 (4): 307–26.

Seidman, S. (1983) 'Beyond Presentism and Historicism: Understanding the History of Social Science', *Sociological Inquiry*, 53 (1): 79–94.

Wrong, D. (1961) 'The Oversocialized Conception of Man in Modern Sociology', *American Sociological Review*, 26 (2): 183–92.

9

SIMMEL AND PARSONS RECONSIDERED

Donald N. Levine

When Talcott Parsons unveiled *The Structure of Social Action* (hereafter *Structure*) in 1937, he was seeking to replace two conceptions of the sociological tradition with a novel vision of that tradition.[1] The first conception, then dominant in the United States, was epitomized in the influential text by Park and Burgess, *Introduction to the Science of Sociology* (1921). Deriving ultimately from Comte, their account told the story of the discipline as a progressive displacement of vague, speculative ideas about social phenomena by precisely observed and rigorously represented facts. In the memorable words of Park and Burgess, 'the period of the "schools"' . . . was giving way to 'the period of investigation and research', and so 'the first thing that students in sociology need to learn is to observe and record their own observations' (1921: 44, v).

A contrasting view appeared seven years later in Pitirim Sorokin's *Contemporary Sociological Theories*. Although Sorokin agreed that the scholar's primary task is 'to deal with facts rather than theories', he nonetheless deemed it crucial to offer the novitiate sociologist a reasoned inventory of the diverse schools of sociological theory, since those theories had 'been appearing like mushrooms after rain . . . [and] the field of sociology is overcrowded by a multitude of various and contradictory systems' (1928: xvii, xix). Accordingly, Sorokin's pluralist account distinguished nine major schools and their numerous branches, thus representing a wide array of the primarily European authors whom Sorokin knew so well.

In countering these modes of representing the field, Parsons argued, against the empiricist approach, that rigorous observation could not suffice to establish a scientific discipline but that independently elaborated theoretical assumptions were also necessary. Against the kind of theoretical pluralism represented by his senior colleague at Harvard, however, Parsons argued that the time had come to unify the divergent theoretical traditions in sociology behind a single theoretical scheme, one that could in fact be justified by purely scientific developments in the discipline during the previous half-century.

So it was, as Jeffrey Alexander has colorfully characterized the effort, that Parsons sought to overcome the dilemma of having 'a nation without a theory' and 'theoretical traditions without a nation'. He sought to reconstruct European sociology by 'providing a synthesis which would eliminate the warring schools which had divided it' and so provide American sociology with an intellectually respectable theoretical charter for its investigative activities.[2] In pursuit of this 'ecumenical' ambition, Parsons aspired to develop 'a theory to end all theories' (Alexander, 1987: 21, 238).

Although Parsons's achievement in *Structure* must still be seen as substantial, his ecumenical aspiration was doomed to failure. On philosophic grounds alone this failure could have been predicted, indeed on the basis of Parsons's own expressed assumptions about the independent variability of theoretical constructs and, later, of the culturally generated symbolic foundations of cognitive schemes. Historically, the failure was evident in *Structure*'s strikingly partial account of the utilitarian tradition (Camic, 1979); its lack of attention to the French tradition before Durkheim and to the entire American tradition; its highly selective appropriation of the work of Marx, Durkheim and Weber; and its nearly complete neglect of the work of Georg Simmel.

Although many of these omissions could be attributed to ignorance, carelessness or legitimate selective emphases, one must raise the question whether or not some of them reflected an early waning of the ecumenical impulse. Commenting on the vicissitudes of this impulse in his fine-grained interpretation of the Parsonian *œuvre*, Alexander argues that Parsons's later work – the development of interchange theory – represented his 'final and most significant approach to theoretical ecumenicism, to his hope of producing a multidimensional and synthetic sociological theory'; but in fact it was with interchange theory that 'Parsons turned decisively from ecumenicism to theoretical imperialism, from synthesis and bridge-building as a conscious theoretical strategy to the tactics of theoretical exclusivity' (1983: 152, 160). Whether or not that is so, we have ample documentation that the exclusionary tactic was already manifest at the time of writing *Structure*. Just before publishing that work, Parsons made the decision to exclude a substantial essay on Simmel from his grand synthesis of the resources of classical theory.

As late as 1935 Parsons had expressed an intention to include Simmel in the grand synthesis, describing him as one of the three writers from the idealistic tradition, along with Weber and Tönnies, who had been 'most important' in the evolution of his views (1935: 282–3). He went on to draft a 16-page section on Simmel for inclusion in *Structure*. His decision not to publish that material reflected an exclusionary impulse which surfaced from two sources. For one thing, as Parsons recalled in a letter written a few months before his death, he had been engaged in competition for the honor of being the principal importer of German sociology to the United States:

[Simmel's] position had been used as relatively few people are still aware as the takeoff point for an attempt to build social system theory which I considered to be fundamentally mistaken. This began in Germany with a large work by Leopold von Wiese, with the title, *Beziehungslehre*. This appeared somewhere near the time I was a student in Heidelberg. . . . It had a certain vogue there but the theme was taken up by the late Howard Becker. Becker built it into a large book which was an adaptation of the Wiese position and went under the title *Wiese-Becker*. Indeed, for a few years, Becker and I were rivals for the leadership of the introduction of German sociology into this country. If I played down Simmel, certainly Becker even more drastically played down Weber. (Parsons, 1979: 1–2)

Beyond this concern for competitive advantage, Parsons apparently came to realize that, despite certain points of affinity with Simmel, their methodological and substantive differences proved so fundamental that it was not plausible to accommodate Simmel under his ecumenical umbrella. As Parsons acknowledged in the letter cited above, 'The decision not to include [the section on Simmel] had various motives. . . . It is true that Simmel's program did not fit my convergence thesis.' In the unpublished material, Parsons indicated some aspects of their incompatibility by maintaining that Simmel's mode of abstraction was only descriptive, not analytic in the manner Parsons espoused, and consequently Simmel's 'mode of abstraction . . . directly cuts across the line of analysis into elements of action which has been our main concern' (1936: 9). No less important, Parsons had come to affirm common values as the essential ingredient of social organization, not interaction as such – the more Simmelian notion which he had employed just a few years earlier, when he wrote: 'By sociology, I should mean a science which studies phenomena specifically social, those arising out of the *interaction* of human beings as such, which would hence not be reducible to the "nature" of those human beings' (1932: 338; emphasis in original).[3]

Parsons's understanding that Simmel did not fit his convergence thesis had a number of serious consequences. For one thing, it freed him to pursue the grand design of his action theory without being encumbered by the complex issues which would have dogged him had he tried to incorporate Simmel's theory at that time. As I observed in 1957, Parsons's failure to devote substantial space to Simmel in *Structure* may have been 'so much the better for sociology', since it gave Parsons more freedom to elaborate his coherent theoretic approach, while sparing Simmel's work the simplification that a Parsonian treatment at that time would undoubtedly have involved (Levine [1957] 1980: lxiii).[4] At the same time, by posing as an authoritative reconstruction of the sociological tradition *Structure* had the effect of establishing a new canon of sociological classics which excluded Simmel, thereby contributing to the eclipse of a major theorist who had been such a stimulating resource for American sociology during the earlier decades of this century (Levine et al., 1976). What is more, it set the pattern for Parsons's life-long lack of attention to Simmel,[5] thereby depriving him of numerous points of support and stimulation in directions where his later thinking ran parallel to Simmel's.[6] Finally, this set the stage for the considerable divisiveness and not always fruitful controversy which

afflicted postwar sociology, with the eruption of a plethora of warring
schools, most of which shared two features: 'a critical stance toward
Parsonian theory, and a programmatic statement in which Simmel was
hailed as a founding father' (Levine, 1984, 361; 1985a, 124).[7]

In recent years the sociological community seems to have been returning
to a more synthetic and ecumenical mode of theoretical work.[8] Notable
efforts have been made to integrate the Parsonian synthesis with ideas
from two of the three main figures most conspicuously absent or underrep-
resented in *Structure*, Karl Marx (for example, by Mark Gould) and
George Herbert Mead (for example, by Jürgen Habermas), as well as with
post-Parsonian developments in American sociology (Alexander, 1987).
Yet the question of the relation of Simmel to Parsons remains nearly as
problematic as it appeared when I first broached the matter more than
three decades ago. This may be a propitious time to review the possibility
of finding constructive ways to relate the legacies of Simmel and Parsons.

Divergences

The task of relating Simmel and Parsons proves particularly formidable
because of one feature which the two theorists shared, a feature which
distinguishes them from virtually all of the other originative sociologists.
Most sociologists, as Raymond Aron has observed, 'generally choose as
their point of departure an analysis of the historical period to which they
belong' (1968: 74).[9] In striking contrast, both Simmel and Parsons took as
their points of departure the strictly academic question of the proper aims
and boundaries of a discipline of sociology, prior to embarking on their
substantive sociological studies. (To be sure, Simmel wrote a few topical
essays before publishing *Über soziale Differenzierung*, but these did not
affect the way he came to conceive of sociology.) As a result, their
epistemic divergences appear particularly formidable because they stem
from deeply pondered and sharply articulated incommensurable presuppositions which protrude extensively in their substantive work, presuppositions which affected their choice of topics for investigation and their
interpretations of social phenomena.

What are these incommensurable presuppositions? I would identify two
above all, one a presupposition about method and one about principles of
social reality. Let me begin with the difference of method.

From about 1933 onward, Parsons never deviated from the goal of
formulating a general theory of action, a general theory based on the clear
articulation of primary elements and the logical derivation of synthetic
theorems from those elements.[10] In his earliest phase, the elements in
question were the structural elements of action: means, ends, conditions
and regulative norms. In his middle phase, the elements were the structural
elements of action systems: motives, roles and symbols. In his later phase,
the elements were the functional requisites of action systems: adaptation,

goal attainment, integration and pattern maintenance. But in each phase, Parsons adhered to a program which used antecedently defined elements to provide the starting points from which the general properties of action were derived. This type of method has been referred to as a logistic method.[11]

Simmel was no less consistent throughout his career in pursuing a radically different type of method. Rather than deriving synthetic theorems from primary elements, Simmel's approach was to identify some particular problem or phenomenal complex and to analyze its essential characteristics. This type of method has been termed problematic or analytic.[12] In contrast to the logistic method, which determines the properties of wholes from their elements – or the dialectic method, which determines the properties of parts by the wholes which encompass them – this method involves the reciprocal determination of parts by their wholes and of wholes by their parts. As Walter Watson has described the contrast:

> [The problematic method] is distinguished from logistic because the elements of the whole are indeterminate until they are organized in the method, rather than being initially determinate so that the method can determine their consequences. . . . This method is distinguished from dialectic because the whole is what it is as the unity of its parts, as a unity of form and matter, rather than being what it is as a part of some larger whole. Its wholes are complete rather than partial. (1985: 91)

For Simmel, then, there were no determinate parts of action from which to generate a grand general theory. His goal was to create what Merton came to call 'theories of the middle range', not as stepping stones to an ultimate goal of systematic general theory, but as ends in themselves, ways of identifying and analyzing phenomenal complexes which observers find of interest.[13] He applied this method in quite different phenomenal domains or worlds – to different personality configurations, different kinds of cultural forms and different kinds of social forms. Rather than reduce all of these formations to a single set of determining elements, he insisted that 'form and content are but relative concepts. They are categories of knowledge used to master the phenomena, and to organize them intellectually, so that the same thing which in any one relation appears as form, as though it were looked at from above, must in another relation, where it is viewed "from below", be labelled content' (Simmel, [1908] 1968: 331; 1955: 172, translation modified).

Given Parsons's commitment to the very different orientation embodied in logistic method, it is no surprise that he came to reject Simmel's proposal to base sociology on the study of social forms, on grounds similar to those he invoked when criticizing Weber – because such a methodology analyzes discrete ideal types instead of constructing a systematic theory based on analytic elements (Parsons, [1937] 1968: 716). Thus, when examining particular phenomena such as friendship, law or economic exchange, Parsons seeks to explain them in terms of their constitutive action elements or systemic functional components, whereas Simmel would seek to analyze their essential defining properties as distinctive types of human formation.

What I term principles here signifies an author's basic assumptions about how to represent (social) reality. For Simmel, the foundational notion is *forms* of *interaction*; for Parsons, *systems* of *action*. These divergent starting points generate two radically different ways to conceptualize social phenomena.

Both authors represent these starting points as instances of abstraction from the totality of observables. For Simmel, the universe consists of innumerable interactions of all sorts – among atomic particles, molecules, organisms, celestial bodies, whatever. What 'society' signifies is an abstraction, from the universe of all interactions, of those interactions that obtain among human beings. A second cut of abstraction separates the energy which drives those interactions from the structures which organize them. Humans come to interact 'on the basis of certain drives and for the sake of certain purposes'. These motives constitute what Simmel calls the 'contents' of interaction. The ways in which those interactions are organized constitute a second dimension of their existence, a dimension which he calls 'forms'. Since the contents and forms of interaction vary independently, such that inquiries into their respective properties can be carried out separately, Simmel assigns to the discipline of sociology the task of identifying and analyzing the constitutive forms of interaction, and to other disciplines the task of investigating the properties of their contents.

Although Parsons applauded Simmel's effort to fashion the discipline of sociology by means of a deliberate act of theoretical abstraction – acknowledging his as 'perhaps the first serious attempt to gain a basis for sociology as . . . a special science' (1937: 772–3) – for Parsons, the way to sociology begins with a different set of abstractions. His first abstraction is the domain of human actions, phenomena which are abstracted from the total universe of phenomena by virtue of possessing some sort of meaning, or relevance to human goals and interests. (In later formulations, Parsons would define action as consisting of those aspects of human behavior which are involved in or controlled by culturally structured symbolic codes [1977: 230]). These meanings provide what Parsons calls an actor's orientations, and an organized plurality of orientations of action constitutes a system of action. The second cut of abstraction for Parsons consists of the orientations which are rational, in the sense of adapting to life conditions and adopting the most efficient means to realize their ends, and those orientations which are governed by norms, and generally glossed as nonrational. The task of sociology, as Parsons defined it in *Structure*, was to study the nonrational, normative dimension of action systems, while economics retained the task of studying the rational dimension of action systems. Even when Parsons later transfigured his basic frame of reference into the four-function paradigm, his point of departure remained that of meaning or purpose, since mechanisms like adaptation and integration were defined in terms of the purposes they fulfilled in maintaining a system of action.

Although each of these formulations harbors a clutch of conflated ideas – confusions which have frustrated generations of readers – in their relatively crude state they can be used to stake out certain core issues that emerge when the presuppositions of Simmel and Parsons are led to confront one another. In comparing them we see something of what Parsons presumably had in mind when he suggested that Simmel's schema 'cut across' his own. For Simmel's schema indicates that both rational and nonrational action orientations belong to the 'contents' of interaction, so that a Parsonian sociology focused on nonrational dimensions of action fails to provide a way to study relational structures; while Parsons argued that by failing to examine the motivational dimension of social interaction in a systematic way, a Simmelian sociology focused on forms fails to provide explanatory accounts of social action. According to Simmel's frame of reference, Parsons neglects forms for contents; in the perspective of Parsons, Simmel neglects contents for forms. As Parsons himself put it, 'My objection to . . . Simmel [concerned] his programmatic formula that the fruitful way to proceed was to construct "formal sociology", that is the idea that *the forms of social relationship should be the center of attention rather than the substantive content of social action*' (1979: 2; emphasis mine).[14]

Clarifications

This gross contrast remains even after one sorts outs the confusions which encumber the accounts of their presuppositions by both authors. In Simmel's work the confusions stem from the radically diverse orders of phenomena which he subsumes under the category of social forms. In the collection of sociological essays Simmel assembled in the great *Soziologie*, he included such disparate topics as superordination and subordination (Ch. 3), conflict and competition (Ch. 4), the stranger and the poor person (Chs 9, 4), secret societies (Ch. 5), group expansion and the development of individuality (Ch. 10) and the quantitative aspects of groups (Ch. 2). In the language of present-day sociology we would describe these under quite distinct categories. Super- and subordination designate a kind of social *relation*; conflict and competition, kinds of *process*; the stranger and the poor, *social roles*; secret societies, a kind of *collectivity*; group expansion, a *developmental pattern*; and group size, a dimension of social organization, hence a *structural variable*. To articulate these distinctions is simply to provide a more systematic account of what a Simmelian sociology of forms encompasses. To analyze the forms of association now means to *look at the structural aspects of phenomena from a variety of angles*. The study of social forms, following Simmel, can focus on relationships, or interaction processes, or roles, or collectivities, or developmental patterns or structural variables. Each of these categories offers a way to represent structural regularities abstracted from diverse purposive areas of human life.[15] Thus, each of the phenomena mentioned above can be refracted into all of these structural categories (see Table 9.1).

Table 9.1   *A neo-Simmelian schema of social forms*

Relation	Process	Role	Collectivity	Developmental pattern	Variable
Super-/sub-ordination	Domination	Superior	Ruling elite	Imposition of rule	Degree of inequality
Enmity	**Conflict**	Enemy	Army	Escalation	Degree of antagonism
Host–stranger relation	Sojourning	**Stranger**	Stranger collectivity	Estrangement	Degree of assimilation
Secrecy	Concealment	Secret-holder	**Secret society**	Declassification	Degree of publicity
Dissimilarity	Social differentiation	Individualized member	Heterogeneous group	**Group expansion and individualization**	**Group size**

Having disentangled the several kinds of phenomena Simmel included in his analyses of social forms, we find his basic principle still at work, but realized in a more transparent and differentiated manner. Any one of the formal categories listed above, for example, could be applied in such diverse substantive areas as art, business, education, health care, politics or religion.

Several confusions pervade Parsons's discussion of his presuppositions. The most serious one, perhaps, appears in Parsons's tendency to equate the rational dimension of action with the pursuit of material interests. This confusion has been amplified by Alexander, otherwise one of Parsons's most perspicacious readers, who has elevated this equivalence into an apical theorem of Parsonian theory. In one of Alexander's recent formulations, he writes:

> Every theory of society . . . assumes an answer to the question, 'What is action?'
> Every theory contains an implicit understanding of motivation. Is it efficient and
> rational, concerned primarily with objective calculation? Or is it nonrational and
> subjective, oriented toward moral concerns or altruism, strongly affected,
> perhaps, by internal emotional concerns? (Alexander, 1988a: 13)

This lumping together of subjectivity, emotionality and morality derives from the fact that Parsons took the economistic model of human action as his point of departure in articulating a theory of action. Yet in making these notions equivalent Parsons ignored a long line of Western thought, evident especially in Hellenic philosophy, Kantian idealism and French social theory, which proceeds from the assumption of a body–mind dualism and holds that reason stands in opposition to desire and that rationality forms the ground of human moral orientations. This construction of rationality was still retained in Weber's notion of value rationality; it figured prominently in the arguments of Dewey and Mead regarding the role of rationality in the domain of public discourse, and has been recovered by Habermas in his notion of discursively argued validity claims. If these distinctions are to be incorporated into a synthetic action theory, then the notions of utility and rationality must be cross-classified rather than equated (see Table 9.2).

While this schema offers a clarified and differentiated account of the orientations of action, it does not affect the question of the relationship between orientations and structure (Simmel's contents and form) in Par-

Table 9.2 *A neo-Parsonian action schema*

Ends of action	Modes of action	
	Nonrational	Rational
Material interests	Appetitive dispositions	Instrumental rationality
Ideal interests	Moral sentiments	Value-rationality, discursive morality

sons's thought. When Parsons discusses structure, he defines it as referring to relatively *constant* features of a system of action, contrasting it with the system's dynamic or processual aspects. But how does he represent structure? In his first phase, structure referred simply to the organization of action orientations. In the middle phase, when he distinguished social systems from other systems of action, he defined it in terms of institutionalized norms: thus, the pattern variables, alternatives of value-orientation, were presented as the main way to represent different kinds of social structure. In the later phase, he emphasized the subordination of structural analysis to functional considerations. Rejecting the appellation of 'structural-functional theory', on grounds that 'the concept function is not correlative with structure, but is the master concept of the framework for the relations between any living system and its environment' (1977: 236), he came to subordinate structural analyses to matters involving the interchange of inputs and outputs among functionally differentiated units. Thus, throughout his work, Parsons found ways to subsume structural considerations under the rubric of meanings – the actor's rational/nonrational orientations, the value-orientations embodied in institutionalized norms, or the purposes embodied in functionally defined subsystems. At no point did he provide a way to represent interactional structures independent of the motivations or purposes of action, although he did provide increasingly rich and differentiated schemata for analyzing the orientations of action.

Simmel, by contrast, provided analyses which could be formalized into the terms of a schema of pattern variables for the analysis of interaction structures. In attempting to articulate such a schema, I once identified at least six such variables (1981). These include group size, social distance, vertical position, valence (positive/negative sentiments), self-involvement and symmetry. That is, any social form can be characterized structurally by specifying how many actors it involves; how close (in various respects) they stand to one another; the degree and type of vertical gradation they exhibit; the respects in which they are positively and/or negatively disposed to one another; the extent of the claims they make on the personalities of their members; and the extent to which the expectations among their members are reciprocal or asymmetrical. On the other hand, for purposes of sociological analysis, Simmel relegates concern for the motivational bases of those structures to what Parsons would have called a residual category.

It does seem that we here confront an irreducible difference between the two approaches. If one's point of departure is to focus on formal structure, purpose becomes residual; if one focuses on purpose, whether in the idiom of actor's values or systemic needs, structure becomes residual. Sociologists tend to divide along the lines of one or the other approach. The division seems accentuated by the fact that some sociologists have tried to embrace both, but only at different points in their careers. Thus, R.F. Bales developed an ingenious schema for analyzing interaction process in terms of functional categories, which he abandoned in favor of a schema that instead measures group structure in terms of Simmelian structural categories such as position (dominance/submissiveness) and valence (friendliness/antagonism); he retained only a single category which designates a functional role (expressiveness/instrumentality). James S. Coleman, on the other hand, initially worked with Simmel-like structural categories in his analysis of community conflict, but turned in his later work to a focus on rational action orientations. Is there anything more to be said on the matter other than that we have apparently reached an impasse in trying to integrate two contradictory perspectives?

Epistemic perspectives

At this juncture I propose to shift the level of discourse and raise a metatheoretical question regarding the status of incompatible theoretical positions, and to advance the notion propounded by those who advocate what has been termed a position of methodological pluralism: the notion that two or more mutually contradictory positions may both be valid. In so doing I want to argue that Simmel and Parsons both have inconsistent positions on the matter. In certain respects, each is a monist; in other respects, each is a pluralist.

When setting forth the principles which ground his approach to sociological investigation, Simmel claimed to be replacing vague and uncertain conceptions of sociology with an unambiguous subject-matter, one governed by a methodologically secure research program. He presents his view of the discipline and its agenda as the only defensible conception. On the other hand, as I argued at length in a recent paper (1989), when discussing the nature of both history and philosophy Simmel showed himself to be an uncompromising and precocious advocate of a pluralist epistemology – in arguments which logically must be extended to cover the domain of sociology as well.

Parsons manifests a comparable inconsistency. Although early on in *Structure* he endorsed Znaniecki's argument that facts about human social phenomena may be represented in a number of different, often cross-cutting schemata, he went on to develop the 'action' frame of reference as the only plausible and all-encompassing theoretical framework for the analysis of human phenomena. Within that framework, he went on to define a uniquely plausible place for the discipline of sociology. While the terms of that definition changed at various points in his career, in every instance he maintained that the role he was assigning to sociology described its mission univocally. Although, in contrast to Simmel, Parsons remained a more consistent monist throughout his career, his later discussions of the constitutive role of cultural symbolism and the independent variability of symbols in shaping all actional dispositions could be drawn on to ground a pluralist position quite at variance with his own predilections.

Those parts of their arguments which Parsons and Simmel advance to ground a position of epistemic pluralism seem to offer the most promising way to resolve the problem generated by their contradictory presuppositions regarding both methods and principles. We may draw on those arguments to construct a view of the sociological tradition that neither reduces it to a trajectory of continually improved empirical techniques nor to a single channel of theoretical formation. They help us to understand that the heritage of sociology is radically pluralistic, in that its range of visions on insights neither can nor should be reduced to a single mold or research program. To say this, however, is not to maintain that· the divergent orientations in sociology have been or should be maintained in antiseptic isolation from one another. On the contrary, the diverse traditions within sociology have taken their shape partly in reaction to one another through progressively developing but contrasting solutions to common problems, and such dialectical interplay makes up a good part of what may be called genuine intellectual progress in the discipline (Levine, 1985b). In the rest of this chapter I wish to suggest ways in which the divergent epistemic approaches of Simmel and Parsons, while arguably incommensurable, may nevertheless be enriched and refined through systematic confrontation with one another.

Connections

Simmel's approach to the study of society is vulnerable in three respects which a Parsonian critique readily reveals. It can remain a distinctive and even more fruitful approach, I submit, by responding to the following criticisms.

For one thing, in viewing the dispositions to engage in social interaction as presocial, Simmel is vulnerable to the objection, voiced long ago by Durkheim, that the 'contents' of association are themselves social facts. In Parsonian terms, dispositions to associate in certain ways reflect processes of socialization and social control which continually shape the motivations of actors – Simmel's 'impulses and purposes'.

What is more, the forms which those associations take receive much of their character and color from cultural patterning. For example, although many properties of conflictual forms derive from factors internal to the conflictual process as such, different cultures produce diverse modes and styles for engaging in conflictual interaction. In some cultures, conflict gets expressed with a great show of aggressive bravado, in others with much emphasis on serious demeanor and respect for one's opponent, in others with a great show of ribaldry and wit.

To say this is to suggest that *part* of what enters into the constitution of social structure is the operation of norms – a fact of which Simmel was fully cognizant. In 'Zur Methodik der Sozialwissenschaft', for example, he considered Rudolph Stammler's argument that 'society is present where the behavior of men is determined not only by laws of nature but also by human normation.' Although he maintained that Stammler's position thereby unjustifiably elevated a mere secondary phenomenon into the essential defining property of society, he still acknowledged that norms provide indispensable conditions of human association.[16] Throughout his substantive analyses, moreover, Simmel shows his awareness of the operation of normative factors – as, for example, in his famous discussion of the way in which conflict unites antagonists by subordinating them to common rules and regulations, or in his discussion of the internalization of moral standards in conscience.

The distribution of different interactional forms, finally, varies from place to place as a function of cultural programming. In some cultures, forms such as hospitality or friendship may be highly valued and omnipresent, whereas they may make only cameo appearances in others. The form of litigation is enormously prized in many societies in East Africa, while in the cultures of East Asia it is avoided as much as possible. Here, too, we should note that Simmel clearly indicated his awareness of the salience of cultural factors for determining the configuration of interactional forms found in a particular setting. As early as his 1894/5 paper on the problem of sociology, he specified that the study of the forms of association should include analysis of the modifications they undergo due both 'to the various stages of production and the variety of dominant ideas of the time'. In Parsonian terms, then, one could say that Simmel acknowledged the salience of norms and cultural ideas, but relegated them to the status of a residual category.

On the other hand, Parsons's approach to the study of society is vulnerable in certain respects which a Simmelian critique readily reveals. If Simmel ignores or makes residual the shaping of interactional structures by values and norms, Parsons fails to identify any features of interactional structure other than those contributed by values and norms. From his earliest essays on role structure on, Parsons consistently defined the social system as consisting of 'institutionalized norms'. This omission can perhaps be corrected by incorporating Simmelian modes of structural analysis while yet maintaining the primacy of value-orientations or systemic functions as points of departure for sociological inquiry.

Thus, one could still take different value-orientations as foundational for major patterns of social stratification, yet incorporate analyses of structural variables like group size, number of status positions, ecological distribution of positions and the like. One could look at norms governing different role sets and still enrich the analysis by considering degrees of intimacy, antipathy and symmetry involved in the relations among those role incumbents. One could identify general values and beliefs associated with the perception of strangers, renegades, middlemen and debtors, and still specify the relational features of those roles in terms that vary independently of those norms. One could accept Parsons's late stipulation that the most important structural components of any action system are the symbolic codes used in communication and decision-making (1977: 237), and incorporate analyses of different kinds of network patterns and other interactional structures which channel that communication.

This kind of reciprocal refinement through dialectical interplay could be extended to the differences of method and other issues on which Simmel and Parsons diverge. The analysis of forms could be recast in terms of a general logistical system which analyzes them in terms of the elements specified in a general theory of action, just as general action theory could be recast in ways which focus on the constitution of type phenomena. Parsons's emphasis on the interpenetration of personality systems, social systems and cultural systems could be enriched by supplementing it with the Simmelian emphasis on the independence and mutual antagonism of the principles animating each of these modes of organizing the contents of human action – the incommensurable, irreducible 'worlds' of self, society and objective culture – and vice versa (see Levine, 1985a: Ch. 9).

Even when it may prove impossible to combine the divergent approaches of the two authors in a single interpretive framework, where one is dominant and the other subordinate, the social analyst may benefit from alternating the two perspectives when considering some particular set of phenomena. Thus, to consider one other axis of difference between Parsons and Simmel, one may look at the professional role, or the pattern of an ideology, now by considering which value-orientation or functional need has primacy in the pattern, and then by looking at it by considering the opposed, dualistic or ambivalent strains which it conjoins.[17]

The general intellectual strategy I invoke here resembles what Walter Watson (1985) has described as 'reciprocal priority'. This entails acknowledging that the choice of a starting point for analysis, since it cannot be determined by the facts, represents some arbitrary element which is nonetheless indispensable for interpretive work. The different approaches are incompatible in the sense that one must use one of them at a time, and not mix them up indiscriminately. But one can use a given principle, like forms of interaction, or systems of action, in ways that take into account many of the facts and constructions highlighted by the other principles, or one can alternate, using the different starting points at different times.

Insofar as both Simmel and Parsons provide arguments to support the position of epistemic pluralism, they can be drawn on to support the type of integration of their respective approaches advocated here. It now remains for us to find the discipline and capaciousness to reach this new kind of ecumenism, and thus move beyond the most recent period of warring schools into discourse cast in a more constructive idiom.

Notes

1. An early version of this chapter was presented at the conference, 'Georg Simmel e le origini della sociologia moderna,' Trento, Italy, 19–21 October 1989. The present version appears in the *American Journal of Sociology*, 96 (5) (March 1991).

2. For extensive elaboration of the metaphor of Parsons's opus as a charter for sociology, see Camic (1989).

3. For further specifying certain issues in terms of which Parsons related to Simmel, I am indebted to Jaworski (1990).

4. For a recent celebration of the sense in which Parsons's skewed historical reconstruction figures as an essential part of his brilliant theory-building, see Alexander (1988b; 1989).

5. This is true despite the inclusion of five selections by Simmel in the two-volume compilation of classic writings on social theory which Parsons co-edited with Edward Shils, Kaspar D. Naegele, and Jesse R. Pitts (1961). The point was later acknowledged by Parsons himself in his preface to the 1968 edition of *Structure*: 'Along with the American social psychologists, notably Cooley, Mead, and W.I. Thomas, the most important single figure neglected in *The Structure of Social Action*, and to an important degree in my subsequent writings, is probably Simmel' (1968: xiv). As Victor Lidz, literary executor of the Parsons estate, observed in a letter about Parsons's subsequent inattention to Simmel: 'My guess is that [Parsons] continued to feel, as he had argued in the Simmel-Toennies draft for *The Structure of Social Action*, that Simmel's theoretical method and . . . substantive theory diverged far enough from the stance of action theory as to make efforts to exploit convergences unfruitful' (personal communication).

6. For example, Simmel, like Parsons, was engaged in a lifelong quest to unite the traditions of naturalism and idealism; he provided an extensive elaboration of a problematic which Parsons would later take up in earnest, the character of money as a generalized symbolic medium of exchange, and pioneered the notion of viewing exchange as a paradigm for all social interaction; and he anticipated Parsons in arguing that self, society and culture were to be distinguished as three distinct, irreducible modes of organizing human experience, and that the concrete individual must be understood as a composite of psychological components, societal components and ideal components.

7. These could be said to include Merton's emphases on middle-range theories, group structural properties and sociological ambivalence; Coser's conflict theory; the exchange theories of Homans and Blau; Laumann's network theory; phenomenological sociology, following Schutz and Garfinkel; and Goffman's approach to symbolic interaction. Of course, the most prominent axis of divisiveness stemmed from the neo-Marxian camp. In Alexander's words, 'the story of sociological theory after World War II is, in one sense, the story of the rise and fall of the "Parsonian empire"' (1987: 281) – a fall occasioned by the rise of divergent positions which assaulted the hegemony of the Parsonian synthesis from different angles.

8. See Neil Smelser's recent observation: 'It seems to me that this phase [of divisive disarray] now appears to be running its course, and that new signs of synthesis are appearing or are on the horizon' (1988: 2).

9. That is, the programmatic ideas of most originative sociologists took shape consequent to their engagement with substantive issues tied to diagnoses of their time. Thus, Comte started his sociology after diagnosing the intellectual and moral confusion of Restorationist France; Tönnies, after observing the dissolution of communal forms of social organization; Durkheim, after confronting the problem of moral solidarity in modern societies; Weber, after confronting the forms of rationalization in the modern West; Pareto, after experiencing what he considered the poverty of rational liberalism; Park, after grappling with the role of the news media in creating modern public opinion.

10. For the evolution of this aspiration in the thought of the young Parsons, see Camic (1991).

11. The typology of methods I employ here derives from the work of Richard McKeon (e.g., 1951; [1952] 1990). For a recent creative exposition of this schema, see Watson (1985). For a more extensive typology of epistemic approaches in the social sciences, see Levine (1986).

12. In my dissertation I called this the method of 'causal resolution'.

13. See Siegfried Kracauer's apt characterization of Simmel's method as a search for *Wesenszusammengehörigkeit* (1920–1), and Maria Steinhoff's depiction of it: 'In all his books . . . Simmel confronts directly the flow of life and, guided by certain cognitive inten-

tions, singles out from its vast fullness individual problems which appear worthy of research, which he then analyzes inductively and *pushes forth in every single investigation to the ultimate layer of the problem*' (1925: 252; my emphasis).

14. In his work on *Structure*, including the unpublished section on Simmel, Parsons dealt with Simmel's cross-cutting emphasis on forms by relegating it to the status of a merely *descriptive* approach. In a significant passage toward the end of *Structure*, he wrote: 'This isolation of descriptive aspects can take place in two main directions, [one of which] may be called the relational. . . . In so far as this *inter*action of the action systems of individuals is continuous and regular these relationships acquire certain identifiable, relatively constant properties or descriptive aspects. One of them is the structural.^{2} [^{2} Simmel's "form".] Another is involved in the relative priority of *Gemeinschaft* and *Gesellschaft*. No attempt will be made here to give it a specific name as a property' (Parsons, [1937] 1968: 744; emphasis and note in original). I would argue that in *The Social System* Parsons came to *transform the theoretical status of relational constructs from descriptive aspects into analytic elements*, analogous to the way he later transformed the status of political science from a descriptive discipline into an analytic discipline. However, the route he chose was to differentiate Tönnies's contrasting types into patterns of value-orientation, rather than to construe Simmel's interactional types as patterns of analytic formal elements – as von Wiese had in effect done.

15. 'A relationship, like superordination-subordination, is a form considered with respect to the kind of connection linking a number of statuses. A process, like conflict, concerns the kind of activity that goes on among the incumbents of those statuses. A status-role, like the stranger, concerns the properties of one party to a relationship. A collectivity, like a secret society, concerns the properties of one party to a relationship when that party consists of a plurality of units. A developmental or dynamic pattern, like group expansion and the development of individuality, is some regularity concerning formal changes exhibited by groups over time. A structural variable, like size, is some dimension of organization, changes in which are accompanied by changes in other aspects of organization.' (Levine, 1981: 68).

16. Simmel wrote: 'Everywhere that human conduct is determined not only by natural laws but also by human normation – that may be termed "society". To say this, however, seems to me to elevate a mere subsidiary phenomenon, a secondary *conditio sine qua non*, into the positive vital principle of society. A religious group . . . takes form as an association not by virtue of "regulation through externally constraining norms", but through the fact that every member knows himself to be one with the other in belief. . . . This psychological interaction in the "invisible church" is what constitutes society. . . . The members of a credit union submit themselves to a certain regulation of contributions and withdrawals, to be sure. . . . However, that is only a limiting condition; the positive principle of their association is the reciprocally extended assistance. . . . A sociable gathering, a "party", doubtless presupposes a large number of external regulations of the conduct of its participants. Even so, even if all of these regulations are fully observed, the sociable gathering becomes a party in the true sense of the term, according to its vital principle – in Aristotelian language: according to its entelechy – only when it becomes a scene of mutual pleasing, stimulating, and cheering' (Simmel, 1896: 579–80).

17. On this general methodological issue, see Merton (1976: Ch.1).

References

Alexander, J.C. (1983) *Theoretical Logic in Sociology*, vol. 4, *The Modern Reconstruction of Classical Thought: Talcott Parsons*. Berkeley and Los Angeles: University of California Press.

Alexander, J.C. (1987) *Twenty Lectures: Sociological Theory since World War II*. New York: Columbia University Press.

Alexander, J.C. (1988a) *Action and its Environments: Toward a New Synthesis*. New York: Columbia University Press.

Alexander, J.C. (1988b) 'Parsons' Structure in American Sociology', *Sociological Theory*, 6: 96–102.

Alexander, J.C. (1989) 'Against Historicism/For Theory: a Reply to Levine', *Sociological Theory*, 7: 118–21.

Aron, R. (1968) *Main Currents in Sociological Thought*, vol. 1, tr. R. Howard and H. Weaver. Garden City, NY: Doubleday.

Camic, C. (1979) 'The Utilitarians Revisited', *American Journal of Sociology*, 85: 516–50.

Camic, C. (1989) '*Structure* after 50 Years: the Anatomy of a Charter', *American Journal of Sociology*, 95 (1): 38–107.

Camic, C. (1991) Introduction to *The Early Essays of Talcott Parsons*. Chicago: University of Chicago Press.

Gould, M. (1987) *Revolution in the Development of Capitalism: the Coming of the English Revolution*. Berkeley: University of California Press.

Habermas, J. (1987) *The Theory of Communicative Action*, vol. 2. Boston: Beacon.

Jaworski, G.D. (1990) 'Simmel's Contribution to Parsons' Action Theory and its Fate', pp. 109–30 in M. Kaern, B.S. Phillips and R.S. Cohen. (eds), *Georg Simmel and Contemporary Sociology*. Dordrecht: Kluwer.

Kracauer, S. (1920–1) 'Georg Simmel', *Logos*, 9: 307–38.

Levine, D.N. ([1957] 1980) *Simmel and Parsons: Two Approaches to the Study of Society*. With a new introduction. New York: Arno Press.

Levine, D.N. (1981) 'Sociology's Quest for the Classics: the Case of Simmel', pp. 60–80 in B. Rhea (ed.), *The Future of the Sociological Classics*. London: Allen & Unwin.

Levine, D.N. (1984) 'Ambivalente Begegnungen: "Negationen" Simmels durch Durkheim, Weber, Lukács, Park, und Parsons', pp. 318–37 in H.J. Dahme and O. Rammstedt (eds), *Georg Simmel und die Moderne*. Frankfurt: Suhrkamp.

Levine, D.N. (1985a) *The Flight from Ambiguity: Essays in Social and Cultural Theory*. Chicago and London: University of Chicago Press.

Levine, D.N. (1985b) 'On the Heritage of Sociology', pp. 13–19 in G. Suttles and M. Zald (eds), *The Challenge of Social Control: Citizenship and Institution Building in Modern Society*. Norwood, NJ: Ablex.

Levine, D.N. (1986) 'The Forms and Functions of Social Knowledge', pp. 271–83 in D.W. Fiske and R.A. Shweder (eds), *Metatheory in Social Science: Pluralism and Subjectivities*. Chicago: University of Chicago Press.

Levine, D.N. (1989) 'Simmel as a Resource for Sociological Metatheory', *Sociological Theory*, 7: 161–74.

Levine, D.N., Carter, E.B. and Gorman, E.M. (1976) 'Simmel's Influence on American Sociology, I & II', *American Journal of Sociology*, 81 (4, 5): 813–45, 1112–32.

McKeon, R. (1951) 'Philosophy and Method', *Journal of Philosophy*, 48: 653–82.

McKeon, R. ([1952] 1990) *Freedom and History: the Semantics of Philosophical Controversies and Ideological Conflicts*. Chicago: University of Chicago Press.

Merton, R.K. (1976) *Sociological Ambivalence and Other Essays*. New York: Free Press.

Park, R.E. and Burgess, E.W. (1921) *Introduction to the Science of Sociology*. Chicago: University of Chicago Press.

Parsons, T. (1932) 'Economics and Sociology: Marshall in Relation to the Thought of his Time', *Quarterly Journal of Economics*, 46: 316–47.

Parsons, T. (1935) 'The Place of Ultimate Values in Sociological Theory', *International Journal of Ethics*, 45: 282–316.

Parsons, T. (1936) 'Georg Simmel and Ferdinand Toennies: Social Relationships and the Elements of Action', Parsons Papers, Harvard University Archives, Unpublished Manuscripts 1929–1967, Box 2.

Parsons, T. ([1937] 1968) *The Structure of Social Action*. New York: Free Press.

Parsons, T. (1951) *The Social System*. Glencoe, IL: Free Press.

Parsons, T. (1977) *Social Systems and the Evolution of Action Theory*. New York: Free Press.

Parsons, T. (1979) Letter to Jeffrey Alexander, 19 January. Parsons Papers, Harvard University Archives, Correspondence 1965–1979, Box 1.

Parsons, T., Shils, E.A., Naegele, K.D. and Pitts, J.R. (1961) *Theories of Society*. New York: Free Press.

Simmel, G. (1896) 'Zur Methodik der Sozialwissenschaft', *Jahrbuch für Gesetzgebung, Verwaltung und Volkswirtschaft . . .* , 20: 575–85.

Simmel, G. [1908] (1968) *Soziologie*. Berlin: Duncker & Humblot.

Simmel, G. (1955) *Conflict* and *The Web of Group-Affiliations*. Glencoe, IL: Free Press.

Smelser, N.J. (1988) 'Sociological Theory: Looking Forward', *Perspectives: The ASA Theory Section Newsletter*, 2 (2): 1–3.

Sorokin, P.A. (1928) *Contemporary Sociological Theories*. New York and London: Harper.

Steinhoff, M. (1925) 'Die Form als soziologische Grundkategorie bei Georg Simmel', *Kölner Vierteljahrshefte für Soziologie*, 4: 215–59.

Watson, W. (1985) *The Architectonics of Meaning: Foundations of the New Pluralism*. New York: State University of New York Press.

10

FROM SICK ROLE TO HEALTH ROLE: DECONSTRUCTING PARSONS

Arthur W. Frank

From sick role to health as medium

Talcott Parsons contemplated issues of health, illness, the sick role and the medical profession from his undergraduate studies in biology through one of the last papers he prepared for publication. His writings on health (principally Parsons, 1951; 1964; 1978) display the extremes of thought that make Parsons continually fascinating. Bourgeois apologies for professional authority alternate with a conception of the body that can be read as postmodern in its implication, whatever its intent. My 'deconstruction' of Parsons researches his texts not to discover an organizing authorial intention that is more or less consistently realized (much less 'verified'); instead I allow his texts to decompose into fragments, and observe these fragments as they circulate among subsequent texts. Thus sociological knowledge is conceived not as an accumulation, but rather as intertextual circulation, perpetually rearranging in new textual orders. One such textual order begins to specify a conception of health, illness and the body that can be called postmodern.[1]

Parsons began with the sick role. In one of his most concise formulations, he defined 'three primary criteria of accepting the social role of being sick' (1978: 21). First, illness was to be regarded as 'not the sick person's own fault'. Second, the ill person enjoys 'exemption from ordinary daily obligations and expectations'. Third, this exemption is qualified by 'the expectation . . . of seeking help from some kind of institutionalized health service agency' (1978: 21; see 1951). A number of objections have been leveled at this conception of sickness (Levine and Kozloff, 1978; Turner, 1987: 45–9), in terms of both its descriptive validity and its prescriptive desirability. I want neither to defend Parsons from these criticisms (see Turner, 1987: 55–8), nor to attempt to revamp the sick role to contemporary conditions of medical practice. Instead I begin with the sick role only to clarify the presuppositions that informed Parsons's later considerations of health.

The sick role recognizes that 'illness is not merely a state of the organism and/or personality, but comes to be an institutionalized role' (1978: 81), which is to say, the sick role is not a condition of an isolated body but is achieved interpersonally within a particular social/cultural milieu. The idea of 'role' adheres to an individual no more than sickness does; both are media of interaction, not properties of persons.

Parsons was clearest about illness as a medium in his late writings on bioethics generally, and the ethics of human subject research in particular. Here we find the alternation referred to above between the bourgeois apologist and the postmodernist. The apologist expressed the fear that 'The rigid insistence on "rights" is essentially a declaration of distrust in the professional complex. Its effect will ordinarily be a "deflationary" or "fundamentalist" restriction of developmental potential' (1978: 64). Parsons goes on to discuss the need for 'inclusion of the "lay" element in the positive functioning of the professional complex', but his quotation marks sustain the essential demarcation of 'lay' versus professional.

Critical and feminist critiques of medicine would label Parsons's worries about 'distrust' as the last gasp of a male, professional elite trying to keep its credibility intact. But Parsons's most regressive moments are often the flip points of his thought. As he writes of distrust being 'deflationary' or 'fundamentalist', he invokes his 'generalized media of exchange'. We move from the patriarchal apologist of the professions to a thinker whose postmodern conception of the body may still elude theoretical grasp.

At the end of his last paper on health, Parsons states that he has treated health 'as a symbolic circulating medium regulating human action and other life processes' (1978: 80). He then illustrates a circulating medium in terms of money:

> a unit in an interacting system – such as an individual or an organ or tissue – must receive an 'income' of the medium in question with which to acquire essential means of its functioning; in the latter process, the unit must 'expend' this resource. This is what is meant by the 'circulation' of the medium. (Parsons, 1978: 80)

Thus health is not 'in' the body, but is the medium of that body's interaction with others.

Health exists only insofar as it is able to 'circulate' – it 'would function only if it is "used" and not "hoarded"'. Health, then, 'must be conceived as bridging both organic and "social"' (1978: 81). Finally, health, like money, has no intrinsic value, but only becomes valuable in exchange. As a medium, 'good health is an "endowment" of the individual that can be used to mobilize and acquire essential resources' (1978: 80).

The conception of media informs Parsons's definition of health. From biology Parsons takes the idea of 'teleonymy' as 'the capacity of an organism, or its propensity, to undertake successful goal-oriented courses of behavior' (1978: 68). Health, then, is

> the teleonomic capacity of an individual living system . . . to maintain a favorable, self-regulating state that is a prerequisite of the effective performance of an indefinitely wide range of functions . . . the capacity to cope with disturbances . . . that come either from the internal operations of the living system itself or from interaction with one [or] more of its environments. (1978: 69)

Illness is simply the obverse of health: 'an impairment of his/her teleono-mic capacity'.

Health is a medium through which an individual's teleonomic capacity can be exercised within an interactive system. Health as 'capacity' circu-lates in the sense of being constantly received as income and expended in the attempt to mobilize and acquire other resources. Most important, health is an endowment of a particular body *only* in that body's interactions with others. Health is a bridge between any one organic body and its social environment; it is a property of neither the body nor the environment, but exists between them. Physiological wellness may be a steady-state internal to the organism, but health links the particular organism with others; again, it exists not *in* bodies but *between* them. Health for Parsons is, as Kroker and Kroker (1987: 29–30) have observed, *outside* the body.

'When conceived as such a medium', Parsons wrote (1978: 80), 'health stands midway between the action level media such as money, power, and language and the intra-organic media such as hormones and enzymes.' On my reading of his work, Parsons gave no other medium this intermediate level position; health is unique, analytically and empirically. Parsons describes this positioning of health as having 'far-reaching significance for the future' and requiring 'a great amount of analytical effort' to develop (1978: 81).

That future has come sooner than he might have imagined. The analyti-cal effort has produced results in which Parsons is neither validated nor disconfirmed, since these concepts define the text as hoarding its informa-tion within itself. Rather his texts circulate as media among other texts in which they are used. In the postmodern theoretical milieu Parsons pro-jected, ideas are not right or wrong in the old sense of validity or reliability. They are more or less mobilized; their 'test' is their continuing capacity for circulation.

A postmodern conception of health disseminates Parsons's recognition of health as a medium. From Michel Foucault, we add that health is a medium of imposed bodily discipline. From Jean Baudrillard, we question whose teleonymy is involved; thus the second modification is 'teleonymy mediatized'. From Jürgen Habermas, we understand that the nature of health as a medium is to be 'non-discursive'. Finally in Pierre Bourdieu we return to Parsons's notion of circulation to suggest health as 'physical capital' (Frank, forthcoming a). These modifications are in no sense discrete from each other, but, as Parsons would be the first to recognize, they interpenetrate.[2]

Health as discipline

Long before Foucault, Parsons framed the sick role within a context of discipline, but only after Foucault do the implications of Parsons become clear. The sick role allowed exemption from normal responsibilities at the cost of the expectation to seek medical help. This help required the ill person to enter into an asymmetrical interaction with a physician, who for Parsons is the core of the 'institutionalized health service agency'. 'Compliance with this [medical] authority . . . cannot be wholly voluntary,' Parsons wrote (1978: 54). Nor did Parsons suggest that doctor/patient relations should be anything but asymmetrical: 'health care cannot be treated as a fully symmetrical relationship in a hierarchical dimension . . . there must be built-in institutionalized superiority of the professional roles' (1978: 29).

Parsons legitimated the hierarchical asymmetry of roles as part of the therapy. The physician had to maintain 'a certain aloofness' and be seen by the patient as 'refusing to respond' to certain patient initiatives. Only in this way could the physician manipulate the reward of his approval (1978: 78). For the physician to enter into a symmetrical relationship with the patient would be to encourage the secondary gain of the exemptions illness brings, as well as to undermine the legitimacy of professional expertise.

The issue is not the empirical adequacy of Parsons's account, for example, whether medical aloofness is a calculated attempt at therapeutic efficacy, or the result of a political economy of medical practice that requires seeing a maximum number of patients. More interesting is what Parsons could not yet comprehend, even as he pointed the way toward it. Parsons never wrote, nor could he perhaps have thought to write, of the 'health role'. He conceived the sick role as strictly transitory, or in the residual case terminal. Parsons defended its applicability to chronic illness (1978: 19), but 'The type case [sic] is, of course, in the episode of specific, acute illness' (1978: 32). The sick role is constructed to move someone out of it as quickly as possible, and the aloofness of the physician is exercised to that end. The 'health role', by contrast, is on-going.

Parsons directs us toward thinking of a health role by suggesting that health is a medium; the actor receives constant inputs, and expends these as outputs. What makes the sick role definable as such is the person's 'adhering to a proper regime and . . . deferring to a competent professional authority in defining what it should be' (1978: 19). Parsons did not foresee that soon the healthy person, no less than the ill one, would also be adhering to a regime and deferring to competent authority for the definition of that regime. It is living one's embodied life in adherence to regimes, and deferral to authority for those regimes, that defines the postmodern health role.

Parsons might have accepted the permanence of the health role, and he might have imagined the application of regimes and authority to the healthy as much as to the sick. What he could not have imagined, and would have resisted, was the physician becoming progressively decentered in the proliferation of regimes. Although Arney and Bergen (1984) display their own Parsonian nostalgia for the physician, they are clear on how the physician's role is changing. Displaying an advertisement from a manufacturer of infant food supplement formula, they comment:

Instead of treatment and cure we see that the problems are to be managed. And we see the problems are to be managed by a system developed by a corporate entity. Where in this image is Vesalius [the physician]? He is no longer visible. He exists only by inference. His presence can be invoked, but he fades quickly to become a component of the overall management system. He has become like a figure in pentimento, a ghostly figure that seeps through the dominant form; he is a figure that can be perceived only on closest inspection. (Arney and Bergen, 1984: 164)

Arney and Bergen's description of a corporate medical complex in which the physician's centrality fades is echoed in the comments of a physician interviewed by Kleinman:

If the patient gets to see you, having fought her way through an obstacle course of receptionists, nurses, social workers, psychologists, and physician assistants set up to protect you – the high-priced specialist whose care is expensive to the system . . . why, then, the system has failed. . . . Now it's disenchantment, like being a worker in a factory turning out a standardized assembly-line product . . . . I don't want to *manage clients*, I want to *care for patients*. I don't want to hide behind bureaucratic regs and physician assistants. I want to do the caring. (Kleinman, 1988: 219)

This physician sees himself 'like a figure in pentimento' and rejects his own disappearance, but the choice is no longer his.

Parsons correctly identified the physician dominating the period of the sick role. As the sick role has become the health role, the physician fades. Health care becomes disenchanted. Parsons's ideals of medical 'fiduciary responsibility' (1987: 24) and 'orientation toward collective values' (1978: 75) are replaced by what Foucault (1988) called a technology of the self. The discipline of health is maintained neither by the physician manipulating rewards, nor by the intermediary workers Kleinman's physician objects to. Ultimately the discipline of health is enforced by the self seeking to fit itself into a definition of health. As Hutton (1988: 135) comments on Foucault, 'Theories of the self [that is, the healthy self] are a kind of currency through which power over the mind is defined and extended . . . power shapes our knowledge of the self.' Health remains a medium, but the medium now uses the person, rather than being used by that person as part of his or her 'teleonymy'.

For Parsons, medical authority was legitimated at the intersection of organic disease and professional competence; the sick role was relevant so long as the latter was used to oppose the former. In the emerging health role, there is no discontinuity between health and illness; instead there is a continuity of regimes defined by a plurality of authorities and enforced by the self as the proper image of what itself should be. Power is decentered without, and practiced within. Here is the future of the health role, as reported on the front page of the *Calgary Herald*:

Albertans who quit smoking and drinking and cut down their weight could be rewarded with lower health care premiums, a major government report suggests.
But those convicted of impaired driving or other offenses could be forced to pay . . . says the Premier's Commission on the Future Health Care of Albertans.

> The $4.2 million report . . . calls for people to take more responsibility for their own health.
>
> And the commission want to force abusers and overusers of the system to go to certain predetermined doctors and possibly take counselling on 'corrective action'.
>
> Every patient's travels through the health care system would be recorded on special plastic debit – or 'smart' cards, which can record up to 62,000 pages of information. (Walker, 1990: 1)

The elements of postmodern health are all here: the reification of self-responsibility to the exclusion of institutional factors that affect health and the cost of its care, the expansion of what 'lifestyle' factors are relevant to health, the double medicalization of 'over-users' whose *Mikado*-like punishment is to be sent for more treatment, and the computerized surveillance system. The disciplinary web is seamless.

Teleonymy as a medium

Teleonomic capacity, 'the effective performance of an indefinitely wide range of functions' (Parsons, 1978: 69), is prerequisite to any action theory; the actor's choice of means and ends requires this capacity. The issue, as it was from Parsons's earliest action theory, is what ends the actor will choose.

In the postmodern period, Parsons's 'normative orientation' is no longer anchored in the history and traditions of the societal community. The image people have of their lives – the ideal to which they seek to adjust those lives – is, in Baudrillard's usage, a simulation of life. In the advertisement Arney and Bergen consider, three babies, looking healthy and happy, wear tee-shirts. These say 'Protein Allergy', 'Common Feeding Problems' and 'Malabsorption'. The caption over the ad reads: 'Now, one *System* manages them all' (in Arney and Bergen, 1984: 164). This advertisement, like most, depends on a curious compression of time. The tee-shirt 'problems' refer to a time past, when the babies were not so healthy or happy. The advertisement compresses the narrative of each baby's problem being diagnosed, 'managed' to produce the present image, and then this management extending into an indefinite future. The babies are now in the '*System*', and when their need for one management product ends, another will begin.

The advertisement is a simulation of infancy in which that infancy becomes Baudrillard's hyperreal (1983; see also Frank, forthcoming b). The hyperreal does not conceal another reality behind or beneath it, as Arney and Bergen describe corporate medicine progressively concealing the physician. The hyperreal conceals the disappearance of the real; it is an image that is so much better than the real that the real simply ceases to exist, if it ever did exist. The hyperreality of the baby advertisement is that *System*-managed infancy becomes infancy itself; who would settle for less?

The actor's 'teleonymy' has become the capacity to achieve and sustain an image, which has its source in mass media. Images are all advertisements, because the means of aligning oneself with the image is invariably some form of consumption. The 'health promotion' advertising that the Province of Alberta has funded for several years typically shows people engaged in activities requiring either specialized equipment (cross-country skis, bicycles) and/or particular access to facilities. At minimum, these people live lives that admit concepts of choice and leisure.[3]

In the narrative compression of health promotion advertising, performance of the activity guarantees health, and 'health' becomes unthinkable outside the image of a high consumption, middle-class 'lifestyle'. The interpenetration is complete: health is the medium of the lifestyle, and the lifestyle is the medium of health. In this government-imagined utopia, the health role becomes the discipline of the good life. Health is the hyperreality of the body and society.

Non-discursive health

The most singular revision to Parsons's theory of generalized media is Habermas's (1987) observation that while influence and persuasion are discursive media, money and power are nondiscursive (see Frank, 1989). Of course Parsons never claimed that the doctor/patient interaction involved Habermasian 'communicative action'. There was no attempt to achieve a consensus; as I quoted above, Parsons believed the interaction must remain asymmetrical. Parsons may have argued that 'In many different degrees and respects, patients are asked to, and they often do, take the initiative in assuming the responsibility for a more active role in the care of their own health' (1978: 25). But they take this 'initiative' within parameters established by physicians; across the unbridgeable gulf of professional versus 'lay', competence is always on the side of the professional.

Parsons never made it the role of physicians to seek consensus with their patients; instead they affect affective neutrality. When Parsons considered the ethical problems of informed consent and protection of privacy in medical research, he concluded that 'the common-sense level of ethical orientation is not only "inadequate", but potentially dangerous in the conditions of a pluralistic modern society' (1978: 64). Parsons wanted to defend the inaccessibility of professional competence to 'lay' persons. Professionals simply cannot be judged by 'common-sense' standards, and therefore 'Professional groups must, to some essential degree, be self-regulating' (1978: 39).

But when Parsons placed physicians beyond the requirement for communicative consensus, he did not imagine the corporate medical management *System* described by Arney and Bergen and reported by the physician quoted by Kleinman. Parsons opened the door to a colonization of health, in the sense that standards of health and sickness would no longer be common-sensical; rather than being grounded in the lifeworld of the societal community, standards would instead become professionalized. He perceived no danger in this, since the profession were individuals whose values were rooted in the same societal community as their patients. Medicine for Parsons was personal and reactive, not bureaucratic and agenda setting.

'Medicalization' has evolved to mean the displacement of physician decision-making by corporate management, and the transition from a medicine that reacts to patient-initiated complaints to one that sets agendas via mass media images. The 'one *System* [that] manages them all' is precisely Habermas's colonization of lifeworld by system. Health is no longer a consensus-determined medium; the teleonymy is not the individual's own, but the *System*'s. In this colonization, Parsons's foundational boundary between 'personality' and 'institutions' is increasingly effaced.

Health as physical capital

Parsons's statement that 'good health is an "endowment" of the individual that can be used to mobilize and acquire essential resources' (quoted above; 1978: 80) clearly anticipates Bourdieu's (1984) notion of 'cultural capital' and his more specific formulation of 'physical capital' (1978). Bourdieu describes how the actor 'invests' capitals like health in order to acquire such resources as marriage partners or jobs (see Frank, forthcoming a). But here also the Parsonian world has been turned inside out. For Parsons, actors would mobilize and acquire resources according to the needs of sustaining the integration and normative consensus of the societal community. For Bourdieu, actors reproduce the class 'habitus' that predisposed them to have certain resources and perceive investment potentials. What is reproduced is not the integration and consensus of the community, but rather hierarchy and privilege.

Again, Parsons opened the door to this thinking, however much he would reject the implications Bourdieu traces out. For Parsons sickness may not be the fault of the ill person, but it is regarded as reflecting an 'element of "motivatedness" not merely in the etiology of the pathological condition, but also in the maintenance of it' (1978: 18). If illness is motivated, then its successful avoidance – health – obviously reflects a person of value. Health is, as Parsons suggests, an investable quality. As Bourdieu allows us to interpolate, the particular value of health as a medium is that it can be 'naturalized'. Health can be invested to considerable gain, but it cannot be taxed as hereditary privilege. The ideology of health formulates it as either natural genetic good luck, or the achieved result of following the proper regime, which brings us back to discipline. Healthy persons are disciplined persons; disciplined, that is, to fit the idealized image of health.

In the 'health role', health is not a medium simply because, as Parsons put it, it is an endowment of the body. *Health is the disciplined capacity of the body to reflect an image of health, and that image is tied to a consumption/management system.* Health displays the person's good citizenship in the discipline of *System* management; the quality that others are willing to receive as an investment is the individual's disciplined malleability to *System* generated images.

Parsons could not foresee how actively people would invest in the health role, or how investable the image of health would become. At Parsons's memorial session at the American Sociological Association meetings in 1979, I could not have imagined a world of video aerobics (a word not found in my 1980 dictionary), lycra as athletic wear, much less as street clothes, or liposuction. Where will it end? Genetic engineering of DNA modification is not yet a reality (so far as we know), but successful heart surgery has been performed on a fetus in the womb; the discipline of achieving health now begins before birth.

As health and illness become an increasingly seamless discipline of the body, that body becomes less an organic being than a medium. The 'health role' is the cultivation of the body, according to a proliferation of regimes (athletic, cosmetic, medical, psycho-introspective and so forth) to meet the hyperreal specifications of an image deriving from a *System* that sells those regimes. The terms of this image are not consensual; it is a non-linguistic ideal, the postmodern superego, the new normative orientation not to family or societal community but to Baudrillard's Simulacrum, the order of images in which the reality (if such ever existed) has disappeared, and the simulation refers only to itself.

Suffering, evil and postmodern health

The broader implications of the 'health role' can hardly be concluded, but some concluding comments on Parsons are possible. I have tried to show how Parsons's thinking about the sick role and health is foundational to the postmodern 'health role'. But after this deconstruction, what is the remainder of Parsons? What is there in his thought that may not yet be disseminated?

In one of his most provocative paragraphs, Parsons links health, now defined as teleonomic capacity, to suffering and to evil. His language is by no means clear:

> If the problem of suffering comes to focus in human exposure to the impact of deprivation independent of individual agency, and that of evil, in exposure to that of consequences independent of active intentions, that of capacity focuses on the fact that, however much we may *want* to do something, we may be prevented to [by?] incapacity from actually doing it. Of course, illness is far from being the only source of human incapacity, but it is a focally prominent and symbolic one, especially in a society with an activistic orientation. (Parsons, 1978: 79)

Suffering and evil both result from an incapacity originating beyond the organism itself, and outside any human intention. All three, suffering, evil and incapacity, are central to what Parsons called 'the human condition'. How they figure into the human condition is, on my reading, opaque, but perhaps Parsons is most valuable to postmodern thought precisely when he is opaque, because then we are free to read him 'against the grain' of what is taken to be his intended project.

Parsons's work can be read as a continuous meditation on the human condition attempting to sustain the viability of intention in the face of internal (organic) and external (environmental) disturbances to the intending 'personality'. The sick role mediates between internal disturbance and external responsibility. The empirical implication of the sick role is to turn the body of the ill person over to medical expertise, without reservation. But what stands out in Parsons's defense of the sick role concept is his commitment to intention, or 'agency', later 'teleonymy', if only as an analytical principle. Parsons's remainder is the reminder that in the postmodern health role, agency has disappeared almost entirely.

Parsons's ideal typical medical patient would be a good example of Garfinkel's (1967) claim that Parsons created a 'judgment dope'. But we reach another flip point; Parsons's final comments on suffering and evil elevate the problem of agency to an existential dimension. Read from the perspective of Parsons's late writings, it is postmodern thought that creates a 'media dope'; at the extreme, postmodernism dismisses any commitment to agency as a nostalgia for the subject. The citizen of Baudrillard's Simulacrum, the status holder within Bourdieu's habitus, Foucault's technologist of the self, and even Habermas's colonized communicator, all lack the agency that Parsons tried, however inadequately, to preserve. Habermas alone has attempted to formulate a remedial praxis, that is, communicative action. The role of praxis in the others is unclear.

Parsons may prove to be of little use in generating a postmodern praxis, but his linkage of illness to suffering and evil is an essential reminder. In the sick role, Parsons treated suffering as another 'figure in a pentimento', scarcely visible behind the professional expertise of the physician. Now the physician is in pentimento, made progressively invisible by the *System*. In the image of the health role, the suffering of sickness is no longer visible; it is a time past or future, compressed out in the present and presence of the image of health. The later Parsons, who brought suffering back in, would have recognized the evil inherent in such a *System*. In the pervasiveness of the *System*, the person becomes the medium of the image. For Parsons, health was the medium of the body; now the body is the medium of health, and health is the medium of the *System*, which has no body. The actor is subordinated to the currency.

Parsons's remainder, the part that does not deconstruct, is his final, perhaps even failing attempts to bring back an agent whose existence depends on knowing suffering and evil. The power of postmodern theory to inform us about the health/illness continuum, and how the self is constituted within it, can distract us from the existential dimension of illness. We forget the fundamental problems: how do we reduce suffering, and what aspects of suffering are properly understood within a concept of evil? These problems are the agenda Parsons leaves to us.

Notes

1. By 'postmodern' I denote a period of time, present and future, and I connote a style. With regard to medicine, the postmodern period seems marked by the increasing effectiveness of medical technology, but also its increasing cost; in response to that cost, increased government and corporate interventions; the public perception of scarce resources for care; and, in the near future, the relegation of ethical issues to questions of 'resource management' (see, for example, 'Experts: Cost will shape bioethics in the 1990s', 1990).

The attributes I believe are central to the postmodern style are those around which I have tried to structure my own text, as a reflexive display of what it describes. Perhaps this reflexive structuring is the essential quality of postmodern style. Ultimately this distinction of period and style deconstructs; the period creates its style, and the style defines the period. Postmodernism is defined in the continual deconstruction of its definitions.

2. None of the four theorists would accept the label of 'postmodern' applied to himself. Their commonality is the reflexive achievement of my own text; they too are being deconstructed.

3. Note also how 'health promotion' has changed. In the 1950s it meant 'early warning signs' advertising; one could interrogate one's body for signs of disease, but do little to prevent their occurrence. Today's messages consist of 'lifestyle' play; one interrogates one's life to see if it fits the image, and a proper fit is assumed to be preventative.

References

Arney, W.R. and Bergen, B.J. (1984) *Medicine and the Management of Living: Taming the Last Great Beast*. Chicago: University of Chicago Press.

Baudrillard, J. (1983) *Simulations*. New York: Semiotext(e) Foreign Agents Series.

Bourdieu, P. (1978) 'Sport and Social Class', *Social Science Information*. 17 (6): 819–40.

Bourdieu, P. (1984) *Distinction: a Social Critique of the Judgment of Taste*. Cambridge, MA: Harvard University Press.

'Experts: Cost Will Shape Bioethics in the 1990s' (1990) *Medical Ethics Advisor*, 6 (1): 1–7.

Foucault, M. (1988) 'Technologies of the Self', pp. 16–49 in L.M. Martin, H. Gutman and P.H. Hutton (eds), *Technologies of the Self: a Seminar with Michel Foucault*. Amherst, MA: University of Massachusetts Press.

Frank, A.W. (1989) 'Habermas's Interactionism: the Micro-Macro Link to Politics', *Symbolic Interaction*, 12: 163–70.

Frank, A.W. (forthcoming a) 'Cancer Self-Healing: Health as Cultural Capital in Monological Society', in N.K. Denzin (ed.), *Studies in Symbolic Interaction*, vol. 12. Greenwich, CT: JAI Press.

Frank, A.W. (forthcoming b) 'Twin Nightmares of the Medical Simulacrum: Jean Baudrillard and David Cronenberg', in W. Stearns and W. Chaloupka (eds), *Jean Baudrillard: the Disappearance of Art and Politics*. New York: St Martins Press.

Garfinkel, H. (1967) *Studies in Ethnomethodology*. Englewood Cliffs, NJ: Prentice-Hall.

Habermas, J. (1987) *The Theory of Communicative Action*, volume II, *Lifeworld and System: a Critique of Functionalist Reason*, tr. T. McCarthy. Boston: Beacon Press.

Hutton, P. (1988) 'Foucault, Freud, and the Technologies of the Self', pp. 121–44 in L.M. Martin, H. Gutman and P.H. Hutton (eds), *Technologies of the Self: a Seminar with Michel Foucault*. Amherst, MA: University of Massachusetts Press.

Kleinman, A. (1988) *The Illness Narratives: Suffering, Healing and the Human Condition*. New York: Basic Books.

Kroker, A. and Kroker, M. (1987) 'Theses on the Disappearing Body in the Hyper-Modern Condition', pp. 20–34 in A. Kroker and M. Kroker (eds), *Body Invaders: Panic Sex in America*. Montreal: New World Perspectives.

Levine, S. and Kozloff, M.A. (1978) 'The Sick Role: Assessment and Overview', *Annual Review of Sociology*, 4: 317–43.

Parsons, T. (1951) *The Social System*. New York: Free Press.

Parsons, T. (1964) *Social Structure and Personality*. New York: Free Press.

Parsons, T. (1978) *Action Theory and the Human Condition*. New York: Free Press.

Turner, B.S. (1987) *Medical Power and Social Knowledge*. London: Sage.

Walker, R. (1990) 'Report on Health Care: Fit Albertan Could Earn Just Reward', *Calgary Herald*, 13 February, pp. A1–A2.

11

THE POLITICAL ORIENTATION OF TALCOTT PARSONS: THE SECOND WORLD WAR AND ITS AFTERMATH

Jens Kaalhauge Nielsen

The work of Talcott Parsons has had a peculiar fate in the field of social science. Parsons succeeded in becoming a dominant and celebrated figure in American social science during the period lasting from the late 1940s to the mid-1960s. On the other hand, his work reached a peak in the years of student rebellion during the late 1960s and the main attack was dominated by strong ideological polemics. Parsons's work was seen as the product of a conservative and nostalgic mind and criticized for its 'static equilibrium theory' and for its basic legitimation of capitalism and bourgeois Western values. Thus during the 1960s and early 1970s a myth was created about Talcott Parsons's political orientation which attained a life of its own and has stubbornly survived until this day. Parsons's political world-view was perceived as opposed to a leftist orientation and Parsons's 'structural-functionalism' became the ultimate symbol of a reactionary type of theory. Theoretical progressivity and anti-Parsonianism became interchangeable concepts.

In the present chapter I will analyze the nature of Parsons's political orientation partly on the basis of his published work and partly through unpublished materials. These materials are of two kinds: Parsons's posthumous papers and other items in the Harvard University Archives, and extensive interviews which I have conducted with Parsons's students, critics, colleagues and family members. This chapter will argue that the established image of Parsons's political orientation and the conservative nature of his theory have neither historical validity nor theoretical substance. In particular, I will examine claims about Parsons's activities in the postwar period which have been raised in an article in *The Nation* (Wiener, 1989).

My attempt to rediscover the real Parsons behind the smokescreen of academic folklore and misinterpretation does not, of course, stand alone. A whole range of scholars have for some time acknowledged the unique significance of Parsons's theoretical contribution and attempted to establish a more sound idea of his theory and its political implications. The most influential and important efforts in this direction have been those of

Loubser et al. (1976), Alexander (1983), Habermas (1987) and Holton and Turner (1986). The present analysis stands in debt to the insights which these attempts have provided.

Parsons's life and early political development

Talcott Parsons was born on 13 December 1902 in Colorado Springs, the youngest of six children. He was born into a family where the values of religious Calvinist Protestantism were combined with an enlightened, progressive openness about scientific and intellectual issues. His father, Edward S. Parsons, had a past as a Congregational minister and had been active in the Social Gospel movement. More specifically, he had been concerned with the challenge which socialism posed for Christian spirituality, and it is possible to see this question echoed in the mind of the young Talcott Parsons, although in a more complex and secularized version. Parsons's family background was, in its own way, to the Left in politics. However, it was a kind of progressiveness which from the very beginning had sources of inspiration other than the axioms of traditional socialism and Marxism.

Parsons graduated from Horace Mann High School in 1920 and then attended Amherst College in Massachusetts – at that time a very experimental and progressive school under the leadership of Alexander Meiklejohn. An event of great significance for Parsons's political socialization occurred when Meiklejohn was dismissed as the President of Amherst College in 1923. This event had a particular symbolic importance for Parsons because his father had six years earlier been forced away from Colorado College by conservative Trustees. Parsons admired Meiklejohn and his fate came as a shock; together with another student, Addison Thayer Cutler, he wrote an indignant defence of Meiklejohn in a national student journal. In the year after this event, young Parsons was given the opportunity to vote for the first time and he cast his vote for Robert La Follette from the Progressive Party, which called for government ownership of railroads and ratification of the child labor amendment.[1] Parsons was also very interested in the implications of the Russian Revolution and the growing strength of the Labour Party in Great Britain. Indeed, Parsons went to England in 1924 in order to study at the London School of Economics, at that time widely known as a center for leftist and progressive intellectualism. Parsons had been originally attracted to the LSE in order to study with the famous socialist Harold Laski, but after his arrival he found Bronislaw Malinowski's courses in anthropology more theoretically compelling. Parsons was also highly concerned about capitalism as a social and theoretical issue and he chose this issue as a topic for his Heidelberg dissertation, reading extensively in Weber, Sombart and Marx (Martel, 1976).

Parsons was a strong supporter of Franklin Roosevelt's New Deal policy in the 1930s and had several disagreements with his friend and mentor

Lawrence J. Henderson about New Deal questions. Henderson was a stout conservative and was almost obsessive in his opposition to the New Deal. Parsons later remembered Henderson as 'dogmatic' on political issues (Parsons, 1977). Parsons appears to have voted for Roosevelt in three out of four elections and was throughout his life a strong defender of a Keynesian type of economy and very much against Milton Friedman's monetarism. Thus, Alvin Gouldner's claim that Parsons was a foe of the New Deal is a complete fabrication (Gouldner, 1970). It is also interesting to note that Parsons's sociological study group in the 1930s was much concerned with the question of class analysis. In fact the issue was discussed intensively. The group also spent much time in an effort to understand the nature of 'propaganda', with particular reference to the Nazi movement in Germany. Parsons's correspondence with his good friend Edward Y. Hartshorne indicates that Parsons was from very early on aware of and concerned about the danger of German and Italian fascism. Evidence shows that it was also part of Parsons's political conviction that measures should be taken in order to get rid of Franco after the war.[2] It was later charged, as part of his loyalty-investigation during the McCarthy period, that Parsons had supported 'communist-sponsored' anti-Franco activities.

Parsons was one of the first in the USA to take an active and uncompromising stand against Nazism at a time when it was not such an easy position to adopt, largely because of the strong influence of the American isolationists. Parsons's outrage against Nazism and the indirect support which Nazism was getting from the isolationists is especially manifest in an exchange that Parsons had with Alan Gottlieb from the Harvard Student Union. Parsons wrote to Gottlieb on 16 April 1940:

> I am sorry that I do not feel I can comply with your request to excuse my class for the peace demonstration Thursday morning. . . . I may add that I have personal reasons for being out of sympathy with the 'Peace' movement which in the circumstances can only mean peace at any price. In the present juncture such agitation plays directly into the hands of the Nazis – I can just hear Goebbels chuckle, as he hears of them. I find it difficult to believe that is the result you really wish to promote.

Parsons became a political activist in this period and played a key role in the establishment of the Harvard Defence Committee, which promoted public awareness of the danger of Nazism and the importance of supporting Britain, which had been at war with Nazi Germany since September 1939. Parsons became chairman of the Morale and National Service subcommittee which was the key subcommittee of 'Harvard Defence'. Parsons exercised a prominent role within this campaign. He even appeared as the main political speaker at a spectacular meeting on campus – a meeting which the isolationists tried to disrupt. Parsons also wrote many letters to Congressmen, attempting to persuade them to take an active stand against Nazism and support Britain. Moreover, Parsons's voice sounded again and again over one of the local radio stations for the Boston area, where he made frequent editorial comments on political events. Parsons focused in these public speeches on the necessity of supporting Britain, and also gave his analysis of internal American politics and on the development of the war. This is clearly not the picture of a detached and removed 'philosopher-king' unable to deal with the issues of 'power' or alien to political activism.

Parsons's work as a member of the Subcommittee on Morale and National Service was not limited to the promotion of general information and agitation. He also initiated a discussion group on German Social Structure which basically attempted to establish a theoretical framework for an understanding of the social causes of Nazism. Those who claim that Parsons was uninterested in empirical analysis of historical events until late in his career should read the long minutes of these meetings and some of his regular correspondence on this issue. Parsons also established at Harvard a group studying the causes of Japanese imperialism.

During the war Parsons worked in the School of Overseas Administration which was formally directed by Carl Friedrich. In practice it was Parsons who ran the school. This work brought Parsons in contact with governmental and intelligence institutions in Washington, especially the OSS, which was the forerunner of the CIA. Many of his Harvard colleagues also worked for the OSS. Parsons was interested in getting declassified materials on the countries about which his school was teaching. Near the end of the war he participated in a conference about the future of Germany, where he argued against a too narrow and historically fixed idea about the 'German Personality Character' and emphasized that the authoritarian personality had been only *one* aspect of pre-Nazi German culture. Parsons also argued against the idea that Germany should be deindustrialized and taken back to a pastoral, agrarian stage. Moreover, he opposed the view that German education and socialization should be directly monitored and administrated by an agency of the United Nations. He was convinced that such measures were not merely unrealistic but that they would nurture the type of political forces which the war had been designed to eliminate. At the end of the war William L. Langer, Director of the Research and Analysis Section of the OSS, offered Parsons a job in that organization. The proposal was that Parsons should follow the American Army in its march into Germany and function as a political adviser on the question of how to administer occupied Germany. Parsons was very interested in the assignment, but he eventually declined Langer's offer because of his increased responsibilities for the postwar development of Social Science at Harvard.

Parsons and the Russian Research Center: the affair of the Vlasov Movement

In 1948 Parsons became a member of the Executive Committee of the newly established Russian Research Center (RRC) at Harvard. The Director of the new center was Parsons's good friend and colleague Clyde Kluckhohn, who was an influential cultural anthropologist. In the summer of 1948 Parsons was sent on a trip to occupied Germany in order to investigate the possibility of the RRC gaining reliable information on the Soviet Union and to make contact with specific individuals. Some of these contacts had been members of the so-called Vlasov Movement, which consisted of a group of patriotic anti-Stalinist officers who in a tragic way had been caught between Hitler and Stalin's totalitarianism. The Vlasov people collaborated with the Germans during the war in order to force Stalin from power in Russia. These people were working for a US Army intelligence school when RRC was informed of their existence.

A historian, Jon Wiener, has written in an article in *The Nation* on the Vlasov people and Parsons's summer trip to Germany in such a way as to build a distorted case based on insufficient and fabricated empirical information (Wiener, 1989). In the article, Parsons is criticized as an unscrupulous person, who knowingly smuggled Nazis and other war criminals into the USA. Wiener's story is built around Parsons's meeting in the summer of 1948 with a Russian collaborator, Nicholas Poppe. The fact of the matter is that Wiener's claims about Parsons's meeting with Nicholas Poppe are a complete fabrication. This event never happened. There does not exist any evidence that Parsons ever spoke with or wrote to, let alone met, Nicholas Poppe.

Wiener makes a particular point of describing the Vlasov people as Nazi sympathizers and pro-Nazis, a claim many will be inclined to accept. After all, are Nazi collaborators not necessarily pro-Nazis and Nazi sympathizers? Yet the real story is much more complex and surprising. The materials available in the Russian Research Center's Collection at Harvard and elsewhere lead to the conclusion that Wiener's discussion presents an unfortunate manipulation of facts and circumstances. The Vlasov people can best be described as leftist-orientated nationalists whose ideology followed the lines rooted in communists' and social democrats' ideas of a highly planned, government-controlled society. The core of the Vlasov people had fought on the Red side in the Russian Civil War and the movement was surprisingly loyal to the basic principles of the Russian Revolution, which they believed had been betrayed by Stalin. Some of them also supported the Kronstadt rebellion, which they saw as a part of the real revolution. The Vlasov movement was, as far as its ideology went, a Red rebellion against Stalin, not a White one. It was a mixture of authoritarian and libertarian tendencies in which the former seemed to have been the strongest (Fischer, 1952: 154). Nevertheless the manifesto of 1944, the so-called Prague Manifesto, spoke about establishing a democracy. Yet the emphasis on democracy might, at least in part, have been a propaganda effort to come to terms with the potentially victorious Western democracies. This is, of course, an issue open to dispute. Most of the Vlasov people were officers who in different ways had been alienated by the Stalinist regime and who, in particular, found that the collectivization program of Russian agriculture had been a terrible mistake. Some of them had friends who had been murdered by Stalin during the purge of the officer corps in the late 1930s. Some had been thrown into jail by Stalin, as was the case with Vladimir Pozdniakov.

The Nazi hierarchy was interested in the Vlasov movement's value as a propaganda tool and had not allowed its members to become comrades in arms. On the contrary, the Vlasov group was consistently subjected to humiliation from the Nazi elite, covering all levels of social interaction. Indeed, the interaction between these Russian nationalists and the German Nazis had very little to do with what one normally associates with the term 'collaboration'.

Vlasov was first allowed to travel in the German-occupied area of Soviet Russia, but, after giving some nationalistic speeches that infuriated Himmler, Vlasov was forbidden by Hitler to travel in the occupied areas, and he was kept in a kind of captivity in Germany during the rest of the war. This and other events constantly alienated the Vlasovs from ever becoming Nazis or Nazi sympathizers. Thus, the Vlasov people were infuriated about SS publications characterizing the Russians as 'subhuman', and it was as a part of the general relationship between them and the Nazis that Himmler gave a public speech in which he called Vlasov 'a pig'. Several of the Vlasov people, who were accused of being communists, were later arrested by the Gestapo, and one of the movement's leading members, Zykov, a convinced Marxist, was apparently murdered by the Gestapo. Consequently almost all the Russian collaborators were very hostile toward Nazi ideology. There were undoubtedly some anti-semitic sentiments among some Vlasov people, but the core of the leadership seems to have been relatively free of this element. One might here recall that anti-semitism at that time was a common pattern in almost all Russian institutions, communist as well as anti-communist; and the Vlasov movement seems not to have been particularly exceptional in that regard. Vlasov himself seems not to have been anti-semitic at all.

The Vlasov people were closely connected to anti-Nazi groups in the German Army and in German Intelligence, groups which included an officer like Claus von Stauffenberg, the man who placed the bomb in Hitler's headquarters in 1944. Von Stauffenberg was one of the most eager promoters of the Vlasov movement's cause and worked actively against some of the Nazi hierarchy's attempts to limit the political operation of the Vlasov movement. The Vlasov movement became at some point an integral part of the anti-Nazi establishment within the German Army. In conclusion, the Vlasov movement was neither Nazi nor sympathetic to Nazi ideology, as measured by any meaningful use of these terms. Moreover, it would be more accurate to call the Vlasov people German collaborators rather than Nazi collaborators, because their real collaboration was with anti-Nazi groups in the Wehrmacht.

As a consequence of their captivity in Germany the Vlasov officers were in no position to commit any war crimes and there exists no indication that any group, while under its authority, committed any such crime. The Vlasov Army existed for only a few months in 1945 and it is remembered for its fight against the SS units that were occupying Prague. Wiener is of course correct that the Vlasov people were called 'war criminals' by Stalin's regime, but what does he expect Stalin to have called some of his most devoted enemies? One can now understand why a title such as 'Talcott Parsons' Role: Bringing Anti-Nazi German Collaborators to the US' would not have worked as a technique for supporting Wiener's crusade against what he calls 'leading liberal scholars' of the Cold War period. I should like to emphasize that in this discussion I certainly do not intend to provide any political-moral legitimation for the Vlasov movement. Whether they were moral or immoral is not the issue here. One might well read my comments as a technical protest against a type of analysis that tries to make a caricature out of complex historical events through simplification and direct distortion. Getting the facts straight is not, however, simply a technical issue. When we are dealing with questions concerning Nazism and war criminals, I believe that we have a *moral* obligation to get the facts as straight as possible.

It is factually correct that the Russian Research Center showed interest in employing Nicholas Poppe as a consultant at Harvard. However, the person who worked with this question and who established these connections was Clyde Kluckhohn and not Parsons. Moreover, the known facts about Kluckhohn's action in this case show that Kluckhohn made a serious attempt to get reliable information on Poppe and that none of this information indicated that Poppe could be associated with any war crime. Whether Poppe was a war criminal is still an unsolved issue. It might of course be proven one day that Poppe actually was a war criminal, but all the available empirical evidence indicates that Clyde Kluckhohn did not have access to such knowledge.

There can be no doubt that the Russian Research Center's activities – in which Parsons was a secondary but committed actor – raise important questions about the general relationship between the academic community and governmental institutions, especially the intelligence community. The real question here is that concerning an appropriate balance between the integrity of a modern university and its desire to be an integral part of the society to which it belongs. One might doubt that there exists any uniquely simple solution to this question, but it is clearly an area in which important moral questions and claims can be raised on a legitimate basis.

It is important to underline the fact that the RRC was from the very beginning tied up with strong intelligence interests and interacted on a regular basis with intelligence institutions like the CIA, the State Department's Intelligence division, Air Force Intelligence and Army Intelligence. The RRC's link to Air Force Intelligence, at that time the biggest intelligence money-spender, was particularly strong. Clyde Kluckhohn's role was here especially important. Kluckhohn was very actively involved in Air Force Intelligence analytical planning and especially in the part of Air Force Intelligence which was concerned with psychological warfare. Kluckhohn's involvement in Air Force Intelligence came, at its peak, closer to that of an administrator than that of a consultant, and there are indications that he also acted as a consultant with respect to Air Force policy during the Korean War. There is no evidence that Parsons participated in any intelligence function. His role was solely that of a member of the RRC's Executive Committee. There is no doubt, on the other hand, that he was fully aware of the integrated network involving the RRC and the intelligence community and that he knew a lot about Kluckhohn's strong involvement in intelligence activities.

All the evidence suggests that Kluckhohn and Parsons simply thought of the collaboration with the intelligence community as a natural extension of the struggle for democracy against fascism undertaken during the war. The fight against the Nazis seems to have served as an appropriate legitimation for a close interaction between the academic world and governmental institutions, including the intelligence part. Large segments of the intelligence community, and especially the OSS, had been built up with Parsons's and Kluckhohn's own colleagues from the Ivy League, elite institutions. Thus in many cases the role of campus professor and the role of intelligence official became entangled. Actually the OSS was during the war and in its aftermath mainly a liberal bastion, recruiting its members from a broad political spectrum. One needs only to be reminded that people such as Herbert Marcuse, Paul Baran, Paul Sweezy and Barrington Moore served in the OSS (Katz, 1989). One should also remember that a scholar like C. Wright Mills served as a special business consultant to the Smaller War Plants Corporation for a period during the war. These wartime connections were institutionalized and simply continued after the war. Moreover, fighting the totalitarian regime of Josef Stalin was a morally and politically legitimate task. The de-stalinization of Eastern Europe and the democratic revolutions of 1989–90 have given further legitimacy to earlier opposition to totalitarianism.

It is impossible to discuss this issue without placing it in an appropriate historical context. One might remember that the events of the summer of 1948 and its aftermath took place in an atmosphere in which war with the Stalinist regime was viewed as highly probable. It was the general feeling that extraordinary things had to be done. It is important to insist that Kluckhohn's and Parsons's concerns about the Stalinist regime cannot be analyzed on a serious scientific basis under the concept of 'Cold War hysteria'. Indeed, 'Cold War hysteria' becomes in Wiener's analysis an indefinitely elastic, residual concept, a conceptual joker, into which all that is in Wiener's opinion 'evil' seems to fit. Today we clearly have a frame of reference other than the Cold War. If one looks at current developments in Eastern Europe, one might find it difficult to say that Parsons's and Kluckhohn's policy was completely without foundation and legitimation.

Parsons and McCarthyism

Few things upset Parsons more than McCarthyism. Parsons became a bold opponent of McCarthy. George C. Homans remembered a dinner with Parsons in the early 1950s in which Parsons could hardly control his emotions over the question of McCarthy, whom he denounced throughout the whole evening (interview with G.C. Homans, 21 April 1988). Neil Smelser has in an interview underlined how hostile Parsons was toward McCarthyism and that he viewed it as 'a running sore in the side of American policy'.[3] Parsons was opposed to the McCarthyist attempt to establish special loyalty oaths in American universities, and he was very active in support of the professors who were involved in the University of California oath conflict. Parsons defended his young colleague Robert Bellah when Bellah was faced with McCarthyist problems. He also ran to the help of Samuel Stouffer when he got into similar political trouble. Finally, Parsons himself was charged with subversive communist activities. One of the results of these charges was that a clearance which was necessary for his participation in an international UNESCO conference was withheld and Parsons was precluded from participating in the confer-ence. Parsons had first to compose a written statement in defence of Stouffer and then to answer the questions of an 'Interrogatory' where he was charged as a communist sympathizer. One must remember that this 'Interrogatory' was a forced statement in which Parsons, for tactical reasons to a large extent, was providing the McCarthyists with the image they wanted to see. Therefore, these statements do not represent a sensitive measure of Parsons's complex attitude to communism. Indeed, the correspondence between Parsons and Stouffer indicates very clearly that the 'Interrogatory' was designed for this very specific purpose. Parsons wrote to Stouffer on 12 February 1954:

> I would not consent to a statement which made me out a 'professional anti-communist'. I stand squarely on the ground that I object to *all* forms of totalitarianism, including that of certain Americans at present. It seems to me that this is the ground on which we academic people *have* to stand. The draft goes as far as I am willing to go in that respect, indeed a little bit farther than I am altogether comfortable about. I feel very strongly about this point.[4]

Parsons had difficulties with Dean McGeorge Bundy's implementation of Harvard's policy during the McCarthy era and his letter of late May 1954 to Bundy expressed his desire for a more aggressive policy on the question of McCarthyism. Parsons participated later in a Committee on Special Freedom and Tenure Cases which was a subcommittee under the American Association of University Professors. This committee conducted an investi-gation of universities that during the McCarthy period had dismissed members for political reasons and, as a result, asked for censure of several institutions. The committee made it clear that 'the mere fact of member-ship in any organization whatever, including the Communist Party, does not constitute adequate ground for dismissal'.[5]

Parsons's attitude to communism and the Soviet Union was complicated. He was clearly opposed to the Stalinist regime and appears to have supported the strategy of containment full-heartedly. There was in that sense a 'realist' element in Parsons's view of foreign policy. It is important to understand that Parsons's view of the communist threat was not in principle different from his opposition to the Nazi threat. They were in his view two historical manifestations of totalitarianism which had to be opposed. Parsons was clearly not more anti-communist than he was anti-Nazi; indeed, he was undoubtedly more passionately anti-Nazi than anti-communist although he disliked them both. People who like to portray Parsons as a compulsive and one-dimensional 'anti-communist' clearly miss the point. He was *primarily* anti-totalitarian and for that reason he was *also* an anti-communist. However, Parsons was much too intelligent to be obsessive about being anti-communist and he clearly discriminated between the Stalinist version of communism and more humanistic forms of that doctrine.

However, one can easily give a misleading impression about Parsons's general analysis of these problems and discuss his 'anti-communism' out of context. Parsons was actually one of the first who supported a *modus vivendi* with the Soviet Union; and he visited the country at the beginning of the 1960s. Parsons at an early stage came to the conclusion that the whole discussion of capitalism versus socialism was inherently inadequate and that this discussion distorted the real issues of the modern world. He was convinced that neither capitalism nor socialism would be the ultimate solution for the modern world. Thus Parsons was one of the first to launch the convergence theory and stressed the similarities more than the differences between the Soviet and the Western systems. The convergence theory predicted that inherent forces within the two systems would 'force' them to move together, and converge into a 'third type'. Parsons's prediction has never been more relevant than in this time of *perestroika* and *glasnost*.

Parsons was very committed to Civil Rights issues and, in an article in 1965, he strongly supported race integration (Parsons, 1965). He was opposed to the Vietnam War, a strong critic of the Nixon administration and with Dean Gerstein wrote an engaged article about the Watergate affair and Richard Nixon's misuse of power. Parsons was sympathetic to the general demands of the so-called youth rebellion of the late 1960s and well aware of the significance of this event within modern history. Parsons and David Riesman were ready to function as political consultants for Senator Eugene McCarthy, if he had been elected at the Democratic Convention in 1968. Eugene McCarthy was a strong opponent of US Vietnam policy.[6] Towards the end of his life, Parsons became interested in Japanese culture and he visited Japan more than once. Shortly before his death at the age of 77, he told his friends that the impact of his discussion with Japanese scholars had convinced him that Weber had overgeneralized his discussion of Buddhism and that Parsons would like to reinterpret his concept of Christianity and his discussion of modern history through a more careful analysis of Sino-Japanese civilization.[7]

Parsons and progressive reform

The history of Parsons's life is certainly not the life history of a committed conservative, an unconditional defender of capitalism, or a person obsessed by consensus. On the contrary, Parsons's life gives us the biography of a man strongly opposed to right-wing politics and the story of an activist against Nazism, McCarthyism and racism. It gives us also the picture of a man who was critical of and unimpressed by the intellectual subcultures which called themselves the 'radical Left'. He often criticized them for being too one-sided, uncritical and unrealistic in their goals; for Parsons, they lacked sophistication in their theoretical and intellectual pursuits. Besides, he had very little sympathy for Marxism which functioned as their basic intellectual ideology, although one might say that he had more respect for Marx than for Marxism. All this convinced the radicals that Parsons (and his Grand Theory) was the prototype of American conservatism. Indeed, they were convinced that the 'abstractness' of his theory in some way or another was a secret weapon for political conservatism – a highbrow conspiracy against good proletarian social empiricism (Mills, 1959; Moore, 1958).

Despite his criticism of certain branches of the Left, clearly the main bulk of Parsons's criticism, explicit as well as implicit, focused on the Right. This point was highlighted by many who came close to Parsons as friends and colleagues. David Riesman has emphasized that 'Parsons had no sympathy for the right at all . . . .'[8] The same point has been made strongly by Neil Smelser: 'Parsons was more hostile to the right than he was to the left . . . . I believe that the people who call Parsons "conservative" do not understand him very well . . . .'[9] Smelser has a valid point. Of the many people Parsons knew well and who became closely connected with him, it has been impossible for me to find any who claim that Parsons was a conservative. The only possible exception might be Norman Birnbaum, but it can be doubted that he was ever in any meaningful sense close to Parsons. The image of a stout conservative is basically the fabrication of people who did not know him very well and who had only the most superficial command of his theory.

Was Parsons a liberal defender of capitalism? First, he did not accept the Marxian idea that modern society was simply 'capitalistic' in the sense that capitalism is a sufficient description of the most essential features and tendencies of modern society. He believed that the economy is embedded in a network of social institutions that place very great strains on what the economy is able to do. Second, Parsons found that one needs analytically to distinguish economic rationality and the market mechanism from 'capitalism' as a socio-economic phenomenon. These are not identical concepts. As Parsons wrote in a letter of 29 January 1975 to Jeffrey C. Alexander: 'Economic rationality, however, as you know as well as I do, is by no means irrelevant to the operation of socialist economy . . . ' Moreover, Parsons's discussion of utilitarianism contains an implicit critique of *laissez-faire* capitalism. In fact, Parsons set out a strategy in *The Structure of Social Action* (1937) in which he attempted to establish the theoretical parameters for a third route between orthodox capitalism and orthodox socialism. Thus it would be very inadequate to portray him, as has often been the case, as a mindless and eager defender of capitalism. As Robert N. Bellah has stated, 'The notion that Parsons was primarily concerned with the defense of capitalism is simply historically wrong. . . . People that talk that way have not made the effort to really understand Talcott's frame of reference.'[10]

Parsons tended to be a friend of progressive reforms and was not compelled by the analytic or moral value of the notion of total revolutions, partly because he found that they tended to nurture extremists of all kinds and partly because he did not believe that *political* revolutions were necessarily all that important. However, Parsons also acknowledged that there was a limit to the utility of pragmatism and that there existed situations in which confrontation was the only possible political and moral solution. When Parsons reached this point, he was invariably uncompromising. This attitude was especially clear in his fight against McCarthyism and is reflected in a letter that Parsons wrote to Samuel Stouffer at the time when Stouffer had been called to an investigation by the McCarthyists, and charged with having close associations with communists. Parsons, at that time located at Cambridge University in England, wrote to Stouffer on 12 February 1954:

> I agree with you that this has to be fought candidly and hard in the interests of everything and everybody we hold dear. It is only a question of the best strategy and tactics. I am in it with you to the death. . . . I am with you in every way and will do literally *anything* I can, even to dropping all the rest of the Cambridge business if necessary.[11]

There is no doubt that Parsons had a great faith in the major American institutions and that, in a sophisticated sense, he was a believer in 'the American Dream'. Parsons had undoubtedly a love affair with what he believed to be the essence of American society. However, does one have to be a reactionary in order to remain committed to the American Dream? Was Martin Luther King not a believer in the American Dream and would we classify him as being on the Right? One might notice that there was a kind of radicalism in this dream of Parsons. It is not accidental that he frequently underlined how much he agreed with Seymour Martin Lipset that the basic American tradition was in a larger perspective a *revolutionary tradition*. Parsons believed that the promise and vision of that tradition was still unfolding. Many American institutions were in Parsons's eyes institutions of revolutionary significance, despite whatever short-term problems and structural contradictions they might have or be associated with. In this way, Parsons had especially high expectations about the function of the modern university as a key player in the process of social transformation.

Parsons was never prepared to accept the type of 'radical' leftist criticism which tended to characterize all the major institutions and all segments of its leadership as morally bankrupt or to reduce everything in modern society and modern culture to the reflection of 'the logic of capitalism' or 'the order of the bourgeois class'. He basically believed that these types of leftist criticism made a caricature of the real problems and the real dangers of modernity. He was annoyed with a lot of leftist critique in the 1960s and 1970s not primarily because it was Left, but because it was, by Parsons's standards, intellectually infantile and reductionist. Parsons's critique of Marxism was very complex, but he regarded it basically as an obsolete theory developed at a time in which philosophy and social science existed in a stage of incomplete differentiation. The limitation of Marx's method and philosophical assumptions created an interpretation of modern society and capitalism that in Parsons's eyes was deeply inadequate and had failed to produce any reasonable predictions of the development of society. However, it would be wrong to leave the impression that Parsons completely rejected Marx's theory. Parsons acknowledged that the structure of the productive forces which Marx had outlined for capitalist society was of real significance, but he insisted that Marx's theory as a whole had been superseded by more sophisticated theoretical approaches.

Parsons's political orientation consisted in a much more complicated and differentiated picture than the one painted by Gouldner, Wright Mills and other radical theorists. His sociology is not easy to classify and Parsons himself does not really fall easily into the classical stereotypes of a Left–Right spectrum. It is safe to classify him as a Left liberalist, but I argue that important parts of Parsons's work fall within the tradition of the humanistic Left which one might distinguish from the communist Left. If one studies Parsons's second Brown Lecture, that he gave on 27 March 1974 at the age of 71 (Parsons, 1974), it becomes clear that he expressed the strongest possible commitment to the unity of mankind and a strong prediction that the time for worldviews based on nation and race was over. Parsons expressed in this way his deepest conviction that the processes of differentiation and interpenetration, so characteristic of modern society, made it impossible in the end for any class, or any nation, or any race to rule the world. It is clear that this view, along with many other indicators, underlines Parsons's commitment to an uncompromising humanistic universalism.

There can be no doubt that Parsons had sympathy for the democratic and humanistic variants of the socialist tradition. Jeffrey C. Alexander concluded in an interview: 'I do not think that there is any great opposition between Parsons's theory and democratic socialism.'[12] Parsons represents a uniquely American route to many of the same qualities that characterized the European tradition of democratic socialism. Although his values were framed within the vocabulary of a Calvinistic activism and other values characterizing the American WASP tradition, Parsons's strong commitment to universalism has many similarities with the idea of socialism. However, Parsons's version of a good society differs from certain socialist versions to the extent that his political orientation has a clear anti-utopian cast and was solidly grounded in the values of a liberal tradition. Parsons was convinced that the good society was already under construction underneath existing power structures and social calamities. The new order was already embodied in some of the most basic mechanisms and institutions of the existing society. This was a crucial part of Parsons's famous optimism. Progress was occurring and was not something which could materialize only through an explicit political revolution.

His consistent disagreement with certain branches of the Left approach suggested to many critics that Parsons was basically satisfied with society and condoned the *status quo*. Nothing could be more false, and Parsons did not conceal his opinion about this part of the general anti-Parsonian folklore. In a letter to Professor William C. Mitchell, who was preparing a book about Parsons's political theory, Parsons complained about Mitchell's manuscript again and again, because the manuscript suggested that Parsons was basically satisfied with the general state of affairs in American society:

> There are a good many statements about satisfaction with the American state of affairs. You are quite right that I very deliberately refrained from attacking a great many of the targets of the American radical left, and you enumerate them – the modern corporation, mass culture, and [unreadable word]. On the other hand, I do not think that you can rightly accuse me of being satisfied with the present state of affairs. Not only is there the kind of worry about the radical right that the McCarthy paper showed; but for example, I could not feel more strongly than I do about the Civil Rights problem about anything. And I feel almost equally strongly about the general poverty situation. I also feel very strongly, indeed, about international responsibility in peace. I am not satisfied with the state of affairs. My difference from the left is that I am much more willing to give the responsible leadership elements a certain benefit of the doubt.[13]

Guy Rocher was on safe ground when he expressed the following view about Parsons's political orientation: 'He can be described neither as a conservative nor a radical, but rather as a liberal imbued with the spirit of the Welfare State, the New Deal, and the mixed economy. He believed neither in the virtues of the *status quo* nor of revolution, but placed his confidence in the structure and dynamism of his society and in the progress of human rationality' (1974: 231). I think that the existing historical data allow us to go one step further than Rocher, to suggest that Parsons is not only located on the left side of the liberal tradition, but that it is not unreasonable to consider him as a part of the modern leftist tradition in a broader sense. This does not deny that Parsons was a liberal, but it emphasizes the idea that he shared many values with the historical tradition which I have called the humanistic Left. This includes the assessment articulated by Jeffrey Alexander about Parsons's close relationship to social democratism.

Conclusion

This discussion of Parsons's political orientation is clearly relevant to current historical events. What we witness in these years of apparent post-communism is more than just the ideological and organizational collapse of state-bureaucratic regimes as the legacy of Stalin and his successors. It also entails an increasing awareness of the analytical bankruptcy of an orthodox definition of the Right–Left spectrum. One wonders what the meaning of the orthodox idea of Right and Left might be in a time when, for example, revolutionary soldiers, workers and intellectuals in Bucharest remove a statue of Lenin as a symbolic expression of their own liberation. Yet, the change in our ideas of Left and Right, and the search for a new way to classify the pattern of modern political forces, might have some impact on the established image of Parsons. While it might have been unthinkable to view Parsons as a leftist humanist in the time before *perestroika*, it might be an idea which is now ripe for consideration.

Notes

I should like to express my thanks to Jeffrey C. Alexander, Victor Meyer Lidz, Martin U. Martel, Roland Robertson and Bryan S. Turner for their encouragement and helpful commentary on earlier versions of this chapter.

1. Interview with Charles Parsons (Talcott Parsons's son), 20 May 1988.
2. Parsons's correspondence with Allan Chase (TPC/HUA).
3. Interview with Neil Smelser, 14 May 1988.
4. The Loyalty Investigation (TPC/HUA).
5. Letter from Talcott Parsons to David W. Bailey, 23 February 1956 (TPC/HUA).
6. Letter from David Riesman to Talcott Parsons, 8 July 1968 (TPC/HUA).
7. Interviews with Victor Lidz, 28 June 1988, and Harold Bershady, 29 June 1988.
8. Interview with David Riesman, 24 August 1988.
9. Interview with Neil Smelser, 24 May 1988.
10. Interview with Robert Bellah, 25 May 1988.
11. TPC/HUA.
12. Interview with Jeffrey C. Alexander, 31 May 1988.
13. Letter from Talcott Parsons to Professor William C. Mitchell, 29 June 1964, p. 3 (TPC/HUA).

Bibliography

CKC/HUA   Clyde Kluckhohn Collection, Harvard University Archives
RRC/HUA   Russian Research Collection, Harvard University Archives
SRC/HUA   Social Relations Department Collection, Harvard University Archives
TPC/HUA   Talcott Parsons Collection, Harvard University Archives

Alexander, J.C. (1983) *Theoretical Logic in Sociology*, vol. 4, *The Modern Reconstruction of Classical Thought: Talcott Parsons*. Berkeley and Los Angeles: University of California Press.

Andreyev, C. (1987) *Vlasov and the Russian Liberation Movement*. Cambridge: Cambridge University Press.

Breman, R.T. (1988) 'The Making of the Liberal College: Alexander Meiklejohn at Amherst', *History Quarterly*, 28 (4): 569–97.

Fischer, G. (1952) *Soviet Opposition to Stalin*. Cambridge, MA: Harvard University Press.

Foss, D. (1963) 'The World View of Talcott Parsons', pp. 96–126 in M. Stein and A. Vidich (eds), *Sociology on Trial*. Englewood Cliffs, NJ: Prentice-Hall.

Gouldner, A.W. (1963) 'Anti-Minotaur: the Myth of a Value-Free Sociology', pp. 35–52 in M. Stein and A. Vidich (eds), *Sociology on Trial*. Englewood Cliffs, NJ: Prentice-Hall.

Gouldner, A.W. (1970) *The Coming Crisis of Western Sociology*. London: Heinemann.

Habermas, J. (1981) 'Talcott Parsons: Problems of Theory Construction', *Sociological Inquiry*, 51 (3–4): 173–96.

Habermas, J. (1987) *The Theory of Communicative Action*, vol. 2, *Lifeworld and System: a Critique of Functionalist Reason*, tr. T. McCarthy. Boston: Beacon Press.

Hacker, A. (1961) 'Sociology and Ideology', pp. 289–310 in M. Black (ed.), *The Social Theories of Talcott Parsons, a Critical Examination*. Englewood Cliffs, NJ: Prentice-Hall.

Holton, R.J. and Turner, B.S. (1986) *Talcott Parsons on Economy and Society*. London and New York: Routledge & Kegan Paul.

Katz, B.M. (1989) *Foreign Intelligence: Research and Analysis in the Office of Strategic Services, 1942–1945*. Cambridge. MA: Harvard University Press.

Kennan, G.F. (1967) *Memoirs 1925–1950*. New York: Pantheon.

Loubser, J., Baum, R.C., Effrat, A. and Lidz, V. (eds) (1976) *Explorations in General Theory in Social Science*, 2 vols. New York: Free Press.

Martel, M.U. (1976) 'Dialogues with Parsons (1973–74)', *Indian Journal of Social Research*, 17 (1): 3–4.

Mills, C.W. (1959) *The Sociological Imagination*. New York: Oxford University Press.

Moore, B. Jr (1958) 'Strategy in Social Science' in his *Political Power and Social Theory*. Cambridge, MA: Harvard University Press.

Parsons, E.S. (1989) 'A Christian Critique of Socialism', *Andover Review*, 11: 597–611.

Parsons, T. ([1937] 1968) *The Structure of Social Action*. New York: Free Press.

Parsons, T. (1951) *The Social System*. London: Routledge & Kegan Paul.

Parsons, T. (1961) 'The Point of View of the Author', pp. 311–63 in M. Black (ed.), *The Social Theories of Talcott Parsons*. Englewood Cliffs, NJ: Prentice-Hall.

Parsons, T. (1965) 'Full Citizenship for the Negro American?' *Daedalus*, 94: 1009–54.

Parsons, T. (1968) Introduction to the paperback edition, *The Structure of Social Action*. New York: Free Press.

Parsons, T. (1974) 'Religion and Science in the Modern World', lecture transcript, Martin U. Martel Private Collections.

Parsons, T. (1977) 'On Building Social System Theory: a Personal History', pp. 22–76 in T. Parsons, *Social Systems and the Evolution of Action Theory*. New York: Free Press.

Parsons, T. (1978) *Action Theory and the Human Condition*. New York: Free Press.

Parsons, T. and Cutler, A.T. (1923) 'A Word from Amherst Students', *The New Student*, 3 (3): 6–7.

Parsons, T. and Gerstein, D.R. (1977) 'Two cases of Social Deviance: Addiction to Heroin, Addiction to Power', in E. Sagarin (ed.), *Deviance and Social Change*. Beverly Hills, CA: Sage.

Parsons, T. and Vogt, E.Z. (1962) 'Clyde Kluckhohn 1905–1960', *American Anthropologist*, 64: 140–8.

Parsons, T., Bales, R.F. and Shils, E.A. (1953) *Working Papers in the Theory of Action*. New York: Free Press.

Ranelagh, J. (1987) *The Agency: the Rise and Decline of the C.I.A.* New York: Touchstone.

Read, A. and Fisher, D. (1988) *The Deadly Embrace: Hitler, Stalin, and the Nazi-Soviet Pact,*

1939–1941. New York: W.W. Norton.

Reitlinger, G. (1957) *The SS: Alibi of a Nation*. New York: Viking.

Rocher, G. (1974) *Talcott Parsons and American Sociology*. London: Nelson.

Schrecker, E.W. (1986) *No Ivory Tower: McCarthyism and the Universities*. New York and Oxford: Oxford University Press.

Simpson, C. (1988) *Blowback*. New York: Weidenfeld & Nicolson.

Snyder, L.L. (1989) *Encyclopaedia of the Third Reich*. New York: Paragon House.

Steenberg, S. (1970) *Vlasov*. New York: Knopf.

Strik-Strikfeldt, W. (1970) *Against Stalin and Hitler: Memoir of the Russian Liberation Movement, 1941–1945*. London and Basingstoke: Macmillan.

Wiener, J. (1989) 'Talcott Parsons' Role: Bringing Nazi Sympathizers to the US', *The Nation*, 6 March: 1–2.

Winks, R.W. (1987) *Cloak and Grown: Scholars in the Secret War, 1939–1941*. New York: William Morrow.

12

NEOFUNCTIONALISM AND THE 'NEW THEORETICAL MOVEMENT': THE POST-PARSONIAN RAPPROCHEMENT BETWEEN GERMANY AND AMERICA

Bryan S. Turner

By the time Talcott Parsons died in 1979 in Munich, his standing in American and, more generally, world sociology had been thoroughly challenged and partly eclipsed by new developments in sociological theory. In fact the high point of his career and influence had occurred relatively early in his life during his presidency of the American Sociological Association and with the publication in 1951 of *The Social System*. In the subsequent decades before his death, structural-functional sociology – the theoretical movement to which Parsons's name became ambiguously attached – had been subject to various powerful critical onslaughts from symbolic interactionism, conflict theory and ethnomethodology (Alexander, 1987; Smelser, 1988). This situation created a paradox in American sociology (to which we can see the 'new theoretical movement' [Alexander, 1988a] as a delayed reaction). Apart from Mead and Dewey, Parsons was one of the few genuinely American (as contrasted with European writers who happen to have migrated to the United States such as Marcuse, Znanieki or Sorokin) sociologists who had not only achieved international standing, but had created a systematic general theory of social systems, which also offered a fundamentally interdisciplinary perspective. But the national community of American sociologists had, generally speaking, turned against Parsons. The scene of academic revenge against the modern Father of American sociology, who had himself contributed to the slaying of Spencer, had genuinely Freudian overtones. Who was going to represent Americanism in the world of international social science scholarship? C. Wright Mills was perhaps too local, too Midwestern; Alvin Gouldner was too pugnacious and controversial to assume a national role of leadership. Erving Goffman's work, while brilliant and ethnographically unmatched, had not produced a systematic theory. The result was that there was an absence at the centre of American social science. It is only in the late 1980s that American sociology is 'beginning to understand the project of the most methodical and comprehensive American theorist' (Sciulli and Gerstein, 1985: 373).

In the meantime, the Europeans – mainly French and German – had produced a galaxy of stars – Louis Althusser, Jacques Lacan, Michel Foucault, Pierre Bourdieu, Jean Baudrillard, K.-O. Apel, Jürgen Habermas, Niklas Luhmann, Norbert Elias and many others. The international situation was even more complicated and intriguing because while the Americans had been busy forgetting Parsons the Europeans were rediscovering him. In particular, in Germany even Habermas was forced to confront Parsons's work (Habermas, 1981) and Luhmann was developing his own powerful version of systems theory (Luhmann, 1982). Germany was also producing major commentators and interpreters of the Parsonian legacy such as Richard Münch (1987; 1988). Even Parsons's unpublished early work was appearing in German; for example, *Aktor, Situation und normative Muster* (Parsons, 1986). There were also a number of French sociological interpretations of Parsons's work such as François Chazel's *La Théorie analytique de la société dans l'œuvre de Talcott Parsons* (1974) and François Bourricaud's *L'Individualisme institutionnel* (1977). Although these developments were an authentic response to Parsonian sociology, they were also in a covert way a form of colonization of the Parsonian legacy by the Europeans.

In this perspective, we can see the recent Parsonian revival in the United States as an attempt to come to terms with the absent American core, an attempt to re-establish some coherence in American sociology but also to give it (once more) a global status, and to repossess the spirit of sociology as more than simply an aid to government policy. In this chapter, various aspects of the so-called Parsons revival are examined through an extended discussion and evaluation of the theoretical contribution of Jeffrey C. Alexander.

The work of Alexander has been obviously important in this renewal of sympathetic attention to Parsons's sociology. While clearly critical of Parsons, Alexander has seen that the importance of Parsons's systematic theory was as a response to the divisive 'warring schools' in sociological theory. The Parsons revival is also bound up, therefore, with rebuilding (American) sociology on a firm, systematic basis. This goal of reconstruction requires a general theory which will transcend the false dichotomies of the classical tradition (individual versus society, conflict versus consensus) while also overcoming many of the problems of Parsons's own solutions. Thus, Alexander is critical of the conservative bias of much of Parsons's work, its formalism in theory, its inability to come to terms with conflicts over interests, and the problems of Parsonian sociology in relation to the explanation of contingent historical change. There is as a result an ambiguity in Alexander's sociology: if Parsons's work was so flawed with difficulties, what is the nature of the Parsons revival? Is it going beyond, while also incorporating, the past; or is it a rejection of Parsonian sociology *tout court*? If the functional paradigm of social change (social differentiation) was so problematic, how can we explain the current enthusiasm for new theories of differentiation in the work of Smelser (1985) and Luhmann (1982). Is it post-Parsonian sociology, or is it neofunctionalism or neo-evolutionism?

Whatever sociologists decide to call these changes in theoretical orientation, it is clear that this renewal of theory will have to take place over a broad theoretical front. It requires answers to the macro-micro link (Alexander et al., 1987); it needs a new version of the theory of structural differentiation (Smelser, 1985); and it will need a theoretical means of bridging the gap between abstract formulations of theory and empirical research (Alexander, 1988b). It requires a new assessment of Parsons's legacy, not only with respect to European social theory, but also to those features of the American tradition which Parsons either ignored or suppressed (Levine, 1980). In the case of Alexander, it may also require a political stance in which sociological theory engages with public issues, such as Watergate (Alexander, 1988c) and with university politics (Alexander, 1988b). The sociologist finds his or her true theoretical fulfilment in the world of political action (Warner, 1988). Although Alexander has produced in rapid succession a number of volumes in the 1980s, it is important to start this examination of his contribution to the re-evaluation of Parsons's legacy with the four-volume basis of the renewal of theory, namely with his studies of the 'theoretical logic' of sociology itself.

To summarize the claims of this opening commentary, Alexander's four-volume study of sociological theory has to be seen in the following context: the traditional dominance of positivist empiricism in American sociology; the partial and inadequate reception of classical European theory in the United States; the excessive factionalism, both ideological and theoretical, within sociology which Parsons referred to as the warring schools; the ambiguous national status of the legacy of Parsonian structural-functionalism; and finally, the failure of sociology to achieve analytical coherence as a result of basic and unresolved tensions between agency/structure, conflict/consensus, instrumental/normative and idealist/materialist perspectives. These volumes are contributions to a renewal of interest in the sociology of Parsons which has been labelled, somewhat problematically, as 'neofunctionalism'. Alexander has himself played a considerable role in establishing the intellectual credibility of this movement.[1] However, the exact relationship between functionalism and neofunctionalism remains open to doubt, or at least open to further theoretical specification.[2]

The task to which these volumes is addressed is that of rejuvenation: sociology has to secure a firmer grasp on the promise of classical sociology, but also to transform that legacy. The context and ambition of *Theoretical Logic in Sociology* (hereafter *TLS*) are thus strikingly similar to those of *The Structure of Social Action*, although it would be a profound mistake to think of Alexander's contribution only in terms of an exegesis of Parsons, or as only a restatement of structural-functionalism.[3] We may briefly state the core argument of Parsons's early work in order to grasp more fully the character of Alexander's enterprise. Parsons attempted to criticize rationalist positivism on the grounds that positivist social theory could neither provide an adequate account of normative order nor incorporate voluntaristic action and the notion of normative selection of ends within its rationalist assumptions. Positivism reduced values to external conditions and different types of human action (traditional and affective) were forced into the mould of instrumental rationality. Positivism could never solve the Hobbesian problem of order, and value-laden actions tended to be regarded as purely irrational. When the various versions of rationalistic action theory (especially utilitarianism in economic theory) came to confront the problem of order – for example, the question of fraud and force in the contractual relations of economic exchange – in the analysis of social relations, they were compelled to resort to *ad hoc* assumptions (such as the 'hidden hand' of history) which were incompatible with their theoretical presuppositions. Parsons developed a very subtle theoretical strategy in order to analyse the weak links in such arguments by concentrating on 'residual categories'. Parsons subsequently exploited this theoretical strategy to great effect in, for example, his work in the sociology of religion, where he showed how the residual category of magic had been fundamental in the development of sociology as a whole.

Parsons attempted to show that these analytical instabilities in Weber, Durkheim, Pareto and Marshall resulted in a convergence towards a voluntaristic action framework, the elaboration of which Parsons saw as his life-long commitment. Alexander believes that Parsons ultimately failed to carry through the task of developing a multidimensional sociology and that criticism of Parsonian sociology in the 1950s and 1960s had much validity. These volumes attempt therefore to take us into a post-Parsonian sociology by settling accounts with classical sociology. In his more recent work, Alexander (1987) has argued that we have in fact already moved into post-Parsonian sociology. The 'new theoretical movement' (Alexander, 1988a) is now free from the Parsonian legacy to establish a new terrain of research. There are some interesting parallels here between the Althusserian idea of an epistemological break, which has revealed a new space for theory, and Alexander's own approach to paradigm developments in theoretical sociology, which he has illustrated ably in *Twenty Lectures* (Alexander, 1987).

TLS had a very mixed and largely inadequate reception in the United States and Europe. It had been enthusiastically pre-reviewed by Lipset, Eisenstadt, Gouldner, Coser, Jay and Bell. This positive pre-reviewing may have been paradoxically responsible for some aspects of its negative reception. One assumes that what unites Coser, Lipset and Gouldner in their appraisal of these volumes is a common rejection of positivistic sociology and its institutional backers. However, many American sociologists remained sceptical as to the real value of *TLS* and to the importance of neofunctionalism (Camic, 1986; Ritzer, 1985). Within a European context, Alexander's work has been partly ignored and partly dismissed as simply an elaboration of Parsonian sociology (Holmwood, 1982). These differences in evaluation are, to some extent, a function of context, and it may be that one weakness of Alexander's survey of sociology is its failure to grasp these national divergences. As a general rule, postwar European sociology had not been so dominated by a scientific, positivist, quantitative or survey-oriented model of professional social science which has been by contrast the hegemonic paradigm in American sociology. In fact it is doubtful whether within any single European society, or within Europe as a whole, there has ever been a dominant paradigm equivalent to functionalism in America in the 1950s (Smelser, 1985; 1988). The present generation of European sociologists has been thoroughly exposed to the epistemological and philosophical difficulties of 'scientific sociology' through various engagements with neo-Marxism, semiotics, post-structuralism, deconstructionist methodologies, critical theory, phenomenology, neo-Nietzschean theory and neo-Weberian revivals. For reasons which have yet to be fully explored, European sociologists acquired a profound legacy of philosophy of science through the incorporation of the works of Gaston Bachelard and Georges Canguilhem into the Marxism of Louis Althusser, the philosophy of Michel Foucault (Lecourt, 1975), and to a lesser extent the critical tradition of Wittgenstein (Winch, 1958). European sociologists probably suffer from a superfluity of anti-empiricist paradigms. Given this immature abundance, it is perhaps not surprising that some European commentators believe that Alexander is merely rehearsing conventional arguments rather than actually developing sociological theory. In many European circles *TLS* has been dismissed as an unimaginative rewrite of *The Structure of Social Action*. In addition, Alexander's analysis and evaluation of Parsons may appear less original now that there has been growing interest in Parsons's sociology in Europe (Bourricaud, 1977; Habermas, 1981; Hamilton, 1983; Luhmann, 1982; Savage, 1981) and elsewhere (Buxton, 1985; Holton and Turner, 1986).

Alexander takes the problem of order and the problem of action as the major foci of any sociological theory. These two problems are approached via an analysis of the theoretical instability of the classical tradition. To some extent, Alexander substitutes a discussion of Marx for Parsons's unpicking of Pareto, but both Alexander and Parsons have curiously ignored Simmel (Levine et al., 1976). Both Parsons and Alexander, in very different contexts and with rather different theoretical objectives, have attempted to provide a viable theoretical alternative to positivism. To dismiss Alexander via a rejection of Parsons is, however, a mistake. For one thing, Alexander does not see classical sociology in terms of a convergence, because it never in practice resolved the tensions between order and action, or between normative and instrumental theories. These issues were typically conflated, whereas Alexander argues for an anti-conflationary multidimensional theoretical strategy (Collins, 1985). These theoretical tensions remained unstable in the classical tradition and their instability has been worked out in various revisions of Marx, Weber and Durkheim. In addition, Alexander's grasp of the historical unfolding of the sociological theories of Weber and Durkheim is far more accurate textually and more perceptive than Parsons's discredited convergence thesis. Alexander also writes with the benefit of historical hindsight. Neofunctionalism is thus more than a correction of Parsons, and in this sense it is not simply post-Parsonianism.

The contradictory evaluations of Alexander are, however, in themselves interesting, because they reflect the continuing crisis of sociology which is a crisis not of premature ageing, but characteristically of destructive factionalism. Modern sociology requires, if it is to survive internal division under the impact of academic competition and external liquidation under the auspices of monetarist pruning, a mature statement of the core tradition which will overcome and transcend our (often) trivial ideological and theoretical differences (Turner, 1989). This defence of sociology may come successfully from a Parsonian, progressive and multidisciplinary social science of action. It is only within this context that we can come to a proper evaluation of Alexander's reprise of the classical inheritance. It is perhaps only in retrospect that we will come to see *TLS* properly as an early statement of the conditions which are necessary for some theoretical rapprochement in sociology, for example, between micro-macro foundations (Alexander et al., 1987).

TLS is, then, a serious and important contribution to sociology for the following reasons. First, sooner or later, modern sociology has to come to terms with Parsons's legacy. The paradox is that, although he has often been dismissed (frequently by commentators who seem to assume that he wrote nothing after 1951), Parsons simply is the most important American social theorist of the twentieth century. This claim is made on the basis of the scope, relevance, internal organization and global impact of Parsons's sociology. In a more developed evaluation, it would be necessary, for instance, to demonstrate that social philosophers like Habermas show less systematic grasp of empirical social issues. Habermas's work over the last decade has become increasingly a second-order commentary on theory rather than a substantial development of critical analysis of modern societies. For example, much of *The Theory of Communicative Action* is an extended commentary on Weber (in volume 1) and on Parsons (in volume 2). While Habermas has written extensively on capitalism as general system at an abstract level, it is not clear how Habermas's work relates to concrete social and political problems, because it is not clear how Habermas's analysis of communicative action in microsocial contexts applies to macroinstitutional arenas. It is true that Habermas has contributed to edited works on German society (Habermas, 1979), but this is not a systematic development of his theory. To make another comparison, within economic theory, *The Structure of Social Action* cannot be placed intellectually on the same level as Keynes's *General Theory*, but it has to be taken, along with Parsons's other economic studies, as a serious theoretical contribution to economic sociology. Few other social scientists have displayed the same analytical consistency, the range of empirical interests or the serious engagement with the problem of human existence. From this perspective, Habermas's evaluation of the stature of Parsons was both generous and correct. Referring to Parsons's academic life, Habermas commented that it provides an 'impression of the continuity and cumulative success of the efforts that this scholar devoted to constructing a single theory over the course of more than fifty years' (Habermas, 1987: 199). In this sense, Parsons developed a genuinely general theory of action. Anybody who doubts these assertions should read Parsons's contribution to the discussion of cybernetics, death, economic problems, university development and religious symbolism in the late 1970s.

In terms of another comparison, Parsons's sociology compares favourably with Luhmann in terms of developing a systematic general theory, while also developing a broad range of research into empirical issues in politics, religion, society and international affairs. Luhmann's range of interests is as extraordinary as Parsons's own very catholic taste for topics: for example, power (Luhmann, 1979), law (Luhmann, 1985), religion (Luhmann, 1984) or love (Luhmann, 1986). The main difference between Luhmann and Parsons may lie in Luhmann's radical attempt to expunge any reference to human action from his systems theory, in the sense that he regards human beings as part of the environment of social systems; a social system thus is made up of communicative acts. By contrast, Parsons's analysis of social systems was grounded in a theory of action, and he saw the goal of his own theoretical activity to be the construction of a general theory of action which would provide the basis for the social sciences as a whole. In this respect, Habermas's criticism of the analytical divisions and tensions in Parsons's work between an action theory in *The Structure of Social Action* and a theory of value-integration of systems in *The Social System* is itself highly problematic.

Thus, Alexander's work offers an important context within which modern sociology might work out its identity via an engagement with the total contribution of Parsons. Alexander offers a comprehensive overview of Parsons's development (in volume 4), but more importantly he locates the Parsonian problematic within the total movement of modern sociology's theoretical logic.

Turning to the second reason for regarding *TLS* as an important contribution to contemporary sociology, these volumes provide a theoretical strategy which shows persuasively that many of the disputes in modern social theory – between Weberians and Marxists, for example – are largely irrelevant, because they have been typically conducted at the wrong theoretical level. Alexander's approach to sociology thus provides a possible resolution of adolescent factionalism through an evaluation of the sociological tradition from a multidimensional perspective on action and order.

Thirdly, these volumes provide a paradigm for how to develop theoretical interpretation and theory construction. Alexander establishes what any theory of society would have to address in terms of general presuppositions and then traces various attempts to resolve ambiguities and contradictions in these presuppositions at every level of sociological inquiry. The result is a careful, detailed and scholarly exegesis of the classical tradition.

Volume 1 (*Positivism, Presuppositions and Current Controversies*) establishes the theoretical framework for the subsequent volumes; it is impossible to understand the later volumes without grasping the fundamental structure of volume 1. Alexander argues that any scientific theory is a continuum of components which starts with observations about the empirical environment and moves through a hierarchy of increasingly abstract activities (such as correlations, laws, classifications, definitions, concepts and models) to a metatheoretical environment of general presuppositions. These components or layers are interrelated, but also relatively autonomous. Alexander's study is concerned with the general presuppositional level of sociology and he argues that the two most important presuppositions in theory are concerned with action and order, which are two distinct bases of social analysis. Presuppositions relating to action are concerned with the characterization of motivation; social theory has been typically bifurcated around one tradition which defines action in terms of its rational, instrumental and purposive features, and another tradition which emphasizes its normative, nonrational and value-laden character. Presuppositions relating to order are similarly divided into sociological idealism (in which order is perceived as internal, subjective and normative) and sociological materialism (in which order is external, objective and coercive). These two problems of order and action are separate questions and should not be conflated. Order refers to the pattern of units, while the action problem essentially refers to forms of motivation. However, the important issue is that every social theory must by definition broach these problems and make presuppositional decisions. This analysis is broadly what Alexander means by a 'multidimensional' sociology (Collins, 1985; Warner, 1988).

Having established these distinctions, Alexander proceeds to identify a number of problems in modern sociological theory. It often lacks adequate generality and debates often fail to address the presuppositional level; it often conflates levels or components of the theoretical continuum; or it is reductionist at the presuppositional level in failing to keep separate the questions of action and order. In short, sociology is typically one-dimensional in approach. Sociological materialism treats order and action in a determinist perspective in which action is instrumental and order is imposed; it precludes any adequate analysis of the role of norms, values and commitments. Sociological idealism approaches order as normative and action as voluntaristic to the exclusion of any appropriate analysis of material constraints and conditions. The alternative approach to these traditional dilemmas is a multidimensional sociology:

action should be conceived not as either instrumental or normative, but as both. Furthermore, this action should be conceived as ordered both through internal and external structures. Only such a dialectical criticism of the presuppositional dilemma enables us to conceive of social theory in a multidimensional way, and multidimensionality is the standard by which I propose to evaluate theoretical logic. (Alexander, 1982a: 123)

Thus, much of the debate between Marxists and sociologists over conflict, consensus, ideology and functionalism is unidimensional and unproductive, since there are often basic presuppositional agreements between, for example, scientific Marxism and structural functionalism, despite disagreements at the level of ideology, classifications and empirical observation (Holton and Turner, 1986: 194ff). The point of a multidimensional approach is to transcend the inadequacies of both sociological idealism and materialism by going beyond sterile debates over one-dimensionality.

Subsequent volumes attempt to work through and work out the presuppositional dilemmas of classical sociology in the work of Marx and Durkheim (volume 2), Weber (volume 3) and Parsons (volume 4). Alexander is acutely aware of the problem of interpretation and the special difficulties which arise in reading classical texts, where there is endless dispute as to meaning, significance and relevance. Alexander attempts to avoid the pitfalls of partisan readings of these major sociologists by concentrating on their presuppositional decisions and on how these influenced the whole development of their work and later revisions by their followers.

It would be impossible to review in any detail Alexander's treatment of specific texts and authors, but these three volumes follow a basic pattern which can be outlined. First, he divides the works of these authors into early and later phases. Unfortunately this simple division often fails to capture the complex development of the analytical schemes of these sociologists. Alexander secondly shows how unidimensional were the approaches of Marx and Durkheim in presuppositional terms. Their failure to resolve these problems led inevitably to revisionism. Thus, Marx never resolved the contradictions between a voluntarist and normative theory of action, and a deterministic and materialist perspective on social order. The analytical role of 'alienation' was implicitly to mask this contradiction: human beings are active and conscious, but under conditions of alienation they lose their sensuous, practical character.[4] The concept of alienation provided a false solution to the freedom/determinism contradiction in Marx, but the solution was obviously paper-thin. Durkheim had the same difficulty, but in reverse. Social order is seen in a collectivist and determinate perspective, but the social world is also normative. Although Durkheim wanted a science of social reality conceived in terms of moral facts which are external and objective, he also had a strong sense of the individual as a moral agent. Durkheim's sociological work was an unstable mixture of positivistic medical sciences, moral statistics and anti-utilitarian social philosophy (Hirst, 1975). The instability of Durkheim's position was illustrated in his changing and erratic approach to religion and the sacred. Alexander extended his analysis of Durkheim in a subsequent volume (Alexander, 1988c).

In Alexander's scheme, Weber represents an ambitious attempt to re-solve these presuppositional dilemmas. In his analysis of action, religion, class and urban culture, Weber developed a genuinely multidimensional approach, but, especially in his later political writings, he retreated into unidimensionality by emphasizing the instrumental side of action and the coercive nature of social order. It is perhaps worth noting here that if Weber moved towards a vision of social action in terms of coercion and interests towards the end of his life, we should hardly be surprised, given the context within which Weber was living (Mayer, 1944). The collapse of the German Reich was not a political context in which one would expect a sociologist like Weber to turn towards a theory of cultural integration! Alexander (1983: 122) provides a (largely implicit) critique of Weber's nostalgic liberalism of despair in which Weber's pessimistic view of bureau-cracy results in a unidimensional view of history. There is an argument for taking this theme of fatalism as a major dimension of Weber's ironic sociology of the negative effects of human action (Turner, 1984).

In the sociology of Parsons, we find also an attempt to reconcile the perennial dilemma of the idealist/materialist dichotomy, an attempt which was nevertheless incomplete. Furthermore, the criticisms of Parsons as a conservative theorist, who could not provide a satisfactory account of conflict, social change and power interests, eventually undermined the influence of Parsons in America – a theme which Alexander has pursued in *Twenty Lectures* (Alexander, 1987). The task of *TLS* is thus an open-ended search for a general, multidimensional theory of action and order which is neither conflationary nor reductionist.

Volume 4 is clearly the most important component within this diagnosis of sociological theory. It is probably the most systematic study of Parsons's sociology in contemporary social theory which we possess. François Bour-ricaud's study[5] does not attempt to cover Parsons's work as a whole, while the Althusserian framework of Savage's study (1981) now looks increasingly archaic. As a balanced and full study of Parsons's theoretical work as a whole, Alexander's work is particularly useful in its scholarly treatment of the various phases in Parsons's work. For example, Parsons's early work is seen as a phase in which Parsons (in *The Structure of Social Action*) established the basic presuppositional requirements of a volun-taristic theory of action. In the middle period, Parsons was (in *The Social System*) mainly concerned with the multidimensional character of the processes of allocation and integration at the societal level. In the later period he was concerned (in *Societies* and *The System of Modern Societies*) to explore issues in the interchange theory from a comparative and histori-cal dimension. A number of commentators on Parsons now see this focus on political freedom and the rules of democracy as his crucial contribution to contemporary sociology.[6]

In his critical evaluation of Parsons's work, Alexander considers various methodological and presuppositional errors. For example, the formalism of Parsons's style and the dependence on 'analogic isomorphism' (Alexander, 1984: 162) (such as the analogies between the flow of power and the circulation of economic commodities) substituted formal and tautological description for genuine sociological analysis and causal explanation. These models often acted as 'decoys' (Alexander, 1984: 167) which generated a lot of spurious debate (for example, about the logical relationship between the interchange model and thermodynamics). At the presuppositional level, Alexander detects a persistent and inadequate 'sociological idealism' in Parsons's analysis (for example, of social change). While sympathetic to Parsons's account of the origins of modern democratic systems, Alexander argues that Parsons's view of history is a modern version of the old Hegelian unfolding of *Geist* in history. Thus 'modernization' presents a consistent and successful process of 'upgrading' and 'inclusion' (Alexander, 1984: 210). The task of neofunctionalism is to address, in a theoretically sophisticated manner, the problems of contingency in social history (Camic, 1986). Because of the emphasis on the normative aspects of social order, Parsons consistently downplayed the instrumental features of social action and social order. The result is that Parsons failed to live up to the multidimensioned scope of his original theory. The task of modern sociology is to pursue the goal of multidimensionality in sociological theory, and this quest will take us beyond Parsons into a post-Parsonian synthesis. In fact, in this sense we are already, according to Alexander (1987), in a post-Parsonian sociology.

I will concentrate on general problems in Alexander's basic theory. Although he is very aware of the problems of relativism in the interpretation of texts and clearly identifies the difficulties of 'reading', he appears in practice not to confront the epistemological difficulties which have been raised by semiotics, French structuralism, deconstructive critiques and modern literary criticism. Specifically he does not address the problems raised by deconstructive methodological strategies and postmodern attacks on conventional modernist readings. Although he confronts Althusser's reading of *Capital*, he does not address the wider problems of interpretation, which in a general way follow from Saussure and which have been developed through Lévi-Strauss, Lacan, Foucault and Derrida. In addition, a variety of hermeneutic approaches have given rise to new interpretations of Marx, Durkheim and Weber which Alexander does not consider. From this perspective, Alexander's own characterization of sociology could be regarded as positivist and rationalist. In this respect I would follow Sica (1983) in arguing that Alexander adopts unproblematically a foundationalist view of science, which can be challenged from a variety of positions. Alexander's respect for the rationality of science is a feature of his approach which was also fundamental to Parsons's own work. However, the autonomy of the empirical level, even in the natural sciences, is a questionable position (Cohen and Schnelle, 1986). Of course, Alexander would not be alone in this respect, since we can argue that sociology as a whole has yet to respond adequately to the type of deconstructive analysis associated with de Man and contemporary textual and literary criticism. Putting this comment in its most general context, contemporary (especially American) sociology has yet to come to terms with the wide range of issues which, for want of a better terminology, we may put under the heading of 'postmodernism'.

There are many aspects of the theoretical formation of classical sociology which Alexander neglects and which are brought into the foreground by alternative readings of the classics. My examples would include the impact of Cartesian thought and positivist medicine on Durkheim, or the relationship between Nietzsche's pessimism and Weber's philosophy of history, or the impact of philosophical anthropology on German social theory (Stauth and Turner, 1988). Alexander offers one footnote on Nietzsche in volume 3 and Simmel receives no commentary at all. Rather like Parsons, Alexander perhaps fails to take seriously the American theoretical traditions which flourished both before and after *The Structure of Social Action*, namely Peirce and Dewey (Levine, 1980). Alexander has also been criticized (Holmwood, 1983) for following Parsons in treating Marx as a utilitarian economist – a perspective which has often been challenged (Gould, 1981). Alexander's treatment of the secondary literature on Marx, Weber and Durkheim is often selective and narrow. Avineri, Althusser, Giddens, Lukács and Olmann are discussed in relation to Marx, but important alternatives are missing (such as the Hungarian Circle of Ferenc Feher, Agnes Heller, Istvan Meszaros or Gyorgy Markus). The result is that Marx's historical materialism is presented as deterministic and reductionist. Insufficient weight is given to the impact of Feuerbachian anthropology, for example, on Marx's view of praxis. In the case of Durkheim, in British sociology the contributions of Mike Gane (1983a; 1983b) and Paul Q. Hirst (1975) point to radically different and more interesting interpretations of Durkheim's contribution to the theory of language in which 'order' is an effect of classificatory systems (like 'sacred/ profane').[7] Recent interpretations of Durkheim by S.G. Meštrović (1989; 1991) also help us to locate Durkheim within a far broader intellectual context. In the case of Weber, it is unfortunate that the work of Karl Löwith is confined to the footnotes and Frederic Jameson receives no consideration. Unfortunately Alexander's study appeared after the publication of Hennis's interpretation of Weber's historical analysis of 'characterology' (Hennis, 1986).[8]

The conflict between a deterministic theory of social order and a voluntaristic theory of action in Marx, Weber and Durkheim has been the subject of endless debates in social science. Alexander may well be correct to argue that an adequate sociology has to see order as both internal and external, and must approach action as both voluntaristic and constrained. The real question is how in actual practice these dimensions are combined; to say that they stand in a 'dialectical' relationship lacks specific content, and therefore the programme for multidimensionality requires a more vigorous and systematic statement.

The 'scientific continuum and its components' which appears in volume 1 (p. 3) and forms the key to the whole study is also either arbitrary or at least open to dispute. For example, general presupposition stands at the top of the continuum as being the ultimate location of theoretical decisions which determine lower order procedures (such as definition). But what determines general presuppositions? In the case of Marx, Durkheim and Weber, it was their ethical view of the problem of Man (in the generic sense) in the modern world. The conflict in Weber between his individualist approach to action and his deterministic view of structure was an effect of a 'religious' view of the world: good motivation typically has negative structural effects (Turner, 1984). What lies behind 'general presuppositions' are moral commitments, values, world-perspectives and ultimate concerns. These types of 'moral decision-making' should not be placed outside the scientific continuum, since they are the driving forces of sociology itself. In fact it is not entirely clear where Alexander would place ethical world-views in relation to scientific activity. For example, 'ideological orientations' (p. 40) stand next to 'models' in terms of generality, but the 'metaphysical environment' is outside the continuum of the components of science. What makes a great sociologist is more than mere theoretical coherence with respect to order and action; these theoretical movements have to be seen within a wider context, which would include even deeper decisions about ontology and meaning. These deeper structures may be called 'passion' or, to use Nietzsche's term from *Die fröhliche Wissenschaft*, 'joy'. This is ultimately the driving force of science. Without such a discussion, Alexander might himself be accused of making a positivist separation of fact and value, because his model does not allow either for the possibility that 'facts' are constituted by theory, or that theory is an effect of prior moral commitments, or at least that it is not clear whether facts and theory connect with each other on a single continuum. In short, it is not clear that Alexander has given a clear account of the 'transformation problem' which makes empirical observations amenable to theoretical analysis. More importantly, we have yet to see how neofunctionalism will deal with postmodernism, deconstructive strategies and anti-foundationalist epistemology.

In his introduction to 'Talcott Parsons on Religion' in *Sociological Analysis*, Roland Robertson wrote that mere exegesis of Parsons is not enough – 'the challenge is to do the work which Parsons began. This must mean that Parsons's work has to be critically elaborated – extended and refined analytically and used with respect to empirical and historical problems' (1982: 284). This task is the real legacy of Marx, Durkheim, Weber and Parsons: not to rehearse theory, but to do it. In order to appreciate Alexander's contribution to sociology, one must therefore go beyond these four volumes to consider his application of a multidimensional sociology to the understanding of empirical issues – a task which he has undertaken principally in *Action and its Environments* (Alexander, 1988b). *TLS* will continue to be criticized, but one indication of a major contribution to sociological theory is that it invites, and indeed invokes, critical attack. Parsons's *The Structure of Social Action* and *The Social System* would be two pertinent illustrations. The critical reception of these volumes is therefore an indication of the recognition of the seriousness of Alexander's own 'presuppositions' which are, as Warner (1988: 653) recognizes, to provide a sociological theory which can be a guide to action in the reconstitution of democratic society. Alexander has not only provided a systematic analysis of classical theory, but he has helped to rescue Parsons from naive criticism as a conservative social theorist. In this respect, Alexander has redirected sociological theory towards liberal-political engagements which are theoretically informed.

How might we evaluate this rehabilitation of Parsonian sociology? In one respect, current interpretations still appear somewhat short in their evaluation of Parsons. In order to understand Parsons, it is important to see him in terms of the battles against economic reductionism which were current at the time. Parsons not only wanted to establish sociology as an independent and theoretically coherent discipline, he also wanted to place sociology in the context of an interdisciplinary effort in the social sciences. The point of the voluntaristic action theory was to create an analytically viable basis for collaborative and constructive work within and between the major social science disciplines – especially sociology, economics, psychology and politics. Of course, Parsons's efforts here were not always entirely successful. For example, it is not entirely clear whether he saw sociology as the general social science *par excellence* (a modern-day version of the queen of the sciences), or whether sociology was that discipline which was to carry out research on the integrative subsystem (of the famous AGIL scheme). It is important to try to understand Parsons's work in this light.

For example, this perspective on Parsons allows us to make some useful comparisons between the Frankfurt School's version of interdisciplinarity and that presented by Parsons in the general theory of action. The Frankfurt School saw materialism as the essential platform of interdisciplinarity, whereas Parsons proposed a (Kantian) action theory as the most promising basis for interdisciplinary work. Recent interpretations of Parsons have rather neglected this aspect of his contribution to the educational development of the social science curriculum in the universities.

Alexander can be criticized for neglecting this dimension of the renewal of Parsonian sociology. The new-movement theorists can also be criticized for seeing neofunctionalism in terms which are so broad that it is often difficult to see who would fall outside its domain. For example, there is a tendency to see Luhmann as, in some respects, a German version of neo-Parsonianism or neofunctionalism, insofar as he has dropped the assumptions about value-cohesion and normative integration. Thus Luhmann formulated a radical version of functionalism. However, while Parsons and Luhmann may have shared a common view about the nature of cybernetics and communication systems, it is difficult to reconcile Parsons's action theory with Luhmann's version of functionalism. The boundary of the social system for Parsons was not based on a division between human beings and social systems; Parsons retained a much stronger sense of action as the basis of the social sciences.

Although sociology has, since Saint-Simon first formulated his vision of the new religion of humanity, had a global perspective, it has also been part of national culture. In the conflict between different types of sociology, therefore, we also see the conflict between nations. Neil Smelser's *Handbook of Sociology* (1988) was explicitly a statement about the national development of American sociology; it was seen as a volume 'on sociology as it stands in the United States' (Smelser, 1988: 15). While Habermas and Luhmann are in many respects critical of German society, their sociology within the international academic situation gives expression (perhaps covertly and unwillingly) to the current resurgence of German culture as a global culture. Perhaps only the British have given up all interest at global communication and internationalism – if we are to take the recent special issue on British sociology in the *British Journal of Sociology* (Halsey, 1989) as a guide to the most recent version of the British view of social reality.

Much of Alexander's recent work has been the product of joint meetings of the theory sections of the American and German Sociological Associations. One can only hope that this fruitful meeting ground will lead to a less nationalistic version of sociology. Here again perhaps the shadow of Talcott Parsons is rather long. During the Second World War, Parsons was important intellectually in keeping the channels of communication between American and German culture open. Nevertheless, Parsons saw American culture as the cutting edge of world culture. To be successful, the neofunctionalist revival will have to be more than merely an American theoretical revival. It will require multiculturalism as well as multidimensionality.

Notes

1. Neofunctionalism (Alexander, 1985) has a more determined commitment to the analysis of change, conflict and ideological critique, addressing itself to empirical issues in contemporary political processes. It is assumed to embrace successfully the standard criticisms of Parsons while going well beyond them. In his most recent work, Alexander has been less concerned with these labels, and has concentrated more on the issue of developing an autonomous theoretical movement.

2. Turner and Maryanski (1988) have argued that neofunctionalism, by abandoning the notion of 'functional prerequisites', is no longer genuinely functionalist, but in turn has abandoned explanation in favour of description.

3. Contrary to Sica (1983), it is inadequate to regard Alexander's sociology as merely a refurbishing of the Parsonian framework. I shall, however, subsequently agree with Sica's critique of Alexander's view of science and the relationship between theory and empirical fact.

4. The basic problem was that the more Marx established the alienation of the working class in capitalism, the less credible a working-class revolution appeared (Duncan, 1973).

5. Bourricaud's study (1981) first appeared in French in 1977 two years before Parsons's death with the title *L'Individualisme institutionnel*; Bourricaud was a graduate student of Parsons at Harvard.

6. This aspect has been developed by David Sciulli (1988) under the notion of 'societal constitutionalism'.

7. The commentaries of Mike Gane (1983a; 1983b) are particularly useful in establishing an innovative interpretative framework for the textual analysis of Durkheim's *œuvre*. In defence of Alexander, his edited collection on *Durkheimian Sociology* (Alexander, 1988c) is itself an innovative presentation of Durkheim's contribution to cultural sociology.

8. Hennis's work became available after the publication of Alexander's study of Weber (Alexander, 1983). Hennis's essay (1983) on Max Weber's 'central question' was first delivered as a public lecture at Nuffield College, Oxford, in May 1982. A translation of Hennis's *Max Webers Fragestellung* (1986) appeared in 1988 as *Max Weber: Essays in Reconstruction*.

References

Alexander, J.C. (1982a) *Theoretical Logic in Sociology*, vol. 1, *Positivism, Presuppositions and Current Controversies*. London: Routledge & Kegan Paul.

Alexander, J.C. (1982b) *Theoretical Logic in Sociology*, vol. 2, *The Antinomies of Classical Thought: Marx and Durkheim*. London: Routledge & Kegan Paul.

Alexander, J.C. (1983) *Theoretical Logic in Sociology*, vol. 3, *The Classical Attempt at Theoretical Synthesis: Max Weber*. London: Routledge & Kegan Paul.

Alexander, J.C. (1984) *Theoretical Logic in Sociology*, vol. 4, *The Modern Reconstruction of Classical Thought: Talcott Parsons*. London: Routledge & Kegan Paul.

Alexander, J.C. (ed.) (1985) *Neofunctionalism*. Beverly Hills: Sage.

Alexander, J.C. (1987) *Twenty Lectures: Sociological Theory since World War II*. New York: Columbia University Press.

Alexander, J.C. (1988a) 'The New Theoretical Movement', pp. 77–101 in N.J. Smelser (ed.), *Handbook of Sociology*. Newbury Park: Sage.

Alexander, J.C. (1988b) *Action and its Environments: Towards a New Synthesis*. New York: Columbia University Press.

Alexander, J.C. (ed.) (1988c) *Durkheimian Sociology: Cultural Studies*. Cambridge: Cambridge University Press.

Alexander, J.C., Giesen, B., Münch, R. and Smelser, N.J. (eds) (1987) *The Micro-Macro Link*. Berkeley, CA: University of California Press.

Bourricaud, F. (1977) *L'Individualisme institutionnel*. Paris: Presses Universitaires de France.

Bourricaud, F. (1981) *The Sociology of Talcott Parsons*. (Translation of *L'Individualisme institutionnel*.) Chicago and London: University of Chicago Press.

Buxton, W. (1985) *Talcott Parsons and the Capitalist Nation-State: Political Sociology as a Strategic Vocation*. Toronto: University of Toronto Press.

Camic, C. (1986) 'The Return of the Functionalists', *Contemporary Sociology*, 12 (5): 692–5.

Chazel, F. (1974) *La Théorie analytique de la société dans l'œuvre de Talcott Parsons*. Paris: Mouton.

Cohen, R.S. and Schnelle, T. (eds) (1986) *Cognition and Fact: Materials on Ludwig Fleck*. Dordrecht: D. Reidel.

Collins, R. (1985) 'Jeffrey Alexander and the Search for Multidimensional Theory', *Theory and Society*, 14 (Fall): 877–92.

Duncan, G. (1973) *Marx and Mill: Two Views of Social Conflict and Social Harmony*. Cambridge: Cambridge University Press.

Gane, M. (1983a) 'Durkheim: the Sacred Language', *Economy and Society*, 12 (1): 1–47.

Gane, M. (1983b) 'Durkheim: Woman as Outsider', *Economy and Society*, 12 (2): 227–70.

Gould, M. (1981) 'Parsons versus Marx: an Earnest Warning', *Sociological Inquiry*, 51: 197–218.

Habermas, J. (ed.) (1979) *Geistigen Situation der Zeit*, 2 vols. Frankfurt: Suhrkamp.

Habermas, J. (1981) *Theorie des Kommunikativen Handelns*. Frankfurt: Suhrkamp.

Habermas, J. (1987) *The Theory of Communicative Action*, vol. 2, *The Critique of Functionalist Reason*, tr. T. McCarthy. (Translation of *Theme des Kommunikationen Handelns*.) Cambridge: Polity Press.

Halsey, A.H. (ed.) (1989) 'Special issue: Sociology in Britain', *British Journal of Sociology*, 40 (3).

Hamilton, P. (1983) *Talcott Parsons*. London and New York: Tavistock.

Hennis, W. (1983) 'Max Weber's "central question"', *Economy and Society*, 12 (2): 135–80.

Hennis, W. (1986) *Max Webers Fragestellung*, Tübingen: J.C. Mohr.

Hennis, W. (1988) *Max Weber: Essays in Reconstruction*. (Translation of *Max Webers Fragestellung*.) London: Unwin Hyman.

Hirst, P.Q. (1975) *Durkheim, Bernard and Epistemology*. London: Routledge.

Holmwood, J. (1982) Review of Alexander, *Theoretical Logic in Sociology*, vol. 1, *Sociology*, 16 (4): 599–601.

Holmwood, J. (1983) Review of Alexander, *Theoretical Logic in Sociology*, vol. 2, *Sociology*, 17 (3): 392–4.

Holton, R.J. and Turner, B.S. (1986) *Talcott Parsons on Economy and Society*. London and New York: Routledge & Kegan Paul.

Keynes, J.M. (1936) *General Theory of Employment, Interest and Money*. London.

Lecourt, D. (1975) *Marxism and Epistemology: Bachelard, Canguilhem and Foucault*. London: NLB.

Levine, D.N. (1980) *Simmel and Parsons: Two Approaches to the Study of Society*. New York: Arno Press.

Levine, D.N., Carter, E.B. and Gorman, E.M. (1976), 'Simmel's Influence on American Sociology, I and II', *American Journal of Sociology*, 81 (4–5): 813–45 and 1112–32.

Luhmann, N. (1979) *Trust and Power*. New York: Wiley.

Luhmann, N. (1982) *The Differentiation of Society*. New York: Columbia University Press.

Luhmann, N. (1984) *Religious Dogmatics and the Evolution of Society*. New York and Toronto: Edwin Mellen Press.

Luhmann, N. (1985) *A Sociological Theory of Law*. London: Routledge & Kegan Paul.

Luhmann, N. (1986) *Love as Passion: the Codification of Intimacy*. Cambridge: Polity Press.

Mayer, J.P. (1944) *Max Weber and German Politics: a Study in Political Sociology*. London: Faber & Faber.

Meštrović, S.G. (1989) 'Moral Theory Based on the "Heart" versus the "Mind": Schopenhauer's and Durkheim's Moralities of Compassion', *Sociological Review*, 37 (3): 431–57.

Meštrović, S.G. (1991) *The Coming Fin de Siècle: an Application of Durkheim's Sociology to Modernity and Postmodernity*. London: Routledge.

Münch, R. (1987) *Theory of Action: Towards a Synthesis Going Beyond Parsons*. London and Boston: Routledge & Kegan Paul.

Münch, R. (1988) *Understanding Modernity: Towards a Perspective Going Beyond Durkheim and Weber*. London and Boston: Routledge & Kegan Paul.

Parsons, T. (1937) *The Structure of Social Action*. New York: McGraw-Hill.

Parsons, T. (1951) *The Social System*. London: Routledge & Kegan Paul.

Parsons, T. (1966) *Societies: Evolutionary and Comparative Perspectives*. Englewood Cliffs, NJ: Prentice-Hall.

Parsons, T. (1971) *The System of Modern Societies*. Englewood Cliffs, NJ: Prentice-Hall.

Parsons, T. (1986) *Aktor, Situation und normative Muster: ein Essay zur Theorie und Handelns*. Frankfurt: Suhrkamp.

Ritzer, G. (1985) 'The Use of Micro-sociological Theory', *Sociological Theory*, 3: 88–98.

Robertson, R. (1982) 'Talcott Parsons on Religion: a Preface', *Sociological Analysis*, 43 (4): 283–5.

Savage, P. (1981) *The Theories of Talcott Parsons: the Social Relations of Action*. London: Macmillan.

Sciulli, D. (1988) 'Foundations of Societal Constitutionalism', *British Journal of Sociology*, 39 (3): 377–408.

Sciulli, D. and Gerstein, D. (1985) 'Social Theory and Talcott Parsons in the 1980s', *Annual Review of Sociology*, 11: 369–87.

Sica, A. (1983) 'Parsons Jr', *American Journal of Sociology*, 89 (1): 200–19.

Smelser, N.J. (1985) 'Evaluating the Model of Structural Differentiation', pp. 113–30 in J.C. Alexander (ed.), *Neofunctionalism*. Beverly Hills: Sage.

Smelser, N.J. (ed.) (1988) *Handbook of Sociology*. Newbury Park: Sage.

Stauth, G. and Turner, B.S. (1988) *Nietzsche's Dance: Resentment, Reciprocity and Resistance in Social Life*. Oxford: Blackwell.

Turner, B.S. (1984) *For Weber: Essays in the Sociology of Fate*. London: Routledge & Kegan Paul.

Turner, B.S. (1989) 'Some Reflections on Cumulative Theorizing in Sociology', pp. 131–47 in J.H. Turner (ed.), *Theory Building in Sociology*. Newbury Park: Sage.

Turner, J.H. and Maryanski, A. (1988) 'Is "Neofunctionalism" Really Functional?', *Sociological Theory*, 6: 110–21.

Warner, R.S. (1988) 'Sociological Theory as Public Philosophy', *American Journal of Sociology*, 94 (3): 644–55.

Winch, P. (1958) *The Idea of a Social Science and its Relationship to Philosophy*. London: Routledge & Kegan Paul.

13

HOW TO READ PARSONS

Bryan S. Turner and Roland Robertson

In our conclusion to this collection of papers on Talcott Parsons, we briefly outline a number of reasons for a different approach to the reading of his work and academic career. Our aim has been to present Parsons's contribution to modern sociological theory and to social theory in the broadest sense. In our conclusion we turn to an assessment of the significance of Parsons's work as a whole. Thus, we will not comment directly on the range of topics covered by the chapters of this study, but will turn instead to a final appreciation of the general character of Parsons's sociology (although we do, almost inevitably, draw upon our own individual contributions, as well as our jointly-written introductory chapter).

Our principal argument about Parsons's sociology is that it is modern, and that Parsons as an intellectual personality was a modernist. We use the word 'modern' here not to contrast Parsons with postmodernism, but mainly in order to suggest that Parsons was not a nostalgic thinker, that he was continuously conscious of the overall uniqueness of continental European encounters with modernity, and that his work directly embraced the full complexity and trauma of American civilization. Both of us have argued elsewhere that Parsons's work is not characterized by the nostalgic romanticism which has been characteristic of much classical sociology, especially in the German tradition where the problem of community and social change was paramount (Holton and Turner, 1986; Robertson and Turner, 1989). In fact we claim, not merely that German theory has largely set the scene for most of general sociology in the twentieth century (alongside a considerable number of French structuralist and postmodernist counter-movements), but that Talcott Parsons, from the time of his own first visit to Germany in the late 1920s, was deeply conscious of this problem. To take another contrast, whereas Durkheim's sociology (Durkheim, 1957) was greatly affected by the problem of communal values and civic virtues, especially in relation to the medieval guild system, Parsons's work was relatively free from any backward-looking evaluation of a lost community. Although it is perfectly obvious that Parsons was primarily concerned with a problem of values in modern society, he did not look towards a pre-modern community for inspiration in attempting to analyze or to promote any system of values. Hence his emphasis on the generalization, as opposed to the restoration, of values.

It is clearly the case that Parsons was inspired by his reading of Christian culture and was obviously influenced, somewhat selectively, by the legacies of Ancient Israel and Greek civilization (Parsons, 1977), but he did not look back to such socio-cultural systems as a direct resource for the analysis of the modern world. It was this modernism which in fact offended critics such as Gouldner (1970), because they appeared to be a naive legitimation of modern, especially American, values and social institutions. However, although Marxist, neo-Marxist and post-Marxist critics claim to be focused on modern reality, there is within Marxism itself an inherently nostalgic paradigm in which there is a commitment to communal values and assumptions which are pre-modern rather than modern. Parsons's modernism, when combined with his optimistic version of American civilization, drew criticism, even anger, from his opponents, who claimed that he was merely legitimizing American civilization. In contrast to such intellectual positions, we have praised Parsons for his unambiguous embracement of the modernist project, and it is therefore not surprising to note Habermas's recent interest (Habermas, 1987) in the work of Parsons. As others have observed, there are important convergences in the work of Parsons and Habermas, but the specifics of the relationship between their defenses of the modern has received little or no attention.

This debate on the modern clearly centers upon Parsons's enthusiasm for America (and Habermas's faith in Old Europe). It is impossible to discuss Parsons's modernism without an evaluation of his analysis of America, an analysis which was necessarily incomplete (Parsons, 1989). The USA was to Parsons the cutting edge or the leading sector of the process of modernization, since it was in America that the processes of differentiation, secularization and fragmentation had developed fully. American culture had produced styles of living, values and forms of interaction and organization which had largely created the modern system and provided the framework within which the rest of the world developed in the post-1945 period. This theme of America runs throughout the entire body of Parsonian sociology, from the earliest essays on economics to the final aspect of his work in the study of the meaning of life.

Parsons wrote in the aftermath of the Second World War, when it appeared that 'the American Way' had been largely responsible for the global rejection of both Nazi totalitarianism and Stalinist communism. It is therefore interesting to speculate on how Parsons's work might have developed and changed in the context of the debate about the decline, not only of the American economy, but of the USA as such. That is, it would be interesting to consider how Parsons would have responded to the growing global economic presence of Japan and Germany as well as to Japanese and German values.

Given what we have said about the primacy of America in Parsons's sociological perspective, we might surmise that Parsons would not have been able to accept the demise of America. Nevertheless the alleged (and global-thematized) demise of the American system does represent a challenge to Parsons's views on differentiation, secularization and the processes of modernity. It is for this reason that Parsons's writings on Japan are important and that they have unfortunately been neglected in secondary commentary on his work. Equally neglected has been Parsons's attitude towards communism and his predictions about the decline of communism and the emergence of a postcommunist world (Parsons, 1964). Parsons's prediction about the collapse of communist systems has been validated by events in Eastern Europe and to some extent the Soviet Union in the late 1980s, and therefore more attention should be given to Parsons's political sociology.

We have drawn attention to the distinctively modern aspect of Parsons's work, since we believe it is the most salient dimension of his sociology. While critics and supporters have drawn attention to the abstract or general quality of Parsons's sociology, we have attempted to argue that the theme of modernity is the most significant thrust of his entire work. Our second main orientation to Parsons, however, is to emphasize the scope and range of his intellectual work and academic interests. The majority of critics have traditionally addressed themselves to merely a fragment of Parsons's project. They have concentrated on small aspects of his general sociology, and it is only in recent years that evaluation of Parsons has begun to take note of his entire intellectual production.

Parsons attempted to analyze almost every major institutional sector of modern societies in the now famous and much maligned AGIL system. Within this broad framework, Parsons wrote on the family, kinship systems, love, economic exchange, entrepreneurship, political systems and cultural aspects of social integration. In addition, he wrote many important articles on specific historical and political topics. We have given emphasis to this aspect of his work because we believe that Parsons has been mistakenly categorized or even dismissed as merely a theorist. We have gone in the opposite direction in order to emphasize the empirical nuances of his work and its objective. Any critical evaluation of Parsons necessarily requires this general overview of his entire sociological production.

To return to the comparison with Habermas, we believe there is an essential difference between Habermas and Parsons on this overall issue. Although Habermas's work has the universal and general characteristics of Parsons's general sociology, Parsons has, in our view, said much more about the empirical workings of contemporary societies. In that perspective Habermas, like most prominent social theorists, remains a somewhat traditional philosopher.

Parsons is not technically a sociologist because his work is very general in its scopes and ambitions. Parsons was a social theorist to whom the entire world and its concrete history was an object of empirical inquiry. Thus, while America was a specific focus of his personal values and research program, Parsons also wrote extensively on Japan, on Russia, on Nazi Germany and on medieval societies. Therefore we would argue that, while America was Parsons's ostensible preoccupation, he was in fact attempting to develop a sociology of world society. He was developing a historical sociology of the development of the modern world as a whole. In short, while Parsons has been heavily criticized for the alleged unhistorical quality of his work, we believe quite the opposite to be the case; namely, that Parsons's sociology is essentially a historical overview of the conditions which have produced the modern world and the historical development of modernity and globality.

Therefore, while their intellectual orientations and style of work were entirely different, it is appropriate to compare the work of Norbert Elias with that of Parsons. Although Elias's study of the civilizing process (Elias, 1978; 1982) is unambiguously a historical study of a major pattern of social change, especially in the European context, we believe that Parsons's sociology should also be read as a major contribution to the historical unfolding of modern social systems. While Elias took what he called the civilizational process as the key dimension of change from medieval Europe to modern times, for Parsons the processes of modernization (especially secularization, differentiation and growing complexity) were major components – actually an alternative set of dimensions of 'civilization'. We are not particularly interested, however, in insisting on the historical character of Parsons's sociology. We simply wish to argue that the question of global change dominated his intellectual activities. It was that problem which led Parsons into the analysis of German social structures, into the commentaries on Japan and Russia, and into his general interest in such matters as the development of the modern university system. Thus, against his critics, it is bizarre to challenge Parsons on the grounds that either he had no interest in 'social change' or that his sociology could not explain it.

It is interesting, therefore, to compare Parsons with yet another major exponent of global sociology: Herbert Spencer. It is now almost a ritual for works on Parsons to start with Parsons's own question from the beginning of *The Structure of Social Action* (1937) where Parsons, following Crane Brinton, asks the question, 'Who now reads Spencer?' This seemingly innocuous question has often been used against Parsons in order to ask another question, 'Who now reads Parsons?' There are, of course, many similarities between their work: the interest in developing a general theory, the concern for patterns of social differentiation, the interest in the modern world as an industrial system, the propensity to draw examples from a wide variety of disciplines, and finally, and ironically, a common interest in Japan. It is interesting and important therefore to go back to Parsons's (1962) foreword to Spencer's *The Study of Sociology*, where he recognized a greater dependence on Spencer than he had originally conceded. Perhaps then alongside the growing interest and appreciation of the work of Parsons, there might be a re-evaluation and reappraisal of Spencerian sociology. While Spencer has been long rejected and criticized as a rather naive exponent of both positivism and functionalism, the scope and generality of Spencer's work, for example in *Principles of Sociology*, becomes increasingly cogent. The comparison with Parsons is thus quite proper and appropriate – as is the original Spencerian starting point of Georg Simmel's sociology.

It is thus appropriate to comment on Parsons as an intellectual while commenting on the general character of his sociology, because so much has in recent years been written about the decline of the intellectual or, indeed, the end of the intellectual (Jacoby, 1987).

A review of Parsons *as an intellectual* is timely. A number of interesting things strike one immediately about the character of Parsons as an intellectual. First, there is the strong interdisciplinary thrust of his theory and teaching – the attempt to forge significant links between sociology and economics, between sociology and Freudian psychoanalysis, between the sociological analysis of culture and cultural anthropology, between theology and sociology, and so on. Secondly, as we have already noted, Parsons's intellectual work is characterized by its generality and its range, so that Parsons cannot be regarded, in any sense whatsoever, as a specialist or as a specialized sociologist. His work breaks and destroys disciplinary boundaries, whilst still retaining its essentially sociological character. Thirdly, Parsons was definitely an engaged – if you will a political – intellectual. He has, of course, been rather often regarded as detached from the analysis of contemporary issues – as a general theorist whose abstract notions have no purchase on reality (Dahrendorf, 1958). Alternatively, Parsons has been frequently presented as an apologist for either capitalism as such or for the specific American version of capitalism. As we have shown in this study, Parsons was in fact directly engaged with the problem of German reconstruction, of Japanese development, with the enhancement of racial equality in America, and with questions of equality and citizenship generally, and was involved in the development of sociology as a major component within the social science curriculum of the modern university. However, there is one particular feature of Parsons's work which is important in this context; namely, his alleged failure to address the Marxism which became prominent in the Western academy in the 1960s. Mark Gould (1981) has very clearly demonstrated Parsons's mistaken assumption that Marxism was merely a new version of utilitarianism. However, there is another aspect to this argument, which is that Parsons did not consistently write against any particular framework of analysis. The great majority of intellectuals develop their work in opposition to others and organize their work around a unified debate or fashionable discourse. Although Parsons was specifically opposed to economism in all its forms, it cannot be argued that his work was constructed entirely in opposition to utilitarian-positivistic modes of reasoning. He was thus engaged, but not necessarily engaged *against* any particular mode of analysis. He was, of course, clearly politically engaged against totalitarianism, which he attacked in both practical and intellectual terms.

In our third positive commentary on Parsons, we would note certain similarities between his work and the development of postmodern social theory. We suggest two particular areas in which this is most obvious. First, as François Bourricaud (1981) has shown in his work on individualism, Parsons's social theory was in many respects decentered in a way which suggests a postmodern strategy. Secondly, Parsons was very clearly aware of a major shift in modern culture towards expressivity, emotion and feeling, and therefore perfectly aware of the critique of instrumental rationalism which is embedded in the postmodern critique of modernism. Thus Parsons's essay on the expressive revolution is a major contribution, although a small article, to an understanding of a major transformation in the development of modern culture towards the expressive and the symbolic. Although Parsons clearly wrote consistently about the idea of a social system, he was consciously aware of the fragmentation and differentiation of modern cultural systems and the shift towards more expressive modes. Although Parsons was *par excellence* a modernist, we simply note the fact that certain aspects of his work may well have anticipated a number of features of the modern-and-postmodern debate.

Having defended Parsons at some length, it is appropriate to ask what criticisms of Parsons we would now make. The most obvious problem about Parsons's sociology is that it is in many respects very inaccessible. The great majority of Parsons's volumes are daunting in their size and scope. They were written in a language which was often obsessively technical. Parsons's literary style does not have the sparkle and wit of contemporary French social theory, the obvious and immediate interest of the work of someone like Erving Goffman, or the 'spiritual wisdom' of the Germans. There is in addition the very special problem of *The Social System* (1951). Many readers of Parsons stop at *The Social System* and have failed to go beyond his mid-life formulation of systems theory to explore other aspects of his work. Probably *The Social System* was too ambitious in scope and would have been more appropriately written, with rich illustration, after Parsons had covered many other aspects of the field. In short, we believe that, while *The Social System* is the most well-known of Parsons's work, in some respects it is the least representative.

The question therefore arises: How does one read Parsons's sociology? Given our modernist interpretation of Parsons as a sociologist whose primary interest was to develop an understanding of America as an advanced social system, our argument is that special attention has to be given to Parsons's political sociology and to those aspects of his work which attempt to trace out a view of the world system of societies. Recognizing the analytical complexity and stylistic difficulties of *The Structure of Social Action*, *The Social System* or *Toward a General Theory of Action*, we claim that Parsons is most accessible in his early essays on fascism, in the papers which analyze strains in the American system, in the work on professionalization and in his studies of the sick role. Therefore, in our reading of Parsons, a special place is given to *Societies: Evolutionary and Comparative Perspectives* (Parsons, 1966) and *The System of Modern Societies* (Parsons, 1971). However, these works are not only the most accessible, they are also central to Parsons's sociological project as a whole, which was to describe the system of modern societies, of which America was the focus. It is for this reason, among others, that we have included Parsons's outline of the American value system.

These works are Parsons's contribution to first-order theory, that is to the development of social theory which attempts to understand social processes and social structure. By second-order theory, we understand those branches of sociology which reflect upon existing theories. For example, this volume is a second-order theory which examines Parsons's place in contemporary sociological theory. While this level of theory is clearly crucial to sociology, and while it is a legitimate scientific activity, it should be seen as merely preparatory to first-order work. Parsons's own second-order theory, such as *The Structure of Social Action*, is a major contribution to sociological theory, but its principal aim was to establish sociology as a viable intellectual discipline, rather than make a contribution to the analysis of society. Parsons is in this perspective primarily a first-order sociologist, despite his confession that he was an incurable theorist, whose main research focus remained a sociology of American democracy within the system of modern societies.

Although we have defended Parsons as a first-order theorist of democracy, especially American democracy, his critics have condemned him as a Cold War liberal whose sociology existed to serve the interests of the American Dream. Of course, in retrospect there may be currently much more sympathy towards such Cold War defenders of Western democracy in the light of recent revelations over the degree of suppression in Romania, Albania, East Germany and other Soviet satellites. As Jens Nielsen has shown in this volume, accusations against Parsons as pro-National Socialist activist are obviously groundless. Parsons's critique of and objections to Stalin's version of communism should not be taken as a right-wing position, but as a liberal objection to authoritarian rule.

Was Parsons a naive supporter of the American Dream? That is, was he indifferent to the negative or reactionary features of American society? In answering this question, it is important to keep in mind Parsons's commitment to citizenship for black Americans, his appreciation of the crucial educational revolution and his genuine commitment to democratic processes. Parsons was clearly conscious of the continuity of inequalities in American society; in fact, he wrote about stratification ceaselessly. Whether Parsons was sufficiently critical of all aspects of American foreign policy is both questionable and difficult to assess, since the extensive Parsons archive at Harvard has yet to be fully analyzed and published. It is obvious that Parsons supported the use of American military power in international affairs; he supported strongly the intervention of America in World War II. How Parsons would have charted and responded to the potential erosion of American influence in the world, the relative economic decline of the American economy in relation to Japan or, as we write, America's dangerous and potentially disastrous involvement in the

Middle East, is unclear. It is difficult to imagine that Parsons would have opposed American intervention in international affairs. What remains equally obvious is that, with the collapse of 'actually existing socialism', there is no real alternative for the foreseeable future to the capitalist economies of Western democracy. Although there can be debate about different *types* of capitalism, alternatives to capitalist systems appear remote and uncertain. Thus, Parsons's commitment to the idea that markets are the most efficient forms of economic behavior and democracies are the most sensitive means for achieving political support remains potent. Thus, for Parsons, the American Dream was radical, democratic and feasible.

References

Bourricaud, F. (1981) *The Sociology of Talcott Parsons*. Chicago and London: University of Chicago Press.

Dahrendorf, R. (1958) 'Out of Utopia', *American Journal of Sociology*, 64 (2): 115–27.

Durkheim, E. (1957) *Professional Ethics and Civic Morals*. London: Routledge & Kegan Paul.

Elias, N. (1978) *The Civilizing Process: the History of Manners*. Oxford: Blackwell.

Elias, N. (1982) *The Civilizing Process: State Formation and Civilization*. Oxford: Blackwell.

Gould, M. (1981) 'Parsons versus Marx: "An Earnest Warning . . . "', *Sociological Inquiry*, 51: 197–218.

Gouldner, A.W. (1970) *The Coming Crisis of Western Sociology*. New York: Basic Books.

Habermas, J. (1987) *The Theory of Communicative Action*, vol. 2, *The Critique of Functionalist Reason*. Cambridge: Polity Press.

Holton, R.J. and Turner, B.S. (1986) *Talcott Parsons on Economy and Society*. London and New York: Routledge & Kegan Paul.

Jacoby, R. (1987) *The Last Intellectuals: American Culture in the Age of Academe*. New York: Farrar, Straus & Giroux.

Parsons, T. (1937) *The Structure of Social Action*. New York: McGraw-Hill.

Parsons, T. (1951) *The Social System*. London: Routledge & Kegan Paul.

Parsons, T. (1962) 'Foreword' to H. Spencer, *The Study of Sociology*. Ann Arbor, MI: Michigan University Press. (Original work published in 1873.)

Parsons, T. (1964) 'Communism and the West: the Sociology of Conflict', pp. 390–9 in A. Etzioni and E. Etzioni (eds), *Social Change: Sources, Patterns and Consequences*. New York: Basic Books.

Parsons, T. (1966) *Societies: Evolutionary and Comparative Perspectives*. Englewood Cliffs, NJ: Prentice-Hall.

Parsons, T. (1971) *The System of Modern Societies*. Englewood Cliffs, NJ: Prentice-Hall.

Parsons, T. (1977) *The Evolution of Societies*. Englewood Cliffs, NJ: Prentice-Hall.

Parsons, T. (1989) 'A Tentative Outline of American Values', *Theory, Culture & Society*, 6 (4): 577–612.

Parsons, T. and Shils, E.A. (eds) (1951) *Toward a General Theory of Action*. Cambridge, MA: Harvard University Press.

Robertson, R. and Turner, B.S. (1989) 'Talcott Parsons and Modern Social Theory – an Appreciation', *Theory, Culture & Society*, 6 (4): 539–58.

Spencer, H. (1969) *Principles of Sociology*, abridge and edited by S. Andreski. London: Macmillan. (Original volumes published 1874–96.)

INDEX